KNOWLEDGE AND COGNITION

KNOWLEDGE
AND COGNITION

EDITED BY LEE W. GREGG
CARNEGIE-MELLON UNIVERSITY

 LAWRENCE ERLBAUM ASSOCIATES, PUBLISHERS

1974 POTOMAC, MARYLAND

DISTRIBUTED BY THE HALSTED PRESS DIVISION OF

JOHN WILEY & SONS

New York   Toronto   London   Sydney

Lawrence Erlbaum Associates, Publishers
12736 Lincolnshire Drive
Potomac, Maryland 20854

Distributed solely by Halsted Press Division
John Wiley & Sons, Inc., New York

Library of Congress Cataloguing in Publication Data

Symposium on Cognition, 9th, Carnegie-Mellon University, 1973.
    Knowledge and cognition.

    "Collection of the papers presented at the ninth annual Symposium on Cognition."
    Bibliography: p.
    1. Cognition – Congresses. 2. Knowledge, Theory of – Congresses. I. Gregg, Lee W., ed. II. Title.
BF311.S83 1973   153.4   74-16105
ISBN 0-470-32657-3

Printed in the United States of America

CONTENTS

PREFACE

This volume is a collection of the papers presented at the Ninth Annual Symposium on Cognition, held at Carnegie-Mellon University in May 1973. The subject of the symposium was *knowledge,* or rather its internal representation in human memory, or in computer systems. Of all the recent symposia in this series, this one represents a meeting of the minds, in that all of the participants were strongly oriented toward information processing theories of cognition. No attempt was made to induce an old-fashioned *S-R* Hullian to mystify the audience with Rube Goldberg mediators. No magical hand-waving from the Piagetian school was allowed. No blind faith in the control of behavior by radical Skinnerians shaped up the proceedings. Just plain old, hard-nosed, deterministic (for the most part) descriptions of thinking and problem solving were presented.

Two of the papers were presented at the Midwestern Psychological Association Meetings at Chicago, Illinois, a few days before the conference. The Simon and Lea paper, Chapter 5, was an invited address entitled "What Problem Solving Has to Say to Concept Learning." A different title was attached to the final version. Greeno introduced the notion that comprehension and learning are similar processes in a talk that he gave at an MPA symposium.

The first chapter presents an overview of recent theories of semantic or long-term memory. This general paper surveys work in the developmental area, in the perceptual learning domain, and in language acquisition, as this work relates to the organization of human memory. Chapter 2, by Greeno, examines the notion that comprehension and learning are both processes that create structures in working memory. Hence these two important aspects of human behavior are seen in a unified framework. Working memory is that memory which is longer than short-term memory, but not yet a part of the organized concepts of long-term semantic memory. What Greeno has done is to analyze the conditions of preliminary knowledge that make the acquisition of further knowledge possible. This is a complex area where Greeno's search for unity in mental processes takes him through what he has termed "the new mental forestry".

Pitz's presentation at the conference generated a great deal of discussion. In contrast to the rather deterministic ideas of cognitive organization, Pitz attempts to characterize that imprecise knowledge on which so many decisions are based. How uncertain are we of facts and figures which we can only roughly estimate? Pitz's formulation presents an information processing analysis that challenges the subjective utility schemes of Ward Edwards and others.

Chapter 4 presents a paper by Egan and Greeno. In contrast to Greeno's earlier view of unity, these authors explode the picture of human mental function, arguing that concept learning, rule induction, and problem solving require distinct internal representations and hence distinctive solution methods. This view is challenged by Simon and Lea in Chapter 5, who argue that cognitive behavior in these tasks is not all that different. These authors distinguish between problem solving in a space of rules versus problem solving in a space of instances. Essentially the same cognitive processes operate in each. The task environments differ only in terms of content.

In Chapter 6, Hunt counteracts decades of psychometric nonsense about human intelligence. He shows how programs (processes) can account for differential performance on a "culture fair" IQ test, Raven's Matrices. Hunt's GPS-like approach spells out the precise requirements for exhibiting differential intellectual performance on the test. His title is "Quote the Raven? Nevermore!"

Chapter 7 is a discussion by Garlie Forehand (now of Educational Testing Service) in which he attempts to communicate these research findings to the educational specialist, provides a coherent picture of the work to date, and relates these analyses to educational goals. Educators use the term 'knowledge' in a narrow way, usually to refer to facts acquired and stored. Forehand's discussion provides a perspective on the interplay between fact and method.

Chapters 8 through 11 are intended as examples. These chapters show the implications of psychological research on semantic memory for the design of computer systems that understand. And vice versa. Hayes and Simon discuss how human problem solvers construct a problem space for a particular problem-solving task, and then show how a computer program that unifies syntactic, semantic, and other sources of knowledge can create the same internal representation of the problem. Differences in problem-solving behavior depend on differences in the internal representation of the problem. What knowledge the problem solver brings to bear is critical in determining his success.

Moore and Newell, in Chapter 9, outline the criteria for a computer system, called MERLIN, to understand. MERLIN is the complete thinker, but falls far short of the stringent conditions that Moore and Newell set for understanding. However, the techniques that these computer scientists have introduced carry us a long way toward highly sophisticated semantic systems.

Reddy and Newell, in Chapter 10, present a progress report on HEARSAY, a speech understanding system, bringing into sharp relief the knowledge required for understanding human speech by machine. These authors draw an important distinction between speech recognition and speech understanding. Understanding implies that the system draws on broad sources of knowledge to interpret the patterns of sound.

Kenneth Mark Colby, a psychiatrist by trade, has been working with computer scientists to develop and test a simulation model of paranoid thought processes. His paper makes several points. First, the knowledge required to synthesize paranoid information processing is based on the structure of belief systems in the patient. Belief systems are organized. There is a structure of strategies governed by delusional-paranoid-belief systems. Colby's model is a theory of how such malevolent belief systems generate verbal replies to natural language inputs. Thus, Colby characterizes his model as an I-O, Input-Output, theory of paranoia. In evaluating the model, an interesting set of dimensions emerges when judges are asked to rate or to determine whether an actual case history, or a computer-generated I-O sequence, is presented. In fact, we see recapitulated in Colby's tests most of the semantic elements that a trained psychiatrist would use to discriminate among normal and abnormal thought processes.

The papers by Forehand and Klahr integrate complex theoretical issues and research findings. I want to thank them for leading the discussion sessions in a stimulating and provocative manner.

I also wish to thank Mrs. Betty Boal, for her outstanding job in arranging, coordinating, and managing the conference as well as these proceedings; and my colleague, Sylvia Farnham-Diggory, for her help with editorial chores.

Individual contributors have noted their sources of support in footnotes. Research on cognitive information processing psychology has been supported for many years by a United States Public Health Service Research Grant MH-07722 from the National Institute of Mental Health.

1
PERCEPTUAL STRUCTURES AND SEMANTIC RELATIONS

LEE W. GREGG
Carnegie-Mellon University

Models of memory must specify the organization of information and the processes that make possible communication and problem solving. In this paper, I will examine some tentative organizational principles which have led us to characterize the information content of memory as *semantic* versus *perceptual.*

The major processes that make use of these data bases are recognition and memory search. Recognition is related to problem solving to the extent that stimulus elements in the problem space suggest appropriate things to do. We see a chess configuration, and a move generator is invoked. We see a mathematical formula, and the appropriate arithmetic manipulations are suggested. Memory search is involved in problem solving when more devious pathways must be taken in constructing a problem space, or in applying problem-solving operators. Language comprehension is a problem solving task wherein we must sometimes examine alternative hypotheses about the meaning of a sentence. Clinical diagnosis is an example of memory search where causal or correlational relationships among symptoms must be explored.

Semantics refers to the meanings of words in a language. The meaning of a word depends not only on the object or event it symbolizes, but also on its relationship to other words. These relationships of word to word, in particular sentential forms, impose an organization. A recent attempt to capture the essential aspects of linguistic organization is one proposed by Schank (1972).

Perception, on the other hand, refers to the meanings or interpretations attached to sensory data. Although some of us (Simon & Siklóssy, 1972) prefer to use the term semantics in relation to the entire collection of symbolic structures comprising human memory, I will argue that perceptual acts, as in recognition memory, use information whose structural characteristics set them apart from memory organization based on linguistic concepts.

This work was supported by United States Public Health Service Grant MH-07722, from the National Institute of Mental Health.

It is important to distinguish between the perceptual act of recognizing a familiar word and extracting its meaning. Thompson and Massaro (1973) state the issue in terms of letter and word recognition. Letter discrimination or classification is directly related to the visual configuration of letter and word. In contrast, knowledge of letter sequences constrains the allowable patterns for whole word recognition. This higher order information was presumably acquired through experience with the language. However, the redundant information about letter patterns is a different kind of datum from the features providing perceptual cues.

If word recognition has both perceptual and semantic stages, then comprehension of larger units—i.e., sentences—must also require two or more stages. Word order redundancy is to sentences, as letter order redundancy is to words. A perceptual-semantic "two-process theory" is discussed in most theoretical overviews of memory. It appears in the distinction drawn by Kintsch (1970) between recognition and recall, but is then promptly lost in Shiffrin's (1970) analysis of memory search. Although Shiffrin recognizes that the memory images are made up of related "smaller units of information [p. 376]," he fails to specify whether or not he is talking about perceptual or linguistic information. Norman and Rumelhart (1970) carefully examine the flow of information from perception to memory and propose a "naming system" to link the perceptual front end to the long-term memory data base. However, by 1972 the same group (Rumelhart, Lindsay, & Norman, 1972) had so far lost sight of the perceptual domain that they proposed to create a pattern recognizer based solely on a semantic retrieval network.

These are examples of the confusion that can arise when metatheories create constructs that are also names of objects in the set of phenomena. Consider the famous *"John"* who *"hit the ball."* In the sentence structure, *John* as a noun, and John as a boy-to-be-recognized have quite different properties. The noun comes first in relation to other words in the sentence. It has special linguistic relations to the verb. But in the visual world, John is a boy. What he is doing may or may not be related to our recognition of him.

Put simply, our knowledge of the visual world and our knowledge of the language used to describe it are different. Our characterization of linguistic knowledge is in terms of formal relations describing strings of words. Our characterization of the visual world may use this linguistic knowledge only in part and unsystematically.

The goal of the LTM modelers was to create a system that would understand natural language inputs. They organized their data bases in terms of an analysis of linguistic relations. The structure of the data base was therefore organized along dimensions appropriate for dissecting sentences, but not necessarily appropriate for analyzing the perceptual world. This is true even though those linguistic strings may sometimes describe the aspects of the visual world. The data base for recognizing an object in the real world—i.e., the bases of perception—may or may not be organized in the same way.

We cannot approach this question without considering the developmental history of the organism.

DEVELOPMENTAL EVIDENCE

Piaget's (1970) work on the growth of percepts and concepts and Herbert Clark's (1973) paper on "Space-Time Semantics in Children" provide a developmental framework for analyzing the differences between perceptual and semantic data bases.

Piaget postulates two kinds of memory. He calls one, *the memory of recognition,* which operates only in the presence of an object—i.e., sensory experience. Secondly, there is *the memory of evocation*—conjuring up an image of an object in its absence.

In information processing terms, Piaget's recognition memory could be described as a tree of elementary perceptual tests, and his evocative memory, as a reactivation of portions of that tree, plus a retrieval of some of its verbal descriptors. Semantic memory in general may grow through the gradual replacement of evocative memory structures by verbal structures. In this way, certain elementary, sensorimotor meanings would be formally preserved.

It is not clear whether Piaget would agree with that formulation. In examining the relationship between percepts and concepts, he has described four "situations" where perceptual and conceptual behaviors interact (Piaget & Inhelder, 1970, pp. 44-48). They are illustrated in Fig. 1.1 (author's graphs, not Piaget's).

Piaget's first case has to do with the onset of object permanence, which he says occurs at about 18 months to 2 years of age. He claims that object permanence, the concept, precisely matches object permanence, the percept. The percept *is* the concept. Obviously, the linguistic behavior that the child, age 2, is capable of exhibiting is little more than naming an object presented to his senses. Only within the framework of the perceptual behavior can we know that the child recognizes a cup passed behind the screen as the self-same cup that emerges on the other side.

Judgments of perspective are an example of perceptual development that diverges from a conceptual framework. Before children can represent the concept of perspective in their drawings, they can make constancy judgments quite accurately. In other words, they know what perspective means perceptually. Interestingly, when the concept of perspective has reached its highest level of development, as evidenced by the child's ability to coordinate viewpoints that are not his own, perceptual constancy judgments have deteriorated. When asked to judge what size a rod must be in order to be a particular size at a particular distance, the nine-year-old will make poorer guesses than a six-year-old.

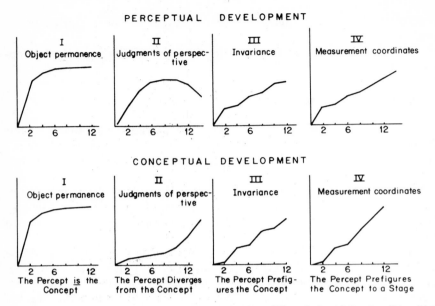

FIG. 1.1. A graphical, hypothetical schematization of Piaget's four "situations" in which rates of perceptual and conceptual development can be compared.

The implication is that language structures—i.e., semantic relation-ships—can evolve without reference to perception. However, in this case, as in the other three "situations" illustrated in Fig. 1.1, the perception has in fact created a stable internal representation that comes before the linguistic expression.

This is precisely the point that Clark (1973) makes in his discussion of perceptual space and the use of spatial terms in English. We argue, as Clark does, that the perceptual tests are a function of the biological make-up of the perceptual system and the environment in which we find ourselves. Properties of the P-space, the perceptual space, are not complicated. When one is standing up, the so-called canonical position, P-space consists of three reference planes and three associated directions. Ground level is a reference plane, and *up* is positive. There is a vertical left-to-right plane through the body, and reference is *forward*, positive. Then there is a vertical front-to-back plane, as a reference plane through the body, both left and right are positive directions. The language space (L-space) in English maps directly onto the P-space, and is the same as the P-space.

> Spatial terms in English reveal that the L-space, the language space, has properties identical with those of the P-space [Clark, 1973].

That is, there appears to be one-to-one correspondence between the perceptual representations and the componential analysis of the words. What is important to our discussion is Clark's argument that the P-space comes first, and that the language maps onto it.

What happens to this during subsequent learning? What operations control the growth of language in relation to perception? Are early perceptual tests changed by the acquisition of new verbal concepts? Just how modifiable are these relationships?

These and other questions will not be answered quickly or simply. However, there are some suggestions that can be made about the nature of the changes that occur in the semantic space. These changes are more malleable than the perceptual tests according to the view we are here proposing. In Chapter 2, Greeno addresses the issue of constructing semantic, or, as he calls them, conceptual structures. Greeno suggests that an intermediate term memory (ITM) can hold newly formed conceptual structures, at least temporarily. Residence time in the ITM may be up to several hours or several days. The structures Greeno describes are those which result from learning processes like those of serial or paired associate verbal learning. We can speak of the growth and changes during acquisition where the association memory processes in aggregate consume about 8 seconds per chunk (Gregg, 1972). The fate of these associations has been little studied beyond the briefest of intervals, although a few speculations about the reorganization of them have been described (Michon, 1972). The changes in relation to previous long-term structures have not been investigated.

MODELS OF PROCESS AND STRUCTURE

One of the fascinating things about some of the recent theoretical work in cognitive psychology has been the development of theories independent of tasks on which the theories can work. Schank (1972) talks about testing a theory of natural language understanding by having a human communicate with a computer. Seventy-five pages later, he gets around to suggesting that the topic of conversation might be a psychiatric interview. Rumelhart et al. (1972) have created a semantic retrieval network, and then cleverly thought of using it to retrieve recipes in the kitchen. Perhaps the first order of business should be to examine task requirements in task environments that are real. For example, in the previous section we noticed that quite specific information processing demands were placed on the child in identifying the permanent object, or in performing operations on spatial terms. Functionally, we can describe a very large number of real tasks based on the sequence of cognitive events in memory search and recognition, and on whether or not an external name of an object is available. For example:

1. Name an object (external name exists).
2. Recognize an object as familiar.

3. Describe an object given its symbolic name, that is, remember something about the object (*a*) physical properties of the object (*b*) functional properties of the object.
4. Decide which of two particular objects is familiar, most recent.
5. Decide which of two names belongs to an object.
6. Categorize objects in classes based on (*a*) physical properties of the object (*b*) functional properties of the object.

We might suppose that each of these represents a component task in a larger problem-solving scheme. We must say what the data bases are and what the programs are that operate on them. Fig. 1.2 is my version of the kinds of processing interrelationships that are needed to account for such real-world task behaviors.

The figure shows that the process of feature extraction leads to a recognition, whereas concepts invoked by the recognition process itself, or by names generated after recognition has occurred, generate the interesting problem solving behavior. Although both are motor responses, the *language generator* is split off from the *function generator*, which may produce a rich variety of actions—such as pointing and drawing.

The perceptual structures at the front end may or may not include the naming process. Norman and Rumelhart (1970) choose to include naming as the final stage of the perceptual system. I believe that there are concepts that can be invoked for which no simple names exist—as in the child's dimensional naming of objects, e.g., "Give me the big red one."

Internal names may or may not have the status of being symbols in a language. There are two ways of accessing a concept: (*a*) the immediate perceptual cues, or (*b*) the intermediate communication through language. One can recognize an exemplar of the class of trees, by direct viewing; or, a skilled poet can index the same node verbally. Names generated after recognition has occurred are part of our problem-solving behavior. Verbal

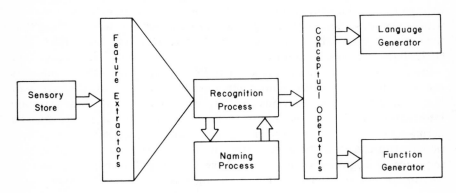

PERCEPTUAL   STRUCTURES   SEMANTIC   RELATIONS

Fig. 1.2. Long-term memory processes from recognition to search.

protocols generated during problem solving behavior represent our own attempts to search semantic spaces to find appropriate functions (operators).

Language generation—speech production—is a complicated motor response of the cognitive system. Complicated patterns of information and precise timing characterize the overproduction of language. Similarly our ability to sketch, to draw, to point and manipulate objects in our environment can be characterized through special encodings of sequential information. Both language generation and other motor functions are motor responses. Why, then, are they separate? They are separate because the intentional organizations are quite different. What moves us around in the space of the language generator, before action, is an entirely different set of dimensions than those of the other sensorimotor skills. Semantic organization involves action and modification, whereas sensorimotor coordinations reflect spatial and temporal patterns.

The boxes in Fig. 1.2 indicate processes. These processes need data on which to operate. The perceptual structures and the semantic relations are the data bases.

Perceptual Structures

The mechanism for perceptual recognition is not a hypothesis testing one; it is not one that involves judgment or decision processes. Recognition memory is a rapid analysis or intersection of sensory data on the long-term storage using the features of familiar objects. Our preference is to say that an EPAM-like sorting tree can do the job. EPAM structures are not restricted to binary tests. Feigenbaum's first model used visual characteristics of letters, curved-ness or straight-linedness, and the test was for the presence or absence of the feature. But there is nothing in EPAM that restricts us to binary tests.

In fact, the span of absolute judgment suggests that we can make discriminations of up to 9 or 10 branches at a test node. A perceptual organization of 7 levels, at 10 values per level is 10^7 or 10 million. Thus, we could have a completely static test structure, 7 levels deep, where at most each test would take 100 milliseconds (nothing happens in less than 100 milliseconds). In .7 of a second, without context any one of 10 million identifiable, familiar objects could be recognized. I have not gone around counting how many things there are in my environment, but I have only 100,000 words in my whole vocabulary. We can perceive at least 100 times as many things as we have words for them. On the basis of tests like the ones shown in Table 1.1, we can sort environmental objects. These perceptual tests may be built into the biological hardware of the visual system. Some surely are—depth perception based on retinal disparity (Julesz, 1970), for example.

A sorting net does whatever is asked of it, at each test point along the way. Suppose that we are trying to deal with a raw sensory input. It seems to

TABLE 1.1

Summary of Perceptual Structures

Modality linked (Parallel or very rapid—less than 50 milliseconds)	
Sensory organization	
Visual tests	Auditory tests
depth	localization
contour	segmentation
texture	harmonic quality
density	volume
brightness	loudness
flicker	flutter & roughness
motion (looming)	perceived variation in pitch & loudness
Perceptual organization based on symmetries	
tilt	sound quality of speech, etc.
form perception & pattern	melody & pattern
size	rhythm
volume of 3-D object	expressive

me that the first question we would ask is, "What modality?" And if the answer is *vision,* that represents one of a number of choices that funnel the sorting operation, the input to the memory system, in a particular direction, in a particular way, perhaps to area 17 or 18 of the occipital lobe. Now what happens to the coded object when it arrives at the association cortex? How do I know that this object that I'm looking at is a human face? There must be some judgments that we make that are fast and simple. What can the tests for humanoid features be?

The role of context. It turns out to be the case, of course, that we make mistakes when we are out of context, and so an alternative proposition—an alternative theory, that I do not know how to test at the moment—is that context selects, say, four or five particular kinds of tests and brings them up front, thereby priming the perceptual system. Under these circumstances, we can recognize the thing in context in 400 or 500 milliseconds.

Is that context verbal? Certainly we deal with context in a semantic space. In reading a book, a kind of hypothesis-testing behavior must go on in anticipating what the next paragraph is about. Perceptual context is not the same thing. It may be based on the size of print on a page or on the expectation of pictures. It may be provided by consistency of style, or by the presence of formulas that gauge my speed, or by whether or not I have made an overall judgment—certainly a semantic judgment—of reading difficulty. And I may be setting some attentional gates or some timing expectations.

But what is crucial is the list of tests that are primarily perceptual in nature and that because of the processing time demand—because of the speed required for processing percepts in recognition memory—must be simple, general, and easily processed by a simple processor. In other words, the feature extraction program that operates on the sensory input must either be hard-wired, or, if some kind of control is involved, exceedingly simple.

Semantic Relations

The number of semantic relations may be very large. A word can be related to any other word through another word concept. The humor or lack of humor in English puns suggests this. Guilford's (1959) remote associate test is another example, since in fact people were able to find remote associates. One outcome of the research on semantic networks has been the search for a small but powerful set of concepts for tying words together. One of the earliest computer systems, Raphael's SIR (1964) used only five basic concepts—*part-whole, possession, logical and, logical or,* and *identity.* Quillian (1967) expanded the number of possible relations by admitting arbitrary associative links, modification and subject-object-relation triads. The content of a Quillian-type semantic memory therefore depended on the particular dictionary definitions of the word concepts.

More recently, Schank (1972), profiting from Fillmore's (1968) case grammar, has expanded the set of basic concepts to 27 categories. Notice that in Table 1.2, most of Fillmore's explanatory power comes about from the meaning of the verb in the sentence. Thus, the expansion of cases comes about through whatever choice of classification for verb meanings one can generate. For example, we can have action verbs or state verbs; or we can have peculiar configurations of interaction, as in communication with another person.

As still another alternative, Table 1.3 shows some items from a list of functional utterances, collated by Slobin (1969), representing semantic categories invented by children in 30 languages.

There is no reason to expect that the way nouns are used in a syntactic structure—a sentence—should go along with the functional use of language by children. However, both represent appropriate organizations for semantic relations, the functional ones giving a clue to the earliest information processing requirements of communicative acts. The analysis of case provides a more sophisticated organization, based on broader experience and the nuances of verb meanings.

If the developmental evidence is correct, we might suppose that certain semantic features are closely linked to the perceptual tests of recognition memory (Table 1.4). We can only suppose that language symbols are mapped

TABLE 1.2

Fillmore's Cases

Type	Description
Agentive (A)	The case of the typically animate perceived instigator of the action identified by the verb.
Instrumental (I)	The case of the inanimate force or object causally involved in the action or state identified by the verb.
Dative (D)	The case of the animate being affected by the state or action identified by the verb.
Factitive (F)	The case of the object or being resulting from the action or state identified by the verb, or understood as a part of the meaning of the verb.
Locative (L)	The case which identifies the location or spatial orientation of the state or action identified by the verb.
Objective (O)	The semantically most neutral case, the case of anything representable by a noun whose role in the action or state identified by the verb is identified by the semantic interpretation of the verb itself; conceivably the concept should be limited to things which are affected by the action or state identified by the verb. The term is not to be confused with the notion of direct object, nor with the name of the surface case synonymous with accusative.

onto the basic outcome of perception. One category of semantic relations, therefore, must be the perceptually dependent relation "name-of." Other relations in this class are category naming, where the test is on the physical properties of objects, and dimensional naming, where the value names along perceptual dimensions, point to internal memory representations.

A second general class of semantic features are perceptually correlated concepts. The outcome of a single, immediate recognition memory is insufficient where volume and size are appropriate. The individual must coordinate two separate observations, or observations made at two different points in time. Meaning depends on the coordination of two or more separate observations. Cause and effect—the comprehension of causality—depend upon the coordination of an agent and some observable outcomes, at two or more points in time.

Finally, there are verbal concepts based strictly on nonsensory data, as in the case of taxonomies that are learned after verbal labels are assimilated. A child may never have seen a live birth, or watched anything lay an egg, but he can learn that birds and mammals are two different kinds of animals.

Conceptual dependencies include the linguistic concepts of Table 1.2 and 1.3 and the memory of abstract dimensions produced through formal education.

There are six ways, according to Fillmore (1968), that nouns can be related to verbs. Miller (1972) has recently analyzed verbs of motion, and found 20 categories describable in terms of 12 componential dimensions. By my calculation, there are either $6 \times 20 = 120$ or $6 \times 12 = 72$ distinct possibilities for searching a memory structure organized along these lines. The program to do it would have to be smart and have a lot of placekeepers. Searching long-term memory must be a slow process.

EMPIRICAL EVIDENCE

Up to this point I have fallen into the same trap that has gotten the others. I have talked glibly and globally, without respect to any particular task or use of the knowledge base. Let me now describe the first of a series of studies that we hope will add to our understanding of semantic memory.

TABLE 1.3

Slobin's Categories of Semantic Universals

Function	Utterance
locate, name	there book
	that car
	see doggie
demand	more milk
	give candy
	want gum
negate	no wet
	no wash
	not hungry
	all gone milk
describe event or situation	Bambi go
	mail come
	hit ball
	block fall
	baby highchair
indicate possession	my shoe
	mama dress
modify, qualify	pretty dress
	big boat
question	where ball

TABLE 1.4

Organization of Semantic Relations

1. Perceptually dependent
    Spatial terms (near-far, above-below, etc.)
    Directions (up-down)
    Name of permanent object
    Name of value on dimension (over generalized)

2. Perceptual derivatives
    Time expressions (based on spatial metaphors)
    Seriation
    Conservation
    Color (multidimensional)
    Shape
    Number (subitizing at low end; density estimation at high end)

3. Conceptual dependencies—arising from descriptive possibilities, logical inferences,
    and conventions of language.
    Taxonomies (class names of formal categories)
    Logico-deductive (propositional, combinatorial operations)
    Associative linguistics (contrast, similarity, completion)

We hypothesized that word recognition depends on the analysis of the visual features of letter groups. Since we used 4- and 5-letter words in these experiments, the spelling patterns are similar to the letter clusters proposed by Gibson (1969). The rationale for the study was based on the hypothesis that the higher-order features for word recognition are scanned by the feature extraction program in a left-to-right scanning order. There is recent evidence in an illusion reported by Sekuler, Tynan, and Levinson (1973) that such a scanning mechanism exists independent of hemisphere and retinal hemifield. We therefore presented individual letters in their correct spatial location in words, one at a time, either in the correct sequential left-to-right order, or in random temporal sequences. In the latter condition, features of adjacent letters would be disrupted. Three letter durations were used: 60, 80, and 100 milliseconds. Thus, for a 4-letter word, total word duration was 240, 320, or 400 milliseconds. Reaction times were obtained from a voice key, after which the subjects were requested to type out the letters that they had seen. There were eight subjects per level of letter duration. Each subject received 100 4-letter words, and 100 5-letter words in a single session, in counterbalanced order.

The results are presented in Fig. 1.3 and 1.4. The data for 4- and 5-letter words are combined. The proportion of correct responses, as a function of letter duration, increases from about .60 to .75 when the letters are presented in their correct serial order (see Fig. 1.3). However, when the order in which

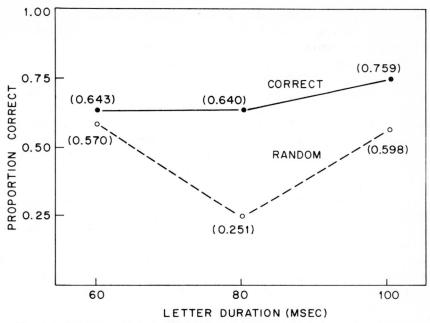

FIG. 1.3. Proportion of correct word recognition as a function of the duration of single letters appearing in correct (left to right) or random order.

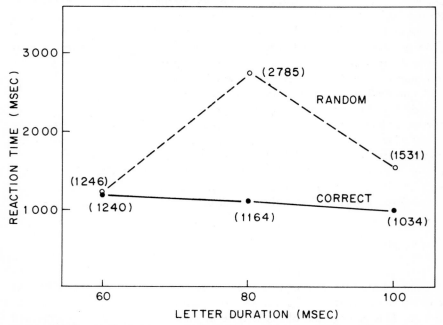

FIG. 1.4. The relation between word recognition reaction time and letter duration.

the letters appear, still in their correct spatial location, is random, a remarkable decrease occurs in the proportion of correct responses at 80 milliseconds per letter.

The phenomenon undoubtedly results from what Mayzner and Tresselt (1970) term *sequential blanking*. Our interpretation of this effect, however, rests on the assumption that information cannot be transferred from an iconic store to the short-term memory at the same time that visual information is being read into that iconic store. Of particular interest in these data are the similar proportions of correct responses at 60 milliseconds, where, presumably, visual information about the word is equally analyzable, whether the letters appear in correct or random order. In Fig. 1.4, we notice that the reaction times for word recognition are highly similar at 60 milliseconds, suggesting that a fast recognition process has occurred. At 100 milliseconds per letter, the proportion of correct responses is less for the random condition than for the correct letter order condition. Furthermore, the reaction times are about 500 milliseconds greater for the random condition. Thus, we interpret these results as showing a memory search process for the correct spelling of the words, a process that is quite different from recognition memory for the words. I believe that the scanning mechanism is confirmed by the marked differences in reaction time and in the proportion of correct responses that we see at 80 milliseconds.

As a simple demonstration, this experiment argues for a real distinction between two kinds of information on which memory processes operate. Posner and Warren (1972) make a similar point. A physical code must represent the structural details of printed letters or words, and automatic processes operate in just a few hundred milliseconds to produce a recognition of the object. Conscious processes, on the other hand, are required to sort out information about the proper spelling of a word, or the semantic features that would allow us to determine whether it is a synonym, a coordinate, or a subordinate to another word. Of course, we still do not know what the particular features are of letters or words that the recognition process takes as input. Our written language provides a rich visual environment where we might expect a large alphabet of features to exist. However, we know from studies of perception in chess (Chase & Simon, 1972) that years of experience with the visual patterns of a chess board make it possible for the chess master to recognize a very large number of patterns.

The Paradox of Perception

In chess perception, for example, we find that the distinguishing capacity of a Grand Master is the vast store of prior, and well-learned, chess configurations that enables him selectively to choose new, but appropriate, moves. This elaboration of his long-term memory allows him quickly and accurately to do this. The fundamental idea of *more* is that the additional information must be assimilated into the system. If we add more books to a library, there are more that must be searched through to find a particular book. If I know more chess games, how is it that the knowledge helps me respond quickly? Why not more slowly?

The paradox of perception is the apparent contradiction in the acquisition of new information that reduces search, facilitates selectivity, and increases speed and precision in identifying appropriate outcomes. Somehow or other, *more* is *less*. The fact is that the new knowledge is not simply added on to the memory like a new book in the library. The effect of knowledge acquisition is to sharpen and make more appropriate the perceptual tests that we use.

There are several ways that we can characterize the facilitation due to knowledge acquisition. First, the dimensions that we use to slice up the world are more efficient because we are able to see the limits, and extensity, of the instances that must be classified. A midwesterner who knows only cottonwoods along the creek and elm trees around the square has a very incomplete tree recognizer. While he may be able to identify those exemplars quickly, slight variations lead to problem solving rather than perception.

The second outcome of a broadened knowledge base is the concomitant necessity for systematic treatment of the space of knowledge. I mean that with only two kinds of trees to classify, there is little demand for organizing tree-like properties. The organization of perceptual tests that pushes the range of one's discriminative powers increases efficiency.

Semantic relations and the data base for language generation involve higher-order conceptual relationships. The uncertainties of conceptual linking make semantic information processing slower and more difficult.

Trade-Offs in the Memory Structures

Current approaches to semantic memory have not disentangled the perceptual part from the semantic part of the system. Only by examining particular problem solving or performance tasks, can we answer questions about the relative effects of perceptual recognition and inferential search. Much of our work at C-MU has used a particular strategy, namely, to put a subject in a concrete task environment, to discover his representation of the task, and then to model the information processes that generate his overt behavior. Both semantic relationships and perceptual structures interact in generating an internal representation of the task environment. How the subject instructs himself to describe the environment—the visual displays and the objects he has to manipulate—and how he puts together a problem-solving program, to use either semantic relationships or perceptual structures, is a function of his experience. The fact is, either or both kinds of representation systems can be used. We want to know which one is invoked, how, and when.

An experiment carried out along these lines (Gregg, 1967) showed that where the display is impoverished, very little learning occurred until a relatively rich verbal description was used to characterize the combination of switches on a box. In fact, some students from the drama department of our university were the best learners in this task that had a highly technical flavor, while some of our engineers, whose formal education provided specific coding schemes that could have been used in solving the problem, nevertheless failed to learn.

CONCLUSIONS

We have argued that semantic relations come about as a result of mapping language onto prior perceptual structures. Recognition memory depends on the structure of the perceptual data base refined through years of experience with our visual world. The formal concepts that we learn through language are the source of semantic relations. This knowledge can be characterized in terms of the relative directness of correspondence to the outcomes of perception. A more general view of semantics is that any symbolic structure that has to do with representing an external task environment has meaning. Therefore, semantics is the study of the relations among the meanings of these structures. Presumably, it is this interpretation that has led to the search for a universal set of semantic concepts for natural language understanding. Unfortunately, purity of thought, in the absence of an external source of environmental stimulation, rarely occurs. Daydreaming may not be a fruitful source of cognitive materials for semantic analysis. Rather, we might better approach the study of knowledge bases by examining particular problem solving tasks. When we do, a sharp demarcation line becomes apparent between perceptual and linguistic behavioral domains.

2
PROCESSES OF
LEARNING AND COMPREHENSION

JAMES G. GREENO
University of Michigan

The suggestion of this paper is that the main processes of comprehension and learning are fundamentally similar. To understand the major psychological features of each process, we need to understand the mechanism by which individuals construct cognitive representations of meaningful information. This involves finding relational patterns among input concepts, and representing these patterns in memory. I will mention a few experimental studies of comprehension and learning. These were selected because they can be naturally interpreted as building cognitive structures based on conceptual relations. I do not intend that this should be taken as strong evidence for the claim that learning and comprehension are fundamentally similar; rather, the experiments are intended to illustrate the potential usefulness of the idea that processes of comprehension are important in learning situations and to support the intuition of a strong analogy between the two theoretical problems.

COMPREHENSION

The general principles of a theory of comprehension are becoming familiar in the work of several investigators. Apparently the main process is finding a set of semantic relationships in a linguistic input. This idea has gained increasing emphasis since Sachs' (1967) early study opposing semantic and syntactic features of sentences read by subjects. Her results indicated that semantic features were better remembered than syntactic ones. Schank (1972) has developed a system for identifying the semantic relationships represented by a sentence. A simple example is in Fig. 2.1 which shows the structure that Schank's system stores in memory or the sentence, "I gave the man a book." In general, the system identifies the main subject and main verb of the sentence, and specifies relationships among the

This research was sponsored by the National Science Foundation under Grant GB-31045.

to ──►man

I ◄── *(past)* ──►give ◄── *(obj)* ── book ◄── *(recip)*

from ──◄ I

FIG. 2.1. A cognitive structure representing semantic relations in a simple sentence. (Adapted from Schank, 1972.)

concepts referred to in the sentence, including such information as tense, object, and recipient of actions.

Another example is shown in Fig. 2.2. The sentence is from Bransford and Frank's (1971) study, and the representation is constructed by Rumelhart, Lindsay, and Norman's (1972) system using principles developed in Fillmore's (1968) analysis of semantic relationships. An important finding by Bransford and Franks was that the form of this structure seemed to be about the same whether subjects heard the sentence all at once, that is, "The rock that rolled down the mountain crushed the tiny hut at the river," or if they heard smaller sentences, like, "The rock rolled down the mountain," "The rock crushed the hut," "The hut is at the river," and "The hut is tiny," with sentences involving different content presented in between.

The studies that we have carried out at Michigan on this problem have extended the evidential support for the idea that comprehension is primarily a process of developing a cognitive structure that represents conceptual relationships. The first study that I will mention was conducted by David

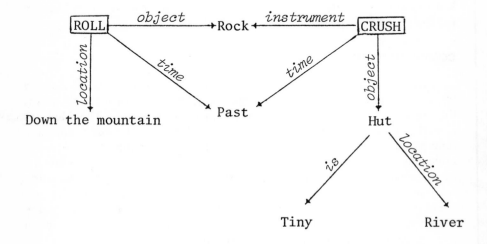

FIG. 2.2. A cognitive structure for a more complex message. (Adapted from Lindsay and Norman, 1972.)

King. King's study used an experimental paradigm developed by Kintsch and Monk (1972), who showed short paragraphs for less time than it takes to read them, and then asked questions that subjects could answer only if they had read and understood two or more items of information in the paragraph. Kintsch and Monk's main result was that the time used to answer questions correctly did not depend on the syntactic form of the paragraph read. The result is explained most simply by the hypothesis that while syntactic variables can influence the ease with which subjects assimilate the conceptual relationships in a message, they do not affect the form of the cognitive structure that subjects build.

Computability Judgment Requirement

King's experiment was very similar to Kintsch and Monk's, using somewhat different kinds of materials, and adding the experimental manipulation of conceptual contiguity. King used stories about hypothetical automobile trips. Each story contained some quantitative information, relating to variables in the following formulas.

$$\text{Distance} = \text{Mileage} \times \text{Fuel used}$$
$$\text{Distance} = \text{Average speed} \times \text{Driving time}$$
$$\text{Average speed} = \text{Average force}/\text{Weight}$$
$$\text{Driving time} = \text{Duration - Stop time}$$

Each subject saw 18 paragraphs of approximately equal length, each containing six items of information. From two to four of the facts in a paragraph were values of quantitative variables from the formulas. The other information included the name of the traveler, the traveler's destination, the purpose of the trip, and an item the traveler took along—when the letter items were needed to fill out a six-item paragraph. After the paragraph had been shown for 15 seconds, the paragraph was replaced by a question that could be answered yes or no. Two-thirds of the questions dealt with the quantitative information, requesting computability judgments of the form, "From the information given can you compute...?" The other questions dealt with the descriptive information, such as, "Did he go to visit his grandmother?"

There were two variables used in presenting paragraph information. One was the syntactic complexity of the sentences. The other was the contiguity of information related to the quantitative variables. To illustrate, the following is a paragraph having two items of quantitative information; the syntax is simple in this paragraph and the quantitative information is not contiguous.

Greg maintained an average driving speed of 70 miles per hour. He drove all the way to Detroit. He went there to look for a job. He brought with him a letter of recommendation. His car used 35 gallons of fuel on the way.

TABLE 2.1

Proportion Correct Response on Computability Items

	Simple syntax	Complex syntax
Contiguous information	.77	.73
Noncontiguous information	.68	.60

The following paragraph has the same information, but the syntax is complex and the quantitative information here is contiguous.

In Greg's driving all the way to Detroit, where he went in order to look for a job bringing with him a letter of recommendation, an average speed of 70 miles per hour was maintained while 35 gallons of fuel were used by his car.

In general, each complex paragraph was a single sentence constructed with as many syntactic barbarisms (such as embedded clauses and passive voice) as possible. Simple paragraphs were composed of short, declarative sentences. Contiguity was manipulated with as much contrast as possible.

The results of the experiment consist of correct response proportions, and correct response latencies (Table 2.1). The 6% difference due to syntax is about the same as the difference found by Kintsch and Monk (1972); it was only marginally significant in King's data. The 11% difference due to contiguity of information was a statistically reliable result.

The main result of the experiment is in Table 2.2—the times taken for correct responses. The differences shown are all far short of significance, with F ratios less than 1.0 for both main effects and the interaction. This result is consistent with Kintsch and Monk's findings, and we interpret it in the same way they did. If the cognitive structure built by the subject were dependent on the format of the input, then complex or disconnected input would not only lead to more errors, but also to slower inference time. Since the inference time was unaffected by either syntactic complexity or semantic contiguity, the result is consistent with the hypothesis that the subject's cognitive

TABLE 2.2

Mean Time (in seconds) for Correct Responses
on Computability Items

	Simple syntax	Complex syntax
Contiguous information	10.4	9.5
Noncontiguous information	10.1	10.5

structure, built to represent the information in the paragraph, is independent of these format variables.

Reading Time Study

The second study that I will mention here was carried out by David Noreen, and is reported more fully elsewhere (Greeno & Noreen, in press). In Noreen's experiment we measured the time taken by subjects in reading sentences. The question we asked was whether the difficulty of assimilating the information in a sentence would depend on a structure built by sentences read previously. The relationships among sentences used in one of the conditions are diagrammed in Fig. 2.3. The two hierarchies in the figure represent concepts that are related by set inclusion, with $a \supset b \supset c$. For example, in one set of sentences the top concepts (a and a') were tall buildings and short buildings. There were tall office buildings (b_1) and short office buildings (b_1'). Included in office buildings were department store buildings specified as tall (c_1) and short (c_1'). At c_2 and c_2' there were banks, with the Midwest Bank said to be a towering structure (c_2) and the National Bank said to be shorter (c_2'). The b_2 had high-rise apartment buildings while b_2' denoted shorter apartment buildings, and the entries below b_2 and b_2' were special cases, as on the other side.

Each sentence specified a relationship between corresponding concepts in the two hierarchies. In the paragraph about buildings, the top-level sentence was, "The tall buildings in Midwest City usually seem to be built

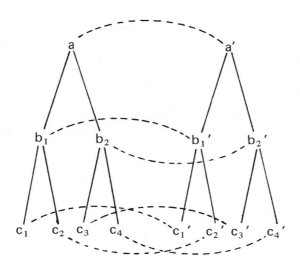

FIG. 2.3. Relations among concepts used in experiment on time to read semantically related sentences.

TABLE 2.3

Mean Time (in seconds) to Read Sentences

	Top-down order	Bottom-up order
Top level	6.5	5.8
Bottom level	8.5	12.2

less soundly than the shorter buildings." The sentence linking the concepts at level b_1 was, "The office buildings with a small number of stories are generally more well-built than those with a large number of stories."

Each sentence was presented for the subject to read, and the time used by the subject was recorded. After each sentence was finished, the subject counted backward for about 10 seconds and then stated the meaning of the sentence to the experimenter. After all seven of the sentences that related to a given topic were completed, the subject answered seven true–false items about the sentences. Each of the true–false items was either a sentence that had been read or the contradiction of one of the sentences.

There were two experimental variables of interest. First, the sentences were presented in different orders: a top-down order starting with a, then b_1, then c_1, c_2, b_2, c_3, and c_4; and a bottom-up order starting with c_1, c_2, b_1, c_3, c_4, b_2, and finally, a. The other experimental variable involved the consistency of the sentences. In one-half of the paragraphs all the sentences specified the relationships going in the same direction. In the other cases there was an exception at the c_1 node.

The effect of ordering on reading time is shown in Table 2.3. These sentences were not all the same length—the fact that it took longer to read low-level sentences is not interesting in these data. The interesting fact is that it took only about two-thirds as long to read the low-level sentences if they were preceded by the sentences that were above them in the hierarchy. The relationships involved in the low-level sentences are consistent with more general relationships given in the higher-level sentences, and when those general sentences were read first, the low-level sentences were made easier.

Of further interest was the time necessary to read sentences that were inconsistent with material read earlier. The comparisons in Table 2.4 are between corresponding sentences in paragraphs that had no exceptions to the general trend of the comparison, and sentences in paragraphs that included an exception. The exception was always sentence c_1. Thus, in the top-down order c_1 contradicted expectations built up by the earlier sentences. That exceptional sentence, and the one following it, took longer to read than was the case when no exceptions occurred. In the bottom-up order, the exception came first, so it was not seen as an exception when it appeared. But since two sentences following it were inconsistent, *they* took longer to read.

TABLE 2.4

Mean Time (in seconds) to Read Sentences

	Top-down order (c_1 and c_2)	Bottom-up order (c_2 and b_1)
Consistent	8.2	9.8
Inconsistent	11.6	14.0

King's and Noreen's results add to the evidence that in comprehending linguistic input, we build structures of semantic relationships. Comprehension may be a process of building those structural trees in memory, as in theories being developed by Schank (1972) and Winograd (1972).

LEARNING

Learning, like comprehension, is primarily a process of constructing conceptual relationships. To demarcate the discussion, it is useful to have a concept that refers to intermediate memory storage. The box diagram in Fig. 2.4 labels a memory system with larger capacity and longer holding power than short-term memory, but which has not necessarily become a part of semantic memory. This part of the box diagram has been called working memory by Feigenbaum (1970) and Reitman (1970).

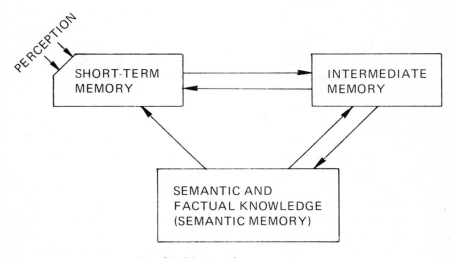

FIG. 2.4. Diagram of memory systems.

Processes for Organizing and Storing Information

Intermediate memory is a system with holding times from several minutes to several hours. Most of our knowledge and understanding of learning mechanisms are at this level. We know practically nothing about processes of increasing and modifying long-term stores. We do know, of course, that some of the information in intermediate memory becomes part of the learner's permanent organized knowledge, and some does not. However, what brings about that transfer is as yet not understood, and I do not intend to deal with that problem here.

Much classroom evaluation involves knowledge stored in intermediate memory which does not become transferred in detail to permanent semantic memory. When a professor prepares a lecture, he generally reviews material or prepares notes by referring to articles and books. That is, material stored in long-term semantic memory is usually not sufficient; structures must be generated in intermediate memory to ensure that the desired information will be included and presented intelligibly. Similar preparations are standard practice for businessmen before they present complex information at meetings, and for attorneys before they present arguments at court. The processes of organizing and storing information in intermediate memory are found in a broad range of important situations where human cognition is exercised. Understanding these processes is a worthy enterprise, and is one about which we have a great deal of scientific knowledge, based on the experimental study of free recall, paired-associate learning, and serial learning.

Free recall. For many years we thought that the free-recall process consisted mainly of forming new associations between individual items, or between items and contextual stimuli. However, work carried out in the last decade, notably by Mandler (1967) and Tulving (1962), has made it clear that free recall is primarily a process of organizing integrated retrieval systems. General discussions of this process, related to hypotheses about the structure of semantic memory, have been given by Kintsch (1972) and Rumelhart et al. (1972), and a formal model of the process of developing the structure has been developed by Anderson (1971).

Paired-associates. The evidential status of hypotheses about organizational processes is not as strong for paired-associates learning as it is for free recall (Postman & Underwood, 1973). However, the idea that subjects develop relational retrieval systems has been applied to the study of interlist transfer and forgetting (Greeno, James, & DaPolito, 1971; Greeno & Scandura, 1966; Polson, 1972). It is well known that relations of similarity and category membership affect the learning of paired associates lists (Batchelder, 1970, 1971; Feigenbaum, 1963; Hintzman, 1968; Polson, Restle, & Polson, 1965; Restle, 1964). The general idea shared by all these analyses is that encoding processes generate retrieval and chunking cues. General mechanisms that construct cognitive structures with some of these features have been developed by Feigenbaum (1963) and Hintzman (1968), and it seems likely that the notion of an EPAM net probably is an important component of a theory about organizational processes in paired-associate memorizing.

Serial learning. It is interesting to recall that Ebbinghaus (1913) used serial learning tasks in order, he thought, to examine processes of forming associative connections between items in the list. During the 1950s, rote serial learning was studied with considerable energy, in an effort to achieve a satisfactory analysis based on the idea of stimulus-response association. The desired analysis was never achieved; a good statement of the theoretical outcome has been given by Jensen and Rohwer (1965). It is easy enough to see what the serial *response* is, but much evidence has accumulated showing that the *stimulus* is not just the preceding item. Many experimental studies were carried out in an effort to find the effective functional stimulus in serial learning, but no one ever found it.

As with free recall and paired-associate memorizing, evidence is developing that serial memorizing includes an important component of cognitive organization (McLean & Gregg, 1967). Recent studies by Martin and Noreen (1973) have employed analyses that allow measures of trial-to-trial consistency in subjects' performance. Recall that organizational processes in free recall were revealed by Tulving's (1962) measurement of trial-to-trial consistency. Martin and Noreen's seriograms support the same conclusion regarding serial learning; that is, subjects are organizing cognitive structures, rather than forming interitem associations, or learning list-position cues.

Learning and Complex Cognitive Structures

If we assume that subjects in rote learning experiments build cognitive organizations in intermediate memory, then it is useful to examine experimental tasks that can be organized in interesting ways. An especially nice example may be found in Restle's (1970b) investigation of number pattern learning. A sequence with a simple organization is shown in Fig. 2.5, along with the structure of operators that Restle proposed as a likely cognitive hierarchy. When a subject learns such a sequence, he develops a structural representation of it in intermediate memory. An appropriate theory of learning is thus a theory of the process by which the cognitive structure gets built.

The current state of theory about building complex cognitive structures is the topic of a review presented by Dennis Egan and myself elsewhere in this volume. As that review indicates, most of our knowledge is about the kinds of structures that subjects acquire, and we understand the process of acquisition only in relatively simple cases, such as learning single dimensional rules for classifying stimuli.

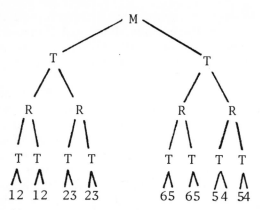

FIG. 2.5. Cognitive structure corresponding to a sequence of numbers. (Adapted from Restle, 1970.)

Learning and Problem Solving

A series of studies in our laboratory has dealt with learning relatively simple computational formulas from probability theory. In most of our experiments subjects learned the binomial formula. Some of our earlier experiments led to a distinction between propositional and algorithmic aspects of acquired knowledge. Propositional aspects correspond roughly to the understanding of concepts; and algorithmic aspects refer to appropriate sequences of actions (Greeno, 1973a). In a recent experiment, Richard Mayer has obtained a result that indicates an important distinction between different aspects of algorithmic knowledge.

In Chapter 5 of this volume, Simon and Lea distinguish between two aspects of cognitive processes during problem solving. One involves attempts to find operators or rules that give progress in the problem and the other, search for information in the problem environment. In calculation, this distinction appears in an especially clear form. To solve the problem, subjects must carry out computations using given quantities. Thus, the subject must identify quantities in the problem with variables in the computational formula, and then do the appropriate calculations. The process of identifying variables probably evokes mechanisms like those in Bobrow's (1968; also see Paige & Simon, 1966) model STUDENT, which translates quantitative information from English text into algebraic equations. Knowledge about the computational operations includes memory of which operation to use at each stage, as well as procedures for carrying them out. Theories about computational procedures have been developed recently by a number of investigators (Dansereau, 1969; Groen & Parkman, 1972; Restle, 1970a; Suppes & Morningstar, 1972).

In a recent experiment on binomial probability in our laboratory, the problem-solving stages were separated experimentally, making the task into a serial anticipation learning problem. Subjects received a series of problems requiring calculation of binomial probabilities, and learned an ordered set of calculations. The steps in solving the problem were of two kinds: (a) identification of a quantity—for example, reading the text of a problem and determining that the value of "p" in the formula is .25; (b) computation—such as multiplying two numbers, raising a fraction to some power, or finding the factorial of a number.

Mayer used two kinds of pretraining with different groups of subjects. In one procedure subjects were given some conceptual background. There was discussion of what a trial is, what an outcome is, what the probability of an event is, and so on. In the other procedure, subjects were trained to write the formula for binomial probability, with the steps in writing out the formula treated as items in a serial list. Following one of these pretraining procedures, subjects learned to compute binomial probability by the method of serial anticipation.

The data in Table 2.5 are the mean number of errors made by the groups with different pretraining on the two kinds of steps involved in the computation. Note that the identification steps were somewhat easier for the group given conceptual background. This would indicate that the processes of finding information in a problem text is aided by appropriate structures in semantic memory. However, the computational steps were much easier for the group previously trained to encode the binomial formula. The result empirically supports the idea that some things we know affect our ability to extract information from a problem situation; and other things we know affect our ability to apply that information correctly.

CONCLUSION

In the section on learning, I have tried to illustrate the important role played by cognitive organizational factors, in both the experimental psychology of rote memorizing, and in more complex tasks involving problem solving and concept instruction. If this analysis is correct, it follows that a central component of learning theory is a set of principles describing how individuals represent relational structures in the material they learn. That theoretical problem is exactly the one dealt with in current theories of comprehension processes.

TABLE 2.5

Mean Errors during Learning of Computational Sequence

	Identification steps	Computational steps
Trained on concepts	5.2	17.2
Trained on formula	7.0	3.8

Should we conclude that learning theory and comprehension theory are identical? At this moment, I am prepared to accept that assertion. There are differences, to be sure. We tend to think of comprehension, rather than learning, if the relational structures built in intermediate memory are of a familiar kind. We tend to refer to learning in tasks where new kinds of relational structures are formed. But that distinction is quite soft, and would not stand up to energetic attack. More meaningful ways of distinguishing between comprehension and learning may emerge as we clarify the process of modifying semantic memory. But at this point, I propose the working hypothesis that the same cognitive principles are operating in both comprehension and learning. We are far from knowing what all those principles are, although the current active state of research on these problems, and the solid gains that have been made in recent years, have brought some of them within view.

3
SUBJECTIVE PROBABILITY DISTRIBUTIONS FOR IMPERFECTLY KNOWN QUANTITIES

GORDON F. PITZ
Southern Illinois University at Carbondale

Uncertainty is an inescapable characteristic of man's environment. "One thing at least is certain—this life flies. One thing is certain, and the rest is lies."[1] That may be overstating the case a little; yet there are many aspects of our knowledge that are imprecise, many propositions, the truth of which we cannot indicate with certainty.

Take as an example the proposition, "The population of Brazil exceeds 85 million." Most people have some vague idea of what the population of Brazil must be, and could give limits within which they are quite sure that the true population must lie. Usually, however, they are not willing to commit themselves on the truth of this particular proposition, or of others like it. In this paper, I shall be concerned with methods for characterizing the degree of uncertainty that is associated with such propositions. I would like to suggest a tentative framework for describing uncertain knowledge, and to offer some methodological suggestions for measuring uncertainty.

DETERMINING SUBJECTIVE PROBABILITY

An Experimental Statement of the Problem

To introduce the issues, let me first describe the results of a simple experiment. The subjects were 19 undergraduate psychology majors, who were asked to indicate the extent of their uncertainty about the populations of 23 countries in North, South and Central America. For each country, they were asked to give two values, say, x_1 and x_2. These values were to be chosen

Research was supported by the National Science Foundation, through Grant GB-28708X. Assistance in conducting the studies reported was provided by Rosemary Schwartz, Cheryl Richardt, Steven Zang, and Willbann Terpening.

[1] *Rubaiyat* of Omar Khayyam.

in such a way that the subject was equally sure that the true population was (a) less than x_1, (b) greater than x_2, or (c) between x_1 and x_2. A classically educated friend insists that the correct term for these values is *tertiles*, i.e., values that divide a probability distribution into equal thirds.

The hyperprecision effect. One might expect that, if subjects had any appreciation for the degree of their uncertainty, the tertiles should include the true value approximately one third of the time. In fact, the number of trials on which the true value of the population fell between the two values given by the subjects was less than 16%. This phenomenon is referred to here as a *hyperprecision effect:* Subjects believe the accuracy of their knowledge to be greater than is warranted by empirical reality.

A rational approach. Since uncertainty must be a characteristic of the environment of any living organism, it is reasonable to assume that organisms develop some mechanism for coping with this uncertainty. One might first ask, therefore, how a perfectly designed organism would handle the problems of uncertain knowledge. One solution to this problem begins with an axiomatic characterization of what is considered to be "rational behavior." Such axiom systems have been proposed, for example, by De Finetti (1937) and by Savage (1954). From the axioms, the theory of personal probabilities follows as a normative prescription for behavior. A working hypothesis may be proposed, that uncertain knowledge can be represented adequately by a set of probability distributions.

By probability, I mean a degree of belief that characterizes the observer of an event, rather than a characteristic of the event itself. The problem of measuring these personal probabilities is for the most part a psychological one.

Choices among gambles. One approach is to give probabilities an operational definition through choices between gambles. For the proposition, "The population of Brazil exceeds 85 million," a person's probability may be measured by offering him several gambles. One of these would pay off if the proposition is true, and the others would pay off on the basis of some random process such as the throw of a die. The numerical probability for the proposition can be determined on the basis of the person's choices.

From a measurement point of view, this procedure may be quite satisfactory, but it leaves unanswered two important questions. The first is psychological: By what process does one arrive at the decision to choose one of the gambles? The second is normative: How does one determine that the judgment is a wise one?

Describing the Behavior

Information processing ability. First, let me point out the obvious fact that a person's processing of uncertain knowledge must take place within the limitations of his general information processing abilities. A person operates with a working memory that is of limited capacity. Within this working memory, operations must take place serially, and only two or three elements can be held in memory for simultaneous comparisons (Newell & Simon, 1972). These limitations impose serious constraints on the extent to which a person can deal with uncertain knowledge, and may account for the fact that a normative theory of rational behavior is not necessarily an adequate descriptive theory. This idea has been pursued by Slovic (1972).

Multistage probabilistic inference. Fig. 3.1 shows a probability tree, with three possible outcomes at the final stage. The equation gives the usual method for computing the compound probability of a given outcome. This equation requires a weighting and summing procedure that would be very difficult for an organism that has a limited working memory and that operates serially. With a tree of any greater complexity, the process would be impossible. It should not be surprising, therefore, that in multistage inference tasks subjects use strategies more appropriate to their abilities (Snapper & Fryback, 1971).

A decision model representation. I shall try to show how one might construct a more accurate description of a subject's behavior. Starting with a very simple, single-stage decision, a serial choice process is postulated. That is, a list of alternatives is generated by the subject, and then considered serially.

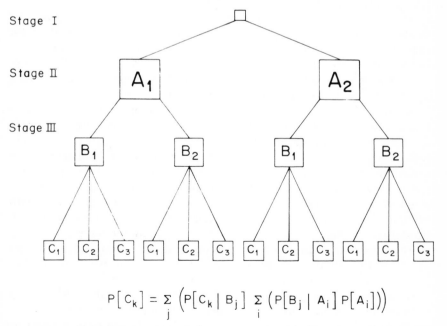

$$P[C_k] = \sum_j \left(P[C_k \mid B_j] \sum_i \left(P[B_j \mid A_i] P[A_i] \right) \right)$$

FIG. 3.1. An example of a probability tree with the usual equation for compound probabilities.

Such a process can only be appropriate for the simplest of decision tasks. Decisions and judgments that use uncertain knowledge are more complex, and are more closely related to the multistage inference task described in Fig. 3.1. In these tasks, a terminal decision is reached through a chain of cascaded inference, and each step is uncertain. Such a task is probably a good model for the way in which people evaluate uncertain quantities such as the population of Brazil. A choice at each stage leads to a consideration of the alternatives at the next stage, until a final decision is reached.

I have assumed, then, that uncertain knowledge is structured in much the same way as is a multistage probabilistic inference task. There is not necessarily only one such structure for a given problem, but it is assumed that only one structure can be handled at a time. For example, the proposition, "The population of Brazil exceeds 85 million," might be evaluated in the following way: First, is "millions" the appropriate unit? Second, how does the size of Brazil compare with that of the USA? Third, what is the population of the USA? And so on.

The statistician, D. V. Lindley, tells the story of a general whose prescription for military decision making was, "First, decide what is the most likely thing to happen. Then take the action best suited to that outcome." This is an irrational, but probably common mode of decision making, and is an inevitable consequence of the serial nature of information processing. The normatively correct way of treating such a task is to compute the probabilities of each terminal event by means of the usual equation for compound probabilities. The fact that, instead, subjects use the serial processing method was demonstrated by Steiger and Gettys (1972). They proposed what they call a "Best Guess" model to account for the results, which is essentially the same model as the serial structure.

Alternative judgments of uncertainty. It is important to emphasize at this point that there are two quite different questions one might ask of a subject when he is confronted with uncertainty. One is to request a decision, a best guess, a point estimate. The other is to ask for a judgment of the degree of uncertainty that is involved. These two questions define two kinds of tasks, analogous to the statistical problems of estimating a mean and giving a statement of probable error. This paper is primarily concerned with tasks that require subjects to evaluate their uncertainty. However, I shall suggest that, in these tasks, the decision process plays a central role. The subject is first and foremost a decision making organism; he is not accustomed to evaluating uncertainty, and I suggest that, when required to do so, his strategies are dictated by his decision processes.

Estimating degree of uncertainty. How, then, would a subject who uses a serial decision process estimate the degree of his uncertainty? One possible method is to determine the subjective probability of each branch point at each node of the tree and aggregate these probabilities. I am inclined to rule out this mechanism, primarily because it would seem to place an undue computational load on the working memory. A more likely strategy consists of estimating uncertainty through a judgment of the variability of terminal decisions. This might be done by multiple replications of the decision process, which might involve the subject's constructing several different representations for the problem. He would then estimate the uncertainty from the variability of the decisions that are reached that way. For example, one might be able to think of several different methods for estimating the population of Brazil. The degree of uncertainty would be a function of the variety of different answers one can produce.

Knowledge and variability. One consequence of the suggestion made here is that one might expect more restructuring, or more variability, of a multistage inference process when the subject has more relevant knowledge that he can use. If this is the case, the knowledgable subject is less likely to show a hyperprecision effect. That is, the more information a subject has, the more variability he can anticipate, and the less likely he is to exhibit overconfidence.

Slovic (1972) has suggested a process of adjustment, using the initial decision as an anchor point, to account for some data from an unpublished study by Tversky and Kahneman. There is no doubt that a preliminary judgment or decision is an important determinant of subsequent processing. Hence, it is likely that the restructuring process that I am suggesting here will be done with the first terminal decision playing an important role as an

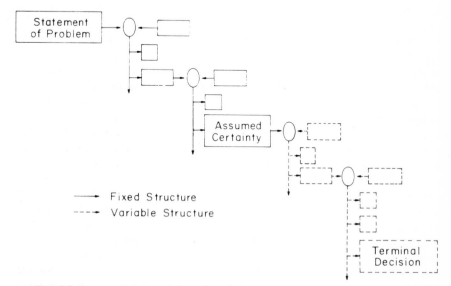

FIG. 3.2. A representation of the point of assumed certainty. (Variability occurs in the structure of decision processes beyond the point of assumed certainty.)

anchor point. The important assumption is that it is primarily through making a series of decisions that a subject is able to appreciate the degree of uncertainty associated with his knowledge. A normative model, of course, states the principle in reverse: A decision should be determined by one's estimate of the degree of uncertainty involved.

Assumptions of certainty. When the decision tree contains many nodes, there is a good deal of evidence that subjects tend to eliminate much of the uncertainty by assuming that only one alternative is possible at some of the nodes. For example, at least one of our subjects apparently decided that "billions," not "millions," was the appropriate unit in which to express the populations of American countries. Slovic (1972) has pointed out that such a process will account for many of the reports of a hyperprecision effect. A schematic representation of this process is shown in Fig. 3.2. It is assumed that, in searching for different ways to structure the problem, the subject will work only with that part of the structure that follows the point of assumed certainty.

SOME EMPIRICAL RESULTS

As a theory, the representation given here is clearly incomplete. Nevertheless, it may be useful in interpreting data from experiments concerned with uncertain knowledge. I shall review some empirical results in the light of these comments about the structuring of uncertain knowledge. In doing this, I shall also comment on some of the methodological problems that are involved. It may become clear that there does not yet exist a perfect method for studying uncertain knowledge.

Direct probability estimation. One technique that has been very popular in recent years is the method of direct probability estimation. Subjects may be asked to express their uncertainty as a probability, a number between zero and one. There is an appealing directness to this approach, but there are inevitable problems in making inferences about psychological processes from numerical responses. These problems are compounded when the response scale is one with which most subjects have little familiarity. These issues were discussed elsewhere (Pitz, 1970), with reference to the so-called phenomenon of conservatism (Edwards, 1968).

Conservatism. Criticism of the use of conservatism as a theoretical construct has been offered by Green (1968) and by Pitz, Downing, and Reinhold (1967). As a descriptive concept, conservatism tells us little about the judgmental processes involved in probabilistic decision tasks. Hence, I would like to suggest that, rather than compare numerical responses with some criterion such as Bayes' theorem, it may be more useful to ask how much information (in the information theory sense) a direct probability estimate transmits about the external stimulus. If conservatism is the only way in which probability judgments depart from optimality, perfect information is being transmitted; it is a trivial matter to rescale the judgments in such a way that they conform to the details of a standardized probability scale. It might reasonably be said that, in such a case, the subject has an appreciation for the relevant attributes of the stimulus. However, Pitz et al. (1967) and Kahneman and Tversky (1972) have suggested that in many cases the relevant aspects of the stimulus from the subject's point of view are not those that would be used by an optimal processor of information.

Some interesting data that illustrate this point are presented in Fig. 3.3. Probability judgments were obtained from a group of 38 subjects. For each possible probability judgment, we computed the proportion of times that the event being judged turned out to be true. Note that conservatism would show up as an S-shaped series of points, with a slope steeper than one. However, any strictly monotonic function would indicate the subjects were able to reflect empirical reality in their judgments. The two sets of data were obtained from the same subjects, at the same time.

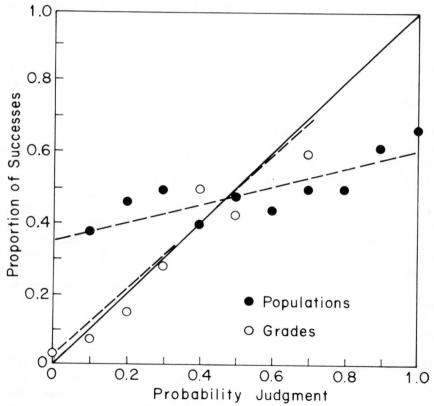

FIG. 3.3. The relationship between probability judgments and empirical reality under conditions designed to minimize information transmitted (populations) and to maximize information transmitted (grades).

The points with the flat slope were obtained under conditions designed to minimize the amount of empirical information transmitted by the judgments. The stimuli were 12 statements of the form, "The population of Brazil exceeds 85 million," with the numerical values being either 20% lower or 20% higher than the true value. The subjects were students in an experimental psychology course, whose knowledge of the populations of foreign countries was assumed to be slight. It was expected that there would be few structural representations of the problems available to them, and that there would be many unwarranted assumptions of certainty. It may be seen that there was no relationship between the judgments and empirical reality, except at the extremes of the judgment scale, and even at the extremes there was a great deal of overconfidence.

The second set of points concerned events for which it was assumed that the subjects would have a rich knowledge base from which to structure the problem. The judgments were taken one week before the final examination in the course, and concerned the grade that the student expected to receive from the course. The information being transmitted by these probability judgments is rather high.

Fractile estimates of probability. Direct judgments need not be given as probabilities. One may also ask subjects to give fractiles for their subjective probability distribution, when the response will be a value for the quantity that possesses a specified cumulative probability. There have been a few recent studies that have used this method. In an unpublished study at Harvard, Alpert and Raiffa asked subjects to give first and 99th percentile values for a variety of quantities. The result was a general hyperprecision effect, of the variety mentioned at the beginning of this paper. Rather than the percentiles including the true value 98% of the time, the figure was less than 50%.

It is probably not the case that probability judgments and fractile estimates give identical measures of uncertainty. Fig. 3.4 presents data from another study in which 44 students in a statistics course were asked to give both probabilities and fractiles for their final exam scores. The circular points show the empirical validity of the probability judgments. The square indicates what happened to the fractile estimates; in this case they were to cover a range with 90% probability, but actually included the true value less than 50% of the time. The fractile estimates produced a hyperprecision effect much greater than that shown by the probability judgments.

One result from this study supports the contention that the broader the base of relevant knowledge, the more restructuring the subject can do and the less will be the hyperprecision. When subjects were divided into two groups on the basis of their final exam performance, the hyperprecision was less for those whose performance was better. The percentage of scores included within the 90% range was 64% for the better students and 33% for the poorer students. This is not to say merely that people who do well can

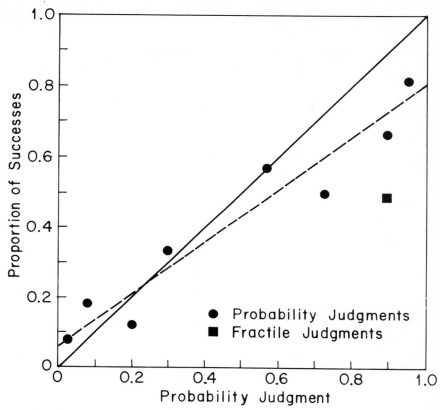

FIG. 3.4. The relationship of probability judgments and fractile judgments in reflecting empirical validity.

better estimate their performance than those who do poorly. They probably can; the point is that they are also better able to assess the possible variability of their performance. Of course, since this was a course in statistics, there is a serious confounding that prevents one from taking the results too seriously.

Previously I described an experimental study of hyperprecision that used tertile estimation methods. From a methodological point of view, tertiles may be more useful in measuring uncertainty than are other fractiles. In studies of fractile estimation like that of Alpert and Raiffa's, one is forced to define a fractile in terms of a numerical probability, and one is faced with the problem that subjects may not be familiar with probabilities. It is easier to define tertiles for the subject, since they can be explained purely in terms of equally likely regions. Quartiles have the same property, but subjects find that estimating two tertiles is easier than estimating three quartiles. The first use of tertiles to assess subjective probabilities, as far as I can determine, was by Peterson and Phillips (1966).

Knowledge and the hyperprecision effect. In one study using tertile estimation methods, three different kinds of quantities were used, varying in the extent to which the subjects were expected to possess relevant knowledge. One set of questions dealt with populations, one dealt with the heights of well-known buildings, such as the John Hancock building, and the third with the ages of well-known people, such as Golde Meir. As expected, the hyperprecision effect was greatest for populations, the tertiles including the true values 23% of the time. For heights of buildings, the effect was almost as great, the true value being included by the tertiles 27% of the time. For ages of people, however, the effect was reversed; the tertiles included the true ages 47% of the time. When estimating ages, the subjects overestimated the degree of their uncertainty. The reason, I suggest, is the greater store of relevant knowledge that people possess concerning people's ages, and the greater variation in hypothetical estimates of age that result from the restructuring process.

Decision vs. direct estimates of uncertainty. I have suggested that a decision or direct estimation process is fundamental to the uncertainty estimation process, in that the former is well established, and the latter does not fit comfortably within the natural information processing system. An experiment was conducted by Will Terpening and myself that supports this contention. Six graduate students in psychology gave tertile estimates for a variety of quantities, populations of countries, heights of buildings, etc. These tertiles define several events that presumably have equal subjective probabilities. A few days later, the subjects made choices between pairs of gambles that were based on these events. Every subject showed a strong preference ordering among the events, even though each event presumably had the same subjective probability. Most importantly, there was a strong preference for gambles involving the central region between two tertiles over regions outside the tertiles. The central region, of course, would include the subject's point estimate, and this point estimate was apparently more important in determining their choice than was their judgment of the probability of a region's including the true value.

The idea that decisions are fundamental to uncertainty estimation can be taken one step further. It is possible to construct a decision task that is based upon a subject's probability distribution for some uncertain quantity, and which then permits the estimation of the subjective probability distribution itself. That subjective probabilities for simple events can be measured this way was pointed out by Becker (1962). The technique is extended here to the case of tertiles. The technique is valuable for two reasons. First, a subject is not required to make any numerical responses; second, it is possible to examine directly the relationship between subjective probabilities and decision-making behavior.

Estimating tertiles using a decision task. Suppose a subject is given any two values, not necessarily tertiles, for some uncertain quantity such as the population of Brazil. He may then be offered a number of alternative decisions: He might specify that the true value is located in one of the three regions defined by the two values, or he could indicate that the true value is *not* in one of the three regions. There are, then, three possible positive responses and three negative responses that he could make.

The decision made by the subject can be used in an iterative fashion to provide estimates for his tertiles. The payoffs can be manipulated so that positive and negative responses give different information about the underlying subjective probability distribution. Following a decision, the two specified values can be altered in such a way as to make the probabilities of the three regions more alike. This sequential estimation technique has been programmed for a PDP-12 computer, and we have used the method in a number of exploratory studies.

In one study, 24 subjects were run, using the populations of four countries and the ages of four well-known people as the uncertain quantities. Since a decision task was used to estimate the uncertainty, one would expect some degree of hyperprecision to occur. The decision-based method does not encourage the subject to take into account the probability of a range that includes his point estimate. For example, a region that includes the mode of a distribution does not necessarily have a very high probability. Nevertheless, it is likely that in a decision task, subjects will tend to ignore the probability of the range, and attend exclusively to the point estimates. The results support this hypothesis; the final tertile estimates included the true population values 18% of the time, and the true ages 34% of the time. The degree of hyperprecision was somewhat greater using this technique than with the direct tertile estimates.

I shall describe one more study that was designed to investigate the hypotheses being suggested here. There is an obvious difficulty in studying uncertain knowledge by asking the subject what he knows, for example, about the population of Brazil. The relevant information that the subject possesses is unknown, and in any case it varies so much from person to person. In the final study, the relevant information was defined during the course of the experiment. The subjects were 10 graduate students and faculty in psychology; they were given descriptions of causal models for the prices of three hypothetical stocks on a stock market. The most complex model is illustrated in Fig. 3.5. One of three normal distributions was selected on the basis of a three stage probabilistic model. The compound distribution of prices is shown at the bottom. The other two causal models were created by omitting either the first stage, or the first two stages of the model shown in Fig. 3.5. The models were not presented in this way to the subjects, but were described verbally.

After studying the descriptions of the three models, the subjects participated in the decision task described previously. The task was presented to them as an experiment in the buying and selling of stocks. From

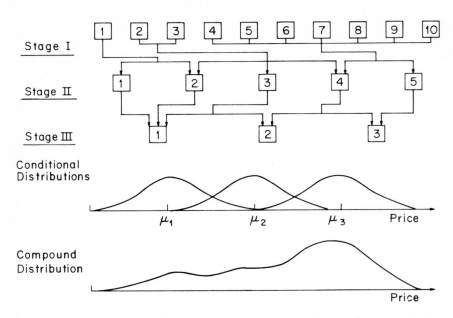

FIG. 3.5. A description of the most complex causal model for the prices of three hypothetical stocks, and the distributions of prices used in an experiment designed to investigate the effect of information available on degree of hyperprecision.

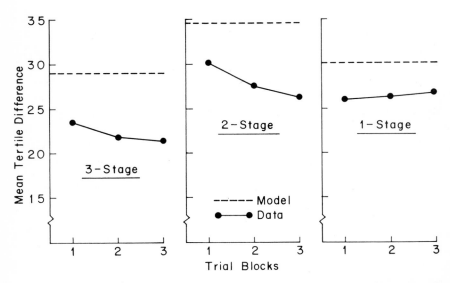

FIG. 3.6. Tertile judgments of uncertainty as a function of complexity of causal model assumed and as a function of trial block.

their decisions it was possible to estimate tertiles for their subjective probability distributions. On the basis of the hypothesis suggested earlier, it was expected that the degree of hyperprecision shown by subjects would be greater for the more complex causal models. The relevant data are shown in Fig. 3.6. It may be seen that there was some slight support for the hypothesis. Of particular interest is the fact that the degree of hyperprecision increased over trial blocks for the multistage models, but not for the single-stage model. However, individual differences were extremely large, and it will be necessary to extend this experiment further before placing much confidence in the results. It is likely, for example, that the most complex model was not complex enough to cause great difficulty for the subjects. Furthermore, the obvious role of random processes in determining the stock prices may lead to important differences between the subjects' processing of these models and their processing of other uncertain quantities.

CONCLUSION

As a concluding comment, I should point out that there has emerged over the last few years an important technology of decision analysis (e.g., Raiffa, 1968). The purpose of decision analysis is to replace intuitive decision making with a more analytic treatment, using the formal methods of decision theory. The assumption underlying the use of these methods is that decisions based on a formal analysis of probabilities and utilities will be more accurate than those made at an intuitive level. However, in any decision analysis, the evaluation of uncertainty at each stage of the decision is critical to the final solution. Hence, one cannot escape subjective judgments entirely; one can only hope to guide them by pointing out the consequences of each judgment, and by searching for inconsistencies. What I have tried to show here is that, while people may be able to make quite accurate decisions or point estimates, there are serious limits to their ability to assess the probable error of their judgments, and that these limitations stem from fundamental characteristics of the human information processing system.

4

THEORY OF RULE INDUCTION: KNOWLEDGE ACQUIRED IN CONCEPT LEARNING, SERIAL PATTERN LEARNING, AND PROBLEM SOLVING

DENNIS E. EGAN and JAMES G. GREENO
University of Michigan

Our purpose in this paper is to contribute toward theoretical integration in the psychology of learning. We will be concerned with learning that occurs in several experimental tasks, including concept learning, serial pattern learning, and problem solving. In each of these situations, a subject begins the task lacking certain critical knowledge. During performance of the task, the subject may acquire new knowledge structures that provide for reaching a criterion set by the experimenter. The knowledge structures are rules stored in working memory. Subjects abstract the rules by observing one or more examples of the rules in use. We will present a review of theoretical proposals that have been offered to explain learning in all of these situations, and develop an analysis of relationships among those theories.

For each experimental situation designed to study induction, we will analyze three issues. The first issue involves the kind of knowledge structure that is constructed as a result of experience in the task. The theoretical question here is what kinds of structures enable subjects to *perform* successfully.

The second issue involves the kinds of knowledge structures that subjects need as prerequisites for learning rules. The question here is what kind of knowledge base is needed for *learning how to perform* the experimental task successfully.

The third question is how the *process of acquisition* occurs. That is, how does the transition take place from the state in which the prerequisite knowledge is available to the state in which the acquired knowledge structure has been incorporated into the knowledge base.

This research was sponsored by the National Science Foundation, Grant GB-31045.

The general plan of our analysis is as follows. We will take up the experimental tasks in turn, considering in each case the issues of structure, prerequisite knowledge structure and acquisition process.

The acquired structures that we consider are all tree structures, differing mainly in the kinds of operations that are postulated. For concept learning, we follow Hunt (1962; Hunt, Marin, & Stone, 1966) in concluding that the acquired structure is a decision tree, with nodes representing tests of attributes for presented stimuli. For serial patterns, we follow Restle (1970b) and Simon (1972a) in concluding that the general form of the acquired structure is an hierarchy of operators defined on an alphabet of some sort. In the case of problem solving, we conclude that the general form of the acquired structure is an hierarchy of goals, involving transformations of the features of the problem situation. We further postulate that the information retained after problem solving is in the form of a mechanism for constructing a goal structure, such as that constructed by GPS (Ernst & Newell, 1969).

We discuss prerequisites for acquisition of these structures in relation to the theory of semantic memory. For concept learning involving well-defined stimulus domains, the needed structures are described conveniently in notation given by Kintsch (1972), and called *antonymous n-tuples*. The structures used in learning conceptual categories in poorly defined stimulus domains seem more easily specified by semantic structures described by Rumelhart, Lindsay, and Norman (1972). These include specified relations of class inclusion and property attribution. The prerequisite structures needed to acquire a serial pattern are knowledge of the alphabet of symbols and a set of operators defined on the alphabet, such as successor, plus 2, times 3, and so on. To acquire the goal structure of a problem-solving sequence, a subject needs to know the features of objects (as is also necessary for concept learning) and a set of operators for transforming features of objects, making new objects in the process (as occurs in serial patterns).

Our discussions of acquisition processes vary in detail with the extent to which the processes have been investigated. Regarding rules for classification, detailed models have been formulated, and a considerable body of empirical information has been gathered from the analysis of simple cases. Quite specific hypotheses have been developed about more complex cases. Concerning serial pattern learning and learning of problem solutions, much less is known about the process of acquisition. However, we can present some general comparisons between the inductive processes that seem reasonably well justified by present knowledge.

CONCEPT LEARNING SYSTEMS

In concept learning, subjects learn a rule for classifying stimuli. The task typically involves a set of stimuli constructed by fixing j values on each of k dimensions. Frequently there are from five to eight dimensions, with two values each. The experimenter decides on a rule for classifying the stimuli—for example, "Figures that are large, and either red in color, or circular in shape, are examples of the concept." The subject's task is to discover this rule, using evidence based on the classification of individual stimuli provided by the experimenter.

A related task, studied somewhat less frequently, may be called *associative grouping*. The subject is asked to learn associative names to several stimulus items, which may be words or visual forms. The names are not all different, and stimuli that have the same name are similar in some way. If stimuli are words, the grouping may be based on a common property of things named by the words. The list might include names of several red objects—apple, brick, rose—and all these might be paired with a single nonsense syllable. Other items in the list might have stimuli naming small things—atom, mouse—and still another category might be names of smooth materials—silk, satin. The subject's task is simply to give the correct name to each of the items. However, the similarity of stimuli having the same name allows the subject to learn a rule that is simpler than the entire list.

Conceptual Structures

Hunt, Marin, and Stone (1966) described the structure of inferred classification rules as sequential decision trees. At each node in the tree a test is carried out to determine the presence or absence of some feature of the stimulus object to be classified. In general, the feature tested at each point depends on the outcome of previous tests, and this structure of intertest dependencies is determined by the logical connectives in the concept. Fig. 4.1 shows a tree for testing membership in the concept category, "Large, and either red or circular." Note that the same features could be used to define a different concept, such as, "Either large and red, or a circle," and then a different tree would be acquired. By *connective structure* of a concept, we will mean the pattern by which the component features are connected in a tree.[1] In the case of classificatory concepts, the alternative connective structures correspond to logical connectives "or," "and," and so on.

There are relatively strong empirical reasons for accepting Hunt's hypothesis about the structures acquired in concept learning. The best evidence was obtained by Trabasso, Rollins, and Shaughnessy (1971). Their

---

[1] In standard terminology, introduced by Haygood and Bourne, reference is made to attribute learning and rule learning. "Attribute" is ambiguous, since it sometimes refers to a dimension and sometimes to a value on the dimension. We use "dimension" to refer to a class of properties (e.g., color, size) and "value" or "feature" or often just "property" to refer to single properties (e.g., red, large). We also think that the term "rule" is ambiguous, since it naturally refers to the complete decision structure used in classification, but in Haygood and Bourne's usage it refers to a single aspect of the structure. We use "connective structure" to mean the way features are related in a concept, and we use "rule" to refer to the complete structure.

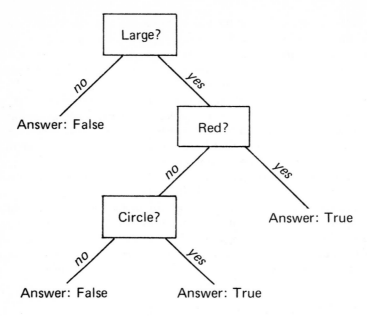

Fig. 4.1. Tree for classifying geometric stimuli in concept learning.

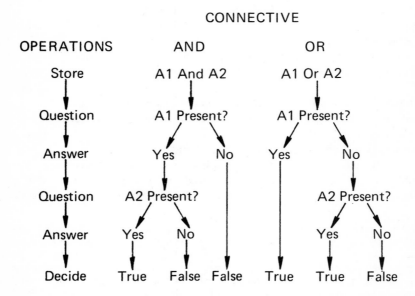

Fig. 4.2. Optimal decision trees for processing conjunctive and inclusive disjunctive concepts (Trabasso, Rollins, & Shaughnessy, 1971).

subjects read statements like, "Large triangle and green circle," and were then shown a triangle and a circle on a slide. The task was to verify whether the statement accurately described the presented objects. Two sets of findings corroborated the hypothesis of a decision based on a tree structure of sequential tests. First, concepts requiring more complex decision trees required more time, both for storing the concept (measured by the time to read the concept's description) and for deciding whether the concept was verified by the picture (measured by time to respond "yes" or "no" after the picture was shown). More detailed evidence was provided, involving the verification times for specific instances. Consider the two decision trees in Fig. 4.2. The time needed to decide "false" for a conjunctive concept is minimal for an instance that has neither of the required attributes, since the first test made by the subject will allow the decision to be made immediately. On the other hand, an instance having one of the attributes will generally take some additional time, since the first attribute to be tested might be present, requiring a second test to determine whether the concept is satisfied. Trabasso's data were generally consistent with predictions based on such considerations, and thus, support the idea that classification rules are represented in cognitive structure as sequential decision trees.[2]

A second source of evidential support is in results of experiments comparing the difficulty of acquiring concepts of varying complexity. Definite predictions about difficulty of acquisition do not follow from the structural model, but it is reasonable to expect that concepts requiring more complex trees—trees with a greater number of nodes—should be harder to acquire. This general relationship is consistent with results of a great many studies (e.g., Bourne, 1970; Haygood & Bourne, 1965; Neisser & Weene, 1962). It should not be supposed that complexity of the acquired tree is the only determinant of learning difficulty. A frequent finding is that rules requiring equally complicated tree structures are not equally easy to learn. For example, Bourne (1970) found that inclusive disjunctions were easier to acquire than conditional rules. Such findings are of value in guiding development of specific hypotheses about the acquisition of classification rules. However, the relationship between complexity and learning difficulty is strong enough to corroborate the hypothesis that the acquired structures in concept learning can be represented as structural decision trees.

---

[2]Trabasso, Rollins, and Shaughnessy (1971) formulated their model as a strictly sequential process. However, formal analysis by Townsend (1972) has shown that parallel processes with rate constants that depend on the amount of processing completed will mimic strictly sequential processes. We have not worked out parallel processes corresponding to sequential decision classifiers in detail, but it seems very likely that such processes could be constructed. Thus, Trabasso et al.'s findings should not be interpreted as evidence for a sequential, rather than a parallel process, although the evidence for the structural features of the decision process seems cogent.

In the case of associative grouping, the structure acquired by subjects probably is simpler than structures of the kind represented in Fig. 4.1. Each grouping of stimuli shares a single feature; the process of assigning a stimulus to one of the groups consists merely of determining which feature it possesses. A tree structure for assigning stimuli to categories is shown in Fig. 4.3. The model is of a sequence of feature tests, similar to the propositional concept model discussed earlier. Another alternative is shown in Fig. 4.4, where a single test node is assumed, with a number of branches equal to the number of categories.

It should be noted that the decision trees postulated for these classification tasks are formally equivalent to the discrimination networks assumed in EPAM (Feigenbaum, 1963) and SAL (Hintzman, 1968). In the tasks given to EPAM and SAL, each item must be discriminated from every other item, so selection of features correlated with response assignments is

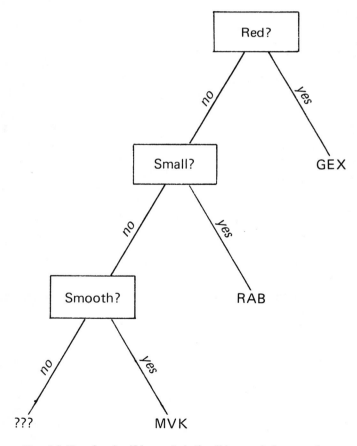

Fig. 4.3. Tree for classifying verbal stimuli in associative grouping.

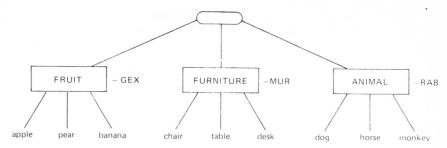

FIG. 4.4. Single level *n*-ary tree for associative grouping.

not involved in the learning outcome. However, it is of interest that the kind of structure postulated for categorical rules is the same as a verbal learning structure in which individual items must be discriminated.

Prerequisite Knowledge

The structure acquired when subjects learn a rule for classification includes features of the objects that are classified. Knowledge of such features, then, probably constitutes prerequisite knowledge for the acquisition of classification rules. There are several schemes for coding the features of a set of objects, including Backus Normal Form grammar (Newell & Simon, 1972). The notation we use here is taken from Kintsch (1972), whose discussion was developed in relation to general properties of the organization of long-term memory. The part of Kintsch' discussion relevant to the present issue is his notation for representing concepts that refer to a partition of some class. Kintsch called such a partitioning set an *antonymous n-tuple*, denoted $(a_1 V \ldots V a_n) \leftarrow c$, where c is the general concept, and the a_i give a partition of the class named by c. The use made of this notation in Kintsch' theory of semantic memory includes representation of concepts that have differing partitions, such as

$$(\text{pet V farm-animal V wild-animal}) \leftarrow \text{animal}, \qquad [1]$$
$$(\text{mammal V bird V insect V reptile}) \leftarrow \text{animal},$$
$$(\text{human V nonhuman}) \leftarrow \text{animal}.$$

Kintsch' antonymous *n-tuples* give a convenient way to represent knowledge of stimulus attributes in well-formed populations—knowledge of what dimensions are varied and what values the dimensions take. In a single example,

$$(\text{color V size V shape}) \leftarrow \text{dimension}, \qquad [2]$$
$$(\text{red V blue}) \leftarrow \text{color},$$
$$(\text{large V small}) \leftarrow \text{size},$$
$$(\text{circle V triangle}) \leftarrow \text{shape}.$$

Note that questions of the form, "Is x an object in the domain?" can be answered with a decision process defined on a knowledge structure like 2. A concept that includes the small domain described by 2 would be (red V blue) ∧ (large V small) ∧ (circle V triangle). A decision tree in the form of Fig. 4.1 could be formed giving the subject a way of determining whether any given stimulus is in the domain. Also note that the rule for any concept specifies a subset of the stimuli in the domain. The decision tree for such a concept has nodes corresponding to properties of objects; therefore, one process involved in constructing the decision tree involves selecting relevant properties. The other process involves discovering the correct pattern of branches and attaching the correct terminal nodes (Haygood & Bourne, 1965).

A subject might start a concept learning experiment with complete knowledge of the stimulus domain, such as that given in 2. On the other hand, he might have to acquire knowledge of the stimulus dimensions and values by observing the experimental stimuli. In the latter case, subjects would need equipment for noticing features of stimuli and for developing a dimension-value structure.

Now consider the knowledge structures needed to acquire rules for grouping verbal stimuli. Two important features distinguish the subject's task. First, the set of stimuli is not a well defined population, constructed by factorial variation of a definite set of dimensions. Secondly, the features that serve as the basis of classification are not detectable in the physical stimuli—i.e., *horses* and *dogs* are not grouped together because of straight lines in the first letter of each word. The shared features are in the subjects' semantic memory structures.

We propose that the knowledge structure prerequisite to learning rules for grouping verbal stimuli is an associative semantic network like those studied by Kintsch (1972), Rumelhart et al. (1972), and Quillian (1968). In these theories of semantic memory there are different kinds of associative connections between concepts. An important distinction is between class inclusion relations and property attribution. Rumelhart et al. designate the relation ISA from a concept to its superset, and the relation HAS from a concept to an attributed property.

A distinction is made in the literature on verbal concept identification between *superordinate* concepts and *sense impression* concepts (e.g., Polson, 1972). Superordinate concepts are groupings of words with shared supersets, such as the categories shown in Fig. 4.4. Sense impression concepts are groupings with shared property associations such as colors, shapes, or textures. Fig. 4.5 gives examples of semantic structures required to identify simple verbal concepts. Note that a basis for grouping Apple with Pear is quite easy to find, since both these concepts are located as subnodes under Fruit in the semantic network. It might be expected that a basis for grouping Apple with Brick might be more difficult to find. Although there is no logical reason for organizing the entries under class names rather than properties,

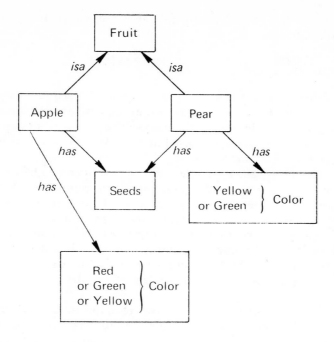

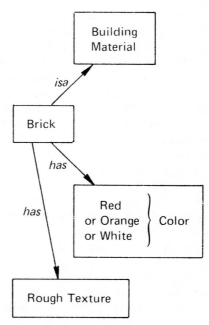

FIG. 4.5. Part of a semantic network.

the available theories have done so, probably because such organization agrees with intuition.

Process of Acquiring Concepts

Rules defined on one dimension. The process of acquiring a simple classification rule is understood thoroughly: Stimuli are classified according to their value on a single binary dimension. The acquired structure is a simple case of the trees shown in Fig. 4.1 and 4.2. When only one dimension is involved, the tree has only one node.

Recent theorizing about simple concept identification has centered around selection of a stimulus attribute for the classification rule. Restle (1962) formulated a rigorous theory based on hypothesis selection. He assumed that selection was with replacement from a constant set of hypotheses. Focussing occurred after correct responses, and resampling occurred after errors. An important theorem is that in this process, all observable properties of the learning system, including the probability of solution following any error, are independent of the size of the sample of hypotheses.

Because of the assumption that subjects resample after errors, Restle's model implies that errors are recurrent events. This counterintuitive prediction was supported in a series of experimental tests carried out by Bower and Trabasso (1964). They showed, for example, that presolution problem shifts did not retard solution. The interpretation of the solution rate as an hypothesis sampling probability was supported by a series of analyses related to the additivity of cues. Trabasso and Bower (1968) presented data involving relevant and redundant cues that were consistent with quantitative predictions based on the sampling assumption about learning rates, and used performance in transfer tasks to estimate that the size of subjects' focus sample was between two and three hypotheses.

The proposition that subjects sample from a fixed set of possible solutions is clearly too simple, and recent work has clarified the selection process. Gregg and Simon (1967) showed that subjects use information available in a stimulus to narrow the set of possible solutions, a procedure they called *local consistency.* Trabasso and Bower (1968) noted that measurements of the hypothesis set obtained by Levine (1967) are reasonably close to the result that would be given by random sampling with local consistency. Any discrepancy from local consistency indicates that an additional memory factor is involved, e.g., keeping track of hypotheses that have been rejected (Chumbley, 1969).

A detailed analysis of the induction of single-dimension classification rules has been made by Wickens and Millward (1971). Their subjects were highly practiced on the stimulus dimensions, and were assumed to consider a small number (s) of dimensions simultaneously, and to eliminate from the sample any dimension whose values were found to be paired inconsistently with responses. When all the dimensions in a sample were eliminated, a new sample was presumably taken. Subjects were assumed to retain information about rejected samples, with a parameter k specifying the number of samples of rejected dimensions that can be remembered. Data were detailed enough to show that no single pair of parameter values for s and k could characterize all of the subjects. However, the values $s = 1$ and $k = 0$ could be rejected for most of the subjects in the experiments.

Associative grouping. Two different experimental procedures are used in the study of associative grouping. In one procedure, subjects study a single list. Items paired with a single response can be grouped together on the basis of similarity. In another procedure, stimuli in different lists that share a feature are assigned the same response.

A theoretical analysis of learning in the single-list procedure has been given by Batchelder (1970, 1971). In Batchelder's analysis, the task is assumed to involve learning at two levels: individual items and relationships between similar items, or rules. An illustration is given in Fig. 4.6. The upper panel shows a tree in which category C_1 is known, with members a_1 and a_2, and response R_1 associated with the category. Individual items b_1 and b_2 are associated with their response R_2, but they are not associated with each other through any common feature. The lower panel shows a modified tree in which both categories C_1 and C_2 are known and associated with their appropriate responses.

In Batchelder's model of the learning process, (a) each item may be in an unlearned state; or (b) in a state where its response is known because it is coded by a feature not shared by other members of the category; or (c) the shared feature of a category may be known. Each presentation of an item presents an opportunity for the item to become learned, if it was not learned previously. Coding a unique feature would produce learning of the individual item. Coding the categorically shared feature would produce learning of the category rule. All members of the category should then be correctly incorporated. Batchelder also assumed that when an individual item was presented, its category rule might be learned. The transitions were assumed to occur in all-or-none fashion. Good agreement was achieved between statistical properties of data and predictions from the stochastic model.

The process of learning to group items appearing in different lists was studied by Greeno and Scandura (1966) and by Polson (1972). Greeno and Scandura found that recognition of a new item occurred in an all-or-none fashion, and that the probability of correctly recognizing its category depended on the variables affecting initial learning, as well as on the obviousness of the categorical connection. In Polson's study, subjects learned a series of lists, each containing one member of several categories. Polson's analysis showed that improvement across lists was related to (a) skill in memorizing individual items; (b) concept acquisition and transfer which

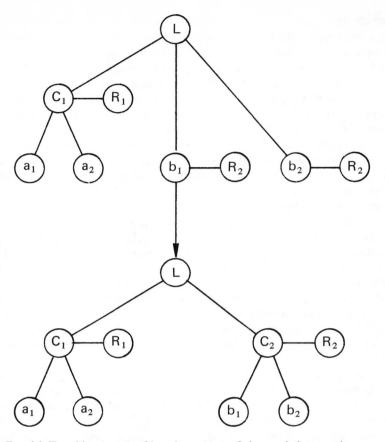

FIG. 4.6. Transition to state of knowing category C_2 in associative grouping.

appeared to occur in an all-or-none fashion; and (c) discovering the general nature of the conceptual categories involved in the task.

The foregoing analyses have provided hypotheses about the process of acquiring a representation of shared features. Correct answers to individual items can be given by subjects whose encoding may not involve shared features. But learning a rule for grouping requires shared features to be encoded.

The available theories are vague on the question of how subjects select features for encoding. Transfer performance measures the probability that shared features are included in the representation, and the effects of some specific factors have been noted. For example, Polson (1972) noted that categories based on shared superordinates are acquired more easily than categories based on shared properties such as colors or sizes. Category dominance, measured by association tests (Underwood & Richardson, 1956b) also affects ease of acquiring categorical rules. The effect of this variable has been related to the parameters of a stochastic model (Greeno & Scandura, 1966). However, other factors, such as the effect of presenting items from a single group in close list contiguity (Schulz, Miller & Radtke, 1963), have not been related to available models.

A more complete theory can be sketched. This theory would specify properties of the subject's short-term encoding, the loss of information from short-term memory, and the effect of both processes on long-term memory representations. The concepts needed for such a theory are available in the literature. Two theories of short-term memory, by Laughery (1969) and by Norman and Rumelhart (1970) analyze short-term feature retention. We need to specify the probability of including a shared feature in the initial encoding of an item, and the rate of loss of features from short-term memory. A simple assumption would be that if shared features occur in short-term memory, the subject will recode them into a category. The situation is graphed in Fig. 4.6. Hypotheses about the features could be related to Quillian's (1968) and Reitman's (1965) discussion of verbal concept activation. Semantic features probably correspond to concepts in semantic memory, an idea that has been used to explain associative clustering (Anderson, 1972; Kintsch, 1970). Quillian's and Reitman's analyses dealt with the simultaneous activation of a semantic node from two sources, and simultaneous activation may correspond to recognition of a shared semantic feature. We believe that the activation features of Quillian and Reitman along with the retention hypotheses of Laughery and Norman and Rumelhart would advance our understanding of associative grouping. Such an analysis might explain the greater ease of acquiring categories involving concepts strongly associated with the items (Underwood & Richardson, 1956a). The stronger associates should have higher probability of being included in the encoding. An explanation could also be advanced for the fact that superordinates provide easier categories than shared descriptive properties (Polson, 1972). Superordinate concepts are relatively strong associates, and in the organization of semantic memory the superordinate entry may be connected directly to the items in an associative group (Rumelhart et al., 1972). Further, analysis of feature loss over time might explain such procedural effects as the greater ease of acquiring categories when items with shared features are presented near each other in the list (Schulz et al., 1963).

Categories based on two or more features. Consider the task of learning a rule for classifying stimuli, where more than one feature is involved in the rule, and where the connective structure is known in advance. Much less study has been given to multifeature rules than to single-feature rules, but there are two relevant analyses.

First, Trabasso and Bower (1964) studied the learning of a classification rule involving four categories determined by two dimensions. The main finding was that the two parts of the category concept each appeared to be acquired in an all-or-none fashion, and the acquisition of the component cues appeared to be independent events.

A detailed analyses of learning the features of a conjunctive classification rule was given by Williams (1971). The memory structures postulated by Williams are similar to those assumed by Wickens and Millward (1971). There is a short-term memory store containing information about a few dimensions, and a longer-term decision store where decisions about dimensional irrelevance are retained. In Williams' model, the subject stores a few property-values of each stimulus in short-term memory, along with their category membership. A trial hypothesis is selected on the basis of information in short-term memory, and is used as the basis of a response to the next stimulus presented. If the response is correct, the subject keeps the hypothesis and adds information about the new stimulus to the contents of short-term memory, losing older information. If an error occurs, the subject tests the dimensions in the trial hypothesis for consistency with the correct classification of the stimulus and tags the inconsistent dimension(s). The effect of this tagging is to reduce the probability on future trials that the tagged dimension will be sampled. Williams assumed that the probability of sampling a dimension increased over trials after it had been tagged as inconsistent according to a linear operator.

Available models of feature learning in multicue classification are strikingly similar to those available for single-feature rule learning. In both cases, short-term memory is used to hold information that generates trial-to-trial responses, and to retain (imperfectly) information about dimensions that have been eliminated from consideration. In the versions developed by Wickens and Millward (1971) and Williams (1971) there are only small differences in detail regarding the way short-term memory is organized and in the exact mechanism of forgetting. Thus, to the best of our present knowledge, the processes of inducing single-dimensional classification rules also operate during multidimensional rule learning. The major difference in the multidimensional case is that subjects do not treat their hypotheses as indivisible entities. When subjects receive information that one part of a current hypothesis is wrong, they generally change only that part of the hypothesis.

Learning the connective structure of a rule. Formal theories of the process of inducing logical connectives have not been developed. Most empirical results have been incorporated into an "intuitive truth table" theory (Haygood & Bourne, 1965; Bourne, 1970). For problems with two relevant dimensions, practiced subjects are assumed to reduce the stimulus population to four categories, corresponding to the four combinations of the presence (true or T) or absence (false or F) of two relevant features. The rule to be learned assigns a response to each of the four categories, For example, the conditional rule requires a positive assignment to TT, FT, and FF, and a negative response to TF. It is proposed that some response assignments are "natural" for subjects, thereby accounting for relative rule learning difficulty, and some transfer effects. It is apparently easy for subjects to assign positive response to the TT class and negative response to the FF category, but the reverse assignments are more difficult.

Ideas that could form the basis of a formal model of rule learning are available. One possibility would be a simple associative model based on the analysis given by Suppes and Ginsberg (1963). On each trial a subject first classifies a stimulus into one of the truth table categories. The correct response assignment is then learned to that truth table class in an all-or-none fashion. Each trial presents an opportunity to learn the response assignment to only one truth table class, and the learning events are assumed to be independent. This aspect of the model is testable, and Batchelder's (1970, 1971) theorems permit testing specific hypotheses about category inter-dependencies. Another possibility is that subjects might be considering alternative connective structures as hypotheses. They might then learn through a process of eliminating connectives found to be inconsistent with the assignments. Such a theory would relate the process of rule learning to the process of feature selection. Results obtained by Wickens and Millward (1971) and Williams (1971) would then be applicable.

Learning features and connective structure. When both features and connecting operations must be discovered, subjects are assumed to begin with a simple hypothesis. If inadequate, it may be set aside and replaced by another, or it may be elaborated. Two main alternative theories both construct hypotheses that can be represented as decision trees, built from the top down. The main difference between the two theories is in the process of selecting the trial hypothesis.

The concept learning systems developed by Hunt, Marin, and Stone (1966) store lists of positive and negative instances in memory, and develop hypotheses about their classification using a computational routine for attribute selection and testing. This early version differs from the later modification by Williams (1971) in that complete information about each instance is available for the process of selecting features and testing hypotheses. Based on the information about instances available in memory, the computational routine tries to find a single feature that will separate all the negative instances from all the positive instances. Failing this, a single feature will be selected on the basis of its frequency among positive instances. The problem is then treated as two subproblems. The computation is recursive, with each of the subproblems treated in the same way that the initial problem was. Variations of this basic scheme were investigated, including several studies of the effect of varying the size and organization of the memory system.

In Hunt's concept learning systems, selecting attributes differs sharply from processes for learning single-dimension rules, proposed by Restle (1962) as well as by Wickens and Millward (1971). Those theories assume features to be selected on the basis of saliency, considered as a stimulus property. Most theories have assumed that saliency is constant, although Falmagne (1970) described the probability of sampling a dimension as affected by feedback. A similar mechanism was assumed by Wickens and Millward (1971) and Williams (1971) to influence retention of decisions that dimensions are irrelevant.

The second main theory about learning both the features and the connective structure of a concept was developed by Johnson (1964). Johnson's model includes a scanning mechanism for selecting features, and assumes that selection is a probabilistic function of saliency. Saliency is determined by a linear operator that takes initial weights for each dimension and adjusts them according to the outcome of a trial hypothesis using that dimension. Selected features are used in subroutines that attempt to construct trial hypotheses; subroutines for attempting conjunctive and disjunctive hypotheses were implemented. Johnson thus incorporates a process of feature selection similar to those used in recent models. The mechanism for learning connective structure is selection from a set of available alternatives. In contrast, Hunt's model bases feature selection on examination of instances, and uses an algorithmic mechanism of rule construction.

Empirical evaluation of models for complete concept learning is not advanced. Both Hunt et al. (1966) and Johnson (1964) presented only general data supporting the plausibility of their models. Johnson's data consisted of protocols that could be compared to simulation output. Hunt et al. compared relative difficulty of problems and found a rough correspondence between the orderings of the model and those of human subjects. Two problems seem to be of importance regarding the way subjects acquire complex classification rules. First, formal analysis should be made of the empirical differences, if any, between Hunt's and Johnson's models. Secondly, experiments to investigate those specific differences need to be carried out.

General characteristics. One way of acquiring a classification rule involves examination of stimuli known to be in a single category, with the relevant features extracted by a noticing mechanism. The other mechanism uses knowledge of potentially relevant features, prior to examination of task stimuli. The process in this case involves selection and testing of trial hypotheses from a known set of possibilities. Most classification learning mixes these two modes of induction.[3] In learning verbal categories, however, the inductive mode is primarily one of scanning and noticing common features. In learning single-dimensional rules for classifying relatively large sets of stimuli, well-practiced subjects use a relatively pure form of

---

[3] Terminology is ambiguous here, also, since "induction" sometimes is used to refer to the first of these kinds of processes, with some term such as "hypothetico-deductive" applied to the second. We prefer the usage in which "deduction" refers to cases where conclusions are derived by formal argument while "induction" refers to cases where use is made of empirical evidence, including such things as feedback given in an experiment.

hypothesis-testing. The more complex forms of categorical rule learning may involve a considerable mixture of processes and strategies.

RELATIONAL CONCEPTS AND ANALOGICAL REASONING

When multiple stimuli are shown, subjects may be asked to learn the relational basis for classifying pairs or larger sets. In the case discussed previously, a single stimulus is shown, and the subject is asked, "Is this stimulus an example of concept X?" The answer depends on whether the stimulus has the defining features of X, and the subject's task is accomplished when those features and their connective structure have been discovered. In a simple task involving a relational concept, a pair of stimuli is shown, and the subject is asked, "Is this pair an example of concept X?" The answer depends on whether the pair has the defining relational feature of X, and the subject's task is accomplished when the relational feature is discovered. To take an extremely simple example, learnable by laboratory rats, (Lawrence & DeRivera, 1954) a pair of stimuli may consist of two solid rectangular figures, one above the other, and the pair is an example of the concept if the upper rectangle is a darker shade of gray than the lower rectangle.

Whether a concept is called relational or not depends on the way in which the domain of objects is characterized. If we consider the domain of objects called angles, the sharpness of an angle is a simple (one-argument) property of objects. If we consider the domain of line segments, the sharpness of an angle is a relational property applying to pairs of intersecting segments. Generally, then, we speak of relational concepts in situations where a person's attention is naturally given to individual objects, and the properties to be used in classification involve two or more of the entities that seem to represent the natural elementary encoding of the system. We do not mean to suppose that properties of individual stimuli are simpler or more direct than relations in any meaningful psychological sense. As Gibson (1966) has argued forcefully, much of our perception probably occurs on the basis of features that he calls higher-order properties of the physical input to our senses, such as gradients of texture. It seems likely that there are many situations where the relations between or among objects or regions are more salient than the properties of individual objects or regions, as Gestalt psychologists were fond of emphasizing. The important point for present discussion is that some properties characterize individual elements, and some properties characterize pairs or larger sets of elements, and n-relational properties can be used to classify n-tuples of elements.

Our discussion of acquisition of relational concepts for classification of n-tuples involves only minor extensions of the preceding discussion. The reason for a separate discussion of relational concepts is to provide an analysis of analogical reasoning. In an analogies task, subjects are given sets of stimuli in the form $A:B::C:(D_1, \ldots, D_k)$, and they are to choose the stimulus D_i that best completes the analogy. The items may be verbal (e.g., mother : daughter :: father: (nephew, brother, son, niece)), or geometric forms.

We will discuss analogical reasoning as a case of relational concept acquisition, involving the process of finding a relational property that characterizes both the A:B pair and one of the $C:D_i$ pairs. In other words, we propose that the solution of an analogy is just the discovery of a categorical rule that permits classifying the chosen $C:D_i$ pair in the same category (of pairs) as the A:B pair.

Relational Structures

A structure that represents a relational rule for classification is just like a structure that represents a rule based on simple properties, except that the properties at the test nodes may be more complex—i.e., they may include knowledge of relational predicates. A formalism that appears useful for the task is that of a relational network, used by Reich (1970) to represent knowledge involved in speaking and understanding language. A simple example is illustrated in Fig. 4.7, representing a relation defined on four elements, consisting of two arithmetical operators. Huesmann and Cheng (1973) studied a task in which subjects induced rules of this kind. The rectangle represents the trinary relation $x = y + z$, and the triangle represents the trinary relation $x = y \times z$.[4] The idea is that a relational structure like Fig. 4.7 may represent the knowledge used by a subject in testing for relational properties. That is, a structure like Fig. 4.1, or any tree representing a classification rule, might have relational properties at its nodes. In that case, the test indicated by such a node would use a knowledge structure something like the one shown in Fig. 4.7.

To our knowledge, in the studies that have been conducted where subjects have learned relational concepts, classification has involved only single relational attributes. Thus, the acquired structure consists of a single test, with a branch to "true" if the test succeeds, and a branch to "false" if the test fails, as in the case of simple single-feature identification.

Now consider the structure developed in the process of solving an analogy problem. The subject's task is to select an answer D_i that has the same relation to C that B has to A; that is, a relational property is found that is satisfied by the pair (A,B) and that is also satisfied by the pair (C,D_i).

In the simplest analogies, the relational structure needed to solve an item involves a single relational property. Easy verbal analogies are of this type; for example, fish : perch :: dog : (Hereford, leghorn, collie, Siamese). A

---

[4] The notation is especially useful in representing operations with inverses; for example, where $X = Y \times Z$, $Y = X/Z$ and if a set of elements satisfies one of the relations, then the same elements (in a different order) satisfy the other.

single semantic relation—roughly, "kind of" or "example"—characterizes the pair (fish, perch) as well as the pair (dog, collie). However, many analogies use more than a single property. Consider the problem mother : daughter :: uncle : (son, daughter, nephew, niece, cousin). The correct answer probably is "nephew," because uncle is the parent of nephew and uncle and nephew are the same sex. Thus, the relational structure used to solve this problem corresponds to a conjunctive concept, with the properties at the test nodes consisting of the relations "parent" and "same sex."

The conjunctive nature of relational structures involved in analogies is especially clear in problems studied by Evans (1968). An example is shown in Fig. 4.8. The most salient relations satisfied by the pair (A,B) and the pair (C,D_2) seem to be (a) the smaller figure is moved from inside the larger figure and placed at its left, and (b) the dot above the larger figure is removed. Implicit in this statement are an important set of relations involving correspondence between figures—for example, the "larger figure" in both A and B is identified with a triangle, and the "dot above the larger figure" is recognized in both A and C despite its being to the left of the median of A and to the right of the median of C.

The kinds of relations that can be sensed and used by people include quantitative relations, specified on dimensions such as size, lightness, and so

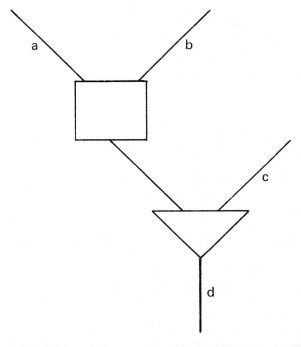

FIG. 4.7. Relational network, representing the relation $d = (a+b) \times c$.

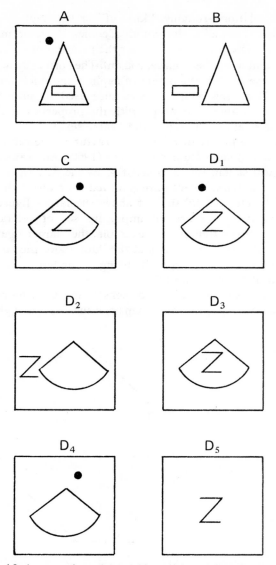

FIG. 4.8. A geometric analogy problem. (Adapted from Evans, 1968).

on. When the features of objects are specified as quantitative values of continuous variables, each stimulus corresponds to a point in n-space, where n is the number of dimensions. Then a relation between two stimuli is a vector. A vector can be considered as a conjunction of n relations, each specifying a difference (distance) on one of the dimensions. In their analysis of analogies involving names of animals Rumelhart and Abrahamson (1971) concluded that subjects develop a relational representation corresponding to the dimensions of semantic space found by Henley (1969). She had subjects rate animal names on the semantic differential, and derived her dimensions from factor analysis. Rumelhart and Abrahamson's results suggest that subjects use quantitative dimensional relations in choosing answers for the analogy problems.

In summary, we think that the structures acquired by subjects who learn to classify sets of stimuli using relational concepts, or who solve analogies, consist of tree structures like those involved in classification of single stimuli. The properties of the test nodes of the trees may themselves be represented by tree structures, and relational networks seem to be a useful way of characterizing them. In the situations studied, the acquired structures appear to be either trees with single test nodes, or trees in which the connective structure corresponds to conjunction.

Prerequisite Knowledge

The main prerequisite knowledge for learning a categorical rule based on relational properties, or for solving an analogy, is knowledge of the relationships involved in the solution. Geometric forms and other pictorial stimuli require ability to detect and classify differences. For example, B is larger than A, and D_2 is also larger than C. In the case of verbal stimuli the needed relational knowledge is contained in the labeled associations of the semantic networks described previously.

When the structure of a relation is complex, as it is in the relation referred to by Fig. 4.7, it seems unlikely that a subject would have all the possible structures in memory. Rather, the simple components of such a structure may be known along with the ability to construct more complex relational properties. Examples of this kind are found in kinship relations, where some combinations of binary relations have simple names (father-in-law, uncle) but others are named only by combinations of relationships (wife's uncle).

Process of Acquisition

One model of the acquisition of complex relational concepts has been developed. Huesmann and Cheng (1973) presented a task in which several sets of numbers were shown, all of which fit some arithmetic formula, such as $(a + b) \times c = d$. Subjects were required to find the rule that the examples illustrated. As they solved the problem, the subjects reported whatever they could about their thoughts.

According to Huesmann and Cheng, subjects work within sets of rules, testing each until the set is exhausted, then moving to another set. The simpler rules—addition, subtraction, multiplication, and division—are tried first; more complex rules are tried later. After a set has been tested, there is some probability that the subject will return to it later if the correct rule is not found. Note that the main structural features of the mechanism for rule induction are the same in the Huesmann and Cheng model as they are in the Wickens and Millward (1971) model and in Williams (1971) model. That is, the subject works with a relatively small set of possibilities, and when elements in that set are removed, new possibilities are generated, with (imperfect) memory of earlier decisions. An important difference is that Huesmann and Cheng were able to specify sets of hypotheses that subjects consider together, based on the complexity of relational properties.

Three models have been given of the process of finding relational structures for solution of analogies. The simplest idea was used by Rumelhart and Abrahamson (1971), who analyzed answers given by subjects to animal name analogies. The analysis was based on a spatial representation of the names, involving three dimensions. According to the model used, the A : B pair of the analogy corresponds to a vector in 3-space. The subject translates the vector so that its origin is at C, then the probabilities of choosing the various D_i alternatives depend on their distances from the end of the vector, with the closer alternatives having higher probability of choice.

A somewhat more complicated mechanism was developed by Reitman (1965) in ARGUS, a general model of cognitive activity that was programmed to solve verbal analogies. ARGUS was provided with an associative memory structure, with labeled associations between concepts. When the A : B pair is presented, the relation that connects those nodes is activated. The problem is solved when a single relation is simultaneously activated by one of the C : D_i pairs. Reitman's model incorporates features of decay of activation over time that we have discussed earlier, but the basic idea is that the relation connecting A and B also can be found as a connection between C and one of the D_i alternatives, and that D_i is the one that will be chosen.

The most detailed analysis of analogical reasoning was given by Evans, who considered solution of geometric analogies. In Evans' program, a relational structure is found that connects A and B, in the form of rules that transform A into B. Similarly, sets of rules are found that transform C to each of the D_i's. The relational structures are then compared, by a routine that removes rules not corresponding between pairs. This leads to the selection of a single alternative D_i, on the ground that the relational structure connecting C with D_i has the greatest similarity with the structure connecting A with B.

General considerations. The same principles appear to govern the induction of relational structures (in relational concept learning and analogical reasoning) as govern the induction of simpler categorical rules in ordinary concept learning and associative grouping. There are cases in which relational properties are known in advance, and induction is a process of selecting the appropriate properties and connecting them. This appears for relational concepts in the Huesmann and Cheng analysis. There are also cases where relational properties are noticed *in situ,* based on a mechanism of difference perception, or of semantic memory activation. These appear in our analyses of analogical reasoning, and are the same general modes of feature selection described in models of ordinary concept learning. Our conclusion is that relational concept learning, and solution of analogy problems, are fundamentally similar to ordinary concept learning, differing only in the kinds of properties dealt with in the two tasks. This is not a trivial difference, but the similarity of cognitive processes in the two groups of tasks seems considerably more important than the difference.

SERIAL PATTERN LEARNING

When a subject learns a sequence, he can extrapolate it to its next member. The simplest case would be a sequence of elements joined by pairwise links. In more interesting cases, sequence elements can be generated from a few rules. The analysis we will give here uses the idea of a relational concept, developed in the previous section. We consider the sequence learned as an *n-tuple* of elements, or a succession of *n-tuples*, and the pattern as an *n*-ary relational structure defined on the elements. As serial patterns are usually studied empirically, the subject learns a single sequence. However, the discussion here will touch on the idea of inducing a structure corresponding to a grammar. This raises questions about classes of sequences that an acquired structure could generate. Accordingly, we will have a few remarks about generalization of serial structure, corresponding to the problem of classification discussed in the previous sections.

Sequential Structures

The simplest cases of series with pattern that we will discuss are a class of sequences studied by Restle and Brown (1970). Define an *srt* sequence as a series of numbers that consists of concatenated chunks, where each chunk is one of the following: (*a*) A constant run, consisting of a series of *j* numbers, all the same—denoted $s(j,i)$, where *i* is the number and *j* is the length of the chunk. (*b*) An ascending or descending run, consisting of a series of numbers starting with *i*, and either ascending or descending in steps of 1—denoted $r(p,k,i)$, where $p = \pm$ (ascending or descending), *k* is the length of the run, and *i* is the initial number in the run. (*c*) A trill, consisting of a series of numbers starting with *i*, in which all the odd positions contain *i* and the even positions contain either $i + 1$ or $i - 1$—denoted $t(p,m,i)$, where *p* is $\pm$ depending on whether $i + 1$ or $i - 1$ is used, *m* is the length of the chunk, and *i* is the initial element. For this discussion, we require the length of an ascending or descending run to be at least two, and the length of a trill to be at least three, thus producing a priority ordering on the chunk structures that

appears to agree with Restle and Brown's data. To illustrate: the sequence
12124654222 would be coded $t(+,4,1)s(1,4)r(-,3,6)s(3,2)$.

As Brown (1971) pointed out, the chunks defined in the *srt* system have a
particularly simple relational structure. A constant run is generated by just
repeating an element the required number of times. An ascending or
descending run is generated by applying the transformation $i_{n+1} = i_n + 1$
or $i_{n+1} = i_n - 1$ uniformly until the needed number of elements is given. And
a trill is generated by applying $i_{n+1} = i_n + 1$ and $i_{n+1} = i_n - 1$ in alternation until the chunk has been generated. On Brown's argument, it is not
surprising that subjects tend strongly to recognize chunks of types *s*, *r*, and *t*
in sequences of numbers, as the evidence indicates they do.

In our usage, the idea of a chunk is a set of elements connected in a
relational structure. Recall from the preceding discussion that a relation
defined on a set of elements may be considered as a component of a complex
concept. The unit we have in mind regarding a chunk in a sequence
corresponds to a set of elements that would be tested by a single decision tree
of the kind shown in Fig. 4.1. It is to be expected that the properties with
greatest salience are those that can easily be expressed as single-node tests. In
that case, the structure acquired when a sequence is learned is the
concatenation of several chunks, each chunk being recognized (or generated)
as a set of elements satisfying a definite relational property. A simple tree
structure representing the sequence 12124654222 is shown in Fig. 4.9. Note
the similarity with Fig. 4.4, representing associative grouping. The structure
is similar, involving in each case a grouping of elements on the basis of a
relation. In associative grouping, the relation is common set membership,
and single elements can be tested for the property involved. Successive
elements within a chunk of a sequential concept are related by a common
transformation. Thus in sequential concepts entire chunks must be tested for
the presence of a relation.

Most studies of serial pattern learning have used either numbers or
letters as elements. In all of these cases (though not only in these cases) the
relations between pairs of elements have the special property that they can be

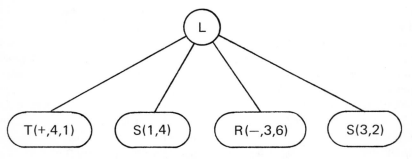

FIG. 4.9. Sequence 12124654222 coded as a series of chunks.

applied iteratively. That is, a relational property applied to x_{n-1} to give x_n can also be applied to x_n, giving x_{n+1}. This property gives the simple structure obtained in runs of consecutive numbers. For example, the chunk 5432 is generated by starting with 5, applying the operator $i - 1$ to obtain 4, then applying the operator $i - 1$ to obtain 3, and finally applying the operator one final time to obtain the last element, 2. Note that this is not a general property of relational systems. For example, in Fig. 4.7, one of the relations of A and B can be stated, "remove dot." This can be applied to A to obtain B, but "remove dot" cannot be applied to B to generate a further element in the sequence.

When the set of symbols is large, a relation can be applied many times to generate a long sequence. The potential length of a sequence can be made infinite by specifying that the sequence is circular—for example, the numbers are defined in such a way that 1 follows 0, 2 follows 1, . . . ,9 follows 8, and 0 follows 9. This circular set allows relations like $i + 1$ to apply to every element, and sequences can be extended indefinitely.[5]

The simplest kind of sequence defined on an infinite ordered set of symbols involves repeated application of a single transformation, for example, 1, 4, 7, 0, 3, ... Sequences generally used in experiments have involved four kinds of complication. First, more than one rule may be used in generating a sequence. Thus, a sequence can be generated by applying the transformations, $i + 3, i - 2, i + 5$ in sequence, so if the initial element is 2, the sequence is 2, 5, 3, 8, 1, 9, 4, 7, 5, 9, ... Secondly, a single rule may have a parameter that changes according to some recognizable sequence. An example is the transformation $i - m$, where m is increased by one each time the transformation is applied. Bjork (1968) studied learning of sequences involving both these kinds of complication, such as $i + 4, i - 2, i + m$ ($m = 1, 2, 3, . . .$), with the transformations applied in rotation. If the sequence begins with 2, the sequence is 2, 6, 4, 5, 9, 7, 9, 3, 1, 4, ...

A structural diagram of a Bjork structure is shown in Fig. 4.10. The subject needs to know the sequence of transformations, and to use the structure the subject needs a memory register to hold the value of m.

A third kind of complication is added in Thurstone series, studied by Simon and Kotovsky (1963) and by Kotovsky and Simon (1973). The extension involves use of two or more sequences that are interleaved to form the series. A familiar example is $a, b, t, b, c, t, c, d, ...$ This is formed from the sequences $a, b, b, c, c, d, . . .$, and the easy sequence $t, t, t, . . .$, with an element of the second sequence inserted after each pair of elements from the first sequence. A structural representation is given in Fig. 4.11. To use this

---

[5] This device allows infinitely long sequences on any set of symbols, including the counterexample given earlier. The relation "plus dot" could be defined so as to add a dot if it is absent, and to remove a dot if it is present, thus making the dot a symbol representing numbers in modulo two arithmetic.

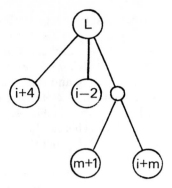

FIG. 4.10. Transformations for generating a Bjork sequence.

sequence, the subject must have memory registers for both i and j, if the sequence is generated in the absence of elements generated in the past.[6].

The fourth kind of complexity involves transformations that take finite sequences as input and return sequences as output. These operations have been studied by Restle (1970), who noted that their structure is represented by an hierarchy of transformations. For example, the sequence 3, 2, 1, 3, 2, 1, 4, 3, 2, 4, 3, 2 has a descending run of three starting with 3, then has that run of three repeated, and then has the resulting sequence of six elements transposed by adding one to each of its members. A structural representation of this sequence is given in Fig. 4.12 in which R represents repetition of a

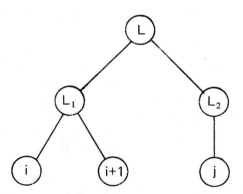

FIG. 4.11. Structure for a sequence formed by interleaving two sequences.

---

[6]Note that Bjork rules may also be interleaved in a similar fashion. Consider the sequence 1,6,2,9,3,8,4,1,5, . . . which is generated by the rules $(i+5)$, $(i+6)$, $(i+7)$, $(i-6)$. This sequence of rules can be represented by interleaving the two sequences $(i+m)$ $(m=5,6,7)$ and $(i-6)$. It is an empirical question whether subjects can learn *srt* chunks when the transformations are defined on rules rather than elements of the sequence.

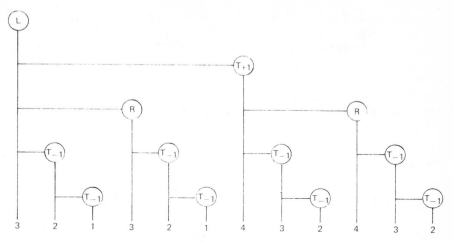

FIG. 4.12. Hierarchical structure of transformations.

subsequence, and T_k represents transposition by k. To use this structure, the subject may proceed in various ways, and an analysis of sequence production based on hierarchical structure is currently in progress by Simon and Greeno.

It should be noted that the structural description of a sequence is not unique. In addition to obvious ambiguities such as the equivalence of + 6 and – 4 in the circle of 10 numbers, there are some interesting alternatives that involve tradeoffs between different sources of complexity in the representation. For example, the sequence a, b, t, b, c, t, ... is coded by Simon and Kotovsky as involving two sequences, with transformations that operate on the current value of the designated sequence. A Bjork structure can also be devised for the sequence, consisting of the operators $(i + 1)$, $(i + m)$, $(i - m)$, $[m = 11, 11, 10, 10, ...]$. The Bjork structure on this sequence has the advantage of using only one working memory for current values, since at each point the operator is applied to the current value. But its sequence of operations is somewhat more complex than that incorporated in the Simon-Kotovsky model.

Our discussion of structures has been limited to relational systems based on symbols from an alphabet with fixed order. Other systems have been studied, notably by Gregg (1967), by Hunt (Chapter 6), by Klahr and Wallace (1970), and by Simon and Sumner (1966). When pictorial stimuli or other patterns are used, a sequence may be represented by transformations in several dimensions. The formal representation of such a sequence would involve transformations consisting of a conjunction of relations such as "add a vertical stripe and rotate 45° ," or some such. It may also be noted that in addition to serial patterns in one dimension, arrays of two or more dimensions can be generated from a set of transformations, when the transformations form an Abelian group. A two-dimensional array would be generated by applying a series of transformations to generate the top row of elements, and then applying a series of transformations to each element in that row, generating the columns of the array. The extrapolation problem for such two-dimensional sequences involves inducing the transformation or transformations for the rows as well as the columns, and presents a rich environment for investigating rule induction, as Hunt's chapter in this volume illustrates.

Prerequisite Knowledge

In any inductive task, the prerequisites include knowledge of a space within which the structure to be induced is contained as a member. As we have noted, that knowledge may be explicit, so that induction corresponds to tests and elimination of definite hypotheses. The initial knowledge about possibilities may be implicit, consisting of the ability to notice and appropriately combine relevant features, or it may be a mixture of these two.

There are two characteristics of serial pattern induction that distinguish it from other forms of relational concept learning. One is the iterative quality of relational systems involved. The other is the nature of connective structures that arise when the relations are used to generate sequences rather than to classify objects. Knowledge that relations defined on an ordered set are iterative may develop as an integral part of such number concepts as transitivity and combination of quantity (cf. Piaget, 1965). In serial pattern learning, principles of concatenation and modification of subsequences make it appropriate to characterize connective structures in terms of formal grammars (Chomsky, 1963; Hopcroft & Ullman, 1969).

The intent of the following analysis is to provide a framework suitable for analyzing connective structures in serial patterns. While our analysis here uses certain formal machinery from the theory of grammars, it is not a complete formalization of serial patterns. We do not go beyond the level of characterizing the four categories mentioned in the preceding section— namely, *srt*-chunked sequences, Bjork sequences, Thurstone sequences with Simon-Kotovsky structure, and Restle-hierarchical sequences. We believe that these classes of sequences might constitute sets of hypotheses. Thus, each grammatical system generates a language of sequences. The learning process would then correspond to a mechanism for inducing a specific pattern within the general class of patterns specified by a grammar. In serial pattern learning these grammars may play the role of truth tables. Just as knowledge of truth tables specifies a set of connective structures, one of which corresponds to the decision tree for the categorical concept, so grammatical knowledge may specify a set of connective structures, one of which may be the target serial concept.

Most of the notation is standard in the theory of formal grammars. However, it is convenient to introduce notation to represent the binary relations that correspond to operators such as $i_{n+1} = i_n + 1$ and the like. The two concepts for which we need notation are the closure of a subsequence and the initiation of a subsequence. We call a subsequence closed when each operation applies to the result of a previous operation. A closed subsequence will be designated by a sequence of operations between square brackets, $[o_1(i) \ldots o_s(i)]$. The variable i in a sequence has to take some initial value, and this will be indicated by the variable name, e.g., $i[o_1(i) \ldots o_s(i)]$ denotes a sequence initiated with some value of i and then operated on successively by $o_1 \ldots o_s$. Exponents will be used to denote repetition, with parentheses added when necessary. For example, $i[o_1(i)o_2(i)]^k$ means that an initial value for i is set, then o_1 is applied, followed by o_2, followed by o_1 and o_2 again, until the pair of operations has been carried out k times. On the other hand, $(i[o_1(i)o_2(i)])^k$ means that i is given an initial value, then o_1 and o_2 are applied, then i is reset to its initial value, then o_1 and o_2 are applied again, continuing until k rounds have occurred. When the number of repetitions is indefinite, an asterisk will be used as the exponent.[7]

We begin with sequences composed of *srt* chunks. The language to be generated is the class of all sequences in which successive chunks are constant, ascending or descending runs, or trills that either rise or fall a single step from their base position. This language corresponds to the set of all sequences, so there is nothing of consequence in being able to generate the language. The point of psychological interest is in generating the set of strings corresponding to the structural descriptions of the sequence.

The grammar has as nonterminal symbols states C, A, and D, representing the conditions of generating constant, ascending, and descending runs, and states U and V which apply while trials are being generated. Additional nonterminal symbols are W, X, and Y, which involve generation of chunk and sequence boundaries. Terminal symbols include (,), [,], *, i, $i+1$, and i-1. It is to be understood that in consideration of a specific sequence, each occurrence of i in the derivation will involve some definite value, rather than the symbol given here, and $i+1$ and i-1 will represent operations to be carried out on the alphabet used in the task. The start symbol is denoted S. The productions are those of a right-linear grammar.

$$Sa \rightarrow (W,$$
$$W \rightarrow [X, W \rightarrow) Y, Y \rightarrow *,$$
$$X \rightarrow iC, X \rightarrow iA, X \rightarrow iD, X \rightarrow iU, X \rightarrow iV,$$
$$C \rightarrow iC, C \rightarrow] W, A \rightarrow i+1 A, A \rightarrow] W,$$

---

[7] There seem to be two uses of the asterisk; one designates sets of strings made up of indicated symbols appearing in any order, the other indicating repetitions of strings with the indicated order preserved each time. The use here is the latter one.

$$D \rightarrow i\text{-}1\ D,\ D \rightarrow]\ D,$$
$$U \rightarrow i{+}1\ V,\ V \rightarrow i\text{-}1\ U,\ U \rightarrow]\ W,\ V \rightarrow]\ W.$$

As an example, the structural description of 12124654 is derived in Fig. 4.13. The structural description generated is $([1\ 1{+}1\ 2\text{-}1\ 1{+}1][4][6\ 6\text{-}1\ 5\text{-}1])*$, corresponding to $((i_1[i_1{+}1])^2\,[i_2]i_3[i_3\text{-}1]^2)*$ in general notation. Compare Fig. 4.9, which shows a more concise tree structure for 12124654222. The grammatical representation, while more cumbersome, has the virtue of making clear the minimal requirements for learning sequences. Since the structural descriptions can be generated from a one-sided linear grammar, only a finite automaton is required for the generating system to operate.

Now we turn to Bjork structures, involving infinite sequences generated by applying a sequence of operations of the form $i \pm c$, where c is a constant, or $i \pm m$, where m advances on each application. Recall that all operations are applied to the element generated most recently, so only one working memory needs to be initiated to produce the symbols that appear in the sequence. However, the increment of each advancing rule needs an initial value and a working memory is required for each advancing rule. The notation we use for the structural description of a Bjork sequence is illustrated by the following: for the rules $i{+}4$, $i\text{-}2$, $i{+}m$ $(m = 1, 2, \ldots)$, we denote the structure $m_1{=}1\ i{=}2\ [i{+}4\ i\text{-}2\ i{+}m_1\ m_1{+}1]*$. The general form of sequences to be derived is illustrated for this sequence as $m\ i\ [i{+}c\ i\text{-}c\ i{+}m\ m + 1]*$.

A one-sided linear grammar will not generate the structural descriptions of Bjork sequences, because of the requirement that a working memory be associated with each advancing rule. The grammar that we give to characterize this system has nonterminal X, terminal symbols i, $i{+}c$, $i\text{-}c$, $i{+}m$, $i\text{-}m$, $m{+}1$, $[,]$, and $*$, and start symbol S, with productions

$$S \rightarrow X]*,\ X \rightarrow i\ [,$$
$$X \rightarrow X\ i{+}c,\ X \rightarrow X\ i\text{-}c,\ X \rightarrow m\ X\ i{+}m\ m{+}1,\ X \rightarrow m\ X\ i\text{-}m\ m{+}1.$$

The derivation for $i{+}4$, $i\text{-}2$, $i{+}m$ is shown in Fig. 4.14. It may be of interest to note that a one-sided linear grammar would suffice if the sequences were restricted to having a single advancing rule, or if all advancing rules used the same sequence of increments. Then only a single memory register would be needed for the advancing rules, and the single initial value of m could be generated without associating it with any of the rule symbols enclosed in the square brackets.

Next we consider the Simon-Kotovsky structures for Thurstone sequences. The need to associate different memory registers with the various sets of operators again requires a context-free grammar. The nonterminals are X and Y, the terminals are i, $i{+}1$, $i\text{-}1$, $[,]$, and $*$. S is the start symbol, and the productions are

$$S \rightarrow X)*,\ X \rightarrow i\ X\ [\ Y,\ X \rightarrow (,$$

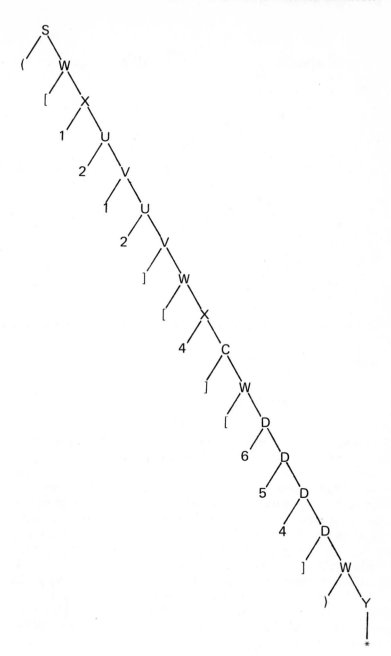

FIG. 4.13. Derivation of structural description of 12124654 using linear grammar.

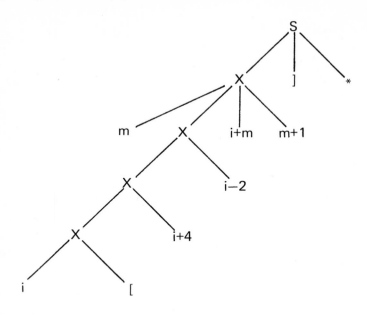

FIG. 4.14. Context-free grammar deriving mi $[i+4$ i-2 $i+m$ $m+1]$* for a sequence 2645979. . . .

$$Y \to i], \ Y \to i+1], \ Y \to i\text{-}1],$$
$$Y \to i \ Y, \ Y \to i+1 \ Y, \ Y \to i\text{-}1 \ Y.$$

The sequence abtbct... would have the structural description $i_2=t$ $i_1=a$ $([i_1 \ i_1+1][i_2])$*. The derivation is given in Fig. 4.15.

Finally, we turn to Restle sequences composed of hierarchies of transformations. These sequences involve operators that are applied to subsequences, and we use the notation $[o[X]]$ to indicate that operator o is applied to the elements of X in turn, generating a new subsequence that is concatenated with X. The notation $[o[X]]^k$ designates that o will be applied to the elements of X, producing X', then o will be applied to the elements of X', producing X'', and so on, until o has been applied successively k times, the complete output being a sequence that is $k+1$ times as long as X.

The patterns to be generated by a grammar for a Restle hierarchical sequence have the form $(i[o_t[. . .[o_2[o_1(i)]^{k_1}]^{k_2}. . .]^{k_{t-1}}]^{k_t}]$*. For example the sequence 321321432432 has the structural description $(3[T_{+1}[R[T_{-1}(i)]^2]^1]^1)$*. A grammar for generating the language of such strings has start symbol S, nonterminal X, and terminals i, o, k, (,), [,], and *. The productions are

$$S \to (iX)^*, \ X \to [oX]^k, \ X \to [o \ (i)]^k.$$

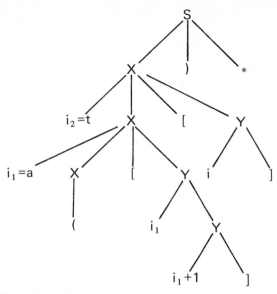

FIG. 4.15. Derivation of structural description of abt bct. . . .

To generate specific trees, rules for replacing i, k, and o need to be specified. i is replaced by symbols in the alphabet, as before. k is replaced by integers, like c in the Bjork sequences. And o is replaced by a set of operators available in the situation, such as T_{+k}, T_{-k}, R, and so on. The derivation of the pattern for 321321432432 is in Fig. 4.16.

Process of Acquiring Sequential Concepts

The grammars given above correspond to machines that can generate the kinds of strings representing learnable serial patterns. The minimal requirements are for a finite state automaton if the sequences are composed of *srt* chunks, or for pushdown storage automata if the sequences involve Bjork structures, Simon-Kotovsky structures, or Restle hierarchical structures. However, human learning systems are probably more complex, involving use of short-term memory as a finite read-and-write tape rather than as pushdown storage, and the use of two or more memory registers for holding information about subsequences. The formal grammatical analysis specifies the kinds of relations that must be found, rather than their generating mechanisms.

To make the learning problem concrete, consider the task of a subject required to learn a sequence generated by repeated application of the same operator—say, 2, 5, 8, 1, 4, 7, ... The task is one of simple relational concept identification. One way to formulate the result is to note that the

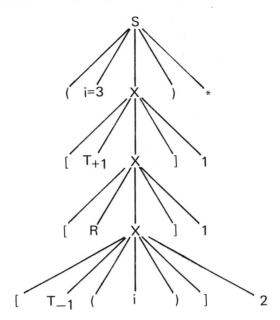

FIG. 4.16. Derivation of a structural description of 321321432432.

solution $(i+3)$ solves an analogy of the form 2:5::5:8::8:1, and so on. The discovery of that solution requires that the subject examine pairs of elements from the sequence, finding a relation between one pair that also applies to the other pairs. If several items are presented at once, then the subject may scan the items, determine relations between pairs, and examine many different pairs in search of consistency. If the items are presented one at a time, the subject must hold a number of items in short-term memory in order to scan for pair relations. Kotovsky and Simon (1973) reported that the relative difficulty of extrapolating Thurstone sequences was about the same using either experimental procedure. Thus, the structural complexity of the sequences is a powerful factor in determining difficulty, and short-term memory for sequence elements and counters is always a factor.

For *srt* chunks, the relation involved in each chunk involves adjacent pairs, but the sequence consists of several chunks having different relations. For Bjork sequences, the relations involve adjacent pairs, but the relation between the nth and $n+1$st elements is not necessarily the same as the relation between the $n+1$st and the $n+2$nd elements. To discover such a pattern, the subject must discover a regular pattern of *differences* between pairs of adjacent items. To do that, the differences must be stored in memory, and comparisons must be made between differences. For Thurstone sequences, two or more patterns of relations operate on different subsequences that are interleaved. Induction requires examination of non-adjacent pairs of elements in the sequence. Finally, for Restle hierarchical sequences, the subject must examine successive relational patterns, and notice that the same structure exists among successive sets of elements. This requires either sets of elements, or relational patterns to be stored in memory and compared with those induced for subsequent sets.

Thus relations abstracted by comparing elements close together in a sequence are learned faster than relations requiring the comparison of elements widely separated in the sequence. For sequences of *srt* chunks, subjects rapidly learn the transformation operating within each chunk, but have difficulty in learning chunk boundaries. Subjects in Bjork's (1968) experiment acquired individual rules in a single stage all-or-none fashion, but learning rates for advancing rules were slower than for constant rules. To learn an advancing rule a subject must make more comparisons of differences abstracted in various parts of the sequence. The difficulty of learning a Thurstone series is directly related to the length of the pattern description of a single period (Kotovsky & Simon, 1973). This fact suggests that recognizing a relationship between two elements in successive periods depends on the organization as well as on the number of intervening elements. In hierarchical sequences, regularities between adjacent elements tend to be recognized first, and later relations between subsequences are noted. Hence, sequential structures like the one in Fig. 4.16 appear to be learned from bottom to top (Restle & Brown, 1970). In some cases the local regularities are so salient that learning of higher level transformations (Brown, 1971) is negated.

A theory of serial pattern learning might assume that subjects try to construct a pattern from noticed relational features. Salience of relational features might thus operate in the environment of serial pattern learning as salience of stimulus features operates in ordinary concept identification. However, it is not clear at this point how to develop assumptions about the search for relations within a single large set.

A fruitful assumption might be that the search goes on within structured subsets of hypotheses about the general properties of the sequence. Such a search process would resemble that assumed by Huesmann and Cheng (1973) in their analysis of relational concept learning. Subsets of relations examined by subjects might correspond to the relations specified in the four grammatical systems given previously. Subjects might hypothesize that the sequence is generated by a system of rules consistent with a grammatical system, and then search for the exact set. Note that each grammatical system corresponds to a nondeterministic automaton, and any definite sequence would be generated by a subset of the rules. The nondeterministic system could thus specify a space of relational structures within which the subject might find a deterministic structure that was satisfied by the sequence at hand. Keep in mind that the grammatical systems are not intended as realistic theories of the learning process. However, they might be realistic theories about subsets of hypotheses examined in the course of learning.

Viewed in this way, the theory of pattern induction given by Simon and Kotovsky (1963) and discussed further by Kotovsky and Simon (1973) represents a theory of search within the subset of possibilities corresponding to the Thurstone sequences. Simon and Kotovsky's model recognizes only "same" and "next" and "backward next" relations in the alphabet, but those relations are examined between pairs of items that are not adjacent. If a relation such as "same" can be applied to items a certain distance apart, then the hypothetical system tests the possibility that the sequence has that period, looking for a pattern of relations that cycles that often. It is important to note that within a set of relations, the various members of the set are probably examined in an order of some kind. For example, Kotovsky and Simon (1973) noted that identity was generally noticed before next relations, and relations between adjacent pairs were noticed before relations between nonadjacent pairs.

A process of finding specific sequential patterns composed of *srt* chunks has been realized in a program written within the framework of the General Rule Inducer (Simon & Lea, Chapter 5).[8] This system codes any sequence into chunks, with priority given first to constant runs, then ascending and descending runs, and finally to trills. Relations are noted by taking the difference between adjacent pairs of numbers in the sequence. The program adjusts hypotheses as long as there is a possibility that the present chunk is a constant, ascending, or descending run, or a trill. When none of those possibilities exists, or when a rule for extending an established chunk conflicts with the next element in the sequence, the code for the preceding chunk is added to the list of rules stored in long-term memory. Repetitions of the sequence are detected by the device of always trying to match the initial chunk stored in long-term memory with any new subsequence encountered, and attempting to use all the chunks stored in memory to generate new instances. The developing new rules are saved as a hedge against future disconfirmation.

It seems clear that similar rule inducing programs can be developed for Bjork sequences and for Restle hierarchical sequences, and made compatible with the Simon-Kotovsky induction program. Interesting theoretical questions will arise when the various programs are integrated into a single system. The various subsets might be searched more or less exhaustively and in sequence—i.e., an inductive program might work from a fixed set of possibilities until the correct one is found. A more interesting prospect is that the system monitors elements stored in short-term memory for whatever simple relations are there. The relations that are found might cue detailed

---

[8]This work was begun at the Mathematics Social Science Board Workshop on Cognition held at Carnegie-Mellon University in June 1973.

examination of a subprogram. Such a program would be similar to Williams (1971) system of feature selection for conjunctive concepts, where selected dimensions are stored in short-term memory, and trial hypotheses are developed by memory scanning.

The hypothesis that relations within subsets are found through a search process is supported by research of Restle (1967) and Vitz and Todd (1967) showing that simple relations among elements in binary sequences appear to be learned in an all-or-none fashion. Restle's (1967) finding that conditional rules are learned in two or more stages is consistent with the assumption that part of a conceptual rule can be preserved when the rule is modified in response to feedback.

Pattern search further provides a way of analyzing generalization. It is known that salience or noticing orders within sets are modified by experience. A sequence that can be organized either in runs or trills will be organized in runs by subjects previously experienced on run sequences; trills will be more prevalent for subjects previously experienced on trills (Restle & Brown, 1970). It seems likely that similar salience effects might occur for more general sets of relational patterns, such as the grammatical structures described here.

INDUCTION DURING PROBLEM SOLVING

In this section we are concerned with induction as it occurs when general properties of a class of solutions are inferred by solving a small number of problems in the class. This kind of induction underlies the development of expertise for a class of problems. Questions of interest concern the way in which an expert's knowledge about a problem is structured, the kinds of activity a novice problem solver must perform in order to gain expertise and the prerequisites for acquiring expertise.

The central concept in our analysis is the idea of problem organization used in GPS (Ernst & Newell, 1969), the goal tree. According to this interpretation, the sequence of actions that solves a problem is organized in a series of subgoals, arranged hierarchically so that if G_1 is above G_2 in the tree, then achievement of G_2 is instrumental in accomplishing G_1. A goal is generally of the form, "Change x to y by doing z," where x and y are situations, and z is some operator or transformation that is allowed in the problem environment. The organization represented by a goal tree specifies a sequence of transformations, each of which modifies one or more features of the situation.

We propose that a person who has mastered a class of problems can construct the goal tree for those problems. This introduces a distinction between the ability to produce a structure and the structure itself. Anyone working through a reasonably complex problem, probably acquires knowledge of the goal tree. That is one sort of knowledge, and we can be fairly definite in characterizing its structure. A person who is said to be an expert for a class of problems can work through new problems in the class with little difficulty. Such knowledge is of a generative nature and allows the expert to construct goal trees in a variety of circumstances.

Solution Structures

For well-defined problems, the subject starts with known initial and desired situations, and finds a sequence of permissible operations that transform the initial situation into the desired situation. As in learning relational concepts, learning to solve a problem involves feature analysis. In particular, the initial stages of both analogical reasoning and problem solving require the analysis of a number of relational concepts defined on two objects. While the person solving an analogy must transfer the relational concept, the problem solver must transform one object into another within the rules of the problem. As in learning serial patterns, problem solving deals with transformations that produce new objects. However, in learning to extrapolate a series, a transformation is applied to the memory of a previous pattern of transformations. In problem solving, the orientation is forward, i.e., transformations are applied to goals later in the problem, rather than retrospectively.

To clarify our discussion we will introduce a few definitions. Any well-defined problem consists of a set of permissible problem states, S, and a set of transformations, T. Problem states can be represented as *n-tuples* in the familiar dimension-value notation used to describe stimuli in studies of concept learning. For each state $s_i \varepsilon S$, $s_i = (d_1, d_2, ..., d_n)$ where each dimension, d_i, has one of a finite number of values. Values may be assigned integers for convenience. There may not exist a unique set of dimensions to represent problem states, but there always exists at least one adequate representation. For example, states in a game of chess might be coded using board locations as the dimensions and names of pieces as values or vice versa. In the Missionaries and Cannibals Problem each state might be represented by the position of the boat and the number of missionaries and cannibals on one side of the river. (For a discussion of procedures for reducing the representation of states in that problem, see Amarel, 1968.)

Each transformation $t_i \varepsilon T$ represents an operation that is permissible in the rules of the problem. These transformations map cylinder sets of problem states into other cylinder sets. Associated with each t_i are its domain c_i and range c_i' each of the form $c_i = (x, x, ..., p_i, x, ..., p_j, ..., x)$. This notation represents the fact that for each permissible operation only a subset of attributes need have specified values, and only a subset are changed by the transformation. While transformations are actually applied to problem states individually, we will use the notation $t_i(c_i) = c_i'$ to make clear the idea that transformations are defined for sets of states.

A convenient way of representing transformations is to employ component vector notation. If $t_i = (0,0, \ldots , v_i, 0, \ldots w_j, 0, \ldots 0)$, then the only features of a problem state altered by t_i are values on the ith and jth dimensions. Suppose transformation t_j is applied at state s_n. Then the resulting state $s_{n+1} = s_n + t_j$. The transformation t_j can be applied legally at state s_n if $s_n \varepsilon c_j$ the cylinder set that is the domain of t_j and if $s_{n+1} \varepsilon S$.

Two further observations are necessary. First, one transformation may follow another only if the intersection of the range of the first transformation and the domain of the second includes the problem state that results from the first transformation. Suppose that at state s_n, $t_i(c_i) = c_i'$ is followed by $t_j(c_j) = c_j'$, then $s_n + t_i = s_{n+1} \varepsilon (c_i' \cap c_j)$. Second, each problem state is the intersection of a finite number of cylinder sets, $s_n = \cap_i (c_i)$. In nontechnical terms, we view the problem solver as selecting a subset of dimensions from the desired problem state, s_d, and trying to transform values of the current state, s_c, to match those in s_d. This corresponds to selecting a cylinder set, say c_j', from the intersection forming s_d, and identifying a transformation, t_j, that will carry the current state into the proper cylinder set. The process of selecting dimensions and the appropriate transformation to modify their values establishes a goal for the problem solver. Once the goal $t_j(c_j) = c_j'$ has been set, the task is to modify the current state so that it falls into the domain of t_j. That of course may require the application of a transformation and the process recurses at a lower level. Eventually, the process will identify a cylinder set c_k' that is produced by t_k where $s_c \varepsilon c_k$. At that point the first operation in the problem can be performed.

Using this formalism, we can define a goal tree as an irreflexive symmetric graph consisting of a set of nodes of the form $t_i (c_j) = c_i'$. These transformations are the goals that modify certain features of the current problem state. In the tree structure subgoals are descendant nodes and represent the operations necessary to produce the conditions under which a higher level goal may be accomplished. When all the subgoals of the goal $t_i (c_i) = c_i'$ have been accomplished the current state at that point in the problem, say s_n, will be in the cylinder set c_i. Clearly the order of executing subgoals is rather strict to insure that problem states fall in the range of appropriate transformations at various stages of the problem. The processing order of this goal tree may be determined by the following algorithm. (1) Process the lowest node on the left that has not yet been executed. (2) If there are unprocessed descendants of the l.u.b. of the goal just executed, return to 1, otherwise go to 3. (3) Process the l.u.b. of the goal just executed and return to 2. One such tree structure of goals with the proper order of processing is given in Fig. 4.17.

The general characteristics of problem solving represented above may be clarified by noting some relationships with GPS. First, recall that GPS has

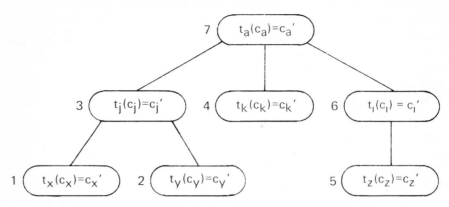

FIG. 4.17. Tree structure of goals with processing order indicated.

the capability of testing the conditions for applying an operator. The pretests for an operator correspond to determining whether the current state of a problem is in the cylinder set that constitutes the domain of the operator. Often a subgoal will be generated to alter the state of a problem in order to meet the requirements of a pretest—that is, to remove a discrepancy between the current state and the domain of an operator. Another point to be noted is that GPS employs an ordering of the differences between states and a table of connections that links transformations to differences that are found. This knowledge corresponds to an ability to generate appropriate nodes in the goal tree on the basis of the problem solver's analysis of features of the situation.

An important feature of problem solving based on generating goal structures is that the entire goal tree need not be held in memory in order to solve the problem. Goal directed moves are possible if a smaller goal stack is held in memory. The goal stack must include the top goal—the root of the tree—as well as the goal being executed and all intermediate goals in the path from the top to the current goal. The goal stack must be ordered in a top-down fashion. The entire goal tree of a problem may be thought of as a record of the contents of the goal stack generated throughout the solution of the problem.

The goal structure of a problem is only one of many structures that might be acquired in the course of solving a problem. We will examine two interesting alternative representations of a problem. Then we will present some data that tend to support the idea that the goal structure is the best characterization of what is learned with experience in solving a problem.

One alternative view of induction during problem solving maintains that the subject acquires a large paired-associate list in which descriptions of problem states are associated with the correct operation to be applied at each state. Specifically, an EPAM net may be constructed for the purpose of classifying problem states. Associated with the terminal nodes of this net would be the correct operation to apply to each set of states. This theory specifies that the bulk of the problem solving effort is of a perceptual and memorial nature. Elements of S are handled as instances in concept learning. Presumably the correct operation for a set of states is learned in a rote fashion.

Evidence comparing chess masters and novices suggests that people do store descriptions of problem states and use that information as the basis of expertise. Analysis of memory for chess positions (de Groot, 1966), eyemovements when scanning a position (Simon & Barenfeld, 1969), and placing pieces to duplicate a chess position (Chase & Simon, 1973) demonstrate that chess masters chunk chess pieces into recognizable patterns. The patterns are defined by chess relations holding between two pieces with a group (e.g., piece A attacks piece B, A defends B, A is the same type of piece as B, etc.). Simon and Gilmartin (1972) have been able to simulate a number of these findings with the Memory Aided Pattern Perceiver (MAPP) program. In this system, a group of pieces is stored in an EPAM net that tests for the presence of particular pieces at particular locations. The terminal nodes of the net contain the label of a cluster or pattern of pieces. This might be something like "Castled king with pawn phalanx." Experienced chess players presumably have stored many patterns, and novices have stored very few.

While MAPP successfully simulates performance in perceptual and memorial tasks, the link between recognizing problem states and producing chess moves has not yet been specified. It may be possible that several clusters can be combined and recognized as a single situation with the best move for that situation learned in a paired-associate fashion. This idea would be similar to Samuel's (1963) proposed rote learning mechanism for storing descriptions of positions in checkers along with information about the best move for each position. A second possibility is that the best move may be determined for each cluster of pieces on a board. Then a selection mechanism would determine which move should be actually carried out. Another possibility is that discrepancies between a stored pattern and a cluster of pieces might generate a move. For example, underdefended pieces might be detected, in which case plans could be made to bring up other pieces to attack or defend (see Simon & Barenfeld, 1969).

A second alternative to the goal structure theory of induction claims that an expert's knowledge about a problem is structured as a serial pattern. In this view, an expert does not construct a tree of goals or analyze the features of problem states, but rather constructs a pattern of transformations (see previous section) that allows the production of the correct sequence of elements in T. To do this, the expert must store lists of correct move sequences, and then be able to extrapolate those in new problems.

There are some cases in which people almost certainly do store sequences of correct transformations while learning to solve a problem. This idea would explain Luchin's (1942) results, where subjects attempted to apply the sequence of transformations that had solved a previous series of water jar problems. When that sequence was inappropriate, subjects had difficulty finding even very simple alternative solutions. Storing move sequences was also the strategy of at least some subjects in the serial switch setting task studied by Laughery and Gregg (1962) and Gregg (1966). In those experiments, the problem was to learn the serial pattern that generated the settings. Subjects did so by acquiring change operators that transformed a base switch setting in sequential fashion. Perhaps the most elaborate model of acquiring move sequences for problems is Hormann's (1965) program GAKU. Its induction mechanism attempts to generalize the sequence of moves that it used to solve a related problem. GAKU's performance has not been tested against human performance.

Thus far we have proposed a goal tree theory of the structure of knowledge acquired when solving a problem. We have also sketched two other theories of the acquired structure. The first claimed that a decision tree was constructed to test states of the problem, and to apply a transformation to that state. The second alternative maintained that a description of the correct pattern of transformations was abstracted and stored.

It might be noted that these three theories of what is learned, when solving a problem, imply very different things about the performance of the experienced problem solver. If a person is solving a problem by way of executing a serial pattern, then he must be always looking backward in the problem. The expert must keep his place on various lists of moves, and base future operations on his memory of previous moves. This "problem solving in the past" can be contrasted with the activity of a solver who learns to recognize states of the problem, and to retrieve the next move in a paired-associate fashion. This activity seems to depend neither on previous sequences of moves, nor on future goals. It is "problem solving in the present." Solving problems by using a goal structure is of course "problem solving in the future," since operations are carried out so that the conditions for future operations may be fulfilled.

To support our choice of the goal structure as the best representation of what is learned while solving a problem, we will present some preliminary results of a series of experiments conducted by Dennis Egan. In these experiments subjects acquired expertise in solving a series of Tower of Hanoi problems. Each problem consists of n disks graduated in size and three pegs for holding stacks of disks. The initial position for the four-disk puzzle is shown in Fig. 4.18. The problem is to manipulate the disks so that they ultimately end up stacked in order on the right-hand peg. The constraints of the problem were the usual ones of moving only one disk from the top of a

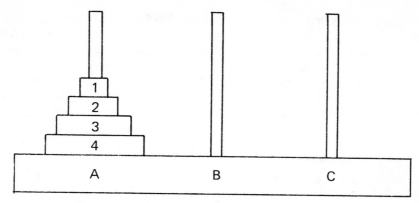

FIG. 4.18. Initial state in four-disk Tower of Hanoi problem.

stack at a time, never placing a larger disk on top of a smaller disk, and attaining the goal in the fewest number of moves possible.

The goal tree for the four-disk puzzle is given in Fig. 4.19. The nodes of the tree indicate the transformation to be carried out. For example, 4AC means, "Transform a state in which Disk 4 is on Peg A by moving Disk 4 to Peg C." The nodes directly under any transformation are the subgoals that must be accomplished to set up the conditions for the transformation. Thus before Disk 4 can be moved from A to C, Disk 3 must be moved from A to B, etc. The goal tree in Fig. 4.19 corresponds to the structure of the reduce-difference goals generated by GPS as it works this problem.

Egan had subjects acquire experience by solving a three-disk and a four-disk puzzle and then transferred them to a five- or six-disk puzzle. The

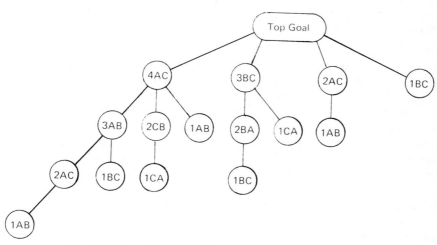

FIG. 4.19. Goal structure for four-disk Tower of Hanoi problem.

smaller puzzles were solved to a criterion of three correct solutions in a row. The procedure was to count as an error any deviation from the unique minimal solution path for each problem. After making an error, subjects were informed of their mistake, were placed back in the previous correct problem state, and then were permitted to continue. When the criterion was reached, the subject began work on the next problem in the series. The criterion for the transfer puzzle was one correct solution. Following that, subjects were given a recognition test in which they viewed selected disk arrangements and had to indicate whether the arrangement shown was in fact one of the states in the correct solution of the transfer puzzle.

An attempt was made to instill different kinds of structural representations for the problems by manipulating the conditions under which subjects solved the two practice puzzles. Briefly, these conditions emphasized either the sequence of moves to get the correct solution, or the major subgoals involved in the solutions, or were ambiguous—indicating only that the subjects should try to learn something from the practice problems, and to apply it to the transfer problem. Subjects in a control group solved the transfer problem with no previous experience on the smaller puzzles. It was generally quite difficult to create differences by pretraining. There are strong indications that acquiring knowledge about the goal structure of problems is the way all subjects benefit from pretraining or general experience.

The error profiles for all groups clearly indicated that subjects performed better as they neared an important goal in the problem. Conversely, subjects tended to have difficulty at points in the problem that were distant from an important goal. This general result is quite consistent with Hayes' (1965, 1966) findings with "spy problems." In those studies subjects memorized a network and then searched it to find a path to a goal. Performance was observed to improve as the subject neared the top goal or a previously defined subgoal. In our Tower of Hanoi studies, subjects apparently abstracted a network of goals on their own initiative.

There were several indications that the network was a goal tree like the one shown in Fig. 4.19. For example, the difficulty of learning the various moves in a problem was linked to the properties of the goal structure used to plan the moves. In these comparisons we will be using data only from the odd-numbered moves in the problems. The odd-numbered moves require a choice among three alternatives: (a) moving the smallest disk to the correct location, (b) moving the smallest disk to a location not on the shortest solution, and (c) moving the disk just moved on the previous trial. The even-numbered moves require a choice between moving the disk just moved on the previous trial and making the correct move. These even numbered moves are easy for subjects to make since they rarely attempt to move a disk twice in a row. The odd-numbered moves always require a decision among three alternatives, and always involve moving the smallest disk. These moves are therefore more difficult to learn and are equivalent in regard to a number of extraneous variables.

If subjects use a goal structure to plan moves, then the difficulty of learning a move should be related to the amount of planning necessary to produce that move in the goal tree. Specifically, if moves are planned using the goal tree in a top-down fashion, then moves made to accomplish high-level goals should be easier to learn than moves that accomplish lower-levels goals. This idea was evaluated using learning data from the Tower of Hanoi studies. The mean number of errors for moves generated at each level of the goal tree was calculated with the result shown in Fig. 4.20.

For the six-disk transfer puzzle, the difficulty of making a move was monotonically related to its depth in the goal tree for levels one through five. This relationship did not hold at the depth of six. The only move occurring at a depth of six in the tree is the first move in the problem. Subjects typically report learning that move by rote memorization. Thus the difficulty of making moves in the problem is related to the difficulty of planning the move using the goal structure in a top-down fashion. Subjects change to a paired associates strategy only for some moves that are very difficult to plan. The corresponding graph for the five-disk transfer problem was virtually identical.

A second fact inferred from Fig. 4.20 is that the three groups with previous experience have a greater advantage on moves that accomplish lower level goals. Initially an inexperienced subject is likely to think that moves accomplishing lower-level goals are arbitrary or unrelated to the higher level goals in the problem. It is only after acquiring experience with the problem that subjects begin to see how the lower-level moves are critical to higher level moves. Ultimately these moves can also be planned, or are just memorized if the planning is too burdensome. These empirical phenomena are also consistent with the idea that top-down planning occurs.

The arrangement of data in Fig. 4.20 refers in a rather simple way to the structural properties of the goal tree. However, those properties do not represent the processes involved in solving the problem. It seems unlikely that the subject would generate a next goal by going back to the top goal and then generating all goals between it and a next transformation. Such a process would not only be very inefficient, but would also make it difficult to solve the problem. An important part of the process of generating goals depends on memory of goals previously generated but not yet achieved.

Alternatively, subjects may keep a record of goals in memory. A pushdown stack seems a suitable device, since the action to be carried out at a given time will generally involve the most recent goal. A system for solving the Tower of Hanoi problem using a pushdown stack to hold goals has been programmed by H.A. Simon and the authors.[9] In this system, as each move

---

[9]This work was carried out at the Mathematics Social Science Board Workshop on Cognition held at Carnegie-Mellon University in June 1973.

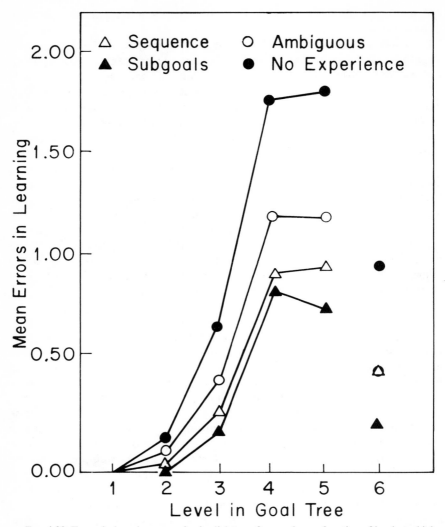

FIG. 4.20. Errors in learning moves in six-disk transfer puzzle as a function of level at which the move was placed in the goal tree.

is planned, a record of the goals generated during the planning process is stored in the form of a stack. Each slot in the stack contains a subgoal along the path from the top goal to the transformation currently performed. As with GPS's procedure for this problem, goals involving larger disks precede goals involving smaller disks. Each time a goal is stored in the stack, the situation is tested to determine whether that most recent goal can be achieved by moving a disk in accord with the restrictions of the problem. When that is impossible, a new subgoal is generated and stored in the stack and tested.

When a move is made satisfying the goal currently in front of the stack, that goal is removed from the stack and the next goal back is tested. Planning moves will not require the addition of any new goals if the moves were planned in the process of generating previous moves. Other moves will require the addition of one or more new goals to the stack.

The process of generating new goals in the programmed system uses features of the goals already in the stack. Each new goal specifies a disk moved from its present location to a specified peg. To determine which peg should receive the disk, the preceding goal in the stack is examined, and the to-peg of the new goal is made different from both the to-peg and the from-peg of the preceding goal. This information in memory turns out to be critical. If memory of the previous goals is removed, requiring generation of the goal stack anew for each move, the program fails to solve any problems involving more than three disks. Without memory for the goal structure leading to a move, the program generates inappropriate goals and eventually goes into a non-terminating loop.

The model of a pushdown storage system for goals can be tested by reorganizing the data previously discussed. In this case errors will be related to the amount of processing thought to occur between two moves. In Fig. 4.21 the mean number of errors on a move is graphed as a function of the number of subgoals between it and the previous move in the goal tree. The greater the number of intervening subgoals, the harder the planning, since more goal-generating activity must be performed. Fig. 4.21 shows a monotonic relationship between the difficulty of learning a move and the number of subgoals intervening between the current and next position. Note how the relationship falls off at points where subjects apparently memorize moves rather than plan them. The graph for the five-disk transfer puzzle was again quite similar. These results are consistent with the finding reported by Thomas (1971) and Greeno (1973b) in their studies of the Missionaries and Cannibals (alias Hobbits and Orcs) Problem. In that problem subjects appeared to plan several moves in advance at various problem states. The first move in the small sequence was very difficult, but the rest tended to be progressively easier.

The analyses in Figs. 4.20 and 4.21 are not independent. However, if each of the independent variables is graphed with the other held constant, a monotonic relationship with errors is observed. Thus, two factors contribute to the difficulty of planning a move in these problems. In the goal stacking model, they are: (a) the number of slots in the pushdown stack required to plan the move; and (b) the amount of goal processing that occurs just prior to making the move. Experienced subjects seem to be better at remembering a large stack of goals and creating a series of goals between two moves.

The remaining data from these experiments concern the recognition test. For simplicity, the data from all conditions of an experiment will be pooled. The general picture is that subjects were not giving familiarity

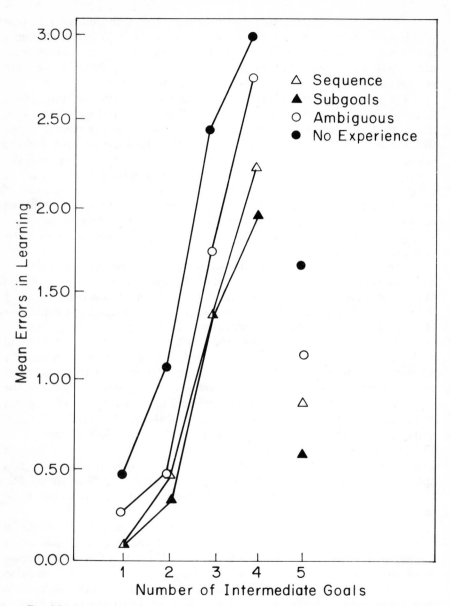

FIG. 4.21. Errors in learning moves in six-disk transfer puzzle as a function of the number of subgoals between the move and the previous move in the problem.

judgments, but were trying to decide if each situation *could* have been involved in the shortest solution. Thus, the test did not have the character of recognizing a list of "unrelated" words, but rather had the character of recognizing a sentence after having read a series of related sentences (Bransford & Franks, 1971).

Consider the way in which subjects reject disk arrangements as not involved in the correct (shortest) solution of the transfer puzzle. Fig. 4.22 illustrates the relationship between the size of the largest disk out of place and the probability of making a false positive error in the recognition test. Subjects could detect rather easily when Disk 6 was not in a proper place. In the shortest solution it is never on the middle peg. Subjects had more difficulty rejecting a position when Disk 5 was not properly placed. In the shortest solution it can be on Peg A or B when Disk 6 is on A, and only on Peg C or B when Disk 6 is on C. Disk 4 is constrained to two positions depending on the positions of Disks 6 and 5. A plausible interpretation of these data is that subjects use the goal tree to assess whether a state could have been in the correct solution of the puzzle. Subjects can detect major discrepancies between a state and the goal tree, but have more difficulty with discrepancies that are more subtle.

The remaining part of the recognition data is consistent with the above interpretation. The problem states that actually occurred in the minimal solution were grouped by the level of the transformation that produced the state. Thus if $s_n = s_{n-1} + t_i$ and $s_{n+1} = s_n + t_j$ and if t_i was performed at Level 1 and t_j was performed at Level 4, then s_n would be classified as a Level 1 state, but s_{n+1} would be classed as a Level 4 state. The relationship between the probability of a miss in the recognition test and the level of the problem state so defined, was found to be monotonically increasing (see Fig. 4.23). Both aspects of the recognition data were replicated in the experiment using the five-disk transfer puzzle.

One interpretation of the recognition data is that after solving a problem, a person either remembers or generates the important components of the problem's goal structure, and uses that information to answer questions about the problem—an idea incorporated in Winograd's (1971) program. That program has perfect memory for the goal structure, whereas the memory of human subjects may be limited to important goals. By important we refer to the number of descendants of a particular goal in the tree of goals. Thus the goal of moving the largest disk to the C peg in the Tower of Hanoi problems has the most descendants, and in fact a subject must spend the first half of each problem accomplishing that goal. A state that violates this goal (i.e., the largest disk appears on Peg B) can be easily rejected as not involved in the correct solution. Further, the state that results from accomplishing this goal is quite easily recognized. Violations of goals with fewer descendants are harder to detect, and resulting states are more difficult to confirm. These findings are similar to those of Kintsch and Keenan (1972), in which propositions with more descendants in a sentence were more likely to be recalled.

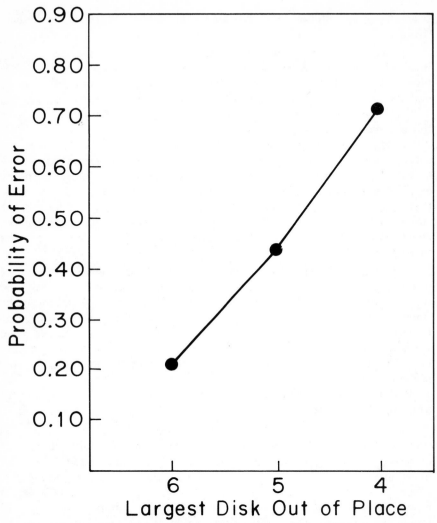

FIG. 4.22. Probability of false positive recognitions for states classified by largest disk out of place.

We began this section by outlining a theory of the structure acquired when solving a problem. The evidence from the Tower of Hanoi studies is consistent with that theory. As people acquire experience with a problem, they can perform "problem solving in the future." Goals are planned to transform the current problem state in the direction of the desired state, and then subgoals are set up to produce a state that is in the domain of the required transformation. The evidence we have cited in favor of this theory is not really hard evidence against the theoretical alternatives previously sketched, but the alternatives are unlikely.

A theory suggesting that subjects base moves on previous moves has little support in these data. The obtained error profiles are difficult to reconcile with the kind of sequential processes discussed in the previous section. While there is a repeating pattern of transformations in the problems (moving the smallest disk in a circular pattern defined on every other move), few subjects report even noticing that regularity. Attempts at emphasizing the sequential pattern in the problem were largely unsuccessful since subjects tended to automatically adopt a forward outlook.

Regarding the theory that subjects memorize state descriptions and associated moves, there appear to be states in the problems where this occurs. However, these states are few in number, and the strategy of memorizing moves seems to be pursued when planning breaks down. The absolute level of

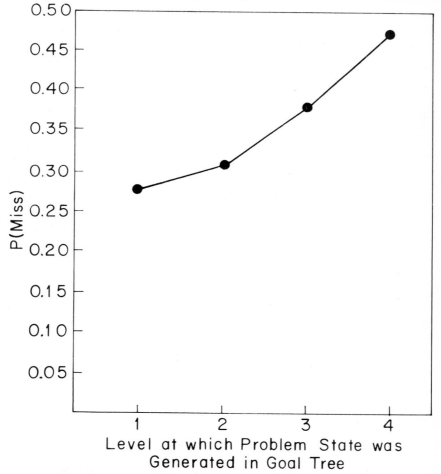

FIG. 4.23. Probability of a "miss" in test of recognizing problem state where states are grouped by the level at which they were generated in the goal tree.

recognition immediately after reaching criterion on the problem seems too low to support widespread use of a rote recognition-retrieval strategy.

Prerequisite Knowledge for Acquiring Expertise

The knowledge that a person acquires during problem solving is a basis for finding one's way through a space of problem states. Any solution is a sequence of actions, but each action corresponds to a relation between a pair of problem states. This provides a parallel between learning in problem solving and serial pattern learning. In serial pattern learning, the subject needs prior knowledge of the alphabet on which the sequence is defined, and also needs prior knowledge of, or ability to notice, the relations from which the serial pattern is constructed. These kinds of knowledge are analogous to those needed for problem solving, and thus for learning during problem solving. The prior knowledge about relations corresponds to knowledge about operators that are permitted in the problem environment. And knowledge about the alphabet corresponds to knowledge about the kinds of objects that can occur as problem states.[10]

Knowledge about problem states may be quite explicit, or may be left to the subject to extract. When explicit knowledge is given, it can be represented as in ordinary concept learning—that is, as lists of dimensions and values. Ordinarily there are also one or more restrictions stated. Consider a few examples. In the Tower of Hanoi problem, the possible states are specified when the subject is given a number of disks and told that no disks are to be removed and no disk may be placed above a disk smaller than itself. The states then consist of all arrangements of the set of disks on the three pegs with no disk above a smaller disk. In the Missionaries and Cannibals problem, the possible problem states are all arrangements involving three missionaries and three cannibals distributed between the two sides of the river, with the boat on one side or the other, with the restriction that on neither side can there be one or two missionaries who are outnumbered by cannibals. The space of possible states in cryptarithmetic is the set of arrangements of letters and digits where some digits have been substituted for letters in the original display, with each substitution applied

---

[10] The notion of a space of problem states used here is quite similar to Newell and Simon's (1972) concept of problem space, but is not identical. A problem space is a set of states of knowledge, where each knowledge state involves a situation as well as the problem solver's knowledge of how that situation was produced, what operators are available, and other factors. The state space that we refer to is just the set of situations that can be produced in a problem environment. In spite of the distinction, much of what is important about problem spaces also characterizes state spaces. In particular, the subject's understanding of the problem environment can produce a limited state space, just as it can produce a limited problem space, and development of an adequate state space (problem space) often is the most interesting process involved in solution of a problem.

to all occurrences of a letter, and no digit being substituted for more than one letter.

In contrast to these explicit specifications, state spaces may have to be inferred or extracted by the problem solver. There is a sense in which Duncker's (1945) candle problem has a describable state space, consisting of all the arrangements of the candle, the wall, and some object that can be fastened to both the wall and the candle. However, it seems more natural to characterize the subject as searching for a way of formulating the problem that leads to a solution. The subject works within a limited state space, and needs to change his knowledge about the problem in order to find a state space containing a solution. This interpretation seems to fit with notions like "restructuring" and "recentering" and finding a "direction" used by Duncker (1945), Maier (1930), and Wertheimer (1959). It also seems closely related to the distinction (Simon and Lea, Chapter 5) between searching for new information about a problem and searching for a solution path in a specific problem space. When new information is found, either in the environment or in memory, and that causes a reformulation of the state space, the subject is said to be engaging in an interesting form of productive thinking (Greeno, 1973a).

Prerequisite knowledge about transformations is generally given in the problem statement, although there are a few cases where interesting productive processes seem to be involved in the discovery of operators. The familiar problem that requires connection of nine dots using four segments involves discovering the operation of extending segments outside the square formed by the dots.

Note that the process of problem solving often coincides with the process of formulating either the space of problem states or the set of the operators. The main process is then the process of acquiring the prerequisite knowledge for problem solving. These cases fit well with the ordinary wisdom that one can often see the solution of a problem as soon as one has found a good way to state the problem. However, there are many cases where a solution does not follow directly from a good statement. The Tower of Hanoi seems to be such a case. A subject may achieve a thorough understanding of possible states and operators and still have something nontrivial to accomplish in the problem. Hayes and Simon (Chapter 8) have given a very useful discussion of the process of extracting what we are here calling the prerequisite knowledge about a problem. Their analysis indicates that in the instructional formats used, knowledge of the state space is relatively easy to extract, while knowledge of the set of operators is harder to achieve. The Hayes and Simon analysis is especially helpful in providing a formal discussion of relationships between general semantic knowledge and the process of developing an understanding of a specific problem, including knowledge of the state space and the set of permitted operators.

Process of Acquiring Expertise

The ideas we can present about the acquisition of cognitive structure during problem solving involve a few facts and a great deal of speculative extrapolation from the other task environments discussed in this paper. It is useful to distinguish learning sequential patterns in problem solving from discovering a good characterization of the problem.

When the solution of a problem apparently depends on finding an appropriate way to characterize the state space and set of operators, the learning problem is essentially one of retaining information. It is hard to imagine a subject who solved Duncker's candle problem later forgetting about the box. Finding the critical features of a problem environment may be quite similar to the process of finding the relevant features of stimuli in concept learning. The subject tries to solve the problem using features that occur to him initially, and if the initial attempt fails, different features are tried. When the critical features of the situation are unlikely to be sampled, the problem is hard. Hypotheses corresponding to problem characterizations may be related to one another hierarchically, so that in some problem environments feature selection may be more systematic than in others. In concept learning, various mechanisms have been proposed to manipulate the salience of features as a function of their use in previously successful hypotheses. A similar mechanism in problem solving would account for "functional fixedness" (Duncker, 1945) in which the critical features of some objects are never even considered because of the salience of other features found helpful in the past.

When subjects must find a sequence of operations within a known space, the learning problem seems to involve more new principles. First, note that any theory will depend on hypotheses about what is learned. If the outcome of learning is thought to be the development of a paired-associate list connecting problem states with specific actions, then EPAM (Feigenbaum, 1963) or SAL (Hintzman, 1968) or some alternative characterization (Greeno, 1970) provides the needed principles. If the outcome of learning is a serial pattern of actions, then the principles of serial pattern learning are the ones we need.

However, the important features of expertise in problem solving may involve something distinguishable from paired-associates and sequential concepts. The characteristic outcome of experience in problem solving is a system for generating subgoals in the problem situation. The process of acquiring such a system is the process of acquiring a set of productions involving (a) conditions in the problem situation and (b) actions that establish subgoals. We know of no formal analysis that deals specifically with the learning of goal-generating productions. However, since that seems to be the central issue for the theory of learning during problem solving, we will offer a few suggestions.

To acquire a set of productions, the subject must identify conditions and select actions—in this case, the actions are the setting of goals. These two factors roughly correspond to the ordering of differences and the table of connections given to GPS. Our proposal therefore resembles one made earlier by Newell, Shaw, and Simon (1960): a system may learn a set of differences and a table of connections. For example, in the Tower of Hanoi, it is important for the problem solver to first set the goal of moving the largest disk onto the target peg. That is, the production system for setting goals gives highest priority to the largest disk not yet on the target peg. Learning this corresponds to learning the appropriate ordering of differences. Learning which goal to set under each condition that occurs corresponds to learning the information given GPS in the table of connections.

In the simplest cases, productions are probably learned in a straight-forward fashion, with each production being added to the list independently. In learning the solution sequence for Missionaries and Cannibals, most components of the solution pattern appear to be acquired in all-or-none fashion (Greeno, 1973b). There are only weak relationships between different stages of the problem (Thomas, 1971). A reasonable hypothesis about this problem is that subjects mainly learn what to do during various states. The determination of "what to do" appears to involve larger units than single moves, but the productions that are learned may well be of the simple form $C \rightarrow A$ where C is a simple description of a state in the problem and A is a short subsequence of moves to be carried out.

The apparent simplicity of learning in Missionaries and Cannibals is probably due to the structural simplicity of the problem. Except for one point in the problem, the subject's alternative responses include only the correct move, the move that returns to the previous state, and moves that violate restrictions in the problem. Thus at nearly every state, the consequence of an incorrect move becomes apparent immediately. Correction of the production leading to that move can take place immediately. Failure to learn the correct solution sequence after solving the problem once probably signifies imperfect information storage and retention.

A more complex structure characterizes many problems, and probably leads to a more complicated process of learning goal-generating productions. An example is the Tower of Hanoi, where a move involving the smallest disk may be incorrect, but this does not become apparent until some moves later, when it turns out that a target peg for some goal has small disks on it, or that a disk to be moved is not the top disk on a peg. In that situation, for the subject to learn what should have been done at the earlier point, a record of the intervening events has to be available.

We propose that an important ingredient in the process of learning the productions for generating goals is the induction of pattern from the sequence of goals and actions that have been retained in memory. When a subject finds that an earlier move has led to difficulty, a connection must be made relating the present difficulty to the previous move. That relationship requires retention of a feature present when the earlier move occurs. In the Tower of Hanoi problem, this relationship has an interesting form. A subject may misdirect a sequence of moves, thereby covering a peg that is to receive something later. The mechanism apparently involves information incorporated in goals that were set when the earlier move was made. Each new goal may have as the target peg one that was neither the target nor the source peg of the previous most recent goal. In this case, then, the feature used as a condition of the production is a characteristic of the subject's goal structure, rather than a characteristic of the external problem state.

This general situation will lead to the forward orientation characteristic of expert problem solving. A typical learning event during problem solving involves a difficulty encountered because of an earlier move, and the induction of a pattern from memory of events leading up to the difficulty. When structures acquired in this way are used later, they will be based on anticipation, and thus will have the characteristic of "problem solving in the future."

SUMMARY AND CONCLUSIONS

Our purpose in this paper has been to review the current state of scientific knowledge regarding the psychology of induction. While we did not set out to develop a single theory of induction, we have attempted to organize our discussion so that comparisons across experimental tasks could be made. Our motive in doing so was in fact to permit a kind of theoretical induction. If similarities among acquired rules, prerequisite knowledge, and inductive processes for a range of experimental tasks are made salient, perhaps ways to fill gaps in understanding performance on individual tasks will be suggested. At the very least, we are able to compare the current level of understanding in each category and show where gaps exist. At best, the comparison could motivate development of theory where it is currently lacking.

The most firmly established facts and theories are available in the study of concept learning. Current explanations of learning sequential rules or rules in problem solving must be regarded as more tentative since these topics have not been studied in as great detail. It is also apparent that across tasks our understanding of the structure of knowledge acquired by induction has reached a rather advanced level. The prerequisite knowledge for inductive processes has not been the subject of much research, and our conclusions regarding that aspect of the learning process are virtually all speculative. For the case of learning simple concepts involving one dimension, the process of rule induction is understood rather well, but for other kinds of rules the process of induction has not yet been thoroughly investigated.

In the tasks we have reviewed, the rules induced all have the form of tree structures, with nodes corresponding to features of stimuli or relations among stimuli. In concept learning, rather impressive evidence indicates that the nodes of a classification tree are tests for the presence or absence of a single feature (value on a dimension). A complex classification rule is a sequence of these tests in which the feature to be tested at some point in the tree depends on the outcome of the previous tests. Relational concepts are tree structures whose nodes correspond to n-ary relations. A test for such a feature may include a conjunction of simpler feature tests. We have taken analogical reasoning to be an example of relational concept learning in which a conjunction of relations is identified and then transferred to a new object. Hence, analogies may prove useful in studying acquisition and use of complex relational concepts in situations requiring relatively rapid adjustment and revision of conceptual structures.

The structures of sequential rules have been characterized as trees generated by the application of productions that include functional operators. In these tasks the nodes of the structural trees are properly called transformations since the task is to produce the next sequence element rather than to classify instances. For the simplest sequences of *srt* chunks, nodes of the tree represent relations holding between adjacent elements within a chunk. In this case, the grammar required to generate structural descriptions of sequences is right linear, whereas a context-free grammar seems to be required for the other types of sequences studied. In the most complex case of hierarchic sequences, the nodes of the structural trees represent transformations of subsequences of elements.

Rules developed in problem solving appear to bring together the ideas of testing an object for required features and transforming the object to obtain the next one in a sequence. In this case the nodes in the acquired knowledge structure are goals or transformations defined on cylinder sets of features. To apply a transformation, the problem state must be an element in the cylinder set that is the domain of the transformation. Subgoals are set to modify features of the problem state so that it will fall into the proper cylinder set. For many problems the construction of subgoals remains difficult even after an appropriate description of the space of problem states has been found. An expert problem solver knows the conditions under which subgoals must be established.

Regarding our discussion of prerequisite knowledge, induction clearly requires coding events by common features so that successive events can be compared. The ability to code features of events implies certain perceptual or memorial capabilities. For concept learning using well-defined geometric stimuli the coded features are of a perceptual nature and the coding is fairly obvious. In verbal concept learning common semantic features of instances are coded. We have taken that to mean that certain structures in semantic memory are required to induce verbal concepts. This idea is supported by the fact that the relative ease of inducing rules based on different semantic features varies in ways consistent with theories of the structure of semantic memory. Learning relational concepts requires the ability to detect relational properties in geometric or verbal instances. Different theories of analogical reasoning suggest somewhat different organizations of prerequisite knowledge. However the theories have in common the idea that subjects have an organized space of instances in which relational properties act as maps between two instances in the space.

For the induction of most sequences studied experimentally, the components of a subject's necessary prior knowledge are rather obvious. If alphabetic material is used the subject must know the ordered set of symbols making up the alphabet as well as certain relations that may hold between two symbols (same, next, backward next). The prerequisite knowledge is more difficult to specify when material not from a standard alphabet is used. Some of these cases would probably have the character of relational concept learning in which the relation used in the sequence can be applied iteratively over some range (e.g., amount of rotation of a figure). The prerequisite knowledge would not be a known ordered set of symbols, but the ability to detect the relations being used. In other cases (e.g., sequences based on a repeating cycle of colors) subjects probably first form an ordered list of elements and use that knowledge to learn the sequence. Finally, we have introduced the idea that a subject may first identify the rule system in use before attempting to induce a specific rule. This knowledge is necessary so that the subject knows the form a specific rule is to take.

Knowledge prerequisite to acquiring rules in problem solving is of two kinds. First, a subject must have an appropriate set of features for organizing the space of problem states. The main requirement in problems solved suddenly by "insight" probably is an advantageous definition of the space of problem states. The requirements for this part of problem solving are quite similar to those for learning a complex concept. The features of problem states must be detected and in some cases this will be largely perceptual but in others will require extensive use of semantic memory. The second kind of prerequisite for learning to solve problems is knowledge about the permissible transformations in a problem. This prerequisite is similar to the requirements of sequential rule induction since each transformation in a problem is a relation defined on two successive problem states.

Concerning the processes of acquiring rules, we have found evidence that two general modes of induction are used. The first of these occurs when the range of possible rules is fairly small and a subject's knowledge of the possibilities is explicit. In these cases subjects can systematically eliminate hypotheses about the rule by an orderly search of the possibilities. The second inductive mode requires less specific knowledge of the possibilities and also applies in cases where the number of possible rules is rather large. In those circumstances we think subjects scan features of successive events in the experiment trying to compare several instances in working memory. In some theoretical mechanisms, changes occur in the saliencies of features, leading to adjustment in the probability that an event will be coded. These general inductive processes rarely occur in pure form. Most induction is probably a combination of feature scanning to verify hypothesized connective structures loosely ordered along a simple-to-complex dimension.

For simple cases of concept learning in which practiced subjects must discover a single relevant feature the explicit mode of induction is apparently dominant. Subjects can consider several hypotheses simultaneously and can keep track of hypotheses rejected as inconsistent on previous trials. When combinations of features must be discovered, it appears that the implicit mode of induction is used. Very little is known about the process of learning the connective structure of concepts. Given the truth table strategy, both rule elimination and learning response assignments by feature scanning are possible. Complete learning of complex concepts almost certainly involves the implicit mode of induction, but may be ordered to the extent that simple connective structures are considered as candidates before more complicated structures. The available data are not sufficient to permit a thorough analysis of that situation.

Evidence has recently been found for an explicit search through ordered sets of hypotheses while inducing concepts involving arithmetic relations. Other kinds of relational concepts have not been analyzed in as great detail. It seems that the process of analogical reasoning might present an interesting combination of the two inductive modes. Comparing the first two objects in an analogy would be a process of scanning for relational properties. Once those were found they might then be applied to the third object so that alternative solutions could be eliminated. Clearly most of what we can presently say about acquiring rules for relational concepts is rather speculative.

The available information on the process of inducing sequential rules suggests that subjects temporarily store sequence elements and then try to find relations among two or more successive elements. This corresponds to feature scanning in concept learning. If a subject has identified the general class of relations used in the sequences to be learned, then the explicit inductive mode is possible. There is a definite noticing order for relations between two elements, and within the classes of *srt* chunks, Thurstone series, or hierarchical sequences only a small number of relations are used. Since the number of possible rules in Bjork sequences is rather large, it is more likely that subjects scan for recurrent relations rather than eliminate rules. That would account for the difficulty of learning advancing rules in those sequences.

We can be least definite regarding the process of acquiring rules for solving a problem or class of problems. In the case of "insight" problems, a feature scanning process that learns in an all-or-none fashion may

TABLE 4.1

Summary of Analysis

Kind of rule acquired	Acquired structure	Prerequisite knowledge	Process of acquisition
Conceptual Classification: Associative grouping (verbal concept)	Decision tree Find which category feature is present	Associations in semantic memory	Scanning instances and noticing common associations
Single-feature classification	Test single feature	Knowledge of or ability to detect features	Selection and elimination of features
Multiple attributives (connective structure known)			Selection of rules or association of response to combinations of features
Connective structure (attributes known)	Conditional feature tests	Truth table combinations	Construction and modification of decision tree
Complete classificatory rule		Features and combinations	
Relational concepts	Test n-ary relational feature	Knowledge of or ability to detect relations (relations in semantic memory for verbal materials)	Search in set of known relations, within subsets ordered by complexity
Analogies	Conjunction of relational features		Note relations and test on alternative answers
Sequential concepts:	Tree structures of relations	Knowledge of alphabet, and detection or computation of relations	Scan sets of elements to identify chunks
srt chunks	Sequence of chunks	Same, next, and backward-next on adjacent elements	Compute and store sequence of differences; compare entries to detect advancing rules
Bjork sequences	Sequence of interval relations	Difference between adjacent elements, and same or next relations on differences	Find period of sequence, formulate rule, and test on elements
Thurstone sequences	Interleaved sequences of interval relations	Same, next, and backward-next on adjacent and separated elements	Identify subsequence chunks and transformations between subsequences
Restle hierarchical sequences	Structure of relations between subsequences	Differences between adjacent elements and between subsequences	Induce pattern in sequence of transformations, including modification of difference ordering and connecting transformations to features of states; modify encoding of problem, if necessary
Solution patterns for solving problems	Structure of transformations defined on sets of states	Space of problem states and set of transformations	

characterize the means by which a subject settles on a useful description of the space of problem states. For serial problems in which a complicated goal structure is necessary, subjects are probably performing several kinds of induction at once. The feature scanning mode may be used to discover the proper difference ordering for the task, while a more explicit search seems possible to connect one of the small number of transformations with each difference. The expert solver has probably acquired his skill at building subgoals by noticing the recurrent features of situations calling for subgoals.

The main points of this summary are included in Table 4.1, and our final remarks concern another kind of prerequisite for induction that is contained only implicitly in Table 4.1. We refer to the critical importance of working memory in every one of the tasks studied. When induction is an explicit search through a set of possibilities, two kinds of information must be in working memory: a subject must be working with a subset of the untested rules, and must know which rules have been rejected previously. The burden on working memory is even greater when induction is less explicit. In cases of feature scanning, information about recent instances is selected and stored temporarily. Additionally, the subject must be able to abstract relations among those features while holding the current hypothesis for possible modification. A further set of requirements involving working memory concern the procedures used to perform the experimental task even after inducing the rule. In concept learning a certain amount of working memory is taken up by the process of sorting a stimulus through an acquired decision tree. Certain sequential rules require keeping track of list markers and pushdown stacks of symbols to generate the sequence correctly. A goal stacking mechanism was proposed to model the process of solving a problem. The point is that procedures undoubtedly take memory, so the working memory required for those procedures is a prerequisite in addition to the long-term semantic memory we have discussed.

5
PROBLEM SOLVING AND RULE INDUCTION: A UNIFIED VIEW

HERBERT A. SIMON and GLENN LEA
Carnegie-Mellon University

Discussions in the psychological literature of cognitive processes generally treat separately a category of behavior called "problem solving," on the one hand, and a category called "concept attainment," "pattern induction," or "rule discovery," on the other. We will use the phrase "rule induction" to refer to any of the diverse tasks in the second category. We find this division already in the 1938 edition of Woodworth's *Experimental Psychology,* where the penultimate chapter is devoted to problem-solving behavior, and the final chapter primarily to rule induction. In explanation of this organization, Woodworth comments:

> Two chapters will not be too many for the large topic of thinking, and we may make the division according to the historical sources of two streams of experimentation, which do indeed merge in the more recent work. One stream arose in the study of animal behavior and went on to human problem solving; the other started with human thinking of the more verbal sort [Woodworth, 1938, p. 746].

Far from merging, the two streams are still treated as quite distinct in more recent works. For example, in his 1968 *Annual Review* survey of artificial intelligence studies and their relevance to psychology, Earl Hunt devotes separate sections to "deductive problem solving" and "inductive problem solving," his categories corresponding closely to those introduced above. Similar categories appear in the principal contemporary textbooks.

This dichotomization cannot be regarded as satisfactory, for it fragments theories of thinking into subtheories with no apparent relation between them. In proposing information processes to account for problem solving, the theorist then assumes no responsibility for the relevance of these processes to concept attainment or other rule induction tasks, and vice versa. It is of course possible that these two kinds of thinking activity are entirely separate and independent, but possibility is not plausibility. It would be

This work was supported by Public Health Service Grant MH-07722, from the National Institute of Mental Health. We are grateful to James Greeno and Allen Newell for helpful comments on an earlier draft of this paper.

much better if we could show just how they are related; or, if they are not related, if we could provide a common framework within which the two classes of activities could be viewed.

Hunt's (1968) dichotomy of "deductive" and "inductive" will not do, for it is easy to show that from a logical standpoint the processes involved in problem solving are inductive, not deductive. Hunt may have been misled by the fact that the earliest artificial intelligence systems for problem solving (e.g., the Logic Theorist) dealt with the task environment of theorem proving. To be sure, the proof of a theorem in a formal mathematical or logical system is a deductive object; that is to say, the theorem stands in a deductive relation to its premises. But the problem solving task is to *discover* this deduction, this proof; and the discovery process, which is the problem-solving process, is wholly inductive in nature. It is a search through a large space of logic expressions for the goal expression—the theorem. Hence, both a theory of problem solving and a theory of rule induction must explain inductive processes—a further reason for believing that these theories should have something in common.

Recent developments in the theory of problem solving (Newell, 1968; Newell & Simon, 1972; Simon, 1972c) give us a clue as to how to go about building a common body of theory that will embrace both problem solving and rule induction, including concept attainment. It is the aim of this paper to outline such a theory. We shall not adduce new empirical evidence, nor even refer to particular experiments in the literature. Instead, we shall take as our starting points the recent formulation of the theory of problem solving mentioned above (Newell & Simon, 1972), and a recently formulated and rather general process model of concept attainment (Gregg & Simon, 1967), and show how both of these relate to the more general framework that is our goal. Since these theories have substantial empirical underpinnings, the discussion will be tied firmly to empirical data, albeit indirectly.

PRELIMINARY REMARKS

Before proceeding, we need to say more clearly what we mean by "common body of theory." A theoretical explanation of the behavior of a subject confronted with a problem-solving task or a concept-attainment task might take the form of a program, an organization of information processes, more or less appropriate to carrying out the task. This is, in fact, the form of the problem-solving theory of Newell and Simon and the concept attainment theory of Gregg and Simon mentioned in the last paragraph. To the extent that two programs explaining behavior in these two kinds of task environments employ the same basic processes, or to the extent that the processes are organized isomorphically, we may say they express a common theory.

But we must be more specific about what is common to them. The fact that two physical theories can both be stated in terms of differential equations connects them only superficially. Even less should we be surprised or impressed to find that two theories of human information processing performance can be written in the same programming language. Computer languages—IPL-V, LISP, SNOBOL—are almost completely general, capable of describing any organization of information processes. Anything that can be done by a Turing Machine can be described in any of these languages. When we speak of a common theory for problem solving and rule induction we intend to assert more than that man is a Turing Machine.

Nor is it sufficient—or very informative—to show that it is possible to write a single program that will simulate and describe human behavior in both a problem-solving and a concept-attaining environment. That kind of generality could be achieved by a "big switch"—a pair of subprograms joined only by a simple test to identify the task environment, and to select from the pair the appropriate subprogram to deal with it.

The generality we seek, then, is not the nearly vacuous generality of either the Turing Machine or the Big Switch. Our aim is to show a much closer relation between problem-solving processes and rule-inducing processes than is implied by either of these. Exactly what this means will become clear as we proceed.

Because "problem solving" and "rule induction" are themselves heterogeneous domains with ill-marked boundaries, we will make matters more concrete by referring to some specific illustrative tasks. For problem solving, we will pay special attention to two tasks analyzed at length in Newell and Simon (1972): cryptarithmetic and discovering proofs for theorems in logic. For rule induction we will use as examples the standard concept attainment paradigms (Bruner, Goodnow, & Austin, 1956; Gregg & Simon, 1967; Hunt, 1962), extrapolation of serial patterns (Feldman, Tonge, & Kanter, 1963; Simon & Kotovsky, 1963; Simon, 1972a), and induction of the rules of a grammar (Klein & Kuppin, 1970; Solomonoff, 1959; Siklossy, 1972).

Our undertaking is a little more ambitious than has been indicated thus far. For, not only have distinct bodies of theory grown up to deal with problem solving and rule induction, respectively, but there has been relatively little unity in theorizing across the whole of the latter domain. In particular, previous theoretical treatments of concept attainment do not include extrapolation of patterned sequences, and theories of sequence extrapolation do not encompass the standard experimental paradigms for studying concept attainment. Here we will aim at a unified treatment of the whole range of things we have here been calling "rule induction," and a comparison of these, in turn, with the activities called "problem solving."

We will begin by outlining the basic features of the information processing theory of problem solving, and then use these features to construct the broader theory.

PROBLEM SOLVING

In solving a well-structured problem (and this is the only kind we shall deal with), the problem solver operates within a *problem space*. A problem space is a set of points, or nodes, each of which represents a *knowledge state*. A knowledge state is the set of things the problem solver knows or postulates when he is at a particular stage in his search for a solution. For example, at a certain point in his attempt to solve the cryptarithmetic problem, DONALD + GERALD = ROBERT, the problem solver may know that the number 5 must be assigned to the letter D, the number 0 to T, the number 9 to E; and he may know also that R is odd and greater than 5. The conjunction of these bits of knowledge defines the particular node he is currently at in his problem space, and the space is made up of a collection of such nodes, each representing some set of pieces of knowledge of this kind.

Problem-solving activity can be described as a search through the space (or maze, or network) of knowledge states, until a state is reached that provides the solution to the problem. In general, each node reached contains a little more knowledge than those reached previously, and the links connecting the nodes are search and inference processes that add new knowledge to the previous store.

Thus, in the cryptarithmetic problem, the solution state is one in which each letter has been assigned a digit and in which it has been verified that these assignments provide a correct translation of the encoded addition problem. The problem solver moves from one state to another by inferences (or conjectures) and by visual searches of the problem display. For example, knowing that $E = 9$ and that R is odd and greater than 5, he may infer that $R = 7$. Or knowing that $E = 9$, he may discover, by scanning, the E in ROBERT, and replace this by a 9, obtaining: $A + A = 9$ (apart from carries) for the third column from the right.

Similarly, in discovering the proof for a theorem, a problem solver organized like the General Problem Solver (GPS) starts with some initial expressions (premises) and the goal expression (the theorem to be proved), and applies rules of inference to generate new expressions that are derivable

$$
\begin{array}{ll}
\quad\ 1 & \\
5ONAL5 & D=5 \\
\underline{GERAL5} & T=0 \\
ROBER0 & R > 5,\ \text{odd}
\end{array}
$$

FIG. 5.1. A knowledge state in a cryptarithmetic task. (The figure shows what the problem solver knows after his initial processing of the sixth, fifth, and first columns of the display.)

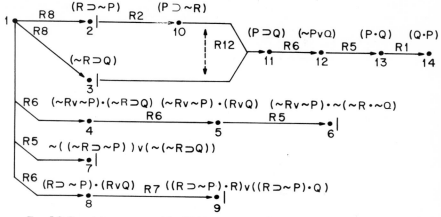

FIG. 5.2. Search tree generated by GPS in logic. (Initial expression (node 1) was (R ⊃∼ P) · (∼R ⊃ Q). Above each node (knowledge state) is shown the new expression that has been derived here. Below each node is shown the order in which it was generated. On each link is shown the operator used to generate the next node. See Newell & Simon, 1972, pp. 420-425.)

from the premises, until an expression is generated that is identical with the desired theorem. In this case, the knowledge states of which the problem space is composed are sets of expressions that have been derived along particular inference paths.

The search through such a problem space is generally highly selective, being guided by the information that becomes available at each successive knowledge state. Given that the problem solver has already visited a certain number of points in the problem space, he can determine the direction in which he will continue to search by two kinds of decisions: (a) selection, from among those already visited, of a particular knowledge state from which to continue his search and (b) selection of a particular operator (inference rule, or "move") to apply at that node in order to reach a new knowledge state.

Means-ends analysis, which appears to be used extensively by human subjects in many problem environments, is a particular kind of scheme for making the choice of operator. It is the key selection mechanism incorporated in GPS. For means-ends analysis, the information in a particular knowledge state that has already been reached is compared with the specification of the solution to discover one or more differences between them. Corresponding to one of these differences, an operator is selected that is known, from previous experience, often to eliminate differences of that kind. The operator is applied to reach a new knowledge state.

We may formalize and generalize this description of problem solving as follows:

1. There is a *problem space* whose elements are *knowledge states.*

2. There are one or more *generative processes* (operators) that take a knowledge state as input and produce a new knowledge state as output.

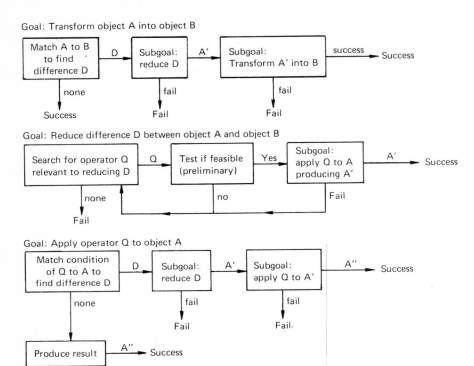

FIG. 5.3. GPS methods—flow diagram. Information in the form of differences between the current knowledge state and the goal is used to select operators that may reduce the differences. (Reprinted with permission from Newell & Simon, 1972, Fig. 8.7, p. 417.)

3. There are one or more *test processes* for comparing a knowledge state with the specification of the problem state and for comparing pairs of knowledge states and producing differences between them.

4. There are processes for *selecting* which of these generators and tests to employ, on the basis of the information contained in the knowledge states.

The crucial points in this characterization are the third and fourth postulates: that information contained in the knowledge state can be used to guide the generation of new knowledge states, so that the search through the problem space can be selective rather than random. The problem-solving process is an information gathering process as much as it is a search process. The accumulation of information in the course of search permits the search to be selective, and gives problem solving in very large problem spaces a chance of success. The processes for using this information to steer the search are generally processes of inductive inference. Being inductive, they do not provide certainty, but have only heuristic value in guiding the search and making it efficient.

Characterizing problem solving as information gathering gives us the framework we need to deal with the whole range of tasks in which we are interested. We shall describe the process for all of these tasks as a search through a problem space guided by information accumulated during the search. And we shall undertake to show that the fundamental search processes (generation, test, and selection processes), as well as the inference processes, are of the same kind in rule induction tasks as in problem-solving tasks, and are organized in a very similar way. Finally, we shall see that the basic *difference* between the two domains is that rule induction involves an alternation of activity between two distinct, but interrelated, problem spaces, while only a single space is involved in problem solving.

Information Gathering in Theorem Proving

Consider the following GPS-like system for discovering proofs for theorems in symbolic logic. Many subjects in the laboratory have been observed to follow essentially this process. The knowledge states are sets of logic expressions that have been derived from the initial premises. Two kinds of information are used to guide the search: (a) the degree of similarity or difference between the expressions contained in a given knowledge state and the goal expression and (b) the specific character of the differences between particular expressions in the knowledge state and the goal expression. The first kind of information measures the progress that has been made in reaching a knowledge state—if it contains an expression that is highly similar to the goal expression, then it can be taken as a likely starting point for further search. The second kind of information suggests how a closer approximation to the goal expression can be obtained—the specific differences that are detected suggest specific operators to remove them (see Fig. 5.3).

Information Gathering in Cryptarithmetic

We shall use the cryptarithmetic task as a "bridge" from the topic of problem solving to the topic of rule induction because it is possible to give an interpretation to the task which places it in either of the two categories. Although the information gathering process in solving cryptarithmetic problems could be described in a manner very similar to our description of information gathering in theorem proving, we shall look at matters in a slightly different way. Let us consider the knowledge states in cryptarithmetic to be made up of two distinguishable components: the *problem display* in which digits have replaced those letters to which assignments have already been made and the *list of assignments* themselves. The problem-solving goal can then be described in two ways: (a) to replace all letters in the display by digits in such a way that the resulting problem in arithmetic is correct or (b) to complete the list of assignments of digits to letters so that each letter has a distinct digit assigned to it. Of course, both conditions must be satisfied to

D O N A L D   D=5
+G E R A L D
‾R‾O‾B‾E‾R‾T‾

Problem Display   List of Assignments
(Instance Space)   (Rule Space)

FIG. 5.4. Dual problem space interpretation of cryptarithmetic task.

solve the problem, but if appropriate consistency checks are made when the display is modified, and when a new assignment is added to the list, then reaching either goal will guarantee achievement of the other.

How is information extracted from knowledge states in the course of solving the problem? Whenever sufficient information has been accumulated in any column in the display, one or more new assignments of digits can be inferred from it by applying simple arithmetic processes. For example, in DONALD + GERALD = ROBERT, if D=5 has been assigned, so that the display becomes: 5ONAL5 + GERAL5 = ROBERT, it can be inferred that the last T is 0, so that T=0 can be added to the list of assignments. The inference is made by a "Process Column" operator that takes the column of the display (together with information about carries) as input, and produces the assignment as output.

Conversely, whenever a new assignment is added to the list, the display can be changed by substituting the assigned digit for the corresponding letter whenever the latter occurs in the display. For example, suppose we have the display 5ONAL5 + G9RAL5 = ROB9R0 and the list of assignments: (D=5, T=0, E=9). Suppose we now add to the list the new assignment, R=7. We can now alter the display to read: 5ONAL5 + G97AL5 = 7OB970. Here, the input is an assignment from the list of assignments, the output is a modified display. The modification is made by a "Substitution" operator that searches the columns of the display for instances of the letter in question, and substitutes the digit for it wherever it is found.

Other inferential processes for producing new information may operate internally to the list of assignments or to the display respectively. As an example of the former, suppose that the list of assignments includes the information: $E = 9$ and $R = 7 \text{ v } 9$. Then, if there is a process for examining the consistency of assignments, that process can draw the inference that $R = 7$, and replace $R = 7 \text{ v } 9$ on the list by this more precise assignment. Similarly, processing column 1 of the problem with the information that $D = 5$, leads both to the inference that $T = 0$, and that a 1 is carried into the second column. The latter piece of information can be entered directly on the display.

The situation can now be redescribed in the following way. We consider *two* problem spaces: a space of sets of assignment *rules* (rules for substituting digits for letters in the display), and a space of sets of *instances* (columns of the display). The goal is to complete the set of rules, so that there will be a distinct assignment rule for each letter. The proposed rules are tested against the instances. Each column of the display, which we are now interpreting as an instance, provides a partial test of the consistency of the rules. The situation so described differs from the usual concept attainment paradigm only in the fact that the instances are not completely independent, but interact through the carries from one column to the next (Fig. 5.5). In every other respect, the task is now a standard concept attainment task. Simply by changing our way of viewing the problem space (or spaces), we have transferred the cryptarithmetic task from the category of problem solving to the category of concept attainment, pattern induction, or rule discovery.

From this example, we hypothesize that *the trademark that distinguishes these two classes of tasks is the presence or absence of more than one distinguishable problem space in which the problem-solving activity takes place.* If there is only one space, we describe problem solving as a search through that space, made more or less selective and efficient by drawing upon the information that is available at each of the nodes that is reached. If there are two spaces, we describe problem solving as a search through one of them (usually, as we shall see, through the space of rules), made more or less selective and efficient by using information available in each space to guide search in the other. By focussing our attention on the processes for obtaining and utilizing information, we can provide the common framework that we have been seeking for all of these tasks.

RULE INDUCTION

If the theory of rule induction is to bear a close relation to the theory of problem-solving processes, then it must be constructed of the same basic modules: one or more generating processes, one or more test processes, and one or more processes to select the generators and tests to be applied, and to determine the order of their application. Newell (1968, 1973) has proposed a

$$
\begin{aligned}
2D &= T + 10C2 \\
C2 + 2L &= R + 10C3 \\
C3 + 2A &= E + 10C4 \\
C4 + N + R &= B + 10C5 \\
C5 + O + E &= O + 10C6 \\
C6 + D + G &= R
\end{aligned}
$$

FIG. 5.5. Space of instances in cryptarithmetic. (Showing interdependence of instances by virtue of carries, C2-C6.)

taxonomy of general problem-solving methods that lists the principal ways in which these modules can be combined into operative systems. By "general methods" Newell means methods that make relatively unspecific demands upon the task environment, and hence, are widely applicable.

Some General Methods

We will be concerned with just three of the methods Newell defines: the generate-and-test method, the heuristic search method, and the induction (or hypothesis-and-match) method. We shall see that the first two of these are characteristic of problem-solving systems, the third of rule induction systems, but that they differ mainly with respect to the information flows among the modules. All of these methods may draw upon one or both of two submethods: the matching method, and the means-ends method.

At a minimum, any goal directed system must include a generator for producing new knowledge states and a test for determining whether a state produced by the generator is in fact a solution state. The simplest solution method is just this minimal *generate-and-test*. The power and efficiency of the method derives from information that is implicit in its structure. If, for example, the generator can produce only a very small set of states, and if this set is guaranteed to contain a solution, the method will be powerful, for the solution will be found promptly. If the test can reject inadequate solutions rapidly—say, by means of a matching process—then the cost of testing will be relatively small.

In the generate-and-test method, the order in which nodes are generated is independent of the knowledge that is gradually accumulating—the information is used only by the test process. Consider next a more sophisticated system, where the generator is no longer insensitive to knowledge that has been produced. Now information flows back from the test to the generator. This feedback requires the test to provide more information than just the success or failure of the match between the knowledge states generated, and the specification of the desired knowledge state (the goal). Using the test information, the generator produces a new knowledge state by modifying a state produced previously in the search. This dependency of generation upon the test outcome characterizes the *heuristic search* method.

We have already remarked on two kinds of information that can be used by the generator in heuristic search: first, information to select which of the previously generated states will be modified to produce the next state; second, information to select which of several available operators will be applied to the knowledge state to modify it. If the latter choice depends on the test's detecting specific differences between a state and the goal state, then we speak of the *means-ends* submethod.

Thus far everything that has been said applies equally well to problem solving and to rule induction. In the former case, the search ends with the discovery of the problem solution; in the latter, with the discovery of a rule that is consistent with a set of instances. In both cases, the key process is a search—an inductive process. The search for a rule can be (and usually will be) a heuristic search, and can employ the means-ends submethod, as we shall see.

What distinguishes rule induction tasks from problem-solving tasks is the nature of the test process. In a rule induction task, the attainment of a solution is determined by applying the proposed rule to objects (*instances*), and by then testing whether the application gives a correct result. The test is not applied directly to the rule, but to another set of expressions, the instances. The evaluation of the rule thus takes an indirect path, and the feedback of information from test to generator retraces this path. A rule is rejected or modified if false instances are associated with it, or if there exist true instances that are not associated with it.

In a rule induction task we can define a space of sets of instances in addition to the space of sets of rules. The test process for the rule induction system operates within the space of instances. It can incorporate an instance generator (unless the instances are generated by the experimenter), as well as instance tests (which may or may not make use of knowledge of results provided by the experimenter). Suppose that the overall test process contains both generator and test subprocesses operating in the space of the instances. These subprocesses and their organization may, in turn, exhibit various levels of sophistication in their use of information—e.g., in the feedback of information from the test subprocess to the generator subprocess. A primitive test process would employ only the generate-and-test method; a more powerful one, heuristic search, possibly including the means-ends submethod.

In Newell's taxonomy, a system uses the induction method if there are separate generators for rules and instances, and a match process to test whether an instance agrees with (is associated with) a rule. Since all heuristic search methods are inductive, as we have seen, it will be better to refer to this method as the *rule induction* method. It is clear that the rule induction method, so defined, is really a whole collection of methods. Nor is the locus of variation limited to the test process, as sketched in the last paragraph. There can also be various arrangements for the flow of information *between* the instance space and the space of rules—i.e., between the test process and the generator process of the entire rule induction process (see Fig. 5.6).

In the most primitive system, there is no feedback of information from test to rule generator (Channel *e*, Fig. 5.6); the test simply eliminates rules that have been generated, but does not provide information to help the generator select the next rule. In this case, the method is a rule induction version of the generate-and-test method, adapted to the dual problem space.

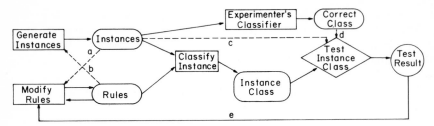

Fɪɢ. 5.6. Information flows in rule induction processes. (Broken lines show information channels used in some, but not all, variants of the rule induction task.)

On the other hand, if the rule generator does not create each rule anew, but produces it by modifying previous rule sets on the basis of information received from the test of instances (Channels *a* and *e*. Fig. 5.6), then we have a rule induction version of the heuristic search method.

Further, the existence of two spaces and two generators, one for rules and one for instances, opens up possibilities for methods that are not available when there is only a single problem space. For example, the instance generator need not be autonomous, but may instead derive information from the rules that have been generated and the previous tests that have been performed—a flow of information from rule space to instance generator (Channel *b*, Fig. 5.6) as well as from instance space to rule generator (Channel *a*). Thus, each new rule may be generated on the basis of the instances constructed up to that point (heuristic search for rules), while each new instance may be generated on the basis of the rules constructed up to that point (heuristic search for instances). This, in fact, is just what is happening in the cryptarithmetic solution method described earlier when we view the columns of the problem display as instances, and the list of assignments as a list of rules.

A General Rule Induction Program

We are now ready to define a formal system that expresses the common theory we are seeking. Fig. 5.7 gives the definition of a General Rule Induction (GRI) Executive Program. In order to make it as readable as possible, the definition is expressed in the informal programming language defined in Newell and Simon (1972, pp. 38-51).

The GRI system is extremely simple, consisting of a subprocess to generate rules, and a second subprocess to generate and test instances. The output of the test (*test-result*) is available as an input to the rule generator, to help guide the next step of generation. Whether this information will be used, and in what way, depends on the internal structure of the rule generator, which is not specified. Thus GRI employs the generate-and-test method. Whether it employs heuristic search or even more elaborate methods depends on the specification of the sub-processes and the information flows between them. Notice that just as the test results are available as input information to the rule generator, so the set of rules is available as input information to the instance generator.

Fig. 5.7 makes patent that the only feature distinguishing a rule induction system from a problem-solving system is that the tests of the rule induction system operate in a different space from the generator. Generator and test use the same space in a problem-solving system. The fundamental generator-test alternation is identical for both kinds of systems, but the similarity between them extends much further. In both problem-solving and rule-induction systems, the selectivity of generators depends upon the feedback of information from the test processes. Because the rule induction system may contain two generators, rather than just one, there is a larger number of possible channels of information flow, hence, a richer taxonomy of possible specialized systems.

In Fig. 5.6, we have shown the flows of information in GRI. Some of these (shown by broken lines) are "optional," in the sense that variants can be devised that include or exclude them. We will illustrate this point in the next sections, when we discuss how GRI would handle some of the standard paradigms for concept attainment, series extrapolation, and grammar induction.

GRI is capable of performing the whole range of tasks just mentioned. We must be careful as to what we mean by this claim. The space of concepts appropriate to the usual concept attainment tasks is different from the space of grammar rules or the space of sequential patterns. For a program to undertake to solve problems in any one of these domains, it will require—in addition to its general mechanisms and organization, common to all the domains—particularized equipment for dealing with the specific domain before it.

The situation here is the same as the situation confronting the General Problem Solver. GPS is a general organization for performing means-ends

```
General Rule Inducer:
1. generate rules (⇒ rules);
   generate instances (⇒ instance);
      classify instance by rules (⇒ instance-class);
      test instance-class (⇒ test-result).
      if test-result = 'correct' tally = tally + 1,
         else set tally = 0;
   if tally = criterion exit,
      else go to 1.
```

FIG. 5.7. Executive program for the General Rule Inducer.

analysis, and for guiding search through a space of knowledge states. Before GPS can go to work on any specific problem, it must be provided with a specification of the problem domain: the objects, the definition of the knowledge states, the operators, the differences, and the associations of operators with differences. The General Rule Inducer needs the same kinds of problem specification in order to tackle specific tasks. GRI itself is an executive program providing an organization within which the specialized subprocesses can operate. We now present some examples of such specialized subprocesses that are applicable to the specific task domains of concept formation, series extrapolation and grammar induction.

Concept Attainment

In the commonest laboratory form of the concept attainment task, the subject sees a sequence of stimuli that differ along one or more dimensions (e.g., "large blue square"). Certain of these stimuli are instances of a concept (e.g., "square"), others are not. The subject guesses whether each is an instance, and is told whether he is right or wrong. His task is to induce the concept so that he can classify each successive stimulus correctly. In heuristic search terms, the subject searches through a space of possible concepts for the right one. The information that guides this search, however, is not information about concepts, but information about whether certain stimuli are instances of concepts or not.

The behavior of subjects in concept attainment tasks of the kinds studied by Bower and Trabasso and others has been formalized by Gregg and Simon (1967) in a family of programs whose individual members differ only with respect to the amount of information the subject is assumed to retain as a basis for guiding the concept generator (Channels a and e of Fig. 5.6). The programs described by Gregg and Simon conform to the organization of the GRI executive.

In those variants of the program where no information is fed back (Channel a inoperative), whenever a guess has been wrong, the generator selects a concept at random from the set of available concepts. A slightly more efficient generator (which, strictly speaking, requires feedback via Channel e only to signal whether or not the last instance was classified correctly) samples randomly from the set of available concepts, but without replacing those already eliminated. A somewhat more efficient generator, using also feedback via Channel a, produces a concept consistent with the correct classification of the most recent instance. A still more efficient generator produces a concept consistent with the classifications of all previous instances. Empirical data in the literature indicate, according to Gregg and Simon, which of these methods will be employed by a human subject depends on the limits of his short-term memory and the availability of time to fixate information or of external memory to record it.

The paradigm described by Gregg and Simon's program does not incorporate a flow of information from the space of concepts to the generator of instances (Channel *b* in Fig. 5.6), since the instances in those experiments are produced by the experimenter independently of the subject's problem-solving processes. The two spaces are linked only through the problem solver's guesses (*Classify Instance*, Fig. 5.6 and 5.7) as to the correct classification of the instances as they are produced. In fact, these guesses are irrelevant, since the information is actually provided by the experimenter's reinforcement of each guess as correct or incorrect. The same problem-solving methods would work if the experimenter simply classified each instance as corresponding or not corresponding to the concept, without demanding a response from the problem solver. The flow of information is entirely from the instances to the concept generator, and not in the opposite direction.

However, in other forms of the concept attainment experiment (Bruner et al., 1956) the problem solver himself generates the instances. He may, of course, generate them randomly; but he may also select instances so constructed as to choose between two classes of hypotheses. This information flow, from the space of rules to the generator of instances (Channel *b*), enables solution methods that are more efficient than any with a one-way flow of information. Notice that the criterion for selection of instances is indirect and sophisticated: instances are valuable for solving the problem (finding the correct concept) to the degree that information on their classification imposes new restrictions on the domain of the rule generator.

The programs of Gregg and Simon do not cover the concept attainment paradigm in which the subject selects the instances. However, it is easy to generalize their programs to cover this case within the executive program of Fig. 5.7. A set of processes that accomplishes this is shown in Fig. 5.8. Each of the four processes—modify rules, generate instances, classify instance, and test instance-class—is extremely simple. The rule generator and instance generator embody particular assumptions about the subject's strategy for using information to enhance selectivity. The rule generator remembers which hypotheses have already been rejected, and also requires the new hypothesis to be consistent with the previous instance. The particular instance generator that is provided here generates instances that are positive for the current rule on half the trials and negative on the other half. As a guarantee of the completeness of the analysis, a SNOBOL version of the program of Fig. 5.7 and 5.8 has been written and tested. By modifying the several processes in simple ways, always employing the executive of Fig. 5.7, a wide range of experimental paradigms and of subject strategies within each of those paradigms can be simulated.

Modify rules (⇒ rules):
    set tally = 0;
1. delete rules from hypothesis-list;
      select item randomly from
         hypothesis-list (⇒ rules);
      classify instance (⇒ instance-class);
      test instance-class (⇒ test-result);
      if test-result = 'right' exit,
         else go to 1.

Generate instances (⇒ instance);
    if parity = 'odd' set parity = 'even',
      else set parity = 'odd';
    produce instance randomly
      from instance-description (⇒ instance);
    classify instance (⇒ instance-class);
    if parity = 'even'
      then if instance-class = 'positive' exit,
         else set complement(rules) = rules in instance & exit;
      else if instance-class = 'negative' exit,
         else set rules = complement(rules) in instance & exit.

Classify instance (⇒ instance-class):
    if rule ∈ instance set instance-class = 'positive' & exit,
      else set instance-class = 'negative' & exit.

Test instance-class (⇒ test-result);
    if correct-rule ∈ instance
      set correct-class = 'positive',
         else set correct-class = 'negative';
    if instance-class = correct-class
      set test-result = 'right'
      set tally = tally +1 & exit,
         else set test-result = 'wrong' & exit.

FIG. 5.8. Program for concept attainment task. (Subroutines for executive program of Fig. 5.7.)

Extrapolation of Patterned Sequences

A theory of how human subjects discover the patterns implicit in sequences of letters or numbers and use these patterns to extrapolate the sequences was developed in the form of a computer program by Simon and Kotovsky (1963). The relation of this theory to other theories of performance in this task and to the empirical data has been reviewed by Simon (1972a). The pattern discovery program is also an instance of the schema of Fig. 5.7.

In the sequence extrapolation task, the subject is presented with series of symbols followed by one or more blanks (e.g., "ABMCDM_"). His task is to insert the "right" symbols in the blanks—that is, the symbols that continue the pattern he detects in the given sequence. The goal object, then, is a sequence of symbols in which all of the blanks have been replaced "appropriately." But to fill in the blanks "appropriately," we must employ the notions of "same" and "next" between pairs of symbols, and perhaps other relations, in order to characterize the pattern as a basis for extrapolating it.[1] If the problem solving is to be characterized as a search, the search goes on in the space of patterns, and not in the space of extrapolated sequences.

To extrapolate the sequence, ABMCDM..., given as an example above, the problem solver must induce the pattern underlying that sequence: in each period of three letters, the first letter is *next* (N) in the English alphabet to the second letter (2) in the previous period (p); the second letter in each period is next (N) to the first letter (1) in the same period (s); the third letter in each period is the constant letter 'M', i.e., is the *same* (S) as the third letter (3) in the previous period (p). The pattern might be described as 'N2p N1s S3p'. The sequence is initialized by supplying the beginning 'A' and the constant 'M'.

Clearly, the elements of the sequence itself in the extrapolation task are the counterparts of the instances in the concept attainment task; while the pattern is the counterpart of the concept. What are the flows of information? As in the simple concept attainment paradigm, the sequence is provided by the experimenter rather than the problem solver. However, in his search for pattern, the problem solver can choose which elements of the sequence he will test for relations at any given moment. If, in the previous example, he is provided with three periods instead of two—ABMCDMEFM...—then, having discovered the second 'M' three symbols beyond the first, he can test whether an 'M' occurs again three symbols later. To this extent, there can be a flow of information (Channel *b*, Fig. 5.6) from a hypothesized pattern component (the repetition of 'M') to a choice of which instance (which part of the sequence) to examine next.

The flow of information in the opposite direction, from sequence to pattern (Channel *a*), is even more critical for the efficiency of the solution method. The problem solver need not generate "all possible hypotheses," but can instead detect simple relations ("same" and "next") between pairs of

---

[1]Ernst and Newell (1969) have proposed an ingenious scheme for handling the sequence extrapolation task as a GPS problem-solving task, that is, in terms of a single problem space that accommodates both the sequences and the patterns. We will not discuss this scheme here, since an analysis in terms of a dual problem space seems more natural and simpler. However, their proposal shows again the close affinity between problem solving and rule induction, as these terms are commonly used.

symbols in the sequence, and then hypothesize patterns constructed from those relations (an example of the *matching* method). Although obviously inductive, the process need not involve any considerable amount of search.

Induction of Grammars

As our final example of a rule induction task, we consider the induction of a grammar for a language, from examples of sentences and nonsentences. This task has received some attention in the artificial intelligence literature (e.g., Biermann & Feldman, 1971; Klein & Kuppin, 1970; Siklossy, 1972; Solomonoff, 1959). In the grammar induction task, the subject generates a succession of symbol strings that may be sentences in a language possessing a formal grammar. He is then told whether or not each string is a sentence. His task is to induce the rules of the grammar so that he can predict infallibly whether any given string will be classified as a sentence. The commercially marketed game QUERIES 'N THEORIES provides a version of this task that is readily adapted to the laboratory.

In this problem domain, the examples of sentences and nonsentences constitute the space of instances, while the grammar rules correspond to the space of concepts. In the most common form of the task, the problem solver selects the sentences against which to test his system of rules, hence there is a flow of information from the space of rules to the space of instances (Channel *b*, Fig. 5.6), as well as a reverse flow from instances to rules (Channel *a*).

Let us illustrate these information flows more concretely. Consider a grammar with two components: a set of base sentences and a set of replacement rules that allow the construction of a new sentence by replacing certain symbols or sequences of symbols, in any sentence where they occur, by a new symbol or sequence. A simple example of such grammar is given by:

$$\text{Base sentence:} \quad Y$$
$$\text{Replacement rule: } Y \leftarrow BY$$

This grammar has a single base sentence, Y, and a single replacement rule, $Y \leftarrow BY$. Applying the replacement rule to the base sentence, then to the resulting sentence, and so on, we obtain, as additional sentences of the language, BY, BBY, BBBY, and so on.

Suppose that it was already known, by previous tests, that Y and BY were sentences. Then, by supplying information from the instances to the rule generator, the possible replacement rule $Y \leftarrow BY$ could be constructed directly. Reversing the flow of information, the rule itself can now be used to generate instances of predicted sentences, and the correctness of these can be checked by the "native informant" (the experimenter).

To match the various concept attainment paradigms, the task could be modified, for example, to supply the set of instances of valid sentences in advance. Or the experimenter could supply instances of sentences and nonsentences, and require the problem solver to classify them. The two classes of tasks are in every way identical with respect to the ways in which information can be made available to the problem solver.

Fig. 5.9 shows processes for performing the grammar induction task that again operates with the GRI executive of Fig. 5.7. These processes are a little more complicated than those of Fig. 5.8, mainly because they must generate and test two different kinds of rules: basic sentences and replacement rules. The specific generators for the two kinds of rules are not defined in the figure. This program, like the one for concept attainment, has also been written and debugged in SNOBOL (with specific versions of the generators for basic sentences and replacement rules). We have begun to gather some data on human behavior in the grammar induction task which, on first examination, fit the program of Fig. 5.7 and 5.9 relatively well, but we will have to postpone detailed analysis of these data to another paper.

The Tower of Hanoi: A Digression

We digress for a moment to comment on the Tower of Hanoi problem, discussed by Greeno and Egan in their paper for this volume, for this task illustrates again how tricky is the distinction between problem-solving tasks and rule induction tasks. The problem as usually stated—to find a sequence of moves that will transfer all the disks from one peg to another, subject to the usual constraints on moves—is clearly a problem-solving task. If demonstration of this is needed, it has been provided by Ernst and Newell (1969), who programmed GPS to solve the problem by the means-ends method.

But the problem can be stated differently: to find a *rule* for transferring the disks from one peg to another. It may also be required that the rule work properly for an arbitrary number of disks. Just as clearly, this is a rule induction task. To solve it, one or more rule spaces must be formulated and searches conducted through these spaces. Knowledge to guide this search may be obtained by manipulating the disks—that is, by searching through the space of arrangements of disks on pegs. Thus *this* Tower of Hanoi problem, as distinguished from the one described in the previous paragraph, involves a dual problem space.

Rules for the Tower of Hanoi can be stated in various forms. One (incomplete) rule is based on the sequence: 1 2 1 3 1 2 1 4 1 . . . , where the digits refer to the disks to be moved. With slight modification, the sequential pattern programs discussed earlier could discover this pattern. The recursive solution to the problem requires a different kind of rule generator—one that understands the concept of recursive definition.

Modify rules (⇒ rules):
   if test-result = 'wrong'
     delete new-rule from rules;
   if basic-sentence-tally = 'done' go to 1,
     else generate basic-sentence (⇒ rule)
      set new-rule = rule & exit;
1. if replacement-rule-tally = 'done' exit,
     else generate replacement-rule (⇒ rule) &
      set new-rule = rule & exit.

Generate instances (⇒ instance):
   if new-rule ∈ basic-sentences
     set instance = new-rule & exit,
     else generate item from positive-instance (⇒ item);
      apply new-rule to item (⇒ instance)
     if instance ∉ positive-instance exit,
      else continue generation;
     if positive-instances exhausted
      set signal = 'finished' & exit.

Classify instance (⇒ instance-class):
   generate basic-sentences (⇒ basic-sentence):
     if instance = basic-sentence set instance-class = 'positive'
     & exit from routine,
      else continue generation;
   generate derived-sentences with length = length(instance)
     (⇒ derived-sentence):
     if instance = basic-sentence set instance-class = 'positive'
     & exit from routine,
      else continue generation;
   set instance-class = 'negative' & exit.

Test instance-class (⇒ test-result):
   if instance ∈ legitimate-instances add instance
     to positive-instances & set correct-class = 'positive',
     else set correct-class = 'negative';
   if instance-class = correct-class
     set test-result = 'right',
     else set test-result = 'wrong';
   add instance to tested-instances & exit.

FIG. 5.9. Program for grammar induction task. (Subroutines for executive program of Fig. 5.7.)

Summary: Application of GRI to Specific Task Environments

Table 5.1 shows how we have interpreted the processes of GRI in the context of the specific tasks we have discussed: concept attainment, sequence extrapolation, and grammar induction. A fourth column in the table shows how the cryptarithmetic task can be handled within the same schema when viewed as a rule induction task; while the fifth column shows which components of the schema have counterparts in a problem-solving task where only a single problem space is involved.

We have shown how the specific processes that describe subject behavior within the executive program of GRI vary as a function of the characteristics of the experimental paradigm and the level of complexity and sophistication of the strategy that the subject adopts for handling the task.

In concept attainment experiments, for example, the subject is usually instructed specifically as to what concepts are admissible, that is, he is given the space of rules. He is also provided with an explicit definition of the space of possible instances. In sequence extrapolation tasks much more is usually left to the subject. The space of rules and the rule generator are not usually discussed explicitly in the instructions, nor *a fortiori,* the test for the adequacy or correctness of the extrapolation. The experimenter provides the instances (the incomplete sequence) and an ill-defined goal (that the sequence is to be extrapolated). The subject evolves the rest: the space of rules and the test for correctness of an extrapolation, as well as the generator and test processes that define his strategy.

Variations in subject strategies relate particularly to the use of information from each of the problem spaces—the rule space and instance space—to guide the generator for searching the other. In paradigms where the experimenter provides one of the generators (e.g., the instance generator in the standard concept attainment paradigm) there is less room for variation in subject strategy than in paradigms where the subject must devise both generators (e.g., in the form of the concept attainment experiment used by Bruner et al., 1956).

CONCLUSION

In this paper we have proposed a conceptualization of problem solving and of rule induction that allows these two arenas of human thinking to be brought within a common framework. We have seen that both problem domains can be interpreted in terms of problem spaces and information processes for searching such spaces. The generators of elements in a problem space may be more or less selective, depending on what use they make of information provided by the tests, and varying levels of selectivity can be observed in both rule-induction systems and problem-solving systems. What chiefly distinguishes rule-induction tasks from problem-solving tasks is that

TABLE 5.1

Application of GRI to Four Tasks

GRI	Task environments				
	Concept formation	Sequence extrapolation	Grammar induction	Cryptarithmetic	Problem solving
Rule space					
Rules	Current hypothesis	Partial pattern	Partial grammar	List of assignments	Node in Problem space
Modify rules	Generate hypothesis	Modify pattern	Modify grammar	Modify list	Apply operator at node
Instances	Instances	Sequence elements	Predicted Sentences	Column of display	—
Instance space					
Generate instance	(Generate instance)	[Generate sequence]	Generate Sentence	Update display	—
Classify instance	Respond	Predict symbol	Query experimenter	Process column	Describe new node
Test					
Test instance-class	[Reinforce response]	Match symbols	[Accept sentence]	Detect contradiction	Evaluate new node

Note. Processes in square brackets are executed by experimenter; processes in parentheses are sometimes executed by experimenter.

the former call for a pair of problem spaces—one for rules and one for instances—while the latter commonly require only a single-problem space. Our analysis of the cryptarithmetic task shows it to lie midway between the two main classes, and hence to provide a useful bridge for translating each of them in terms of the other.

To test the conceptualization, and to guarantee that it is more than a set of analogies, we constructed a formalization, the General Rule Induction program, together with subprocesses for concept attainment and grammar induction that operate within that program.[2] By means of GRI, each of the tasks can be mapped formally on the others. The basic components of these programs are generator and test processes organized into generate-test, heuristic search, means-ends, and matching methods.

---

[2] Since this was written, Dennis E. Egan and James G. Greeno have written SNOBOL routines that operate within GRI for discovering sequential patterns (personal communication). Thus the GRI scheme has now been implemented for the three main rule induction tasks discussed in this paper.

6
QUOTE THE RAVEN? NEVERMORE!

EARL HUNT
University of Washington

How do we assess mental power? This question has posed a major technological challenge to psychology for a century. Two themes recur in the literature. How are we to differentiate between what a person can do and what a person has learned to do? Another way to state the question is "Is performance due to an ability to figure out solutions to novel problems or due to the possession of a store of knowledge about problems analogous to those presented in the testing situation?" This question is by no means a new one. Our failure to resolve it has produced one of psychology's greatest social controversies, the debate over use and interpretation of intelligence tests (Jensen, 1969; Scarr-Salapatek, 1971). The second theme is a more theoretical one; to what extent is there a general factor in intelligence? The two themes are related, since it is consistent to assume that a pure measure of the general factor, *g,* would also be a culture-fair measure. It would not be consistent to test *g* in a situation which required that the examinees utilize culture-specific training.

The purpose of this paper is to examine a well-known psychometric measure, the *Raven Progressive Matrix Test* (Raven, 1965), which is often asserted to be both culture-fair and a measure of *g* (Butcher, 1968; Robb, Bernardoni & Johnson, 1972). Indeed, no less an authority than Spearman (Spearman & Wynn-Jones, 1951) regarded the Progressive Matrix Test as an appropriate measure of the general factor. Jensen (1972) refers to the test as the best single measure of the *g* factor that is now available. Although others have demurred somewhat, since correlations between the Raven test and other intelligence tests range from .4 to .7 (Butcher, 1972; Matarazzo, 1972), clearly the test is widely accepted. As it is easy to administer and score, it has recently appeared as a covariate or independent variable in a number of experimental studies of cognitive ability. For these reasons alone, the task

The research described herein was supported by the National Institute of Mental Health, Grant MH 21795 to the University of Washington. I would like to thank Clifford Lunneborg and Steven Poltrock for their constructive comments during the writing of this paper. The responsibility for errors, of course, remains mine.

demands of the test are worthy of study. Our interest, however, is motivated by a more theoretical concern. Hunt and Lunneborg (1973) argue that it is inadvisable to have a technology for measuring individual differences which stands apart from a theory of cognition. A similar point has been made by Glaser (1972), who regards the general failure to find an interaction between the effectiveness of training methods and the ability of trainees to be evidence that our ability measures are deficient. Hunt, Frost, and Lunneborg (1973) have shown that the conclusions one might draw from a number of paradigms in cognitive psychology, in which individual differences are treated as "random variation," must be tempered if one considers psychometrically measurable differences between individuals. Such observations warn us to look carefully at the information processing demands of an intelligence test before we decide what the test measures. This is what we propose to do. The remainder of this paper is an attempt to answer the question "What sort of computer program could solve Progressive Matrix problems?" We shall be particularly concerned with the psychological principles illustrated by such a program and with the amount and organization of extraproblem knowledge that the program needs in order to demonstrate that it is appropriately endowed with a general intelligence factor.

PROGRESSIVE MATRIX PROBLEMS

All the problems in the Raven test have the same form. The subject is presented with a three by three array of geometric patterns, excepting the lower-right hand element. An example is shown in Fig. 6.1. Symbolically, we will refer to the matrix

$$M = [m_{ij}], i, j = 1 \ldots 3 \qquad [1]$$

of patterns, with the understanding that element m_{33} of this matrix is unknown. Immediately below the array of patterns, eight answer patterns are presented. Let

$$A = \{(a_k)\} k = 1 \ldots 8 \qquad [2]$$

be the set of answers. The subject must find a relationship (or relationships) which holds between the eight known elements of M, and uniquely specifies one of the eight answer elements as the m_{33} pattern. Again reverting to symbols, suppose that a subject observes that there is a relationship (equivalently, an operation) that always holds between successive elements of a row of M. Then for all known elements of M, it is true that f exists such that

$$m_{i,j+1} = f(m_{i,j}). \qquad [3]$$

Therefore,

$$m_{33} = f(m_{32}) \qquad [4]$$

and if there is a k such that

$$a_k = f(m_{32}) \tag{5}$$

then a_k must be the correct answer.

Progressive Matrix problems are often easier to solve than to describe. Refer again to Fig. 6.1, which is the practice problem from Set I of the Advanced Progressive Matrix test, 1962 version. In the terms just introduced, f is the operation "Remove one vertical bar." Other definitions of f are possible. A correct rule will, as this one does, identify Answer Pattern 8 as the missing matrix element. The difficulty of a Progressive Matrix problem depends upon the complexity of the progression rule, f. Thus far we have discussed only simple rules, in order to illustrate the principle of problem construction. To solve a particular problem, the subject may have to discover operations on rows, as in the example, or on columns (a column rule is also possible in the example, or a combined rule for rows and columns, or a rule which regards all elements of the matrix as part of a single pattern.

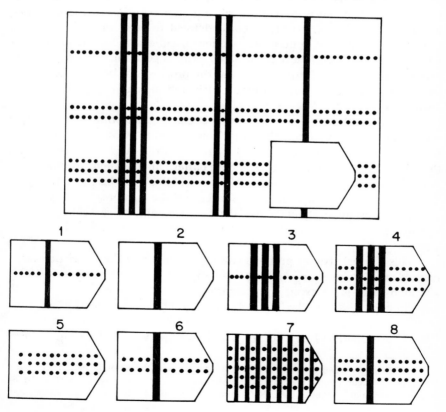

FIG. 6.1. Practice problem from Set 1 of the Advanced Progressive Matrices.

Three versions of Raven's Progressive Matrix Test are in general use. Our discussion will deal with Set I of the 1962 Advanced Progressive Matrices. This consists of 12 problems designed to sort individuals into "dull," "average," and "bright" groups. The test takes about half an hour. Set II of the same test consists of 36 problems, and is designed to make a finer differentiation between adults and older children of above average ability. According to Raven (1965), Set I and Set II tap the same cognitive abilities. A test utilizing colored matrices is also available, but will not be discussed.

BASIC CONCEPTS AND TERMINOLOGY

To summarize the notation format: a problem will be written as a matrix M of three rows and three columns, using conventional matrix notation, i.e., m_{ij} refers to the (geometric pattern) element in row i and column j. A solution to a problem is a selection of a pattern, a_k, from the set $A = \{a_k\}$ $k = 1 . . 8$, of possible answers. The solution is correct if some relationship between matrix elements is maintained when pattern a_k is inserted into the m_{33} position in the matrix. An *algorithm* is defined to be a set of steps which, when executed in the appropriate sequence, either produce a solution or terminate at a defined failure point.[1] The term "algorithm" has been chosen, rather than "program," to indicate that the processes to be described could be mechanized in a computer program, although such a program has not yet been written.

The algorithms to be presented begin by detecting some simple relationship between matrix elements. This is used to create an hypothetical *base element,* which serves as the first *trial answer.* A trial answer is best thought of as a description of a geometric pattern and, as such, specifies a set of patterns. For example, "single, solid vertical line" can be thought of as a description which fits several of the elements of the answer set in Fig. 1. The algorithms progressively embellish the base element, by searching for new relations in the matrix, until the trial answer meets the criteria for a correct answer.

This general style of problem solving is similar to the heuristic search method used widely in Artificial Intelligence research (Nilsson, 1971), although there is no explicit representation of problem solving as a graph searching process. In the psychological literature, the algorithms to be presented could be regarded as examples of Miller, Galanter, and Pribram's (1960) Test-Operate-Test (TOTE) cycle. A third way of looking at these

---

[1] The definition of algorithm as used here is consistent with the use of the term in Computer Science, i.e, an algorithm is a mapping from all strings of an input language to the strings of an output language (Glushkov, 1966). No distinction is implied between "algorithmic" and "heuristic" reasoning in the sense of "always correct" versus "guessing procedure." The algorithms to be presented are defined procedures for generating guesses.

algorithms is to think of them as examples of the hypothesis generation and test method of problem solving described by Newell and Simon (1972). Indeed, the algorithms could be expressed in Newell and Simon's production system notation, although a more conventional flow chart notation will be used here. The precise language chosen to describe the algorithms is probably not too important at the stage of analysis to be presented, although it might be later, in attempting to link these results with other results in the simulation of cognitive processes. What is important is the disparity in the psychological processes being simulated by each algorithm.

Overview of the Problem-Solving Process

Two algorithms will be presented. In formal information processing language, one algorithm represents a Progressive Matrix problem as a plane figure in which certain figures can be detected, and applies physically defined transformations to that representation. The other algorithm represents a problem as an ordered collection of sets of features, and applies logical and arithmetical transformations to these features. In a more traditional language, the first algorithm will be called the *Gestalt algorithm*, as it deals with a problem by using the operations of visual perception, such as the continuation of lines through blank areas and the superimposition of visual images upon each other. The second algorithm will be called the *analytic algorithm*, as it applies logical operations to features contained within elements of the problem matrix. This choice of names is meant to be descriptive without commitment to a particular school of psychology. An interesting alternative naming of the algorithms, which certainly would imply such a commitment, would be to call the first algorithm a *concrete operations algorithm* and the second, a *formal operations algorithm*.

The Gestalt and analytic programs both use, as a subroutine, an *answer evaluation* program. This program makes some nontrivial psychological assumptions of its own concerning the decision to accept or reject an answer proposed by the problem-solving algorithms. Therefore, it will be described first.

ANSWER EVALUATION ALGORITHM

The answer evaluation algorithm accepts as input a pattern description and a definition of the operations used to derive it. The operations must be rules for deriving the m_{33} element of a matrix from the other elements in the third row or column, or from a combination of these. The flow chart of the answer evaluation algorithm is shown in Fig. 6.2. The first step is to determine whether or not at least one of the patterns in the answer set satisfies the description being evaluated. If the answer to this question is "no" the pattern description can be rejected. If the answer is yes, further

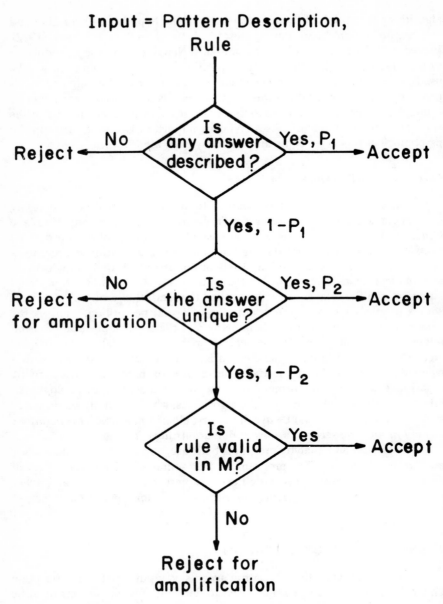

FIG. 6.2. Flow chart for answer evaluation.

processing may be in order. Before detailing what then happens, we pause to consider what we mean by the phrase "A pattern satisfies a description." There are two definitions, one for use with the Gestalt algorithm and one for use with the analytic algorithm.

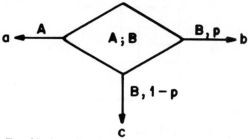

FIG. 6A. A semistochastic branch of a flow chart.

Flow chart conventions for indicating iterative processes (e.g., a FORTRAN DO statement) are all clumsy. Iterative sequences of computations will be indicated by beginning the sequence with a box with curved ends. The last step in the sequence will branch back to the box. Flow of control after the iteration is complete will be shown by the path exiting from the side of the box. The appropriate diagram is shown in Fig. 6B.

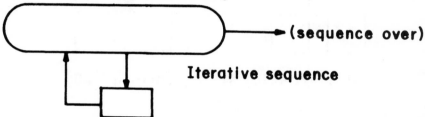

FIG. 6B. Flow chart convention for indicating iterative processes.

Gestalt description. A description is a (visual) figure consisting of lines and darkened areas. A matrix or answer element is similarly described. An element P satisfies a description D if D can be superimposed on P in such a way that all lines and darkened areas of D fall on equivalent lines and darkened areas of P. This definition does not require that D and P be identical, since P may have darkened areas and lines in addition to those covered by D. Fig. 6.3 shows two nonidentical patterns and a description which satisfies either of them.

Analytic description. P and D are sets of features. P satisfies the description D if D is a subset of P.

Evaluation of plausible answers. Suppose that a pattern satisfying the description has been found within the answer set. It is always assumed that answer evaluation will proceed in normal reading order, and that the first satisfactory pattern in A will be chosen as the first trial answer. With probability p_1 this answer is accepted as being correct. (Refer to Fig. 6.2.) With probability $1-p_1$ control will be passed to the next step of the algorithm.[2] At this step the remaining elements of A will be examined, to

---

[2] Some of the flow charting conventions to be used may be unfamiliar. A *semistochastic branch* is defined to be a branch dependent on a test with two possible outcomes, A or B. If Outcome A occurs, Branch a is taken with Probability 1. If Outcome B occurs, Branch b will be taken with Probability *p,* and Branch c with probability 1-*p.* A semistochastic branch is diagrammed as shown in Fig. 6A.

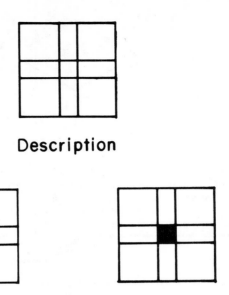

Description

Patterns Satisfying Description

FIG. 6.3. Illustration of Gestalt description.

determine whether the description specifies a unique pattern. If it does not, the answer evaluation algorithm returns control to the answer generation algorithm, indicating that the current description must be embellished in some way. If the answer is unique, then with probability p_2, it is accepted as the correct answer. With probability $1-p_2$ a further check is made. In this check the rule used to generate the answer is applied to the *second* row or column of the matrix, to determine whether the third element of that row or column could be generated. Since elements m_{23} and m_{32} are known, the predicted answer can be checked for accuracy. If the answer generating rule passes this check, then the input description is accepted as an answer. If this check cannot be passed, the answer generating algorithm is instructed to produce a new answer. Note that it is not possible to say whether or not the next answer should be an amplification of the current answer, since the answer evaluation algorithm will have rejected the rule used to select an answer element, but will not have uncovered evidence indicating that the particular answer element chosen is not, in fact, the correct choice.

As will be shown, it is possible that some answer generation algorithms will not be able to generate an answer satisfactory to the answer evaluation algorithm. The behavioral interpretation of this outcome is unclear. Mathematically, the most convenient assumption would be that an answer is chosen randomly from the answer set. In fact, this is unlikely. The Raven test does not require that the subject make any response. Indeed, the instructions encourage the subject to continue on if a particular problem cannot be solved. Therefore, we would expect a substantial number of incomplete answers. It also appears that there are systematic guessing patterns amongst individuals who do not understand the harder problems. Forbes (1964) observed that there were consistent error patterns for Set II problems at the lower levels of ability. Some consistency in error patterns could be obtained from the answer evaluation algorithm by varying the values of the parameters p_1 and p_2, which can be thought of as indices of the extent to which the subject is willing to jump to a conclusion without adequate validation. The present theory, however, does not state what the subject's response should be if no trial answer can be accepted, or if a set of two or more possible answers is located.

THE GESTALT ALGORITHM

The Gestalt algorithm consists of three answer generators and an executive subroutine. The executive applies the answer generators and uses the answer evaluator to accept the results of each generator. The three generators are best thought of as operations on visual images. The generators employ principles of continuation and superimposition.

Continuation. Any visual progression which is interrupted by the blank region replacing the m_{33} element is continued through the blank region. When this is done, the blank region will contain a pattern, and can be regarded as a matrix element or a pattern description. The continuation operation, then, treats the entire matrix as a single visual field. Two types of continuations of visual progressions are allowed: the *continuation of explicit lines* between matrix elements, and the *continuation of visual fields.*

The process of continuing explicit lines is simple, any line drawn between the elements of the problem matrix, M, will, of necessity, be interrupted at the edge of the blank space occupying the m_{33} position. This is illustrated by Fig. 6.1 in which the blank space interrupts one solid vertical line and three dotted horizontal lines. Continuing these lines will fill the blank space with a pattern which, in this case, coincides exactly with the pattern of an answer element.

The process of continuing visual fields is more subtle. Let us regard each matrix element as a view of part of a continuous visual field, located behind the plane of the matrix itself. A row, then, would be similar to a view of a single scene, observed through a wall with three windows in it. A continuation through three elements of a row or column exists if the changes from the first element to the second, and from the second to the third, could be produced by motion of a rigid body across the field of view corresponding to the views through each of the elements. To return to the window and wall example, the views through the available elements are used to construct a hypothesis about the complete visual scene behind the wall. The missing

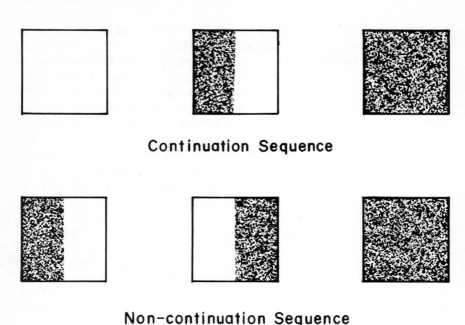

Continuation Sequence

Non-continuation Sequence

FIG. 6.4. Examples of continuation of visual progression.

element is analogous to a window with the shades drawn, and the problem is to guess what would be seen if the shades were to be lifted. Since motion of a rigid body is allowed, the scene could equally well be thought of as showing, in successive row or column elements, the view through a single window over time. Note that the "views" permitted by these interpretations are not identical. In both interpretations changes in the "views" from element to element in the matrix are to be understood by reference to a model of visual scenes in the physical world.[3] An example is shown in Fig. 6.4. The top row would have been produced by successive views through a single window as a rigid body passed behind the wall. (Think of the view through a window into an alley, as a large truck passes by.) By contrast, there is no continuous motion of a single rigid body that will produce the sequence of views shown in the lower row of Fig. 6.4.

Superimposition of whole patterns. Some intuitively easy Progressive Matrix problems cannot be solved by continuation alone. A general characteristic of such problems is that the pattern produced by the continuation operation must be amplified in a fairly simple way. Superimposition operations provide a way in which this can be done. A complete matrix element can be superimposed on another by placing the outer borders

---

[3]A very similar method of analysis is used in computer science to infer the arrangement of three dimensional scenes from two dimensional projections (Clowes, 1971; Falk, 1972).

of the base element (i.e., the trial answer) and some other matrix element in correspondence. In doing so, the algorithm permits distortion of either the x or y scales *of the base element*. The psychological justification for doing so is that human vision is surprisingly insensitive to distortions of scale. An example is shown in the upper half of Fig. 6.5. If superimposition can be achieved on some matrix element, a trial answer is constructed by distorting the matrix element matched to the scale of the original base element. Note that this is equivalent to "coloring in" the base element to match the coloring in the matrix element which it superimposes. Still another way to regard this operation is to say that continuation is used to establish the outline of the answer pattern, and superimposition is used to select a matrix element with that outline. The selected element, appropriately scaled, is the trial answer.

Superimposition based on point matching. Let us refer to the above described operation as *border superimposition*. A second type of super-imposition, *point superimposition,* extends the operation to parts of matrix elements. In some simple Progressive Matrix problems the base element can only be superimposed upon a part of the pattern covered by any one matrix element. An example is Problem 2 of Set I, which is shown in Fig. 6.6. Fortunately, an observation by Attneave (1956) about human visual perception provides us with a psychologically justifiable way to extend the

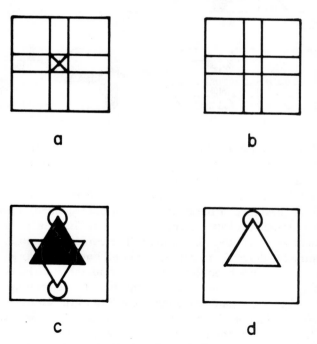

a   b

c   d

FIG. 6.5. Superimposition operations. (Fig. b can be placed on a by border superimposi-tion. Fig. d can be placed on c by point superimposition at circled points.)

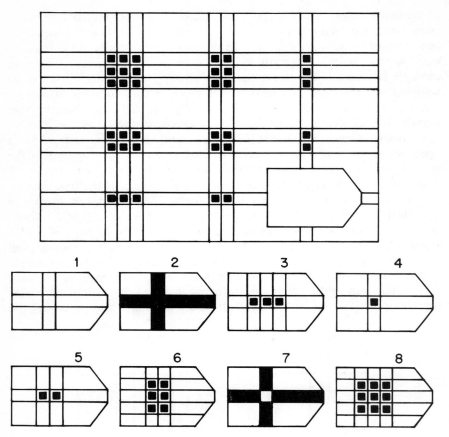

Fig. 6.6. Problem 2 of Set 1.

notion of superimposition to handle such problems. Attneave noted that most of the information about a visual pattern is concentrated in the set of points of maximum curvature along the boundaries of a figure. Using this notion, we define *point superimposition* to be an operation in which the point of maximum curvature of the boundary of a base element is placed on the point of maximum curvature of a matrix element. Changes in the scale of the base element are permitted, if required. The two superimposed figures are then examined to determine whether or not all lines and colored areas of the base element rest upon equivalent features in the matrix element. This operation is similar to the operation involved in determining whether a matrix element satisfies a description according to the Gestalt definition. If description satisfaction is not achieved, superimposition fails. If it is achieved, the region of the matrix element lying under the base element is rescaled to the original dimensions of the base element, and becomes the trial answer.

In spite of the wordiness of its verbal description, superimposition is a very simple visual operation. The lower half of Fig. 6.5 shows an example.

Both border and point superimposition are visual operations, and are most easily thought of as capabilities of a machine that can manipulate optical images. Programming a superimposition operator on a digital computer would certainly not present any conceptual difficulties, although it might be a tedious task. It is necessary, however, to specify which matrix element will be chosen for the superimposition process, as different answers could result from the choice of different matrix elements. At least, this is a theoretical possibility, although there are no such problems in Set I. We have no theory to guide us here, but empirical observations of error patterns in Set II problems (Forbes, 1964) suggest that the elements adjacent to the m_{33} element (i.e., m_{32} or m_{23}) should be used.

The Gestalt Control Algorithm

The flow diagram of the control routine for the Gestalt algorithm is shown in Fig. 6.7. Initially, all explicit lines in the matrix problem are continued through the blank area, forming the first base element. If no explicit lines are found, the extended definition of continuation is applied—first to rows and then to columns to create a base element. Note that there is a semistochastic branch after each application of continuation, so there is always a chance that the program will terminate after an unsuccessful application of continuation. Once a base element is found, it is evaluated as a potential answer and either accepted, rejected, or returned for amplification. If amplification is required, the superimposition operations are used. If they cannot construct a satisfactory answer, the algorithm terminates in failure.

Evaluation of the Gestalt algorithm. Table 6.1 summarizes the performance of the Gestalt algorithm on Set I of the Advanced Progressive Matrices. The procedure is clearly capable of solving problems one through five, although in some cases there is a defined probability of terminating with an incorrect answer. Unfortunately, no published data have been located which indicate what the parameter settings should be in order to mirror human performance. The overall score obtained by the algorithm is in the range which Raven (1965) indicates to be slightly below average performance in the normal adult population.

Problem 6 is particularly interesting from the viewpoint of the Gestalt algorithm. The problem cannot be solved by continuation and super-imposition, as they have been defined here. On the other hand, if one expands the idea of continuation to include completion of "good" figures (the Gestalt principle of *Praegnanz*) and accepts the hypothesis that a triangle is a good figure, then Problem 6 is solvable. The theoretical difficulty, of course, is that the principles of perceptual organization are stated in such a way that an algorithmic definition of them is difficult to obtain.

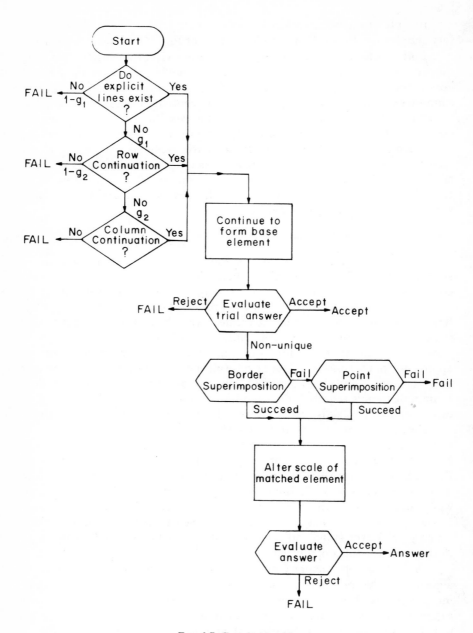

Fig. 6.7. Gestalt Algorithm.

There appears to be no way in which Problems 7-12 of Set I can be solved by the Gestalt algorithm or by reasonable amplification of it.

TABLE 6.1

Operations Applied to Problems 1-6 by Gestalt Algorithm

Problem	Operation applied	Answer selected
1	Continuation	8
2	Continuation	1 (incorrect)
	Point Superimposition	4 (correct)
3	Continuation	3 (incorrect)
	Border superimposition	5 (correct)
4	Continuation	2 (incorrect)
	Border superimposition	1 (correct)
5	Continuation (column)	2 (correct)
6	Continuation (?)	5 (correct)

Note. Problems 7-2 cannot be solved by this algorithm.

THE ANALYTIC ALGORITHM

The analytic algorithm consists of a set of operations and a framework for executing them. When provided with all its operations, the algorithm can solve all the Set I problems. Lesser scores will be achieved if the set of operations is restricted. The basic difference between the analytic and Gestalt algorithms is in the way a Progressive Matrix problem is represented. In the analytic program matrix elements are represented as hierarchically ordered sets of features of subelements, rather than as unitary visual patterns. The operations used by the algorithm are operations on sets of features and properties of subelements, rather than operations on sensory images.

The first "subroutine" of the algorithm is a feature abstraction process. The word subroutine has been placed in quotes, to signify that the feature abstractor will not be specified in detail sufficient to permit programming. Feature abstraction is better thought of as a set of rules for a human to follow while preparing a matrix problem for input to the algorithm. The rules appeal to common human experience and intuition. The subroutine is programmable in principle if one concedes that it is possible to develop a machine to scan a continuous line, to recognize grayness levels, and to recognize the repetition of a particular subelement throughout a region (e.g., upper right quadrant) of a matrix element. We also assume that a machine could be built to recognize common geometric figures, such as a cross, to count the number of times a specified subelement appears in a matrix element, and to measure the major dimensions of a subelement. While many of these operations are difficult or tedious to program on a digital computer, they are all easily mechanizable given appropriate equipment.

Let a feature be defined as a property of a subelement, where a subelement is either a "familiar closed figure," such as a cross or circle, a line, or the grayness level of an area. The properties to be considered for each subelement are presence or absence, continuity of grayness area (graded, dark, light, dotted), location of subelement, breadth, width, and number of subelements. A single subelement, then, can give rise to several features. For example, element m_{11} of Fig. 6.1 can be described by the feature set

$$m_{11} = \begin{array}{ll} \text{present(vertical line)} = \text{true} & [6] \\ \text{grayness(vertical line)} = \text{dark} \\ \text{number(vertical line)} = 3 \\ \text{present(horizontal line)} = \text{true} \\ \text{grayness(horizontal line)} = \text{dotted} \\ \text{number(horizontal line)} = 1 \end{array}$$

In addition to distinguishing between features arising from different subelements, we shall distinguish between *figure* and *ground* subelements. A ground subelement is defined to be a subelement which is extended or repeated over some continuous area from one side to another of a matrix element. Only one ground subelement is permitted in a matrix element. If two elements qualify as grouped elements by the above definition, then the one with the larger area or the lighter grayness value is assumed to be the ground element. This definition suffices to specify a single ground element for all problems in Set I.

The distinction between figure and ground is important because the algorithm will try to produce the m_{33} element first by modifying features arising from figure subelements, and then figures from ground subelements. One can construct a problem for which different solutions would be achieved if different orderings were used.

In some cases the analytic algorithm deals with the features of a row or column, instead of the features of elements of a row or column. In this case the features of the row (column) are simply the union of the features of the elements in the row (column). The figure-ground distinction is retained.

The basic principle of the analytic program can be illustrated by considering its action given an arbitrary ordered set, $\{X, Y, Z\}$ of features of subelements. Normally X, Y, and Z will be the elements of row one or column one. Each set of features will itself be ordered, so we may write

$$X = x_1, x_2, \ldots x_i, \ldots x_k, \tag{7}$$

and similarly for Y and Z. Each of the x_i, y_i, and z_i will have a property type (present-absent, color, etc.) and a value. The dummy value NIL is used for features which do not apply to a particular element, in order to keep the numbering of features consistent across X, Y, and Z. The initial problem is to find a sequence of operators which, when applied to X and Y, will produce Z. Let s be such a sequence, and assume that it has been found. This means that if s is regarded as a single operator, then

$$s(X,Y) = Z. \tag{8}$$

To produce an answer to a matrix problem, the algorithm then considers the triplet of feature sets X', Y', Z', where X' and Y' are known and Z' is not. Normally X' and Y' are the first two elements of the third row or column, and Z' is the m_{33} element. A trial answer is constructed by computing

$$s(X',Y') = Z'. \qquad [9]$$

It is also possible to evaluate s by using a second set of known matrix elements, X^*, Y^*, and Z^*. Normally this will be the second row or column of the problem matrix.

The sequence s must be constructed from individual operations, and these, in turn, must be selected. This is done by a variation of the *means-end analysis* technique introduced by Newell and Simon (1961,1972) and familiar to all students of computer simulation of problem solving.[4] Means-end analysis is guided by an operator-difference matrix. The rows of this matrix correspond to the Set $F = \{f\}$ of operations available to the algorithm. The columns represent possible types of differences which can occur between matrix subelements. Three possible difference types will be considered: presence or absence of a subelement, a difference in the number of repetitions of a given subelement, a difference in the location of a subelement, and a difference in the physical dimensions of two subelements with the same name (cross, star, dot, etc.). Feature Sets X and Y are compared on a feature by feature basis until a discrepancy is found. Let i be the lowest integer such that $x_i \neq y_i$. The algorithm then searches down the rows of the operator-difference matrix until an operator, f, is found which affects the type of difference noted, i.e., a search is made for f such that $f(x_i) = y_i$. Since it might be possible to apply f to several features in X, a particular application will be denoted by

$$f(X,i) = x_1, x_2, \ldots x_{i-1}, f(x_i), x_{i+1}, \ldots x_k. \qquad [10]$$

A sequence consists of one or more concatenated operations $f, g \in F$. It might be that

$$s = g(f(X,i),j) = x_1 \ldots f(x_i) \ldots g(x_j) \ldots x_k. \qquad [11]$$

For simplicity, suppose that this is not necessary and that $f(X,i) = Y$. The next step is to validate f by using it to produce Z from Y. This is done by searching for the lowest integer j such that $f(y,j) = z_j$. Validation is achieved if the relation $f(Y,j) = Z$ is true. If it is not, the algorithm seeks a further operation, g, to complete the sequence as in 11. To predict Z' the value of matrix element $f(Y',j)$ is computed.

These formalisms make precise, but may serve to hide, a simple idea. Consider the set of matrix elements shown in Fig. 6.8. The upper row

---

[4]There is also a strong resemblance between the algorithm described here and Evans' (1968) program for solving geometric analogies.

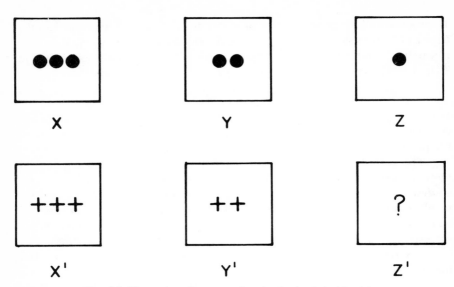

FIG. 6.8. Illustration of set operations in the Analytic Algorithm.

presents the X, Y, Z elements and the lower row the X', Y', Z' elements. The feature sets for the first row are

X = present(circle) = true, color(circle) = black,   [12]
         number(circle) = 3, location(circle) = centered.
Y = present(circle) = true, color(circle) = black,
         number(circle) = 2, location(circle) = centered.
Z = present(circle) = true, color(circle) = black,
         number(circle) = 1, location(circle) = centered.

The analytic algorithm detects that the *number* property of the figure element *circle* has different values in X and Y. An operation which decreases number, subtraction, is applied to the appropriate element and property. This establishes a rule for application to the X' Y' pair; "Locate a figure element for which there is a number of difference between X' and Y', and apply subtraction to that element in Y', thus producing Z'."

The analytic algorithm is as powerful as the operators available to it. The following operations are sufficient to solve all problems of Set I of the 1962 version of the Raven test.

Constancy. If $X=Y=Z$, then $Y'=Z'$.

Supplement/delete. There is an element e_1 present in Y which is not present in X. Determine whether there is also an element present in Z which is not present in Y. If e_1 is present in Y' but not in X', then add e_2 to Y' to produce Z'. The above definition holds for the supplement operation. The delete operation is identical, except that the roles of X and Y, and Y and Z

are interchanged, and e_2 is to be deleted from Y'. Note that a *change element* operation is as a deletion followed by a supplement.

Expansion/contraction. There is a subelement which appears in X and Y, and differs only in the size of its physical dimensions. Assume that the element in X is smaller than the subelement in Y. By expanding the subelement of X it is made identical to the one in Y. (If the contrary assumption is true, contraction applies.) The subelement in Y is sought X', Y' pair is then examined for a similar relationship between subelements. In making this search only figure or ground subelements are considered, depending on whether figure or ground subelements have formed the basis of the relationship in X, Y, and Z. If the search is successful Z' is produced from Y' by expansion or contraction. The choice of the figure and ground sub-elements on which to operate must be identical X, Y, Z and X', Y'.

Addition/subtraction. The operation is similar to expansion/contraction, except that it is applied to a *number* property of a subelement.

Movement. Let R_1, R_2, and R_3 be contiguous regions of a matrix element, such that R_1 borders on R_2, and R_2 on R_3. If subelement e_1 appears in R_1 in X and in R_2 in Y, then predict that it appears in R_3 of Z. (It is assumed that the subelement does not appear in R_1 in Y or R_2 in Z.) If this is true, locate a subelement e_2 which appears in R_1 of X' and R_2 of Y'. Z' is Y' with e_2 moved from R_2 to R_3. Both e_1 and e_2 must be either figure or ground elements.

Composition/decomposition. Subelements which are present in X are absent in Y and *vice versa*. If $X \cap Y = Z$, composition applies and Z' is assumed to be $X' \cap Y'$. If $X = Y \cap Z$, decomposition is applied, and Z' is assumed to be $X' - Y'$.

The operations have been stated as actions on matrix elements. They can also be applied to entire rows or columns, by defining a row or column as the union of the sets of features defining its elements. In applying an operation to rows or columns, however, only the $X'Y'$ pair is known. Therefore, the steps of locating an operation by comparing X and Y, and then validating by predicting Z and verifying the prediction, are no longer possible. Instead the X' and Y' sets are compared, to determine which features must be added to Z'. Any features not actually in Z' (the third row or column) are assumed to be the features defining the m_{33} element.

Table 6.2 shows the operator-difference matrix used by the analytic algorithm. Recall that the order of consideration of differences is first for differences arising from figure subelements, and then for differences arising from ground subelements. The rule that figure differences should be considered first is well grounded in classic studies of perception. The differences arising from a given subelement are considered in the order presence-absence, size, number, and location. This order was chosen because it represents a progressively more abstract ordering, and it is well known that the more concrete aspects of a visual stimulus are reacted to more rapidly.

TABLE 6.2

Operator-Difference Matrix for Analytic Algorithm

OPERATOR	Difference element present – absent	Size	Number	Location
Constancy	X		X	X
Supplement/Delete	X			
Motion				X
Add/Subtract			X	X
Compose/Decompose	X		X	X
Expand/Contract		X		

Finally, the order of the rows in Table 6.2 is important, since this order establishes a list of operators in the order in which they will be used to attempt to reduce a particular type of difference. A different ordering of rows could, on some problems, produce a different sequence of actions and possibly a different solution.

The Control Routine

Fig. 6.9 presents the flow chart of the executive routine for the analytic algorithm. First, each matrix elements is reduced to a set of features. Means-end analysis, as just described, is then applied first to rows and then to columns. (An interesting feature of Set I Progressive Matrix problems is that the same operations and results would occur if the rows and columns were interchanged.) It may be the case that means-end analysis applied solely to rows will produce a trial answer which does not uniquely describe one of the answers in the answer set, and hence, the answer evaluator will return the trial answer for amplification. Means-end analysis is then applied to the columns in order to specify an answer further. If this is done, however, the operator that was successful in the row analysis is temporarily moved to the first row of the operator-difference matrix, so that it will be in a favored position if the appropriate column difference is detected. This step was included to place the phenomenon of problem solving set into the simulation.

In a few cases a single pass through the algorithm will not be sufficient to produce a unique answer. In this case the problem is attacked iteratively, but on the second pass no features are considered which have been used to construct the first trial answer. None of the problems of Set I require more than two iterations through rows and columns.

It is also possible that no operator will apply, and hence no answers will be produced from the analysis of rows and columns. The algorithm then attempts means-end analysis using row and column descriptions instead of element descriptions. As noted previously, this means that only the $X' Y'$

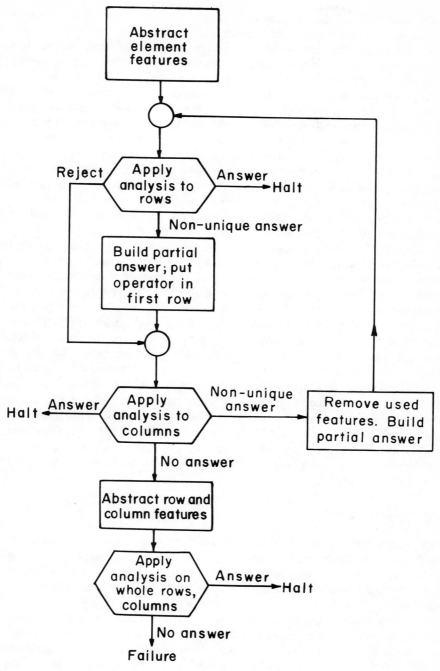

Fig. 6.9. Flow chart of Executive for Analytic Algorithm.

pair, and part of the Z' feature set, will be available and the various operations on sets must be modified appropriately.

A symbolic description of the application of means-end analysis has already been given. Fig. 6.10 shows the sequence of operations in more detail. The constancy operation is always applied first, as the "null difference" is always a subset of the set of differences. Psychological justification for rapid application of this operator is found in the fact that it is essentially an application of a search for a conjunctive solution to a problem. Numerous studies have shown that such solutions are, indeed, favored by humans. (Bruner et al., 1956; Hunt & Hovland, 1960; Neisser & Weene, 1962; Hunt et al., 1966). If constancy fails to produce an acceptable answer, means-end analysis is applied more formally, guided by the operator-difference matrix. The answer evaluation routine is entered whenever possible. This may result in the acceptance of an incorrect answer, but the probability of such an acceptance can be computed.

Evaluation of the analytic algorithm. The analytic algorithm can find the answer to all problems in Set I, if all the operators given above (except movement) are provided. The manner of solution of progressively more difficult problems is of interest, since clearly there must exist some set of operators which will work. Table 6.3 summarizes the results of applying the analytic algorithm to all 12 problems. Only the constancy and addition-subtraction operations are required to produce a score in what the test manual refers to as the "dull" range. By adding the contraction/expansion and supplement/delete operations a score approximating that achieved by the Gestalt algorithm can be obtained, although in a quite different way. In order to solve Problems 7, 8, and 9 the algorithm must act on row descriptions rather than element descriptions, but does not require any new operations, beyond those used in Problems 1-6. A score of 9 is at the upper end of the "average" range. Problems 10, 11, and 12 are solved by the composition/decomposition operations. These problems are said to be solved only by bright adults.

CONCLUSIONS

There are two ways to solve Raven's Progressive Matrix problems, utilizing quite dissimilar psychological techniques. It is particularly interesting that similar scores and similar patterns of correct and incorrect answers would be achieved on Set I by either the Gestalt or (reduced) analytic algorithms. This observation casts some doubt on the interpretation of a Raven Progressive Matrix Test score as a measure of g, since nothing in the psychometric literature leads one to believe that identical general factor scores should be associated with qualitatively different styles of cognition. This is not the first time such a suspicion has been voiced about the Progressive Matrix test. Although he generally approved of the test

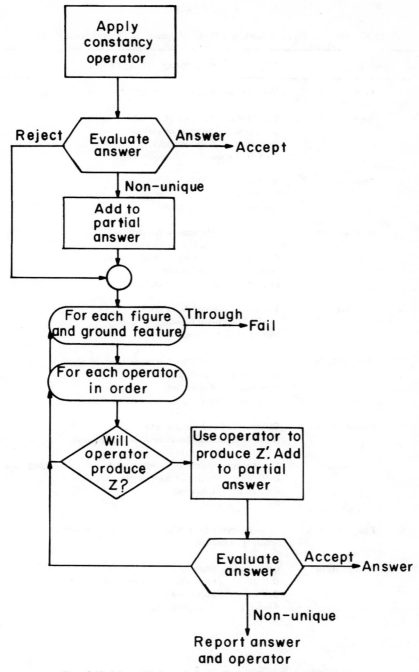

FIG. 6.10. Means-End analysis applied to Progressive Matrices.

TABLE 6.3

Analytic Algorithm Analysis: Solutions of Set I of Advanced Progressive Matrices

Problem		SEQUENCE OF ACTIONS
1	Features:	Number and shading of horizontal and vertical lines
	Row analysis:	Constancy: Number of horizontal lines
		Difference: Number of vertical lines
		Operation: Subtraction
		Predicted answer: 8 (unique, correct)
2	Features:	Vertical lines: Number
		Horizontal lines: Number
		Squares: Number, location
	Row analysis:	Constancy: Number of horizontal lines
		Location of squares
		Difference: Number of vertical lines
		Operation: Subtraction
		Predicted answer: 4 (unique, correct)
3	Features:	Black area: Breadth, height
		Horizontal rays: Number
		Vertical rays: Number
	Row analysis:	Constancy: Breadth of area; Number of rays
		Difference: Height of area
		Operation: Expansion
		Predicted answer: 5 (unique, correct)
4	Features:	Quadrangle height and width
		Number of dotted lines (vertical, horizontal)
	Row analysis:	Constancy: Height of quadrangle, number of dotted lines
		Difference: Width of quadrangle
		Operation: Expansion
		Predicted answer: 1 (unique, correct)
5	Features:	Triangle, symmetric triangle, (presence/absence)
		Shading (location)
	Row analysis:	Constancy: Shading
		Difference: Presence/absence of triangle
		Operation: Supplement
		Answer: 2 (unique, correct)

TABLE 6.3—Continued

Problem		SEQUENCE OF ACTIONS	
6	Features	Squares, number of, location; Lines, number of	
	Row analysis:	Constancy:	Number of lines
		Difference:	Number of squares, location of squares
		Operation:	Subtraction
		Answer:	5 (unique, correct)
7	Features:	Square, cross, dot, dotted background, line background, checker background	
	Row analysis:	Constancy:	Background type
		Difference:	Presence/absence of figure supplement
		Operations:	All fail
	Column analysis:	Constancy:	None
		Difference:	Presence/absence of figure and ground elements
		Operations:	All fail
	Matrix analysis:	Constancy:	Number of figure elements of each type
		Predicted answer:	6 (unique, correct)
8	Features:	Presence/absence of circle, diamond, square Number of interior lines	
	Row analysis:	Constancy:	None
		Difference:	Presence/absence of element Number of interior lines
		Operation:	Supplement/delete fails Subtraction fails
	Column analysis:	Constancy:	None
		Difference:	Presence/absence of element Number of interior lines
		Operations:	All fail
	Matrix analysis:	Constancy:	Number of figures of each type Number of interior line features with value 1,2,3
		Predicted answer:	3 (unique, correct)
9	Features:	Line type, Line number, Line location	
	Row analysis:	Constancy:	Line number
		Difference:	Line orientation type
		Operations:	All fail

Table 6.3—Continued

Problem		SEQUENCE OF ACTIONS
	Column analysis:	Constancy: Line orientation
		Difference: Line number, type
		Operations: All fail
	Matrix analysis:	Constancy: Presence/absence of line types
		Predicted answer: 7 (unique, correct)
10	Features:	Darkened quadrant, present/absent
	Row analysis:	Constancy: Absence of quadrant 3,4
		Difference: Presence/absence in 1,2
		Operation: Composition
		Predicted answer: 8 (unique, correct)
11	Features:	Dots, number of, location of
		Diagonal line, left-right (presence/absence)
		Vertical-horizontal line (presence/absence)
		Background diagonal line (presence/absence)
		Background curved line (presence/absence)
		(Two above each have two types)
	Row analysis:	Difference: Number of dots; presence/absence of dots
		Operations: Addition fails
		Composition: non-unique answer
	Column analysis:	Difference: Presence/absence of figure and ground elements
		Operation: Composition on background
		Predicted answer: 7 (unique, correct)
12	Features:	Circle, 'brand', dot, triangle, present or absent
	Row analysis:	Constancy: None
		Difference: Presence/absence
		Operation: Decomposition
		Answer: 6 (unique, correct)

Spearman himself noted that, introspectively, he saw two ways of attacking it: an *analytic* manner (his terminology!) in which attention wandered from element to element; and a *synthetic* manner, in which the patterns were mentally grouped into larger units, or wholes. Spearman regarded only the analytic manner as a cognitive operation heavily loaded on *g*. (Spearman & Wynn-Jones, 1951).[5] Spearman, as is well known, continued to search for a better operational definition of the general factor. We, on the other hand,

---

[5]This interesting historical fact was discovered after the algorithms were developed.

regard his observation and ours as evidence for a different conclusion. What we require is diagnostic tests which tell us a person's cognitive style in intellectual operations, rather than an index of the person's location in a static Euclidean model of mental power.

A similar argument can be made if one wishes to use Piagetian terms. The Gestalt algorithm can be regarded as a collection of concrete operations, while the analytic algorithm is a vehicle for applying formal operations. The Progressive Matrix test, as now constructed, cannot be used to distinguish between individuals operating at these two levels, for the simple reason that the two algorithms may produce identical results. On the other hand, a collection of Progressive Matrix problems could almost certainly be found that would differentiate between the two algorithms, even at modest levels of ability. We suggest that the construction of such a test might be a worthwhile goal for developmental psychology.

It is often argued that an aptitude test ought to measure what a person can do, not what a person knows how to do. This argument is particularly cogent for tests alleged to be "culture-fair," a property several authors have assigned to the Raven test. Of course, any pure measure of ability uncontaminated by performance variables is impossible. Culture-fair tests are more properly described as tests which minimize the importance of special knowledge possessed by only a subset of the population of individuals upon whom the test is to be used. The algorithmic analysis of the Raven test, however, raises questions about the philosophical definition of culture-fair testing.[6] Tulving (1972) has distinguished between *episodic memory,* a record of the individual's personal life experiences, and *semantic memory,* a record of the individual's general understanding of the relationships which exist in the world. Ordinary intelligence tests are probably quite successful at minimizing the influence of episodic memory, but they intentionally test semantic memory. Culture-fair tests try to minimize the role of semantic memory, testing cognitive operations instead. Our point is that there is a third category of knowledge, *operations memory,* which consists of an understanding of useful problem-solving representations and the operations which can be applied to them. Some parts of operations memory may unfold as part of normal human development; in other cases the expansion of operations memory may be under cultural control. Number systems, for example, have been available for only a short period in the history of our species. Nevertheless, an information processing approach to cognition leads us to the conclusion that intelligence cannot be regarded as a meaningful concept apart from the representations and operations which the person brings to the testing situation. This is not simply a reiteration of the

---

[6]Of course, this is not the first time that the practicality of constructing a culture-fair test has been questioned. Here the issue is not so much the practicality that is questioned as the philosophic basis for desiring such a test.

psychometric maxim that it is impossible to measure ability apart from knowledge. It is an assertion that the attempt to do so is meaningless.

Such strong remarks might be read as a suggestion that the entire concept of intelligence, and with it the technology of intelligence testing, be abandoned because of a faulty theoretical structure. In fact, we regard our analysis as showing exactly the opposite. The approach developed here can be used to develop diagnostic intelligence tests. Such measures would not represent intelligence as a point on a real line, they would indicate what mental algorithms were used by the person examined and what operations were available as subroutines to those algorithms. The following specific pieces of further research are suggested as steps toward the creation of such a test:

1. The analysis presented here must be augmented by an analysis of Set II of the Progressive Matrix test, both because this set is larger and because more item analysis data is available. Such an analysis is now being conducted. We hope to determine whether the error patterns expected by the Gestalt and analytic algorithms can, indeed, be found in population data.

2. The algorithms proposed for solving Progressive Matrix problems are akin to those used by Clark and Chase (1972) and Trabasso et al. (1971) to account for the analysis of logical statements. These authors have shown that time to solution of an individual problem is a sufficiently stable variable to be of great use in revealing the underlying mental processes. The same sort of analysis can be carried out by presenting Progressive Matrix problems under real time computer control. The technology is not formidable, and could provide an intermediate step between paper and pencil testing, where only limited data can be obtained, and the very expensive individual examination procedure.

3. The technology for tracking eye movements has recently progressed to a point at which it is feasible to observe eye movements during various types of problem solving. This technology could be combined with computer controlled test presentation to study further the use of algorithms in the Progressive Matrix and other widely used intelligence tests. It is doubtful that such a procedure will result in a feasible individual intelligence test for measurement purposes,[7] but it should be useful in experimental analyses of proposed tests, to determine what a test measures in terms of cognitive operations. This would be preferable to the present technique of validation based upon correlational evidence.

SUMMARY

The Raven Progressive Matrix test is a widely used psychometric instrument, said variously to be a culture-fair and to be a measure of the

---

[7] The subject must be trained extensively. During testing the individual's head must be held motionless by a bite bar, and the equipment must be recalibrated frequently.

general factor of intelligence. Two algorithms for solving Progressive Matrix problems have been proposed; a Gestalt algorithm which is based on the manipulation of visual images, and an analytic algorithm, which is based on formal operations applied to sets and subsets of element features. The first algorithm can solve half of the problems in Set I of the 1962 revision of the test, a score which is regarded as within the normal adult range. The second algorithm can solve all the problems of Set I; a reduced version of the second algorithm can solve those problems solved by the first algorithm.

This result, by itself, can raise a question concerning the use of the Advanced Progressive Matrices test as a measure of the general factor of intelligence. The result can also be used in support of the position that intelligence can not, and ought not, be conceptualized or measured as something apart from an individual's (partly learned) stock of problem-solving methods. This leads one to regard a psychometric test of ability as a means for diagnosing cognitive style, rather than as a method of measuring an individual's personal loading on one or more factors of intelligence. Specific research suggestions were made for further work which could result in the development of a Progressive Matrix test with the desired diagnostic properties.

7
KNOWLEDGE AND THE EDUCATIONAL PROCESS

GARLIE A. FOREHAND
Educational Testing Service, Princeton, New Jersey

This volume, the ninth in the Carnegie Series on Cognition, prompted a retrospective glance at the first, a collection of papers on problem solving presented in 1965 and published 1966 (Kleinmuntz, 1966). That earlier volume included papers by three of the same authors represented in the present volume (Hayes, Simon, and Newell). In addition, it presented one of de Groot's early papers on perception in chess, a paper which has become a classic, as evidenced by its frequent citation in this volume. It also included presentation on problem solving by several psychologists from the behavioristic tradition (Gagne, Staats, Skinner, and Goldiamond). In the epilogue I wrote for that volume, it seemed appropriate to contrast the approaches of behavioristic and information-processing psychology, and to conclude, somewhat hesitantly, that information processing psychology offered important ways of advancing "psychology's long-promised involvement in the detailed study of complex, integrated, nonartificial human behavior."

In 1965, experimental psychology was gingerly testing information-processing waters. Well before 1973, when these papers were presented, it had taken the plunge. In 1965, information-processing psychologists were at pains to explain the purposes of their models, and to demur from the mentalistic connotations that contemporary experimentalists often ascribed to them. They were a bit apologetic about presenting results from protocol analysis and from experiments with small N's and few conditions. In 1973, they confidently combine models, protocols, and experiments to construct detailed theories of the phenomena of learning, problem solving, perception, and language.

In what seems remarkably few years, information-processing psychology has come to dominate the experimental study of complex human behavior. That rapid success encourages me to speculate that within a comparably short time the approach will have as much of an impact on psychology in the field as it has had on psychology in the laboratory. In particular, its potential for illuminating recalcitrant problems in education seems evident. Some thoughts about that potential, and the work required to realize it, form the focus of this commentary.

A reading of the first seven papers in this volume immediately suggests direct linkages to classical concerns of educational psychology. This commentary will discuss some of these linkages to reading, motivation, teaching methods, and intelligence.

Perhaps no educational problem has proven more frustrating to educators and researchers than reading. The number of published research reports on reading must be well into the thousands. Several journals are devoted exclusively to the subject. Teachers and curriculum designers probably devote more time and effort to reading than to any other educational objective. Yet, the late James E. Allen, when he was United States Commissioner of Education, cited the following conclusions from statistical information collected by the Office of Education.

— One out of four students nationwide has significant reading deficiencies. . .
— There are more than three million illiterates in our adult population.
— About half of the unemployed youth in New York City, ages 16-21, are function-
ally illiterate.
— Three-quarters of the juvenile offenders in New York City are two or more years
retarded in reading.
— In a recent U.S. Armed Forces program . . . 68.2% of the young men fell below
grade seven in reading and academic ability.

The concern inspired by these statistics is increased by the realization that reading is the primary method for any kind of academic learning, and a major requirement for most kinds of learning needed to function in our society.

All of the research and pedagogical effort devoted to reading has not succeeded in providing a convincingly detailed description of the reading process. Analyses often divide reading into components such as word recognition, word meaning, comprehension, and study skill. Unfortunately, neither the results of research on the reader, nor the instructional methods offered to teachers, indicate the cognitive processes that constitute these components. The reason is not difficult to find; several papers in this volume show it clearly. A process such as comprehension involves an intricate array of knowledge and operations. It is difficult to model the process even for a passage of impoverished semantic content. The present papers, however, on the analysis of understanding and perception, offer concepts for achieving a new level of specificity in the description of the reading process.

Greeno suggests that the process of comprehension is one of finding a set of semantic relations among the concepts involved in a linguistic input. He cites persuasive evidence for the definition, both from the studies newly presented here and from the work of other investigators. The definition is consistent with Hayes' and Simon's analysis of a person struggling to understand a set of problem instructions and with the model they developed to represent the development of such understanding. It is also consistent with Gregg's analysis of the memory search process.

This conception, with its supporting results and theory suggests a new approach to the measurement of reading comprehension. The usual reading comprehension test consists of a series of paragraphs to be read, followed by a number of questions concerning facts, relationships, and implications of the content of the passage. Using a similar format, it should be possible to obtain a much more detailed description of the reader's representation of the semantic content. Gregg's analysis of semantic relations suggests that a detailed and specific inventory of the semantic content of a passage can be achieved. A similar description of a reader's representation of the semantic content should be obtainable. A method might be first to record the reader's free recall, and then to follow with probing questions about the relationships among the semantic elements of the passage. The results can be measured against the accurate semantic analysis, that is, the one constructed by experts at leisure. This method should reveal much more about a reader's comprehension than the sometimes arbitrary questions asked after the passage has been read. A carefully constructed set of testing materials could provide a reasonably complete map (*a*) of the kinds of semantic relations that the reader can comprehend by reading; (*b*) of those he systematically fails to grasp; and (*c*) of characteristic intrusion or misinterpretation errors that are part of the reader's personal or cultural semantic conventions.

Information processing can also provide models for diagnosing perceptual disabilities in reading. As Gregg's analysis of perceptual recognition would suggest, some students may fail to achieve comprehension because of defects in the "front end" of the task of accessing long-term memory and in the perceptual and naming operations that generate the concepts to be related semantically. An extended diagnostic procedure would include methods of identifying such defects, perhaps ways of determining what kind of sorting tree a reader uses in recognizing a word or letter and what search procedure he uses. A relatively crude way of detecting whether a particular reader's difficulties lie toward the proceptual or the semantic end of reading might be provided by contrasting his comprehension of written and oral material.

This line of thought also suggests approaches to remediation. It may be supposed that a speaker of the English language has in his repertoire the kinds of semantic relations that the language is capable of expressing—or at least of those likely to be encountered in straightforward prose. If so, and if the reader can recognize the individual words in the passage, his faulty comprehension might signify unfamiliarity with conventions for expressing semantic relations in written form. A conception of this sort, together with appropriate diagnostic information, would render less mysterious and more correctable an individual's "reading retardation."

These papers also prompt speculation about motivational problems. Hayes and Simon remark about the neglect in the study of problem solving of how the subject comes to understand the task he is to perform. Their evidence for a close interaction between understanding and solving suggests that the other side of the coin is equally remarkable. It is rare, except in a classroom or testing situation, that a person is asked to "comprehend" something without affecting what he has comprehended. The protocol reported by Hayes and Simon shows that the subject shifted often from the attempt to understand the rules to the attempt to solve the problem. While the authors have not yet programmed the shift between understanding and solving, it is an explicit part of their theory. Indeed, considering both their protocol and their model, it is difficult to see how such a shifting mechanism can be omitted from a theory of understanding. Without it, the solver cannot test his understanding or learn the full range of states and operations embedded in the problem.

Perhaps not all understanding occurs in the context of problem solving (although one could make a case for arguing that it does). But shifting between attempting to understand and attempting to *use* what is understood, may be a necessary feature of comprehending. If so, many learners experience an *incomplete* learning situation. The "slow reader" is a case in point. For his "faster" schoolmates, the urge to communicate is sufficient motivation to perform the tasks of language analysis and representation. If this communication does not begin relatively early, the learner is confronted with an unappealing task: to "comprehend" the words and sentences before him without a use for his comprehension.

As skill in reading develops, there are many ways of completing the learning situation. The subject matter is sufficiently interesting to motivate the relatively slight strain of comprehension. Or the student may have his own external motive: the science passage satisfies his curiosity, the poem arouses his emotions, the instruction tells him how to accomplish a goal. But if the reader is insufficiently skilled, these satisfactions are unavailable to him. Perhaps the process of instruction can provide additional ways of completing the learning situation. Students might attempt to comprehend rules in order to play a game, comprehend instructions in order to build a model, comprehend a message in order to communicate with a friend. These "extensions" provide a testing procedure for assessing the accuracy of the comprehension. They provide reinforcement for accurate comprehension. But perhaps most importantly, they provide a goal; the comprehension task becomes part of a complete problem-solving process.

The analyses of rule induction by Egan and Greeno and by Simon and Lea offer perspectives on another critical educational concern: the design and conduct of teaching methods. A great many "educational" learning tasks are in fact instances of rule induction. Indeed, if one pursues the generalization that Simon and Lea make to rule induction in multiple-problem spaces, almost any learning experience can be so described. Note that "inductive teaching" does not have a monopoly on education by rule induction. A student responding to the most cut-and-dried, teacher-dominated lecture-demonstration is in fact activating a version of the general rule inducer. The question is not whether a learning situation is or is not inductive, but rather, what inductive learning process is activated by it.

It is informative to think of various teaching methods as instances of the General Rule Inducer. Two fairly extreme cases are linear programmed instruction and inductive teaching. In linear programmed instruction most of the program is in fact carried out by the text. The text states the rule (definition or principle), presents instances (examples), generates new instances for classification by the students (stems) and tests the instance-class (feedback). The student's role is limited to classifying instances (responding to the stem) and modifying rules ("correcting" his understanding of the rule if his response is incorrect). This latter operation—presumably the fruit of the learning process—is left unspecified in linear programmed instruction. Indeed, orthodox programming theory appears to assume it out of existence; if the program is arranged so that the student never makes a mistake, then the student's modification of his learned rule is limited to "adding on" elements as specified by the text.

Rationales stated for inductive teaching techniques usually emphasize two features: "active" learning and induction of principles from the student's own experience. Inductive teaching plans are indeed characterized by greater student participation throughout the process. Different instances, however, vary greatly in the model of the induction process implicit in the method. Two reasonably representative examples might be described as follows. By means of stimulus questions from the teacher or observations by students, a set of instances is generated, and features of the instances are examined. From common features of the instances, a principle is derived. The principle is often the teacher's preformulated rule. Instructional analysis of the concept often stops here. Presumably some students would continue to classify instances, perform tests and modify rules, while others would not. Other versions of inductive teaching carry the process further employing tentative rules (proposed by either student or teacher), testing by means of examples and counterexamples, modifying the concept and recycling. As GRI would see the induction process, the first is a truncated version, the second an iterated one. Other examples fall between.

These examples are primitive but they suggest that GRI can indeed serve as a description of the learning processes that accompanies a range of instructional techniques, and perhaps as a guide to the detailed planning of an instructional sequence. The examples also, however, reveal the poverty of conceptualizations of the learning process that characterize instructional technique. This is not to criticize the educators who designed the techniques; the present volume demonstrates the novelty and incompleteness of such conceptualizations in psychological theorizing. The question is whether the increasingly detailed and specific models of learning theory can provide the link so long sought between learning theory and learning technology. Can the representations used to understand thought also be used to effect it?

Perhaps the most elementary need of instructional models is a concept of what Egan and Greeno call "the kind of knowledge structure that is constructed." Such knowledge, it appears, can quite generally be represented as a hierarchical structure of elements. The elements, depending on the nature of the task, might be features of objects, relations among objects, or operations on goals. The shape of the hierarchy also depends on the nature of the input and the tasks

The very recognition of knowledge as a hierarchical structure casts light on the problem of specifying the expected outcome of a learning experience. So-called behavioral objectives are often small, idiosyncratic segments of the structure. Educators may complain that such objectives are impoverished, but they lack methods of stating (and therefore motive for explicating) more complex instructional aspirations. In fact, hierarchical representations of objectives have been used with success by curriculum developers, usually employing the analysis proposed by Robert Gagne. An information processing hierarchy of knowledge structures offers two new ways of thinking about them. First, that such structures should be represented in terms of a specific task or set of tasks—i.e., the structure should include not only particular knowledge, but also how it is to be used and how the parts ought to relate to one another. Secondly, the information processing approach suggests that an individual's knowledge structure can be revealed in more detail than a series of independent behavioral tests can provide.

Of course, we are far from having the ability to specify the desired knowledge structure for a complex task and to infer the nature of the structure acquired by a student. However, the experiments that Egan and Greeno report suggest that ingenious experimenters can devise probes. Their methods included developing a detailed statement of problem requirements, observing problem difficulty in relation to the requirements and observing the performance of subjects at different stages of learning—again with the model of problem requirements as a guide. While their observations were specific to the problems they studied, their probe strategies are generalizable to other learning tasks.

Ever since information processing theories began to take shape, their potential for illuminating individual differences, particularly intelligence, has been anticipated. The potential has been easier to cite than to achieve. Hunt has now provided a paradigm that not only demonstrates how information processing models can contribute to our understanding of intelligence, but also points the way to fuller development of the approach.

Hunt has shown that two contrasting models can take a particular intelligence test, obtain results not dissimilar to those obtained by persons, and thereby reveal possible explanations of individual differences. Each model has elements that can be varied: representations of problem elements, answer generators, operations, and answer evaluators. By adding to, deleting from, or otherwise modifying these elements, one would produce models of a whole population of individuals. The striking contrast between the two models points to another way of characterizing individual differences. One of the models treats the task as a perceptual one, coding the input as visual elements and relations among elements, and applying perceptual criteria. The second model codes the input as sets of features, and employs analytic problem-solving operations. Each is a plausible model of how different persons might take the test; such individuals would be different not only in the *quality* of problem-solving processes but also in their entire content: coding of the elements, perception of relations, methods of transforming, and criteria for evaluating answers. The distinction suggests the concept of style, as it is used in individual differences. The concept has usually referred to the personality domain; Hunt's models suggest that it pertains to ability as well.

Much research and development is needed to put such a conception to use, but several lines of approach are evident. They include constructing models for a wide range of tasks domains, including other intelligence tests; using models to guide the interpretation of protocols; using protocols to guide the construction of models; and devising ways of making manifest the key features of the individuals' processing.

The theoretical and practical implications of such work are extensive and Hunt has outlined a number of them. One example is suggested by Hunt's discussion of the Raven test as a measure of *g*. Hunt concludes that the comparable success of two different algorithms casts doubt on the interpretation of the test as a measure of *g*. It also suggests a new way of looking at general intelligence. Hunt cites Spearman's earlier speculation that only an analytic approach to the Raven test measures *g*. We might suggest that a test measures "general intelligence" to the extent that the skills used in solving it generalize to other problems. The question becomes not whether intelligence is general, but rather what is the domain of tasks to which a particular set of processes pertains? Such an analysis would make major progress toward the long-sought goal of using intelligence tests to make maximum use of a person's strong skills and remedy his weak ones.

Pitz has introduced an element not treated by the other contributors to this volume, and seldom considered explicitly in educational thought—the effect of uncertainty on thought processes. Pitz is certainly correct that uncertainty is always with us when we use our "knowledge" to make judgments or decisions. It is apparently rare for students to be asked, or taught, to estimate the uncertainty, but the result of the hyperprecision effect is certainly evident to any teacher who has listened to a student extrapolate a psychological theory or historical interpretation. The restructuring that comes with increasing knowledge is also usually evident. If Pitz is correct that dealing with uncertainty is a decision-making process, representable as search through a decision tree, and that increasing knowledge produces more accurate assessment of the extent of one's uncertainty, then it should be possible to use heuristic problem-solving models to teach people to improve their decisions under uncertainty. If the individual differences that Pitz observed are a result of differences in processing strategies, they might help explain the wide variation in quality of judgments made by people with presumably identical information. There is little data bearing on such speculations, but the speculations are intriguing nonetheless.

By using the ideas in these papers as stimuli for my own speculations, I have neglected many details. There are enough fascinating findings, theoretical differences and similarities, innovative methods, and far-reaching implications, to keep a graduate seminar going—and learning—for months. But probably all concerned would agree that theories of knowledge ought to contribute to a wide range of learning problems. I find it encouraging that the paradigms used in this paper generalize so readily to educational problems. Obviously, much research and development is required to test and use and evaluate experimental ideas in complicated applied fields. But the ideas themselves point in promising directions. The effort required to develop educational learning theory that is informed by information processing theory cannot fail to be worth making.

8
UNDERSTANDING WRITTEN PROBLEM INSTRUCTIONS

J. R. HAYES and H. A. SIMON
Carnegie-Mellon University

Psychological experiments are usually carried out as follows: when the subject is brought into the laboratory, he is carefully introduced to the task he is to perform. He receives a set of instructions, written or oral or both, and then a series of practice tasks and examples. The experimenter answers any questions he may raise about points he does not understand. Only after the subject has completed these steps and the experimenter is satisfied that the subject understands the task, does the actual "experiment" begin.

For many experimental purposes, the procedure just described is perfectly reasonable. But if the object of study is the process known as "understanding," then the procedure discards from the data precisely the phenomena that are to be explained—how the subject comes to understand what task it is that he is supposed to perform. In the present research our aim has been to observe and record the behavior of the uninstructed subject—his behavior from the first moment that he receives the experimental instructions until the time when it appears that he understands the task fully.

While it is surely an elementary point that the relevant data for the study of understanding are the records of behavior while understanding is being achieved, for years we have, in our studies of problem solving, been throwing away these data, and examining only the protocols of subjects who have received and absorbed "proper training" in the task they are to perform. Of course we have not been alone in doing this. Studies of the behavior of naive subjects during the period when they are assimilating experimental instructions are almost nonexistent in the literature of psychology.

If a person is to solve a problem, there are several things he must know. First, he must know the set of problem elements—that is, the materials of the problem. Second, he must know the initial state of the problem and its goal.

This research has been supported by Public Health Service Grant MH-07722 from the National Institute of Mental Health and by National Service Foundation Grant GS-38533. The authors wish to express special thanks to Don Waterman who introduced us to the PAS-II system and who spent many hours advising us.

Third, he must know an operator or a set of operators for transforming the initial state into the goal. Finally, he must know the restrictions under which the operator may be applied.

Taken together, these essential items of information define what Newell and Simon (1972) have called a basic problem space. A problem space is a subject's representation of the task environment that permits him to consider different problem situations, to characterize these situations in ways that may help him decide what to do, and to apply the operators for changing one situation into another. A basic problem space is a minimal space that includes just those things that are essential for defining the problem, the solution, and the operators. Subjects may elaborate the problem space to incorporate other kinds of information that may be helpful to a solution. Hence, two subjects who set out to solve a given problem may use different spaces to do so. For example, one of the subjects may solve the problem by relatively inefficient trial and error procedures for searching the basic problem space; while the second, who identifies a cue for selecting the best operator at each step, may solve the problem in this augmented problem space (the space augmented, that is, by the descriptors that provide the cues) quickly and with little or no search. The problem space that the subject constructs will determine the manner of his search for a solution.

When a person solves a problem of a type with which he is already familiar, he will be able to recall and use elements of the problem space that he constructed while working on previous problems. This gives him an advantage over the naive subject who must construct the entire problem space from the beginning by extracting the necessary information (sometimes laboriously) from the problem instructions. Comparison of naive and sophisticated subjects makes it clear that the process of problem space construction may require considerable time and effort.

Our interest in the process of problem space construction derives in part from the above observation—that it is an essential aspect of problem solving which can be an important source of problem-solving difficulty. Our interest also derives from observations that the form of the problem instructions may determine which of several alternative problem spaces the subject constructs. For example, Duncker (1945) has observed that information in the problem description in an active sentence may lead to the exploration of an entirely different set of alternatives than does the same information in a passive sentence. A better understanding of the process of problem space construction should help us to understand the relation between the problem instructions and the problem space that the subject constructs.

In this paper, we will be concerned with the procedures that humans use to construct a new problem space when they are faced with an unfamiliar problem. We will present and analyze, in general terms, a problem-solving protocol, propose a model of the process of problem space construction that appears to be generally consistent with the protocol, and describe a computer simulation of some of the central processes of that model. Finally, we will draw some conclusions from our work about the nature of the understanding process, as this process appears in the understanding of written task instructions.

THE TASK

Our subjects solved a problem called "The Tea Ceremony" shown below.

A Tea Ceremony

In the inns of certain Himalayan villages is practiced a most civilized and refined tea ceremony. The ceremony involves a host and exactly two guests, neither more nor less. When his guests have arrived and have seated themselves at his table, the host performs five services for them. These services are listed below in the order of the nobility which the Himalayans attribute to them.

Stoking the Fire
Fanning the Flames
Passing the Rice Cakes
Pouring the Tea
Reciting Poetry

During the ceremony, any of those present may ask another, "Honored Sir, may I perform this onerous task for you?". However, a person may request of another only the least noble of the tasks which the other is performing. Further, if a person is performing any tasks, then he may not request a task which is nobler than the least noble task he is already performing. Custom requires that by the time the tea ceremony is over, all of the tasks will have been transferred from the host to the most senior of the guests. How may this be accomplished?

The Tea Ceremony was constructed as an isomorph of the "Tower of Hanoi" problem (Rouse-Ball, 1962), the familiar puzzle in which disks of various sizes must be transferred among three pegs subject to restrictions on the set of legal moves. When we say that the Tea Ceremony is an isomorph of the Tower of Hanoi, we mean that it is the same problem as the Tower of Hanoi but disguised in different words. More precisely, we mean that any solution of the Tower of Hanoi puzzle may be translated, step by step, into a solution of the Tea Ceremony and vice versa by using the following correspondences:

TEA CEREMONY	TOWER OF HANOI
Three participants	Three pegs
Five tasks	Five disks
Nobility of tasks	Size of disks

The problem space information that the subject had to identify from the problem description included: (a) problem elements, such as the set of three participants in the Tea Ceremony and the list of five tasks, (b) the initial state in which the host was performing all the tasks and the goal state in which the senior guest performed them all, (c) the operator for requesting and effecting the transfer of tasks, and (d) the complex restrictions contained in Sentences 6 and 7 under which a task could be transferred.

The problem was presented to the subject typed on an 8″ × 11″ sheet. It was organized in two paragraphs—Sentences 1 through 4, and Sentences 5 through 9—rather than in the format shown. Our subject did not recognize that the Tea Ceremony was isomorphic to the Tower of Hanoi puzzle.

PRELIMINARY ANALYSIS OF THE PROTOCOL

The initial segment of the subject's protocol is reproduced in Fig. 8.1. While our discussion will include references to the whole protocol, the later portions have not been reproduced in detail because of its length (a total of 494 lines).

The Processing Sequence

When the subject received the instruction sheet containing the text, he first read through the sentences in their order of presentation, with only a single instance of backtracking (see Fig. 8.1, lines 2-4). We know that he was able to extract a good deal of information from Sentences 1, 2, 3, 4, and 8 on his first pass through the text since he later makes use of information in these sentences before he returns to reread them. Indeed, he never rereads Sentences 1, 2, and 3. In particular, during the first pass, he derives information about the set of participants, about the list of tasks, about the initial assignment of tasks to participants, and about the goal.

After reading through the text for the first time, the subject turns his attention to understanding Sentences 5, 6, and 7, the sentences that contain information about the operator for transforming the initial state into the goal and information about the restrictions under which that operator may be applied (Fig. 8.1, lines 5-35). That these three sentences were relatively more difficult to understand than the others is suggested by the fact that the subject read them from nine to eleven times each in the course of the problem-solving episode. In contrast, he read Sentences 1, 2, 3, 4, and 9 only once or twice each, and Sentence 8, four times.

The subject's behavior in interpreting these relatively difficult passages is of considerable interest. As we interpret them, the relevant sections of the protocol reflect two major processes which alternate with each other. The first is the *Language* process which reads short segments of text and extracts information from them through syntactic and semantic analysis. The second is the *Construction* process in which the newly extracted information is checked against and added to the subject's developing model of the situation described in the problem text. Passages in the protocol which illustrate

The Initial Segment of the Problem Solving Protocol

1. S. Reads sentences 1, 2, and 3.
2.   "Now wait a minute. How many people are here? Let's go back."
3.   Reads sentence 2.
4.   "OK, the host isn't a guest, that's my problem."
5.   Reads sentences 3, 4, 5, 6, 7, 8, and 9.
6.   "Well, I don't understand the problem. Let's go back to the
7.   beginning of the last paragraph."
8.   Reads sentences 5, 6, and 7.
9.   "I'm beginning to get an idea of trying to order these tasks.
10.   Where . . . OK . . . there are five — fire, flames, cakes, tea, poetry."
11. E. "A little louder."
12. S. "OK. A person may request of another only the least noble of the
13.   tasks which another is performing — so if my friend is performing
14.   a bunch of tasks, I can request — wait a minute — something's
15.   fishy here. Look at this sentence. 'Honored Sir, may I perform
16.   this onerous task for you?'. So I'm going to perform a task
17.   for him."
18.   Reads sentence 6.
19.   (pause) "Let me get this straight. Let's assume there's someone
20.   across the table from me and I'm one of the guests and my host is
21.   on the left and the other guest is straight across the table. Now —
22.   now, if I'm the person, I may request of, say, the other guest only
23.   the least noble of the tasks which he is performing. So he is per-
24.   forming a bunch of tasks and I may ask him. . . But if all I can ask
25.   him is 'Honored Sir, may I perform this onerous task for you?' . . .
26. S. Hmm. What does this mean?"
27.   Reads sentence 6.
28.   "I'm not . . . I'm requesting to do something for him — or I am
29.   requesting to do something that he is already doing — for him.
30.   Oh, I see. So he's doing something and I'm going to do it for
31.   him, I guess."
32.   Reads sentence 7.
33.   "OK. So we got both of us here doing something and I can't
34.   ask to do something which is better than I'm already doing."
35.   Reads sentences 8 and 9.
36.   "To the most senior of the guests — I guess that means the oldest."
37.   (pause) "Hmm. OK. So from the host to the most senior of the
38.   guests. Ah. The transfer of the task means the doing of
39.   the tasks, I guess, so the host starts out doing all the tasks
40.   and we want to end up with the oldest guest doing all of the
41.   tasks, I suppose. Ahh . . . Let's think about that.
42.   Let's say the host is doing all five tasks.
43.   He's stoking the fire, fanning the flames, cakes,
44.   tea, poetry and the other two
45.   doing nothing."

FIG. 8.1. The initial segment of the problem solving protocol.

alternation between these two processes may be seen in Fig. 8.1 at Lines 1-2, 12-14, 15-17, 18-22, 23-25, 28-32, 33-35, and 36-42. Each of these eight passages begins with a short direct quote from the problem text. The reading of these quotes signals the initiation of the *Language* process.

The last part of each of the eight passages reflects the subject's attempt to interpret the information extracted from the segment of text he has just read. The subject's interpretations are clearly more than simple paraphrases of the text since they contain information which, while consistent with the text, was neither required nor suggested by it. For example, in Lines 13-14 the subject introduces himself and his friend as participants in the Tea Ceremony. In Lines 18-22, he assigns spatial relations to the three participants which were nowhere suggested by the text. Notice that the subject continues to appear as a participant in all of the passages but the last one. These interpretations by the subject reflect the operation of the *Construction* process.

The transition between the first and the second process is frequently marked by the use of the conjunction, *so*. In four of the eight passages, *so* follows the quote immediately (Lines 13, 16, 24, and 34). In two others, *so* also appears, but only after the meaning of a lexical element has been clarified (Lines 29-31 and Line 37). If we assume, as seems reasonable, that these lexical clarifications are part of the *Language* rather than the *Construction* or some other process, then *so* marks the transition between the two processes in six of the eight cases.

Examination of the sequence in which the subject reads the sentences of the text yields further suggestions about the nature of the processes which he employs in understanding the text. In the segment of protocol shown in Fig. 8.1, there are 22 transitions from one text sentence to another. Of these, 16 are in the forward direction—from an earlier to a later sentence—and six are in the backward direction. In all cases, the forward transitions are from a sentence to its immediate successor in the text—that is, the forward transitions never skipped a sentence. Twelve of the 16 forward transitions occurred without intervening comment by the subject. These appear to reflect the normal process of reading sentences of text in sequence.

Of the remaining four transitions, three were associated with passages which we classified above as reflecting the *Construction* process. In all three cases, the process succeeded in the sense that the subject completed an interpretation of the text segment without discovering a contradiction. The three passages may be found at Lines 16-17, 31-32, and 34-35. In the one remaining transition, seen at Lines 26-28, the subject's comment, "Hmm. What does this mean?", suggests a failure to interpret the extracted information but does not indicate that the subject has discovered a specific area of conflict which might guide his search for new information.

Of the six backward transitions, two occur after the subject has read the last text sentence. At this point, of course, any transition would have to be a backward transition. Of the remaining four backward transitions, three were associated with failures of the *Construction* process. (In Lines 2, 13-15, and 24-25 in Fig. 8.1, there is evidence of the failed construction processes. The fourth transition (Fig. 8.1, Lines 8-12), is not obviously associated with such a failure. The box score is shown below:

		Construction Process		
		succeeds	fails	uncertain
transition	forward	3	0	1
	backward	0	3	1

These results suggest that forward transitions are associated with success of the *Construction* process and that backward transitions are associated with its failure.

While we will not focus on the later stages of problem solution in this paper, we should comment on them here to place the *Understanding* process in appropriate context. The segment of protocol which we have examined above covers the beginning of the experimental session, and is concerned entirely with understanding the problem and not at all with taking steps to solve it. We could as easily have selected a segment at the end of the experimental session which would be concerned entirely with solution and not at all with understanding. Such protocols, like the segment quoted below, consist largely of sequences of legal moves:

—the senior guest will ask to recite poetry from the host. OK. The junior guest then asks to pour the tea from the host. . . .

Between these two extremes in the middle part of the experimental session, the protocol reflects both attempts to understand the problem and attempts to solve it.

The processes of *Solving* and of *Understanding* appear to alternate with one another much in the manner of the *Language* and *Construction* processes described above. That is, failure of the *Solving* process appears to cause the subject to return to the *Understanding* process.

We want to call attention to the rapid alternation between these two processes when the subject is attempting to interpret a difficult section of the text. This alternation of processes provides a key to the subject's procedures for constructing the problem space. A preliminary model of the relations among these processes is described below and summarized in the form of a flow diagram in Fig. 8.2. A simulation which we will describe later provides a detailed realization for the *Extraction* and *Construction* process, although not of the actual alternation process. Inside the boxes in Fig. 8.2 are the names of programs used in the simulation.

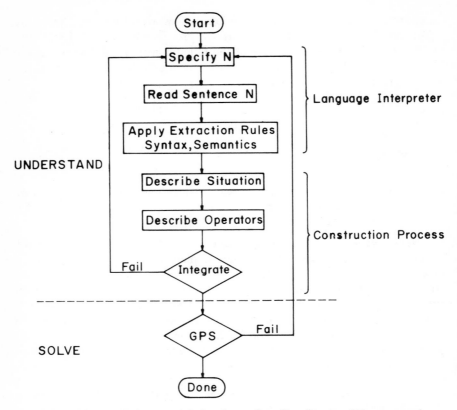

FIG. 8.2. A preliminary model of understanding: flow diagram of the processes.

The Model

In the model (Fig. 8.2), we will view problem solution by the naive subject as employing two complex and interacting processes: an *Understanding* process that generates a problem space from the text of the problem, and a *Solving* process that uses the problem space to explore steps toward solving the problem. A problem-solving episode is assumed to start with the *Understanding* process, to end with the *Solving* process, and to alternate frequently between these two processes in the intervening interval. The *Solving* process is assumed to control problem solving in the sense that it begins to run as soon as enough information has been generated about the problem space to permit it to do anything. When it runs out of things to do, it calls the *Understanding* process back to generate more specifications for the problem space. With this arrangement, the text of the instructions is interpreted only to the extent that is necessary in order for the *Solving* process to arrive at a problem solution. Any parts of the text that are irrelevant to that goal may remain uninterpreted or only partly interpreted.

The *Understanding* process consists of two subprocesses (Fig. 8.2): a *Language* interpreting process and a problem space *Construction* process. The process for interpreting *Language* reads the sentences of the problem text and extracts information from them, guided by a set of information extraction rules. These rules identify the moods of the text sentences, identify noun groups that refer to physical objects and activities, and assign such relations to them as "agent," "instrument," "property," "location," and so on, much in the manner of a case grammar (Fillmore, 1968). In the Tea Ceremony problem, the *Language* process must recognize "the inns" and "a most civilized and refined tea ceremony" as noun groups, "in the inns" as a locative phrase, and so on.

The *Construction* process accepts information, sentence by sentence, from the *Language* interpreting process and builds a representation of the problem space, consisting of two parts: a *Situation* description and a set of *Operators*. The description of the *Situation,* based on information extracted from sentences in the indicative mood, represents the problem elements (e.g., inns, villages, host, and so on), relations among problem elements (e.g., The inns are located in the villages), and the initial and goal states of the problem.

The set of *Operators,* identified from information extracted from conditional statements and sentences in the subjunctive mood constitute a production system in which the conditions are represented as states (or aspects of states) of the *Situation,* and the actions are represented as processes for making changes in the *Situation.* As we shall see, a major responsibility of the *Construction* process is to make certain that the representation of the *Situation* is compatible with the representation of the *Operators,* so that the *Operator* processes will perform correctly in changing the *Situation.*

The problem *Solving* process works by running the *Operators* generated by the *Construction* process under the control of a problem-solving strategy of some kind. If the *Solving* process fails to achieve a solution, either because it runs out of things to do, or because it encounters a contradiction, it calls back the *Understanding* process to elaborate or alter the problem space in order to resolve the conflict.

SIMULATING THE UNDERSTANDING PROCESS

In the previous section we examined the behavior of a human subject in the laboratory, confronted with instructions for a task with which he was not previously familiar. We have observed the subject as he gradually acquired an understanding of the task. On the basis of our examination of the subject's protocol, we then sketched out a model to describe his behavior.

Another approach to the understanding of understanding is to construct a computer simulation of the process. There already exist in the literature a number of examples of "understanding" programs, although these were constructed mainly as explorations in artificial intelligence, and not as specific simulations of the human processes. Before we go on to describe the simulation program we have built to explain human behavior in the Tea Ceremony task, it will be instructive to take a brief look at these earlier efforts.

Previous Understanding Programs

The broad outlines of the understanding program we shall describe here derive from the HEURISTIC COMPILER (1963, 1972), an early exploration of the possibilities of constructing a problem-solving program capable of writing computer programs from English-language instructions. The problem-solving component of the HEURISTIC COMPILER was modeled on the GENERAL PROBLEM SOLVER; that is, it accepted as input a formalized description of the program to be written, and used means-ends analysis to produce code corresponding to the description. The "front end" of the HEURISTIC COMPILER, a rather primitive interpreter of natural language, accepted an English-language description of the programming problem, and produced from it the formalized description that the problem-solving component required as its input.

The HEURISTIC COMPILER's capabilities for interpreting natural language instructions were primarily semantic rather than syntactic in character. It was not capable of handling a wide range of English constructions, but only relatively simple descriptive prose; hence, needed only relatively simple processes to discover the underlying phrase structure and convert the input sentences into internal list structures. Of more interest is the fact that it was capable of expanding these input sentences, supplying various omissions and ellipses, by matching them to information already stored in semantic memory. Thus if the input sentences referred to a "state description," the HEURISTIC COMPILER would find in semantic memory a full and rather elaborate characterization of a state description, and could use the information contained in that characterization to supply missing information about state descriptions that was needed to formulate the programming problem for the problem-solving component of the system. Since we will be using the same techniques in the present system (but with rather more elaborate syntactic capabilities), there is no need to describe here just how the HEURISTIC OMPILER accomplished this semantic analysis. The interested reader is referred to the published descriptions (see Simon, 1972b).

Bobrow (1968) constructed an early program for understanding natural language in algebra story problems in order to set up the equations for solving the problems. His program demonstrated that only relatively simple syntactic analysis was required when the task itself supplied a sufficiently rich semantic environment. Raphael (1964, 1968) constructed a question-answering scheme, SIR, that accepted natural-language questions and used various kinds of stored semantic information to draw inferences and to answer the questions.

Another understanding program, the General Game Playing Program (GGPP), was constructed by T. G. Williams (1972) to show how the information contained in a source like Hoyle's Book of Games could be translated automatically into a program that would play (legally if not well) any one of the games described there. Thus, GGPP was confronted with exactly the same task we posed to our subjects in the present study—to extract from written instructions the description of a task, and to program itself to perform that task. GGPP did not accept natural English text as input; the information had to be put into a proper language for it. But the inputs it accepted contained essentially the same information about the game as was provided by Hoyle. The program had general capabilities for making moves or plays in board and card games, for sorting decks, and for matching patterns, and could store in semantic memory information about decks of cards, and so on, that could subsequently be applied as an aid in interpreting the rules of particular games. (For example, "a bridge hand consists of 52 cards, deuce through ace, in four suits.") GGPP could interpret the instructions for most kinds of card and board games.

An understanding program constructed by D. S. Williams (1972) programmed itself to perform tasks (to answer items on an intelligence test), but avoided the problem of natural language interpretation by inducing the task requirements, instead, from worked-out examples presented to it. Programs constructed by Coles (1972), and Siklossy (1972) had capabilities for understanding natural language input, but employed these capabilities to a rather different end than the one under consideration here. They are relevant, however, to the general problem of using semantic information as an aid to the interpretation of natural language. Coles used information derived from pictures to select the correct interpretations of sentences that were syntactically ambiguous. Siklossy used matched pairs of pictures and sentences, in the manner of the Ogden and Richards "Language Through Pictures" series, to enable his program to induce the grammar of a natural language.

In Chapter 9 of this volume, Moore and Newell describe a system, MERLIN, designed to perform various kinds of understanding tasks, and to explore the general nature of understanding processes. In a later section of this chapter, we will have some comparisons to make between the notions of understanding that are embodied in MERLIN, and those incorporated in the program we are about to describe. The schemes reviewed in the preceding paragraphs, together with a number of other schemes for handling natural language are discussed and compared by Simon and Siklossy (1972), Chapter 2.

The state of the art of natural language processing, as of about 1972, is captured very well by Winograd's (1972) SHRDLU program. SHRDLU interprets statements and questions in English, using a case grammar that facilitates matching syntactic with semantic information. On the basis of the input questions or commands, SHRDLU then provides answers or carries out the commands, using for this purpose a reasoning program, PLANNER. Thus the language-processing component and the problem-solving component of SHRDLU stand in the same relation as the language-processing component and the problem-solving component of the HEURISTIC COMPILER, or of the system to be described here.

All of the programs described in this section are to be viewed primarily as studies of artificial intelligence schemes.

The UNDERSTAND Program

We have written a computer program, UNDERSTAND, as a first approximation to the processes used by our human subjects to understand the instructions of the Tea Ceremony problem. As we stated earlier, the process of understanding a task begins with the presentation of the task instructions to the subject, and ends when the subject has acquired a program that enables him to undertake to perform the task. If the task involves solving a problem, then the product of the understanding process is a problem-solving program appropriate to the task in question.

In the UNDERSTAND program, we have not tried to simulate the alternation of phases betwee *Understanding* and *Solving* that we observed in the subject's protocol, and in this respect the program fails to capture the temporal sequence of the human processing. It seemed to us that, in this first approximation, the initial job was to see how information in the task instructions could be combined with semantic information assumed to be already available to the subject in such a way as to permit the subject to interpret the instructions as an appropriate input to his problem-solving processes. We leave the alternation of phases to a later time when this initial problem has been adequately solved, and we can undertake a second approximation.

The problem-solving program that the subject acquires through the understanding process defines for him: (*a*) a basic problem space in which he can carry on a search for the problem solution, (*b*) one or more operators for moving through the problem space, and (*c*) one or more tests for determining the presence or absence of particular features at any node in the problem space. The problem-solving program that is developed under these circumstances need not be manufactured out of whole cloth. The subject may come to the experimental situation already provided with more or less general problem-solving capabilities. Under these circumstances, understanding means representing the new task to himself in such a way that some of these general problem-solving capabilities can now be used for tackling it. We can imagine the *Solving* processes mentioned earlier as having two components: a more or less general program for solving problems, and a set of specific inputs to that program which define a particular problem for it in such terms that it can go to work on the problem. If such a factorization is possible, then the task of the *Understanding* processes is to provide this second component, in proper format, to the problem-solving program.

In the present instance, we will assume that the problem-solving program which is the target of the understanding process resembles the General Problem Solver (GPS) (Ernst & Newell, 1969), in its general shape. The principal inputs that GPS requires, before it can go to work on a problem, are (*a*) a representation of the successive states of the problem-solving situation (i.e., of the nodes in the problem space), (*b*) one or more processes or actions for changing one of these states into another (for making legal, and possibly illegal, moves), (*c*) a set of differences for describing states and comparing pairs of states, and (*d*) a table of connections between differences and actions, which prescribes the possible actions that may be taken when each kind of difference is encountered. Providing GPS with these four kinds of information about a task environment enables it to undertake problem-solving activity in that environment.

Not all of this information needs to be supplied to GPS from external sources. Equipped with appropriate learning programs, GPS might be expected to develop the third and fourth classes of information by itself; that is, to induce from the description of the problem space a list of differences, and to induce from these and from the operator or operators for changing states a table of connections between differences and actions. Several investigators have discussed learning programs for GPS-like problem solvers that are capable of carrying out these learning tasks—of inducing differences and the table of connections. (A number of such learning programs are described and discussed in Eavarone & Ernst, 1970; Ernest & Newell, 1969; Newell, 1963; Newell, Shaw, & Simon, 1960.)

To strip our problem to its barest essentials, we will assume that GPS is equipped with such a learning program. Hence, what remains for the understanding process is to generate from the problem instructions the representation of problem states, one or more processes for changing states, and one or more tests for the presence or absence of particular features in a state. If the task, for example, were to learn to play checkers from a set of written instructions, the understanding program would have to be able, by reading the instructions, to generate a representation for the checker board and checker positions, and to generate a process for making checker moves.

In the problem before us, the Tea Ceremony, the task for the understanding program is to find a way to represent the successive situations during the ceremony—specifically, to represent the distribution of tasks among the participants—and to construct a program for transferring a task from one participant to another. Moreover, the transfer program must operate properly upon whatever representation has been constructed. The latter is a nontrivial requirement, for we shall see that it is probably most expedient to generate the two main outputs of the understanding program—the representation of situations and the transfer process—more or less independently of each other. Hence, the transfer process must be sufficiently flexible to adapt itself to the particular representation that has been chosen, whatever that may be.

Whether the scheme described above and the program developed out of that scheme actually describe how human subjects go about understanding task instructions is, of course, an empirical question, to be settled by comparing the output of the understanding program with the subjects' protocols. In the present paper we will not undertake a detailed comparison of the UNDERSTAND program with the protocol we presented and discussed in the previous section. Our main concern is to see whether we can in fact produce from the Tea Ceremony instructions an appropriate set of inputs for a GPS-like problem solver. As in other simulation environments, an important first step is to produce a set of processes that are sufficient for the task. Determination of how closely these processes approximate to the human processes can be postponed until this first step has been taken.

Processing Stages

The UNDERSTAND program carries out its work in two discrete stages which correspond to two of the components of the model described earlier (Fig. 8.2).

1. The task instructions are read and reread. They are analyzed syntactically and semantically to extract from them their "deep structure," as linguists use that term. As before, we will refer to the processes that do this as the *Language* processes.

2. The deep structures of the sentences describing the task are analyzed further by matching them against a set of requirements that specify the form of an acceptable input to GPS. We can think of these requirements as a set of templates in long-term memory that provide a model for a well-formed problem, in the sense of GPS. We will call this second set of processes the *Construction* processes.

The input to the first stage is the text of the task instructions, and the output is the deep structure of the text (Fig. 8.5). The input to the second stage is the deep structure, the output is a task specification in a form suitable as input to GPS (Fig. 8.7, 8.8, and 8.9). Since the problem-solving process can now go to work on this task specification, the latter represents the subject's understanding of the problem.

As before, we are oversimplifying when we describe the understanding process as proceeding in two sequential stages. We have seen in the human protocol strong evidences of alternation of processes from the *Understanding* to the *Solving* processes and back, and this surely implies, within the *Understanding* processes, some alternation between *Language* and *Construction*.

Language: Extracting Deep Structure from Text

That portion of the simulation which is concerned with extracting the deep structure from the text has been realized mostly in PAS-II (Waterman & Newell, 1973). PAS-II is a flexible interactive computer program designed as an aid to the process of protocol analysis. In particular, it was designed to take as input a problem-solving protocol and a description of the problem space that the subject used to solve the problem, and from these to trace the sequence of operators that the subject applied in solving the problem. For example, PAS-II will provide an analysis of a cryptarithmetic protocol if it is given a description of the subject's problem space, including both the knowledge elements that the subject identifies in the problem (e.g., letters, digits, parity, and so on), and a list of the operators that are available to the subject (e.g., operators that assign a value to a digit or that process a column).

In the present context, we have made use of PAS-II in a manner parallel to, but different from, its originally intended use. We have used it to accept as input the problem text and a set of text-reading rules, and to generate as output a set of syntactically and semantically interpreted elements from which the second part of the UNDERSTAND program can derive the problem space that is implied in the problem description.

Since PAS-II has convenient facilities for defining sets of processing rules (e.g., segmentation rules, grammar rules) that can be applied in an arbitrary order designated by the user, it is well adapted to this new task. PAS-II also provides compact notations for expressing grammatical and semantic relations, a number of editing, storage, and other utility functions, and interactive capabilities.

General Organization

We have divided the task of extracting the deep structure into three phases, accomplished in sequence: (*a*) a syntactic phase that parses sentences, (*b*) a semantic phase that identifies significant relations and assembles structures that have special meaning (e.g., lists and quotes), and (*c*) a cross-reference phase that handles intersentence relations such as anaphoric reference. The first two of these phases operate on the text one sentence at a time. In the third, or cross-reference, phase, the text is considered as a whole.

The syntactic phase. The syntactic analysis is accomplished by applying three types of rules to the input sentences. These are segmentation rules, grammar rules, and integration rules. The function of the segmentation rules is to break complex sentences into smaller, more easily handled, segments. For example, the segmentation rules separate the subject from the predicate of a sentence by breaking after a noun that is followed by a verb. This separation simplifies the identification of the object of the sentence by preventing confusion between the subject and the object. The segmentation rules also break after commas, colons, semicolons, and relatives such as "which" and "that."

For example, Sentence 2 of "The Tea Ceremony" is broken into three parts by the segmentation rules:

"The ceremony"

"involves a host and exactly two guests,"

"neither more nor less."

The grammar rules assign grammatical classes to words and to groups of words. First, single words are classified as nouns, verbs, adjectives, determiners, and so on. Then more complex units are identified by the ordering and grammatical classes of the words that comprise them. For example, in parsing the segment of Sentence 1, "a most civilized and refined tea ceremony," the words were classified respectively as determiner, adjective, adjective, conjunction, adjective, noun, noun. The string adjective-conjunction-adjective was classed as a conjoined adjective, and the two nouns were classed as a noun string. Then the whole structure, because it consisted of a noun string preceded by an optional adjective string preceded, in turn, by an optional determiner, was classed as a noun-group with "ceremony" as its head. Finally, the structure was reclassified—as are all noun-groups and pronouns that are not possessive pronouns—as an object. The output of the grammar rules for this segment was the element (OBJ CEREMONY).

The output of the grammar rules for the segment, "is practiced, . . ." is the element (VG IS PRACTICED), indicating a verb-group with "practiced" as the main verb and "is" as the auxiliary. When there is no auxiliary, the marker, "aux" appears in the auxiliary position.

In addition to noun-groups and verb-groups, the grammar identifies prepositional phrases (". . . to them . . ." = (PHR TO THEM)), time marks ("When . . ." = (TMARK)), modal auxiliaries (". . . may . . ." = MODAL)), groups defined as a digit followed by a plural noun (". . . two guests . . ." = (GR TWO GUESTS)), and about 20 others. Fig. 8.3 shows the output of the grammar rules for each of the sentences of the problem text.

The integration rules are applied to the output of the grammar rules. These rules serve the function of assembling correctly parsed sentences from

```
                  : : SENTENCE 1
(PHR IN INNS)  (PHR OF VILLAGES)
(VG IS PRACTICED)  (OBJ CEREMONY)
                  : : SENTENCE 2
(OBJ CEREMONY)
(GR TWO GUESTS)  VG <AUX> INVOLVES)  (OBJ HOST)  (AND)
(ADJNEG MORE)  (ADJNEG LESS)  (COMMA)
                  : : SENTENCE 3
(OBJ GUESTS)  (TMARK)
(PHR AT TABLE)  (CONJVG (VG HAVE ARRIVED)  (VG HAVE SEATED))  (OBJ THEMSELVES)
(OBJ HOST)  (COMMA)
(GR FIVE SERVICES)  (PHR FOR THEM)  (VG <VAUX) PERFORMS)
                  : : SENTENCE 4
(OBJ SERVICES)
(LIST)  (EXTD NOBILITY)
(OBJ HIMALAYANS)
(PRH TO THEM)  (VG <AUX> ATTRIBUTE)  (COLON)
(ACT STOKING FIRE)
(ACT FANNING FLAMES)  (COMMA)
(ACT PASSING CAKES)  (COMMA)
(ACT POURING TEA)  (COMMA)
(ACT RECITING POETRY)  (COMMA)
                  : : SENTENCE 5
(COTEMP CEREMONY)
(GROUP THOSE-PRESENT)  (COMMA)
(VG <VAUX> ASK)  (OBJ ANOTHER)  (MODAL)
(OBJ SIR)  (QUOTE)  (COMMA)
(OBJ I)  (MODAL)  (COMMA)
(MEMB THIS ONEROUS TASK)  (PHR FOR YOU)  (VG <VAUX> PERFORM)  (QUOTE)  (QUEST)
                  : : SENTENCE 6
(HOWEVER)
(OBJ PERSON)  (COMMA)
(PHR OF ANOTHER)  (VG <AUX> REQUEST)  (MODAL)
(EXTM LEAST NOBLE TASKS)  (ONLY)
(OBJ OTHER)
(VG IS PERFORMING)
                  : : SENTENCE 7
(FURTHER)
(OBJ PERSON)  (IF)  (COMMA)
(GROUP TASKS)  (VG IS PERFORMING)
(OBJ HE)  (COMMA)  (THEN)
(EXTD TASK)  (VGNEG <AUX> REQUEST)  (MODAL)
(MEMB NOBLEST <ADJ> TASK)  (VG <AUX> IS)  (OBJ HE)  (COMP NOBLER <ADJ>)
(VG IS PERFORMING)
                  : : SENTENCE 8
(OBJ CUSTOM)
(VG <AUX> REQUIRES)  (REL)
(OBJ CEREMONY)  (TMARK)
(VG <AUX> IS)  (FINAL)
(GROUP TASKS)  (COMMA)
(MEMB MOST SENIOR GUESTS)  (PHR FROM HOST)  (VG WILL TRANSFERRED)  (PREP TO)
                  : : SENTENCE 9
(OBJ THIS)  (QWORD HOW)  (MODAL)
(VG BE ACCOMPLISHED)  (QUEST)
```

FIG. 8.3. Output of the grammar rules applied during syntactic processing of the problem text.

the grammatically classified elements. Included among the integration rules are rules that identify sets of objects (defined as a group or an object joined to another group or object by "and"), subsets of sets, and lists (defined as ordered sets). Other integration rules assemble predicates from verb groups, objects, phrases, and time markers, and then construct sentences by adding subjects to these predicates. The output of the integration rules for Sentence 2 is

(SEN CEREMONY INVOLVES (HOST (TWO GUESTS)) D T)
(SET HOST (TWO GUESTS)) (SUBSET (TWO GUESTS))
(NEGADJ MORE) (NEGADJ LESS)

In the first line of the output above, "D" is a placeholder for an indirect object and "T" is a placeholder for a time mark such as "Initial" or "Final". The negative adjectives will be ignored by the program hereafter, since they have failed to find a place in any structure of interest to the UNDERSTAND processes. Execution of the integration rules marks the end of the syntactic phase of the *Language* program.

Semantic phase. Processing in the semantic phase is accomplished by two sets of rules which we will call the Semantic1 rules and the Semantic2 rules. The Semantic1 rules search for sentences that have verbs denoting important relations, such as ASK, DO, and PARTICIPATE, and transform them into the corresponding relations. For example, the segment of Sentence 7, "if a person is performing any tasks, . . ." which the syntactic phase has coded as:

(IF)(SEN PERSON PERFORMING (GROUP TASKS) D T)

is transformed into:

(IF)(REL DO PERSON (GROUP TASKS) D T)

Fig. 8.4 shows the output of the Semantic1 rules for each of the sentences in the problem text.

The Semantic2 rules carry out the final stage of semantic processing. These rules use the special marks left in the text by the earlier processing stages, e.g., (QUOTE), (QUEST), (STRING X), and so on, to assemble complex structures (quotes, questions, and lists—ordered sets). For example, Lines 12-15 in Fig. 8.4 are transformed to:

(REL ASK (GROUP (THOSE PRESENT)) LIT (OF ANOTHER) T)
(REL (ASK DO) I (MEMB THIS ONEROUS TASK) (FOR YOU) T)

In the first line, the marker "LIT" indicates that the object of the relation "ASK" is a quote, the interpretation of which follows in the next line. The relation (ASK DO) stands for the complex relation of "asking to do" constructed from the "ASK" relation and the action of doing involved in the quote that the relation contained. Lines 7 and 8 in Fig. 8.4 are transformed into:

(LIST TASKS NOBILITY ((ACT STOKING FIRE) (ACT FANNING FLAMES) (ACT PASSING CAKES) (ACT POURING TEA) (ACT RECITING POETRY))

SEMANTIC 2 MODE

```
: : SENTENCE 1
(REL LOC INNS VILLAGES)  (REL LOC CEREMONY INNS)
(PRED (IS PRACTICED) CEREMONY D T))
            : : SENTENCE 2
(REL PART CEREMONY (MOST (TWO GUESTS)) D T)
(SET HOST (TWO GUESTS))  (SUBSET (TWO GUESTS))
(ADJNEG MORE)  (ADJNEG LESS)
            : : SENTENCE 3
(TMARK Q)  (REL LOC GUESTS TABLE)  (SEN GUESTS (VG HAVE SEATED) GUESTS D Q)
            (SEN GUESTS (VG HAVE ARRIVED) NIL D Q)
(REL DO HOST (FIVE TASKS)  (FOR GUESTS) Q)
(SET (FIVE TASKS))
            : : SENTENCE 4
(LIST TASKS (NOBILITY A) L)
(SEN HIMALAYANS (<AUX> ATTRIBUTE)  (NOBILITY A)  (TO THEM) T)
(STRING ((ACT STOKING FIRE)  (ACT FANNING FLAMES)  (ACT PASSING CAKES)  (ACT POURING
            TEA)  (ACT RECITING POETRY)))
            : : SENTENCE 5
(COTEMP CEREMONY)  (MODAL)
(REL ASK (GROUP THOSE-PRESENT) OB (OF ANOTHER) T)
(QUOTE)  (INDIR SIR)
(QUEST)  (REL DO I (MEMB THIS ONEROUS TASK)  (FOR YOU) T
(QUOTE)
            : : SENTENCE 6
(HOWEVER)  (MODAL)
(REL ASK PERSON (MEMB ONLY (LEAST NOBLE)  (TASKS A))  (OF ANOTHER) T)
(REL DO OTHER (TASKS A) D T)
            : : SENTENCE 7
(FURTHER)
(IF)  (MODAL)  (REL DO PERSON (GROUP TASKS) D T)
(THEN)  (REL (NO ASK) HE (TASK A) D T)
(SEN (TASK A) (IS (COMP NOBLER <ADJ>))  (MEMB NOBLEST <ADJ> TASK) D T)
(REL DO HE OB D T)
            : : SENTENCE 8
(SEN CUSTOM (<AUX> REQUIRES) REL D FINAL)
(TMARK FINAL) (SEN CEREMONY (<AUX> IS) OB D FINAL)
(REL TRANS (GROUP TASKS) HOST (MEMB MOST SENIOR GUESTS) FINAL)
            : : SENTENCE 9
(QWORD HOW)  (QUEST)  (REL DO THIS OB D T)
```

FIG. 8.4. Output of semantic processing.

Cross-referencing. Currently, cross-referencing is handled by an auxiliary SNOBOL program called JTEA. This program performs two functions:

1. It traces anaphoric references and replaces pronouns with the referenced nouns.

2. It handles words such as "further" and "however" that link sentences together. It does this by (a) matching elements in the two sentences to be sure that the subscripts are assigned in a consistent way across sentences (e.g., that "PARTICIPANT.1" in Sentence 5 refers to the same object as "PARTICIPANT.1" in Sentence 6. The matching is accomplished by searching for an identical verb in the two sentences and establishing that the matched objects bear identical relations to it. (b) It then assembles the two sentences into a single sentence and deletes the linking word.

Fig. 8.5 shows the final result of the processes for extracting the deep structure from the problem text. Now the *Construction* processes must be applied.

Construction: Representation and Transfer Processes

In Fig. 8.5 we show the interpreted text as it emerges from the parsing process, that is, in the form of the "deep structure" of the original problem instructions. In the present section, we describe the portions of the understanding program that take this interpreted text as input and produce a representation for the various states of the problem situation and a process for transferring tasks from one of the participants to another. The latter process will also incorporate tests for guaranteeing that the conditions stated in the problem for a "legal" transfer are satisfied; that is, that the task being transferred is the least noble of the tasks being performed by the person from whom it is taken, and is less noble than any of the tasks of the person who takes it.

Representing the Situation

In preparation for subsequent processing steps, the program examines the text to find the whole set of participants and the whole list of tasks, then converts this set and this list into an appropriate internal representation, assigning to the set and list their types, to the list its ordering relation (ORDER) and to the members of each their respective types. The resulting

```
                               DEEP2 MODE
(REL LOC INNS VILLAGES) (REL LOC CEREMONY INNS)
(PRED (IS PRACTICED) CEREMONY D T)
(REL PART CEREMONY (HOST TWO GUESTS)) D T)
(SET HOST (TWO GUESTS)) (SUBSET (TWO GUESTS))
(ADJNEG MORE) (ADJNEG LESS)
(REL LOCA GUESTS TABLE) (SEN GUESTS (VG HAVE SEATED) GUESTS D Q) (SEN GUESTS
                        (VG HAVE ARRIVED) NIL D Q)
(REL DO HOST (FIVE TASKS) (FOR GUESTS Q)
(SET (FIVE TASKS))

          (LIST TASKS (NOBILITY A) ((ACT STOKING FIRE) (ACT FANNING FLAMES)
                        (ACT PASSING CAKES) (ACT POURING TEA)
                        (ACT RECITING POETRY)))
(SEN HIMALAYANS (<AUX> ATTRIBUTE) (NOBILITY A) (TO THEM) T)
(COTEMP CEREMONY) (MODAL)
(REL ASK (GROUP THOSE-PRESENT) LIT (OF ANOTHER) T)
(REL (ASK DO) I (MEMB THIS ONEROUS TASK) (FOR YOU) T)
(HOWEVER) (MODAL)
(REL ASK PERSON (MEMB LEAST NOBLE (T ASKS A)) (OF ANOTHER) T)
                        (REL (NO ASK) PERSON (MEMB NO (LEAST NOBLE) (TASKS A))
                        (OF ANOTHER) T)
(REL DO OTHER (TASKS A) D T)
(FURTHER)
(IF) (MODAL) (REL DO PERSON (GROUP TASKS) D T)
(THEN) (REL (NO ASK) HE (TASK A) D T)
(SEN (TASK A) (IS (COMP NOBLER <ADJ>)) (MEMB NOBLEST <ADJ> TASK) D T)
(REL DO HE OB D T)
(SEN CUSTOM (<AUX> REQUIRES) REL D FINAL)
(SEN CEREMONY (<AUX> IS) OB D FINAL)
(REL TRANS (GROUP TASKS) HOST (MEMB MOST SENIOR GUESTS) FINAL)
(QWORD HOW) (QUEST) (REL DO THIS OB D I)
```

Fig. 8.5. Deep structure of the problem text.

```
TASK = 'FIRE FLAMES CAKES TEA POETRY  :, TYPE LIST, ORDER NOBILITY'
FIRE = ':, TYPE TASK'
FLAMES = ':, TYPE TASK'
CAKES = ':, TYPE TASK'
TEA = ':, TYPE TASK'
POETRY = ':, TYPE TASK'

PARTICIPANT = 'HOST GUEST.1 GUEST.2  :, TYPE SET,'
HOST = ':, TYPE PARTiCIPANT'
GUEST.1 = ':, TYPE PARTICIPANT'
GUEST.2 = ':, TYPE PARTICIPANT'
```

FIG. 8.6. List structures obtrained for Sentences 2 and 3.

structures, obtained by processing Sentences 2 and 3, respectively, are shown in Fig. 8.6.

The program searches the text for a sentence in the declarative mood that is labeled with a time tag, on the assumption that such a sentence will be descriptive of the situation at some stage in the problem. The first such sentence it discovers in the processed text is Sentence 2, which describes the problem situation at the outset of the Tea Ceremony. The program takes this as the information from which it will undertake to construct a representation of the situation. The sentence asserts a relation between the host and the tasks.

Now the program is ready to create a description of the initial situation. Sentence 2 asserts a relation, DO, between an object of the class, PARTICIPANT, and a list of objects of the class, TASK. The attribute, PARTICIPANT, is associated with the structure, SITUATION; and the list of participants is associated with this attribute as its value. The participant on this list that is synonymous with "HOST" is assigned the attribute, TASK, and the list of tasks that, according to Sentence 2, the host is performing is assigned as the value of this attribute. The resulting description of the situation is shown in Fig. 8.7.

The *Transfer* Process

The program next seeks information about the operators for the Tea Ceremony. Employing as its cue the use of the subjunctive mood, it discovers that Sentences 5 through 7 of Fig. 8.5 have been tagged as a production—that is, as describing an action. In Sentence 5 it discovers the relation ASK:DO having three arguments: the task, the participant making the request, and the participant currently performing the task. That is, ASK:DO is of the form:

$$REL(TASK,PARTICIPANT.1,PARTICIPANT.2).$$

The next step is to search semantic memory for the meaning of this relation—that is for a known process having the same formal structure as

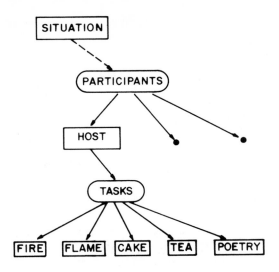

SITUATION = " :, PARTICIPANT L1,"

L1 = " HOST GUEST.1 GUEST.2:, TYPE SET,"

HOST = ":, TYPE PARTICIPANT, TASK L2,"

L2 = " FIRE FLAME CAKE TEA POETRY:, TYPE LIST, ORDER NOBILITY,"

FIG. 8.7. Description of the situation.

ASK:DO, and having associated with it a procedure for actually executing the process. In the present version of the system, the proper formal structure is identified by *Match*, a process that compares the given relation with a relational structure in semantic memory, and determines whether the former is isomorphic with the latter. Here "isomorphic" means that the given relation has the same number of arguments as the relation in semantic memory, and that these arguments are distributed in the same way among arguments of different types. To accomplish its task, *Match* makes use of a subroutine, *Class*, which identifies the types of the arguments in each relation, and counts the number of arguments of each type.

In the instance before us, the given relation has three arguments, one of one type (TASK), and two of another type (PARTICIPANT). In semantic memory, we find the relation, *Transfer*, which also has three arguments, one of the type OBJECT, and two of the type ACTOR. The *Match* process therefore succeeds in mapping REL upon *Transfer*, with TASK corresponding with OBJECT, and PARTICIPANT.1 and PARTICIPANT.2 corresponding with ACTOR.F and ACTOR.T, respectively (see Fig. 8.8).

Associated with the transfer process in semantic memory is a procedure for actually carrying out a transfer. We can now use that procedure, on the basis of the identification we have made of the components of ASK:DO with the components of *Transfer,* to execute the action called for by ASK:DO, that is to transfer a task from one participant to another. However, two things remain to be done: to add to ASK:DO the specific conditions for a legal move in the Tea Ceremony, and to adapt the code for the transfer operation to the particular representation we have chosen for the problem space. We will take up these two points in reverse order.

Fitting process to representation. The coding procedure associated in semantic memory with *Transfer* is very general and flexible. If it is provided with information about the representation that has been selected, the procedure will perform a transfer operation appropriate to that representation. In the case before us, a task is a member of the value list of the attribute TASK of the participant who is performing it. To transfer that task from one participant to another, we must delete it from the list on which it appears, and add it to the list of tasks that is the value of the attribute TASK of the participant who receives it.

The information that *Transfer* needs about the representation is provided by the process called *Describe. Describe* examines the representation of the situation, and produces a description of the way in which the relation between a task and the participant who is performing it is represented (Fig. 8.9). In the case before us, the description would read: TASK MEMBER VALUE TASK, which may be translated, "TASKS are stored as MEMBERS of the list of VALUES of the attribute TASK of the structure PARTICIPANT.X." The description produced by *Describe* also indicates where information about the participants is stored in relation to the structure, SITUATION. In the present case, the description would read: PARTICIPANT MEMBER VALUE PARTICIPANT, which may be translated, "PARTICIPANTS are stored as MEMBERS of the list of VALUES of the attribute PARTICIPANT of the structure SITUATION."

The *Transfer* process uses the latter description to *Find* the structure associated with PARTICIPANT.1, then uses the former description to *Find* the task to be transferred on this structure, and deletes it from the list. The *Transfer* process next uses the second description to *Find* the structure

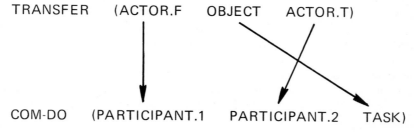

Fig. 8.8. Matching the arguments of the transfer relation into the relation COM-DO.

VSIT = ":, WHICH PARTICIPANTS, PARTICIPANTS MEMBER,
TASKS MEMBER VALUE TASKS , "

FIG. 8.9. The relation between a task and the participant who is performing it.

associated with PARTICIPANT.2, then uses the first description to add the task to the list of tasks associated with this structure.

The *Transfer* process will use the same method to carry out the transfer for other representations of the data—it will *Find* the first participant, delete the task to be transferred, *Find* the second participant, and add the task to those associated with him. The transfer will also be performed correctly if participants are associated with tasks instead of tasks with participants. In this case (which will be disclosed by the output of *Describe*) *Transfer* will *Find* the task to be moved, *Find* the participant associated with it, and change the latter to the participant who is to receive the task.

Conditions for a Legal Transfer

To define a complete process for a legal move (i.e., a legal transfer of a task) in the Tea Ceremony, the program must be able to test whether a particular task is the least noble of the tasks being performed by one of the participants (the donor); and whether this task is less noble than all the tasks being performed by another participant (the one requesting the task). The process LIST('TASK','PARTICIPANT.X') will produce a list, in order of nobility, of all the tasks that are being performed by PARTICIPANT.X. The *List* process, like *Transfer,* is independent of the particular representation that has been selected to describe the situation. It acquires this independence by making use of the description of the situation produced by *Describe* to find PARTICIPANT.X in the structure that describes the situation, and then to find all of the tasks assigned to PARTICIPANT.X. From the list, TASK, it obtains the tasks, ordered by the relation of NOBILITY.

List will operate equally well if the situation is described in terms of tasks and the participants responsible for them, as if it is described, inversely, in terms of participants and the tasks they are performing. In either case it produces an ordered list of those tasks that are being performed by the participant in question.

With the output of *List* in hand, it becomes an easy matter to determine whether a particular task is the least of an ordered list (i.e., its last member), and whether the task is less than all members of such a list. The former test is performed by the function LEAST, the latter by the function LESSA (for "less than all"). Thus to test whether the conditions are satisfied for transferring TASK.4 from PARTICIPANT.2 to PARTICIPANT.3, we first execute the test:

LEAST('TASK.4', LIST ('TASK', 'PARTICIPANT.2'))

and then, if that test succeeds, the test:

LESSA('TASK.4', LIST('TASK', 'PARTICIPANT.3'))

Accommodating the Transfer and Find Processes

Making the *Transfer* process, and the *Find* process that it employs independent of the representation exacts a heavy price in terms of processing time and complexity. Each time these processes are executed, the description of the representation must be reexamined, and a multitude of tests must be carried out to choose the correct path through the routines. The inefficiency is twofold: (*a*) only a small part of the total routine, *Transfer,* or *Find,* is relevant to any particular problem representation and (*b*) tests on the description of the representation to determine which path to follow make up a considerable part of the processing. The processing could be carried out much more rapidly if these inefficiencies could be removed.

The phenomenon we are describing has a clear human counterpart. When a human subject learns a new procedure that is necessary for carrying out a task, he executes the procedure haltingly, stopping along the way to ask himself: "What do I do next?" or "Where am I?" As he executes the procedure repeatedly, he begins to transfer more and more of the steps to long-term memory, so that he can retrace the path "automatically," without these halts, hesitations, and tests. It is our hypothesis that his increasing speed and sureness of performance results specifically from replacing a "general purpose" program, replete with tests for selecting his path in a given situation, with a special program tailored to the current representation he is employing, and omitting the tests as inessential.

To simulate this hypothesized human assimilation process, we assume a gradual transfer to long-term memory of the steps in *Transfer* and *Find* that are actually executed, omitting those steps that are information-gathering tests on the description of the representation. Thus, there are gradually created in long-term memory, streamlined versions of *Transfer* and *Find*—call them STRANFER and SFIND, respectively—that permit automatization of these operations.

RELATION OF PROTOCOL TO PROGRAM

Since the UNDERSTAND program is intended only as a first approximation of the process by which our subject understands the problem text, we did not expect (and have not observed) a detailed correspondence between the behavior of the subject and the behavior of the program. Indeed, we have not as yet attempted to derive a complete problem behavior graph from the protocol. However, we have observed some interesting correspondences between the protocol and some of the global features of program organization which suggest that at least the major processes are grouped together appropriately and that they are arranged in roughly the right order.

Earlier analysis of the protocol focussed on the content of the subject's statements strongly suggested that the subject employs two distinct processes in understanding the problem—a *Language* process which extracts information from short segments of text and a *Construction* process which integrates the information derived from the text into a unified model. This conclusion was supported by two observations:

1. Transition from the *Language* process to the *Construction* process is frequently marked by use of the conjunction *so.*

2. The sequence in which the sentences were read was influenced by the subject's success or failure in finding an interpretation in his model for the information from the text. Thus, the *Language* process appeared to be controlled by the *Construction* process, and hence, to have a role distinct from it.

Further evidence concerning the differentiation of these two major processes may be obtained by examining the subject's difficulties in understanding Sentences 5 and 6 of the problem text. In essence, what we will argue is that information analyzed in an earlier stage of processing by the *Language* process may be reanalyzed and given a new interpretation at a later stage of processing by the *Construction* process.

A major difficulty in interpreting Sentences 5 and 6 stems from the ambiguity of the construction "perform . . . for" in the question "may I perform this onerous task for you?"[1] Suppose that A asks B, "May I pour tea for you?" This may mean that A has responsibility for pouring tea and that he wants to exercise that responsibility for B's benefit by pouring tea into B's cup. On the other hand, it may mean that B has responsibility for pouring tea and that A wants to relieve B of that responsibility. The first interpretation is the one most strongly suggested in the context of Sentence 3. One expects a gracious host to perform activities for the benefit of his guests. Only the second interpretation, however, is consistent with Sentences 6 through 8, since these sentences clearly require that responsibility for the tasks be transferred among the participants. Both interpretations are compatible with Sentence 5.

We believe that the *Language* process assigned the first meaning to "perform . . . for" in Sentences 3 and 5 and the second meaning in Sentences 6 and 7. The disparity between these two meanings first became important when the subject attempted to integrate the information in Sentences 5 and 6 into a single representation. The attempt at integration is first revealed in Lines 13-15 of Fig. 8.2 when the subject says, "so if my friend

---

[1]Webster's Collegiate dictionary (1961) lists 11 definitions of the preposition "for" of which only 3 are appropriately used with the verb "perform." In the first, "for" is synonymous with "instead of"; in the second, it is synonymous with "in behalf of"; and in the third, it expresses duration of time as in "for hours." Only the first two of these meanings are used in the protocol.

is performing a bunch of tasks, I can request—wait a minute—something's fishy here." The subject is in the process of interpreting Sentence 6 and has just assigned some tasks to "the other" represented in his model by his friend. Allowing ourselves to speculate freely about what the subject is thinking at this point, we generate the following scenario. The subject, trying to represent the request mentioned in Sentence 6, imagines himself asking his friend if he may perform one of the friend's tasks. The form of the request that he imagines, however, derives from Sentence 5, and the meaning of "perform" in that request is different from the one required in Sentence 6. At the moment when he says, ". . . I can request . . . wait a minute . . . Something's fishy here," he recognizes that the request as he has formulated it is inappropriate for accomplishing the transfer required in Sentence 6 and thus derives the first clue to the conflict in the meanings of "perform." After reexamining Sentences 5 and 6, he responds to this inadequacy again in Line 25 when he says, ". . . But if all I can ask him is . . ."

The conflict between the two meanings is finally resolved in Lines 29-32. In Lines 29-30, the subject clearly recognizes that the critical difference in the meanings is whether the asker or the person asked has the initial responsibility for performing the task. In Lines 31-32, he chooses the second meaning.

To summarize, what we derive from this sequence is evidence consistent with our position that two distinct processes are involved in understanding the problem; a first process which assigns meanings to sentences taken one at a time and a second process which integrates the meanings of the sentences.

Another example which illustrates the integration of meanings may be found in Lines 31-34 of Fig. 8.1. Senence 6, which focusses on the tasks "the other" is doing, yields the interpretation in Line 31, "So he is doing something. . . ." Sentence 7, which focusses on the tasks which the asker is doing, might be expected by itself to yield an interpretation such as, "So I am doing something. . . ." In fact, the interpretation of Sentence 7 at Line 34 is, "So we got both of us here doing something. . . ." This suggests the integration of information derived separately from Sentences 6 and 7.

Evidence of the operation of a *Describe-Situation* process may be found in Lines 2-4, where the subject identifies the set of participants, in Lines 9-10, where he identifies the list of tasks, and in Lines 40-42, where he states the initial and final conditions of the problem. Evidence of the operation of a *Describe-Operator* process may be found in Lines 39-40, when the subject says, "The transfer of the tasks means the doing of the tasks. . . ."

The evidence that we have presented here is extremely fragmentary and in no sense establishes the reality of the processes we have postulated. Only careful analysis of many problem-solving episodes can provide the kind of evidence we require.

LESSONS FOR UNDERSTANDING

In Chapter 9 of this volume, Moore and Newell provide a general discussion of what it means for a system to "understand." Their viewpoint is that a system understands knowledge to the extent that it uses the knowledge whenever it is appropriate. How well does the UNDERSTAND system that we have been describing in this chapter meet this criterion? And is the identical task with which we have confronted our human subjects properly regarded as a test of understanding?

Does this Task Require Understanding?

With respect to the second question, clearly learning about a task from written instructions is a test of understanding of those instructions. The instructions contain knowledge about the task imbedded in English prose, and the evidence that the subject has used the knowledge appropriately is that, after a time, he is able to try to perform the task. We say "try to perform," because the issue is not whether he can solve the Tea Ceremony problem, but whether he comes to know what the problem is.

The nature of the understanding so achieved is most evident from an examination of the UNDERSTAND program. "Using the knowledge when appropriate" means, in this context, using it to construct a problem representation that will serve as input to a problem-solving program. That the subject also constructed such a representation is evident from his verbalizations of his attempts to operate the model of the situation that he produced. We can say, therefore, that both computer program and human subject understood the task instructions, for they used the knowledge contained in them, successfully, for the purpose for which they were intended.

How Full is the Program's Understanding?

Understanding is not an all-or-none affair. One can speak of degree, range, and depth of understanding. Moore and Newell provide in their chapter a useful checklist of dimensions of understanding. It will be instructive to apply this checklist to the UNDERSTAND program, to see what kinds of generality it possesses, and along what dimensions it is limited. In assessing both generality and limitations, however, we need to bear in mind that the limitations will be of at least two different kinds. Certain kinds of understanding may be unachievable because of limitations built into the very structure of the program. A program might be so built, for example, as to be inherently incapable of forms of understanding that humans achieve through processes of visualization.

Other kinds of understanding may be lacking to a system not because of structural deficiencies but because it does not possess critical specific pieces of information that it needs to perform a task given it. For example, to perform the Tea Ceremony task, a system needs a certain knowledge of English vocabulary and English syntax. The brightest person in the world will not be able to understand the task instructions if he knows no English. But this kind of deficiency is less incorrigible than the kind first mentioned. If the system's structural capabilities are adequate, then it can be supplied with specific information of the second kind as it needs it for any given task.

One should not be too glib about "supplying" information to a system—whether computer or human. Computers are notoriously hard to program, and humans almost as notoriously hard to educate. Nevertheless, the distinction between structural limitations of understanding systems and limitations stemming from remediable lacks of specific information is important for any evaluation of a system's performance and prospects.

Moore and Newell take up eight dimensions of understanding in their analysis: representation (completeness, "grain," multiplicity of representations), ability to convert knowledge to action, assimilation of the external environment, accommodation to the external environment, directionality, efficiency, tolerance of error, and depth of understanding. Let us see how UNDERSTAND fares with respect to each of these.

Representation

UNDERSTAND does not encode information into specialized formats, but holds it internally in the form of list structures, that is, lists and descriptions (alias semantic nets, association networks, colored graphs). It is well known that these are perfectly general structures: anything that can be symbolized can be symbolized with their help.

But to encode something is one matter, to encode it in such a way that it is usable is another. UNDERSTAND has no particular capabilities for selecting a problem representation that will facilitate solving the problem. It is, in fact, closely bound to the stimulus in the representation it constructs. Change in the wording of the text of instructions will cause UNDERSTAND to change its representation of the problem.

By the same token, UNDERSTAND is not capable of constructing more than one representation for a given problem—in the way, for example, that a person solving a mathematical problem may carry along both an algebraic and a geometric version of it. In general, we may say that, although UNDERSTAND can understand task instructions in order to construct a problem representation from them, it does not understand the design and modification of representations as a means for facilitating problem solution. It is not able to apply information toward that goal.

Efficiency

There is little we can say about the efficiency of the UNDERSTAND program, beyond what has already been said in the discussion of representation and accommodation. The chief efficiency issue for a program of this kind is probably not how efficiently it achieves an understanding of the text, but whether the understanding, once achieved, is in such form as to facilitate its subsequent problem-solving efforts.

Error

The UNDERSTAND program has little or no capability for recovering from error. Its chief protection against erroneous interpretation of information is to leave it uninterpreted unless the interpretation is clear. This is an important technique that has not been much exploited in artificial intelligence programs (see Siklossy, 1972), but which is probably much used by humans. When we do not understand a sentence, we can go back and read an earlier sentence that may help us interpret it, or we may continue reading until we gain other information that helps us understand it.

In contrast to the simulation program, the human subject gives evidence of having error-recovery capabilities. For example, he first appears to interpret "for him," in the expression "to do something for him," as meaning "on his behalf." Only after this interpretation leads him into difficulties, does he explore the alternative: "in place of him."

Depth of Understanding

Does a human "understand" arithmetic if he can add two numbers and get the correct sum? Or does he understand only if he can state Peano's postulates for the integers and derive the sums table from them? Or do we have to test his understanding in some other way? We would probably be inclined to say that the second test implies deeper understanding than the first. It implies that the performer cannot merely do something, but that he knows what makes it work.

We could ask a whole host of comparable questions about the UNDERSTAND program. It understands the text of instructions well enough to construct a problem representation, but it does not understand why it wants such a representation. It can "understand" the structure of a representation well enough to write a description of it, for use by the *Find* and *Transfer* processes, but not well enough to manipulate the representation into a more useful form. Understanding in complex environments of this kind is not a unitary thing; it can be tested in many ways, and passing one test offers no guarantee of passing others.

The Program and Human Understanding

If our main interest lay in artificial intelligence, then we would want the UNDERSTAND program to understand in the deepest, most efficient, most flexible way possible. However, we developed this program not as an exercise in artificial intelligence but as an attempt at a first-order approximation to human understanding in this task environment. A human being does not usually understand a difficult problem quickly, deeply, efficiently, and in the most flexible way possible. Part of our task is to identify the limitations—structural limitations and limitations of knowledge—of the human seeking to understand written instructions.

It is probable that humans, like the UNDERSTAND program, are severely stimulus-bound with respect to the particular representation they construct. For many problems—especially puzzle-like problems—finding the good representation is the nub of the problem. What is the human capability for solving problems, like the problem of the mutilated checkerboard, that are of this kind? Inventing a new representation or shifting from one problem representation to a more appropriate one are acts of human creativity that occur rather rarely, even with intelligent persons. A program with strong capabilities of this kind, if we could invent one, would probably not provide a good simulation of human capabilities or limitations.

Similar comments could be made with respect to the other dimensions of understanding we have discussed. The real test of whether the UNDER-STAND program has the right characteristics to simulate humans is to compare its behavior in different task environments with records of the behavior of human subjects. The program may equally well fail by showing too much understanding as by showing too little. We would be hard pressed, until we have carried our analysis much farther than we have to date, to say whether the subject whose protocol we discussed here was more skillful or less skillful than the UNDERSTAND program in understanding the text of the Tea Ceremony instructions.

Converting Knowledge to Action

The UNDERSTAND program has a number of important capabilities for translating knowledge into action. These capabilities exist at two levels. In the first place, the central objective of the program is to translate static knowledge, in the form of English language prose, into an input suitable to a general problem-solving program like GPS. We can view the problem-solving program itself as an interpreter and the input that defines a particular task domain and problem for it as a program to be interpreted. Thus, the translation process dynamicizes the knowledge contained in the static instructions—makes it interpretable.

The second way in which the UNDERSTAND program translates knowledge into action is by assimilating information in the task instructions that refers to task actions or moves (e.g., the transfer of a task from one participant to another in the Tea Ceremony). Stored in the program's long-term memory is information about how to execute certain quite general processes, like the TRANSFER process. Assimilating an action mentioned in the task instructions to such a general process stored in memory gives the UNDERSTAND program the ability actually to execute that action in the context of the problem representation.

Assimilation

The generality of the UNDERSTAND program's assimilative powers depends on the generality of its capabilities for processing the English language, and the repertoire of actions that is stored in its long-term memory. The actual program as it now stands is quite limited in these respects. We have limited its linguistic knowledge and its knowledge of actions pretty much to the specific needs of the Tea Ceremony task. But, in terms of our earlier distinction, the limits are mainly limits of education and not limits of educability.

The machinery of PAS-II makes it quite easy to supplement the syntactical and semantic rules with new or modified ones. To be sure, if we multiplied the amount of information about language now stored in PAS-II by 10 or 100, we would have to reorganize the memory storage somewhat, to avoid lengthy linear searches through it; but methods for searching efficiently through large memories, by providing them with appropriate accessing routes or "indexes" are now pretty well known, and this can hardly be regarded as a structural limitation on the system.

Similarly, while UNDERSTAND now possesses knowledge of only a few active processes (TRANSFER, LEAST, LESSA), there is no in-principle reason why this repertoire cannot be expanded. Moreover, examination of the *Transfer* process, and the matching procedure that underlies its application, suggests that the number of different processes that commonly arise in representing problem situations may not be large. The *Transfer* process as it now stands, for example, can be interpreted to handle all the kinds of processes that are defined as "moves" in common games.

Accommodation

The line between assimilation—taking in information from the external environment—and accommodation—adapting the internal system to the requirements of the external environment—is not easy to draw. If we think of constructing the problem space as assimilation, then the UNDERSTAND program does relatively little that can be interpreted as accommodation. It does not store the results of its understanding in long-term memory in such a way as to facilitate the solution of new problems that may be posed to it. The one process we have described that might be considered to be accommodation is the process for streamlining the *Transfer* process once it has been adapted to a particular problem representation.

Directionality

The UNDERSTAND program's strong sense of directionality derives from its single-purpose nature. It is designed to do just one kind of task: to translate problem instructions into a form that makes them suitable as inputs to a problem solver. It can do whatever the situation calls for, provided that this is what it does call for. This does not mean that the general principle underlying the UNDERSTAND program could not be used in programs with other goals. Indeed, the HEURISTIC COMPILER is an example of an earlier program that used the same idea to another end. The HEURISTIC COMPILER also derived its directionality from templates stored in long-term memory of the kind of object it was seeking to construct. In that case, the desired object was a computer program in a certain format.

Hence, we can say of directionality as we said of assimilation, that the underlying principle of the UNDERSTAND program is quite general, while its present implementation is quite limited and specific.

CONCLUSION

We have set ourselves the goal of describing the processes by which a person understands a set of written problem instructions. This paper reports the first phase of our work toward that goal. We have made progress in two directions. First, through protocol analysis, we have identified, at least tentatively, a network of functions involved in the subject's attempts to understand the problem text. Second, in the UNDERSTAND program, we have provided a set of well-specified processes that perform some of the identified functions. In specifying these processes, we have made some choices that have theoretical implications for psychology. For example, the structure of the transfer process and the nature of the language analysis both make strong assertions about the understanding process—assertions that can be checked against data.

The work reported here represents only a first step toward the goal of discovering exactly how people extract meaning from task instructions. We may list some of the tasks that remain to be carried out:

1. An important feature of our subject's behavior, the alternation between the text-reading and the problem-solving functions, must be simulated. In its present form, the UNDERSTAND program may be viewed as simulating the subject's behavior through his first reading of the text up to the point at which he first attempts to run his model of the problem. The simulation must now be carried forward to include processes by which the

subject's attempts to run the model, either through their success or their failure, provide new information to guide the text interpreting processes in returning again to the problem instructions.

2. We need to carry out protocol analyses formally and in detail, and we need to widen our data base. Data from other subjects and from a wider variety of problems (including variants of the instructions for the Tea Ceremony, as well as other isomorphs of the Tower of Hanoi problem) must be analyzed and compared in detail with simulation programs.

We are encouraged by our progress to date to believe that thinking-aloud protocols of naive subjects trying to interpret the instructions of a new task, combined with simulation programs embodying some of the processes we have incorporated in UNDERSTAND provide us with powerful tools for examining the processes of human understanding.

9
HOW CAN MERLIN UNDERSTAND?

JAMES MOORE and **ALLEN NEWELL**
Carnegie-Mellon University

This paper addresses the question: "How is it possible to understand?". The source of knowledge for what we have to say is a long-standing research effort to produce an understanding program called Merlin. That effort has been one primarily in artificial intelligence and thus this paper will also reflect primarily artificial intelligence concerns. Its appropriateness in a psychological context rests on a view that artificial intelligence is simply part of theoretical psychology (Newell, 1970). Enough evidence for this general view exists that it need not be labored here (e.g., Hunt, 1971; Newell & Simon, 1972).

Since Merlin has not been reported extensively we will start by providing some historical background. This will lead to posing the problem of understanding in a particular way, namely as a series of design issues that must be met by any understanding program. We will briefly illustrate these issues by means of current work in artificial intelligence. What little can be said about the issues from current data in psychology will become clear in passing. With these issues as background we will then discuss Merlin and the design decisions that characterize it (including those still open). We will summarize by attempting to answer how it is that we expect Merlin to understand.

SOME HISTORY OF MERLIN

Merlin was originally conceived (with the name CSA, standing for almost nothing) in 1967 out of an interest in building an assistance-program for a graduate course in artificial intelligence.[1] The task was to make it easy to construct and play with simple, laboratory-sized instances of artificial intelligence programs. Because of our direct interest in artificial intelligence,

This research was supported by the Advanced Research Projects Agency of the Office of the Secretary of Defense (F44620-70-C-0107), which is monitored by the Air Force Office of Scientific Research.

[1]The original group included Richard Young in addition to the present authors.

the effort transmuted into one of building a program that would understand artificial intelligence—that would be able to explain and run programs, ask and answer questions about them, and so on, at some reasonable level. The intent was to tackle a real domain of knowledge as the area for constructing a system that understood.

Artificial intelligence might appear to be too advanced a domain of knowledge. On the contrary, it has some properties that make it quite attractive. It involves discrete symbolic structures, thus avoiding the continuous three-dimensional world of time and forces. There is little highly developed theory in artificial intelligence, so that much of its knowledge is embedded in programs, which exemplify various important concepts and issues. Thus, "understanding artificial intelligence" can be replaced by "understanding artificial intelligence programs" with a consequent gain in specificity of the domain of knowledge. The entire project was cast as one of intelligent computer assisted instruction (CAI).

A memory structure was developed (of which much more later) and an extended attempt was made to explore the properties of this structure (Moore, 1971). The high point of that study was the representation of a version of LT (an early theorem proving program for the propositional calculus) in this generalized memory structure, such that the system (by then called Merlin 1) could put it all together and prove trivial theorems. The memory structure (which might be viewed in one way as a semantic net) was highly unstructured so that the problems addressed through these first years were basic ones of operating within such a generalized structure and were not at all ones of CAI. However, work was done at the same time on how to represent the programs of artificial intelligence in a way appropriate to being understood (Newell, 1969).

The goals of Merlin require progress on many of the central problems in artificial intelligence (though instantiated in a particular guise). We settled down to explore these as a basis for designing a full-bodied Merlin. We put together a Merlin 2, a Merlin 2.5 and currently are working on a Merlin 3. These are not to be looked at as complete programs for an understanding system, but as explorations of various facets of the design. Many of these facets will come out below in discussing one or another aspect of an understanding system.

Meanwhile (since 1967 was some time ago) other developments in artificial intelligence programs have occurred. Most notable from the standpoint of Merlin have been the planning languages, Planner (Hewitt, 1969, 1972) and QA4 (Rulifson, Derkson, & Waldinger, 1972), along with Winograd's (1970) program realized, in part, in Microplanner. Also important were the continued developments of semantic nets (e.g., Carbonell, 1970; Quillian, 1968, 1969) and related conceptual structures (Shank, 1972). We have needed to understand Merlin in relation to these developments and the underlying structure of this paper reflects that attempt.

THE NATURE OF UNDERSTANDING

Any attempt to analyze directly the nature of understanding must be seen as a preliminary and approximate venture. A general lesson of work in artificial intelligence is to lean heavily on the analysis of the structure of programs that accomplish specific tasks, and to treat less seriously general analyses of the nature of intellectual functions. Still a certain amount of framework is useful. Let us stipulate, then, that we wish to construct an understanding program. How shall we comprehend our task?

The Essence of Understanding

Let us attempt to state directly what we might mean in saying of Subject S that he (or it) understands. First, we take understanding to refer to knowledge, not to things directly. To say that S understands object or activity X is elliptical for saying that S understands knowledge *about* X. The shift leaves hanging the ambiguity of what knowledge is understood. Thus, to artificial intelligence is associated an imprecisely defined domain of knowledge and to understand artificial intelligence is to understand some, but not necessarily all, of that knowledge.

Second, we take the ultimate criterion of understanding of knowledge to lie in its use:

> S *understands knowledge* K *if* S *uses* K *whenever*   [1]
> *appropriate.*

This might seem vague, invoking terms such as "use" and "appropriate," which appear to be no way better defined than "understand" itself. In fact, most of the concepts in Statement 1 can be successfully explicated. The vagaries in applying the statement to specific cases lie in lack of empirical knowledge about the system under comment or in lack of analytical ability.

The basis for these assertions lies in the analysis of computer programs and their behavior. The knowledge that a program has is defined in terms of an agreed-upon encoding. This can be done successfully even when the encoding is in the structure of the program, rather than the content of particular data expressions in a memory. Whether a program has or has not a certain bit of knowledge on a particular occasion can be settled directly by an examination of its code and data structures. A program uses knowledge in the production of some external behavior when the representation of that knowledge forms part of the processing sequence for producing the behavior. The complexities of programs—their size, conditionality, self-modifiability, and capability for irrelevant processing—all complicate the analysis, but do not change its character.

The notion of appropriate can also be given precise statement. We posit of certain information processing systems that they have goals. This may be an externally imposed stipulation, though it can be grounded in the agreed-upon interpretation of the system's internal structure (that certain data structures operate as goals). Whether behavior is appropriate is determined by whether it serves to obtain the goal (or goals). This determination requires an analysis of the task environment and, from it, an objective determination of the courses of action that could possibly serve to obtain the goals. Given the objective analysis, it can be further determined whether the specified knowledge could have been used to produce one of these behavior sequences. A complication in the analysis is that generally no single item of knowledge is sufficient to produce goal-obtaining behavior. Thus the appropriate use of an item of knowledge is always against the background of a larger collection of knowledge that is sufficient to produce the total behavior. This implies a competence model of the system, which characterizes capacities solely in terms of total knowledge. The entire analysis is complex, with distinct possibilities for error. But there does not seem to be conceptual difficulties with it.

As noted, the claims that all these characterizations and analyses can be carried out rests in part on the everyday practice in computer science and artificial intelligence in analysing computer programs. It receives strong confirmation in the intensive and successful work over the last five years in program verification (see London, 1972). The task of formally verifying that a program accomplishes a given process or possesses specified properties (e.g., it will terminate) requires formalization of most of the above scheme. These techniques have grown up in a situation where the internal structure (both data and program) of the information processing system is completely known. When we turn to the analysis of human behavior, we are in the position of conjecturing the internal structure. As such, additional sources of error open up—in the inputation of goals, of knowledge, etc. But these complications do not affect the basic adequacy of this concept of understanding.

The above account takes understanding as a step-function: the system either understands or it does not; if it does then it always uses the knowledge when appropriate. Clearly we need to augment Statement 1 with another:

> *Understanding can be partial, both in extent (the class of*   [2]
> *appropriate situations in which the knowledge is used)*
> *and in immediacy (the time it takes before such under-*
> *standing can be exhibited).*

The two qualifications are directly related: the more time we allow, the more understanding the system may be able to demonstrate, given that it has the knowledge. However, the relationship is not simple and in artificial systems especially, knowledge is likely to be bound into structure in ways that make it available only in limited situations, independent of the amount of processing allowed.

The above analysis seems to us essentially correct—that one need not seek further for an explication for the intellectual function of understanding. By itself, however, it does not help much in developing an understanding program such as Merlin. Part of the difficulty is in the lack of any good notion of extent. To this matter we now turn.

The Extent of Understanding

If the study of understanding is approached in the same way as the study of other intellectual functions in artificial intelligence, a task environment is sought such that performance in the tasks of the environment indicates that the program understands. Thus, we generate chess playing programs, integration programs, particular puzzle solvers, etc. For understanding, this strategy does not quite work. The issue is the requirement for diversity of task. To understand is to be able to reveal that understanding in use in the context of any task, providing that other requisite understanding is available. Diversity of task, not sheer numerosity, is clearly the important consideration.

To our knowledge there exists currently no satisfactory approach to a taxonomy of tasks by which to assess diversity. The ultimate source of difficulty in obtaining such a taxonomy undoubtedly comes from the requirement that it reflect the structure of the problem solvers who are to perform the tasks. There is no trace at the moment of such a theoretically-based taxonomy. There are, however, two distinct approaches that should be mentioned, one based on natural language, the other based on the use of function terms.

It is no accident that much work in artificial intelligence on understanding systems is simultaneously an effort in natural language understanding (from Raphael, 1968 to Quillian, 1969, to Winograd, 1971). To trade on a metaphor: Take care of the language and the problems will take care of themselves. Put another way, natural language encompasses an immense and immensely diverse space of problems, though one that is unknown and uncharacterized in any independent way. Therefore, a problem solver that understood natural language would seem to be capable of being posed problems of sufficient diversity for assessing understanding just by means of language, without prior analysis or commitment to a task environment. Some of the surface appeal of programs such as SIR (Raphael, 1968) is exactly this: you speak various facts to it of your own choosing, thus creating your own microworld, and then pose problems within that world.

There are difficulties with this view, of course. Understanding of task domains may be a precondition for understanding linguistic utterances about them—simply reversing the aphorism above. Large classes of problems cannot be posed via language, e.g., those involving direct interaction with the environment. Linguistic analogues of physical problems (to give them an imperfect name) already commit to encodings of the environment, which may constitute an essential component of the problem. Nevertheless, the use of natural language provides one approach to describing task diversity, though it does so by finessing much of the problem.

The second approach is to obtain a set of function terms that appear to span all tasks. By a function term we mean a highly abstract term, usually a verb, that contains a means-ends notion. "Support" is a good function term, so is "Comprehend," though the means-end orientation is somewhat more subtle. No good theory of function terms exists, which describes how they describe human intellectual activity or how they might perform similarly in artificial systems (however, see Freeman & Newell, 1971, for some discussion). But collections of function terms seem capable of spanning entire spaces of possibilities without providing an operational definition of the space.

A good example of a functional taxonomy can be found in the work in the early fifties of a Committee of College and University Examiners to put together a taxonomy of educational objectives (Bloom, 1956).[2] Fig. 9.1 gives the taxonomy in outline, though without the supporting definitions and documentation developed by the Committee. The taxonomy, though developed intuitively, was tested both on many existing statements of educational objectives and (more important) on its ability to classify large numbers of test items from existing tests of mental abilities.

The claim of such a taxonomy is that it comprehends all mental activities or skills without positing an underlying structural space in which these can be rigorously defined. Function terms, such as "analysis" and "comprehension," cover an indefinite set of situations. The very strength of such functional decompositions (to cover without being precise) also constitutes their main disadvantage from our current view (namely, to understand what it is to understand). For there is nothing in the taxonomy that helps discern the attributes of an understanding system. For instance, one hardly wishes to create an understanding system that has components corresponding to the separate domains of the taxonomy—that is, an analysis faculty, a synthesis faculty, an evaluative faculty, etc. It can conceivably be used evaluatively to organize the assessment of the diversity of the task domains of a given understanding system. But in its present state of development it does not seem capable of doing much more.

The rather unsatisfactory state of describing spaces of diverse tasks makes unattractive the principal methodological strategy of initially specifying the task domain and then programming to meet the demands of that domain. We turn then to an alternative strategy.

---

[2]We are grateful to Stuart Card for pointing out the relevance of this work to us; he is making a much more thorough investigation of the use of such a taxonomy in the study of understanding systems.

1.00 KNOWLEDGE
    1.10 Knowledge of specifics
        1.11 Knowledge of terminology
        1.12 Knowledge of specific facts
    1.20 Knowledge of ways and means of dealing with specifics
        1.21 Knowledge of conventions
        1.22 Knowledge of trends and sequences
        1.23 Knowledge of classifications and categories
        1.24 Knowledge of criteria
        1.25 Knowledge of methodology
    1.30 Knowledge of universals and abstractions in a field
        1.31 Knowledge of principles and generalizations
        1.32 Knowledge of theories and structures

2.00 COMPREHENSION
    2.10 Translation
    2.20 Interpretation
    2.30 Extrapolation

3.00 APPLICATION

4.00 ANALYSIS
    4.10 Analysis of elements
    4.20 Analysis of relationships
    4.30 Analysis of organizational principles

5.00 SYNTHESIS
    5.10 Production of unique communication
    5.20 Production of a plan, or proposed set of operations
    5.30 Derivation of a set of abstract relations

6.00 EVALUATION
    6.10 Judgments in terms of internal evidence
    6.20 Judgments in terms of external criteria

FIG. 9.1. Taxonomy of intellectual functions.

Design Issues

One way to reveal the nature of understanding systems is to ask what design decisions they incorporate with respect to a set of key issues. What are these issues? Like the taxonomy of Fig. 9.1 they will be intuitively defined and will in general be described in functional terms. Unlike the taxonomy, the functions will correspond to a view of how an understanding system must be structured and what mechanisms are required to solve the problems an understanding system must face. They can reflect both difficulties and opportunities that arise from pervasive features of task environments or from the nature of information processing as we currently understand it. Another way to look at such a list is to ask what one wants to know when confronted with a new understanding system, so as to assess its distinctive contributions.

Fig. 9.2 presents the list of design issues. They fall under eight main heads. Within some of these there are listed a series of subissues. These issues are not meant to be exhaustive, but rather those that have some bearing on the particular questions to be raised in this paper.

Let us run briefly over the list in the abstract, though it is partly self-explanatory. All information processing systems have knowledge by virtue of an international REPRESENTATION. There may be more than one such representation; indeed most systems split their knowledge between a data representation and a program representation. Thus the first thing to know about an understanding system is the set of representations it uses.

Several issues arise about representations. The first is that of *scope:* what knowledge can be represented, what cannot. The general question here is easily settled, for with only a few constructs, a sort of conceptual completeness is obtained. These constructs are those of the first-order predicate calculus: propositions formed from predicates by conjunction, disjunction and negation, with the predicates themselves dependent on variables ranging over a given domain of discourse and subject to universal and existential quantification. With this much, realized in any of many forms, all of mathematics and physical science is formalizable, and by extension most anything else one can become definite about. This claim is of necessity informal and really amounts to showing that apparently more expressive mathematical systems (especially set theory) can be formulated within first-order calculus. It need not detain us, except to note that questions of the completeness of expressive power do not in general discriminate among current understanding systems (though a few early ones were highly limited).[3]

The second issue is that of *grain.* One way of viewing a problem solver is that he has a developing state of knowledge about his problem: each action that he takes generates some more partial knowledge. To be able to add this partial knowledge to his current total state requires a representation that can encode it. If the stock of concepts is not adequate, the problem solver is forced to approximate the knowledge in some way. The net effect of this

---

[3] An important special issue is the extent to which the system can represent its own strategies of action to permit processing other than evocation. We will not be able to deal with this here.

REPRESENTATION: What internal representations of knowledge are used?
  Scope Issue: What knowledge can be represented?

  Grain Issue: What sorts of partial knowledge can be represented?

  Multiple Representations Issue: How does the system capitalize on the fact that ease of knowledge use is a strong function of how it is represented?

ACTION: How does system convert knowledge into behavior?

ASSIMILATION: How does the internal structure of the system make contact with the external task environment?

ACCOMMODATION: How does external structure become converted into new internal structure?

DIRECTIONALITY: How does the system use its knowledge appropriately for the task?
  Keep-progressing Issue: What do you do when you don't know what to do?

EFFICIENCY:
  Interpreter Issue: Inserting interpreters degrades performance multiplicatively.

  Immediacy Issue: Certain general methods (mostly involving search) are precluded as the requirement for immediate response increases.

  Formality Issue: Formalism introduces inefficiency by forcing uniformity of processing.

ERROR: How does the system cope with the ubiquituous existence of error?
  Frame problem: When the world changes, once-true encoded knowledge becomes false.

DEPTH OF UNDERSTANDING: How is knowledge brought to bear whenever it is appropriate?
  Access Issue: Does the system have access to all implications of the knowledge cast in the representation?

FIG. 9.2. List of design issues.

approximation is inevitably to introduce the possibility of error, which shows up in many problem solvers as search, with its resultant combinatorial explosion.

An example will help. In a cryptarithmetic puzzle (Newell & Simon, 1972) the problem solver must ultimately assign digits to variables (e.g., R will be 0, 1, ... 9). If at a certain point the problem solver infers that R must be odd, then if he has the concept of odd he can augment his knowledge state appropriately. However, if all he has is the ability to represent the integers, then he must overcommit, so to speak, and indicate that R is 1 or 3 ... . Even if he has the concept of disjunction, so he can remember that R is 1v3v5v7v9 this may not avoid the consequences, if his only way of dealing with assignments is in terms of digits (i.e., he does not have the equivalent of odd + odd = even). The combinatorial explosion arises because enumeration of the alternatives in partial knowledge is the general way to deal with being unable to represent (and manipulate) a partial state directly.

The final representation issue is that of *multiple representation*. This rests on the common observation that how a problem is represented is often a major aspect of solving it. Thus finding an appropriate representation for a problem should be an important activity. Unfortunately, the current art is not up to handling multiple representations within the same system. Thus, the import of this issue is whether a proposed understanding system has any devices for capitalizing on multiple representations.

The second main design dimension, ACTION, concerns the fundamental problem of how a system derives behavior from the knowledge that is encoded statically in its structure. A range of options are available, from the application of inference rules, to the use of language interpreters (note that a program is as much a static representation of knowledge as a data base). Behavior, refers not only to ultimate external behavior, but also to internal behavior used mediately in generating final behavior.

The third dimension, ASSIMILATION, reflects another fundamental problem for any understanding system. At a given point in time all that the system knows is encoded somehow in its internal structure. An encounter with a task in its environment brings the system into contact with another body of structure. How are the two to make contact? If the external environment were of only small variety with respect to the total amount of structure in the system, one might imagine that the system could be prepared to recognize any particular environmental structure it was encountering. But the reverse is generally true: the amount of structure in the system is small compared to the amount of structure in the environment and is in no way capable of encoding it all, no matter how indirectly. Thus, a primary issue for the system is how it maps the external task into its internal structure.

We call this the assimilation issue, taking the term not only from its everyday use, but also because it corresponds well with the Piagetian use of the term, wherein a child assimilates aspects of its environment to the child's internal schemas (e.g., Piaget & Inhelder, 1969).

The status of assimilation mechanisms is rather peculiar in artificial intelligence. Every system must contain some mechanisms for assimilation in order to work on a population of tasks. Yet often the solution is to code within highly restrictive agreements between the structure of the task environment and the expectations of the internal program, thus not facing any assimilation issues (for an example see GPS, Ernst & Newell, 1969). On the other hand, the task of natural language input, which has received much attention, may be viewed comfortably as an assimilation issue. Similarly, the subfields of vision and speech are devoted to assimilation. Thus, one would think we know a lot about it. But the poverty of mechanisms that deal with analogy and metaphor, or that formulate problems in an environment so they can be tackled by an existing general method (such as the simplex method of linear programming), attest to the primitive state on assimilation.

The category of assimilation leads naturally to ACCOMMODATION, which is the modification of the internal structure of the system to be able to cope with a wider range of tasks. The term is again Piagetian (Piaget & Inhelder, 1969). Both assimilation and accommodation involve a change of internal structure—indeed a system requires internal structure change (i.e., memory) to behave in other than simple ways. But assimilation involves a transient modification that leaves the system with essentially the same bases for further assimilations, whereas accommodation is the general term for the acquisition of new assimilative capabilities. Though the distinction between the two cannot be made sharply in phenomenal or behavioral terms, it is usually extraordinarily clear when the structure of a system is made explicit.

DIRECTIONALITY refers to the problem of how a system organizes itself to do a particular task posed by the environment. A wide range of mechanisms are possible. There can be a single method which is automatically evoked—indeed, which simply constitutes the structure of the program. Alternatively, there can be a collection of methods, which then requires some selective procedure. There can be an apparatus of goals with an explicit goal tree, or the directionality can be distributed in the structure of the program as a series of local decision processes. The system can rely on the recognition of progress after it has already been made, or it can do much processing so as never to try inappropriate courses of action.

A particular subissue is that most methods have only a limited chance of solving a task. Many systems simply give up once they have tried these methods and they have failed. We call the *Keep-progressing issue* the question of whether a system has an indefinite capability for continuing to work on a problem in a relevant way.

EFFICIENCY would seem to be almost self-explanatory. However, as we use the term it needs to be distinguished from directionality. In heuristic search paradigms a central problem is to control the combinatorial explosion. The heuristic devices that do this—by providing effective ways to direct the search—are part of directionality. But beyond such problems are also ones of computational efficiency, especially for high frequency basic processing tasks.

A clear example of efficiency arises with the use of interpreters. As is well known, the use of an interpretive language entails a cost of anywhere from a factor of two to ten over a compiled version of the same language. Analogous degradations occur in large systems when they are constructed with interpreter-like levels. What is purchased for this cost is flexibility and control. In practice the interpretive level can itself be handled interpretively, thus compounding the problem (but presumably also the gain). The

Interpreter issue, then, is whether a system has availed itself of these gains and if so, what design features does it have for controlling the costs.

A second pervasive efficiency issue arises from the constraint of *immediacy*—that the system is forced to exhibit its understanding within a limited time. More generally, we usually assess understanding to be the more complete, the faster it is exhibited. The efficiency issue here shows itself not only in how quickly basic processes can be performed, but in whether the methods used stand a chance within the time limits available. In general, search must be avoided, except in judicious amounts.

A final efficiency issue has been labeled that of *formality*. In fact its point is somewhat speculative. The use of formalisms implies the adoption of fixed conventions for representation and processing, which provide guarantees of various sorts (that computations can always be carried out, that certain algorithms can be proved to give the correct results, etc.). Formalisms tend to the adoption of uniform procedures, which is to say, procedures that are applied unadaptively. Thus the introduction of formalism would seem to be a pervasive source of inefficiency in systems, leading to excessive processing over large domains for which the formalism yields large, complex expressions. There would appear to be a close relationship between this concern and that of multiple representation.

ERROR is ubiquitous. Starting with assimilation, which already implies an approximate relationship between the internal structure of the system and the task environment, errors are possible at every turn in a system. They arise from the methods themselves being only heuristic, from underlying unreliability of processes (which, however, can be brought to very low levels in digital systems), to the fact that knowledge is missing on which to base solution so guesses must be made. Thus, all systems must have mechanisms to deal with error—to detect it, to contain its effects, to correct it.

A special case of the error problem has come to be known as the *frame problem* (Raphael, 1970). In a modifiable environment, knowledge of the environment is not invariant under changes in the environment. This generates error, since once-true data is now false. Its name derives from the notion of a changing frame of reference.

Much of the notion of DEPTH OF UNDERSTANDING seems to be captured in being able to utilize knowledge whenever it is appropriate to do so. The question of task diversity discussed earlier responds to this issue: how to pose a wide enough variety of occasions of use to assess how deep is the understanding of some knowledge. The metaphorical adjective of depth (rather than say breadth) is perhaps a little misleading. Whether knowledge is appropriate and in what way, can vary in obscurity; thus deep understanding implies the ability to use the knowledge in nonobvious contexts. This connotation seems appropriate. But depth is also used when referring to the total knowledge of a topic (as in knowledge of quantum mechanics). Here it refers to the amount and completeness of such knowledge and the ability to answer successive "why" and "how" questions. This connotation is not appropriate, since we have not dealt with understanding of areas or events.

In systems with narrow task domains, knowledge can be organized so as readily to be brought to bear on the task. However, as the diversity of tasks increases, there is no way to pre-organize the system so that the knowledge relevant to each task is already localized—the subsets of knowledge demanded cross-cut each other in too many ways. Thus there arises the issue of *access* to the knowledge in a system, implying by this mostly the discovery of appropriate knowledge, rather than physical access. However, the two are related, since how information is represented has much to do with its access, especially when inferential processes are viewed as an access method (as when the access to $7 > 5$ is made via stored knowledge of $7 > 6$ and $6 > 5$).

Having run through the list of Fig. 9.2, we reiterate its function. It is a list of *design issues*—of the key questions to be asked of any proposed understanding system as to how it works and what expectations might be generated about its viability. The list being functional cannot claim to be a unique decomposition, nor can it claim to be complete. It does cover the main issues we wish to raise in our understanding of understanding systems. It serves to perceive the existing state of such systems in artificial intelligence and to view Merlin as a potential contribution to that evolution.

SOME EXAMPLES

Let us put some flesh on this list of design issues by looking briefly at some existing understanding systems.

Predicate Calculus Theorem Provers

A useful start is the predicate calculus theorem provers—they have simple structure and for many people they seem to be at the opposite pole from systems that understand. Fig. 9.3 shows the layout of a prototypical resolution-style theorem prover. Fig. 9.4 provides an outline description in terms of the design issues.[4]

The representation of knowledge in a Resolution Theorem Prover (RTP) is in terms of propositions, called clauses. Each clause is a disjunction of a set of predicates or negations of predicates, the predicates themselves being functions of variables over a domain of discourse. The entire knowledge in the system is encoded as a set of such clauses (taken to be the conjunction of the propositions), with the exception of the fixed structure (shown to the right in Fig. 9.3) that processes the clauses in a task-independent way.

---

[4]For a straightforward account of resolution theorem provers in their own terms see Nilsson (1971).

Resolution is a formulation of the first-order predicate calculus and thus has the same representational scope. What can actually be represented depends on the particular predicates, but these are defined entirely within the system (by axiomatization in terms of the clauses in which they participate). On the other hand, a serious limitation is that the discourse refers to an external domain and does not permit representation of the strategies of processing or of the current state of the computation.

The representation also has some grain problems. An example shows up in the handling of equality. It can be axiomatized by three clauses corresponding to $[X = X]$, $[$if $X = Y$ then $Y = X]$, and $[$if $X = Y$ and $Y = Z$ then $X = Z]$. However to effect the replacement of equals with equals, a separate clause is required for each variable position of each predicate, e.g., for $P(X,Y)$ one must add two clauses: $[P(X,Y)$ and $X = Z$ implies $P(Z,Y)]$ and $[P(X,Y)$ and $Y = Z$ implies $P(X,Z)]$. These extra clauses increase the combinatorial explosion, since they increase the size of the set of clauses.

A strong feature of resolution theorem provers is their uniform representation for all knowledge. Thus they opt to ignore the benefits of multiple representations. However, the matter is not so simple, for options still exist for how to encode a given task. The freedom lies in choice of predicates. For example, in representing a set of objects in space, one can choose a distance predicate $D(X,Y)$ between objects or one can choose a pair of coordinate predicates, $V(X)$ and $H(X)$. As we know from analytic geometry, the same problem may look very different in the two cases. However, little choice exists for the style that axiomatization takes. In particular we cannot actually adopt a coordinate system and calculate directly within it. Neither can we develop new representations or shift from one to another, since the set of predicates is fixed. (It would be possible to work with several representations simultaneously, though it has never been tried as far as we know.)

The action in resolution comes about through the application of a single rule of inference (called the Resolution Principle) plus the application of a strategy. The rule takes as input two clauses and produces a collection of new clauses (the resolvants) that can be added to the total pool (see Fig. 9.3). The strategy determines which pair of clauses shall be considered next. Essentially all of the research in predicate calculus theorem provers has gone into the discovery of strategies and the establishment of their properties (including therein new rules of inference, which are ways of packaging selection rules). The great virtue of this arrangement is that all of the knowledge in the system (the clauses) can be processed in a uniform way to yield whatever new knowledge the system is capable of.

Assimilation and accommodation can be considered jointly, since an RTP makes no distinction between them. A new task is presented to the system by expressing it as a set of clauses (logically, the negation of the assertion of what is to be found or proved). Once added, these are indistinguishable from any other clauses in the system. Likewise since all

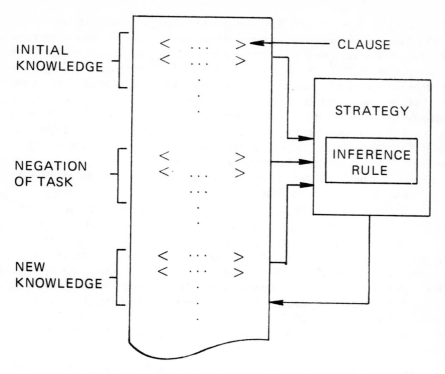

FIG. 9.3. Diagram of stylized resolution theorem prover.

REPRESENTATION   CLAUSES
   SCOPE   COMPLETE (ONLY 1st ORDER)
   GRAIN   IGNORE (e.g., EQUALITY)
   MULTIPLE REPRESENTATION IGNORE
ACTION   INFERENCE, EXTRACTION
ASSIMILATION   ADD CLAUSES, IGNORE ENCODING
ACCOMMODATION   (= ASSIMILATION)
DIRECTIONALITY   TEST FOR DONE, STRATEGY
   KEEP-PROGRESSING   UNTIL FAIL/SUCCEED
EFFICIENCY   IGNORE
   IMMEDIACY   IGNORE
   FORMALITY   ACCEPT
ERROR   NO ERRORS
   FRAME PROBLEM   NO CHANGES IN MODEL
DEPTH   COMPLETENESS
   ACCESS   STRATEGY, LINEAR SCAN

FIG. 9.4. Design characterization of resolution theorem provers.

knowledge is clauses, new knowledge (essentially accommodation) is acquired just by adding clauses to the system, either by an external source, or by permanent retention of clauses generated by the system itself. Thus assimilation and accommodation are both trivial operations (though the determination of what to assimilate or accommodate is not). One would expect, and indeed it is true, that a price is paid for this: The total knowledge structure is an unorganized mass. There are, of course, a number of theorem provers that have deviated from this homogeneous set of clauses. Insofar as they do have assimilation and accommodation, they require processing in order to integrate the new material into whatever organization has been set up. But the basic system, as described, occupies an extreme point with respect to these two design functions.

The above picture of assimilation is incomplete. An RTP is a totally internal system, with no provisions for acquiring problems in the external world and creating the internal representation as a set of clauses. It does not respond to this basic aspect of assimilation at all. In practice, of course, various solutions to this problem have been adopted, ranging from simple interfaces in mathematial notation, to English language interfaces (Coles, 1969), to interfaces that connect the RPT to an external physical environment for a robot (Nilsson, 1969). All of these represent essentially external solutions, so that the system itself cannot be said to face the task of assimilation.

Directionality is achieved in an RPT by a recognition that the answer has been found. The occurrence of a null clause signifies a contradiction (the occurrence of a clause C and another clause $\sim$C) and the system remains continually sensitive for the production of such a clause. This is as minimal a scheme of direction as is possible, for in the basic system no shaping of the generation of new clauses occurs.

Again, some strategies do involve giving preferred status to resolutions that might lead toward the null clause (e.g., the Unit Preference rule) or to these using the clauses corresponding to the task (e.g., the Set of Support strategy). These convey a simple sort of directionality to the system, though they do not amount to a full scale goal system (e.g., that could set up subgoals).

In terms of special mechanisms, efficiency issues are ignored in RTPs, though of course many are coded in machine language to be as fast as possible. With the simplicity of the basic processing scheme, almost all efficiency issues translate into strategic issues of selection of appropriate clauses, which is to say, directionality. The system, of course, is the essence of a formalism. In fact all versions spend most of their time calculating according to the dictates of a particular uniform strategy, and spend essentially no time considering either what to do or whether there are short cuts.

RTPs also ignore the problem of error. They assume the representation as given, and that all acts of inference are valid and that none are preferred to others because of reliability of the premises or whatever.

With respect to depth, however, the situation is different: the nature of the formalism guarantees that if there is a solution to the task within the knowledge that the system holds, then it will be found in due course. This is the essential content of the completeness theorems for the first-order calculus (extended to cover the various selections introduced by the strategies). In terms of our present formulation, we must agree that an RPT understands its knowledge, since in fact it will use it whenever appropriate. Thus, RTPs receive something in return for the various uniformities that underlie them. Of course, this depth of understanding is guaranteed only if time bounds are ignored and in general the RTPs do not respond at all to the issue of immediacy.

This completes our general view of theorem provers according to the general design issues of Fig. 9.2. It suppresses most of the detail of the strategies (wherein much of the research has resided), but reveals a number of gross features that dictate the sort of problems one will have in taking an RTP as an understanding system (as has been done in some of the work in robotics).

We can now introduce a theme that will be reiterated later. It seems to us that an understanding system must come to grips with the entire set of design issues. Thus, one of the functions of the list of Fig. 9.2 is to make it apparent when a particular system is to be taken as only a partial proposal for an understanding system.

Planner-like Systems

An important development in the last few years is a collection of language systems called Planner-like systems after Hewitt's Planner (1972). Another one is QA4 (Rulifson, Derkson, & Waldinger, 1972), and their features are migrating into many additional systems. Although they are languages, they incorporate a set of mechanisms that respond rather directly to the issues in our design list and any system erected within them adopts these solutions. They provide an appropriate contrast point to the RTPs just discussed and indeed some of their features were provoked by the system Zeitgeist provided by the work in theorem proving.

Fig. 9.5 shows the design specifications for Planner-like systems.[5] The representations in Planner-like systems move away from a highly particular structure (i.e., the clause, with a single semantic interpretation) to general data structures. However, they do not go so far as the list languages (such as

---

[5]We will operate from a composite of Planner and QA4, and ignore features of other systems, even where they augment these two.

REPRESENTATION	(LIST, BAG, SET, ARRAY)
SCOPE	UNRESTRICTED QUANTIFICATION
GRAIN	NO POSITION (BASE LANGUAGE)
MULTIPLE REPRESENTATION	PATTERN MATCH
ACTION	PROGRAMS (= LISTS)
ASSIMILATION	PATTERN MATCH
ACCOMMODATION	WRITE PROGRAMS
DIRECTIONALITY	GOALS + WEAK METHOD
KEEP-PROGRESSING	NO POSITION
EFFICIENCY	EQUIVALENCE
INTERPRETER	COMPILE IN BASE LANGUAGE
IMMEDIACY	NO POSITION
FORMALITY	ACCEPT BUT RICH
ERROR	BACKTRACK (+ MULTIPROCESS)
FRAME PROBLEM	UPDATE DATA BASE
DEPTH	
ACCESS	GLOBAL DATA BASE (PATTERN)

Fig. 9.5. Design characterization of Planner-like systems.

LISP) which adopt a single homogeneous data structure. Rather, in an effort to buy both ease of representation and efficiency, they provide a small set of basic data structures. Thus, QA4 provides lists, bags and sets (collections of symbols that are respectively: ordered with repetition of items, unordered with repetition, and unordered without repetition). Planner admits lists, strings and arrays, but not bags or sets. Thus, all structures are still to be composed out of some basic structures, but a small variety is admitted. In this respect they do not come fully to grips with the multiple-representation issue, though there is still the freedom to represent a problem within these basic structures in any way that is desired. Furthermore, as we will discuss below, a strong pattern match capability is an integral part of these systems. This makes the encoding of representations easier, though there are yet no striking examples that show it.

Planner-like systems are not inference systems built around a proof procedure. Rather they are language systems. Consequently the constraints that keep RTPs limited to first order do not apply, namely, technical difficulties in developing matching (unification) for higher order logic (but see Huet, 1973). These systems then permit quantification over anything, i.e., over predicates and processes, and in general provide an omega-ordered predicate calculus (without thereby providing any validity-based proof procedures). Furthermore, in common with other list processing languages (of which they may be considered an extension) they permit self-reference to the programs and evolving data structures.

The Planner-like languages have no special proposals to make about grain and their position on this score is fundamentally that of the underlying list processing systems.

A basic tenet of these systems is that knowledge should be stored in the form of programs rather than in the form of propositions (the phrase used has been "procedural embedding of knowledge"). The position taken on action is to encode knowledge in a form that can be converted directly by an interpreter (of about the complexity of a list language interpreter). Consistent (again) with the embedding in an underlying list processing environment, programs are represented in lists, hence do not introduce a separate data structure.

A second basic aspect to the action is the concept of evoking the next procedure by means of a pattern match. The effect is to produce a form of generalized inference, in which structure X matches program $[X \to P]$ thus evoking (i.e., detaching) P. P itself may present a pattern Y which might match the program $[Y \to Q]$, thus evoking procedure Q. Hence, chains of inferences (either forward or backward) can occur, intermixed with other processing. Since the processing of propositional representations is almost entirely governed by substitution and detachment in various guises,[6] there is no need to distinguish clearly between propositional and procedural forms.

We have now mentioned the pattern matching capability twice, once with respect to multiple representations and again with respect to the mechanization of an inference capability embedded within procedures. Pattern matching arises yet again with respect to assimilation. It is a step in the right direction. The pattern represents structure in the system that is tied to the knowledge about what to do (i.e., Pattern $\to$ Procedure). When a pattern successfully matches the external task structure, then that external structure is assimilated. Not only is the action evoked, but the variable parts of the external structure have been bound to the variables in the pattern (as when the pattern $[X + Y]$ matches the expression $[2 + 3]$ with the binding of X to 2 and Y to 3), thus, becoming external structure that the system can deal with because the system has imposed an interpretation on it, namely, that it fits the pattern.

Thus, to us, the Planner-like languages propose a specific mechanism for assimilation. All the Planner-like systems have very powerful match facilities, meaning by this that the class of patterns they admit is relatively large and complex. However, the pattern match is still a syntactic device in which the mappings that are admitted are those attainable with substitution operators.[7]

---

[6]Indeed it is unclear whether there is any other kind of processing of symbolic structures except substitution and detachment, except for the processes that govern their evocation, storage and transmission (i.e., PMS level processes, Bell & Newell, 1971).

[7]There have been matches that do somewhat more than this. SCHATCHEN, the match in Moses' SIN (1967) matched relative to the commutative law and implicit factors $(X \leftrightarrow 1 * X, X \leftrightarrow 0 + X)$, though as we shall see below this is approached in another way by QA4. GPS (Ernst & Newell, 1969) has a generalized set of so-called immediate operators in its match routine that are difference driven. Thus, GPS would match $A \lor B$ to $\sim A \supset B$. The

The added complexity that arises in a pattern-directed, procedurally oriented system implies an issue of accommodation. Unlike the RTPs, which can add new structure simply by storing clauses in the data base, in Planner-like systems new capabilities imply new programs. The position taken by these systems is that they should engage in the construction of new programs. Some progress has been made on this though it cannot be said that the language systems themselves really provide other than an orientation.

Another major proposal of the Planner-like systems is the incorporation of a goal scheme as part of the basic language system, to provide direction. Thus, these are the first operational goal-oriented programming languages. There is an explicit goal structure that admits a pattern as the defining criterion of the desired object. In addition there is a generalized weak method.[8] This takes the schematic form:

Is there a data structure that matches G?
    If so, quit with goal satisfied.
Is there a program of form [G → P]
    If so, execute it.
    If not, fail.

The procedural expression [G → P] is to be read "If you wish to obtain G, then execute procedure P." P may be any procedure at all, including one that sets other goals. Thus via this generalized method one can evoke more specialized methods, including direct computational algorithms for obtaining the goal.

The Planner-like systems have not been strongly responsive to efficiency issues (except in one important particular, described under depth of understanding). However, one exception in QA4 also makes clear the nature of efficiency issues that do not come under directionality. Often one is dealing with classes of representations that are equivalent under common sets of operations. Naming (especially with bound variables) is one example, so are commutativity and associativity. The establishment of such equivalence often occupies a major amount of processing.[9] Thus, in QA4 expressions are kept in canonical form relative to the known properties of the operations involved. Much effort has been devoted in the system to making this canonicalization efficient.

---

substitution operations were realized by means of these immediate operators. This scheme was also used for commutative and associative matching. See the generalized description of matching in Newell (1969).

[8]See Newell (1969) for the concept of a weak method.

[9]Those familiar with RTPs will note the amount of time spent in dealing with the axioms of associativity, which are complex. They introduce much of the thrashing that goes on in proving simple theorems in group theory.

The Planner-like systems also make a major proposal with respect to error: They incorporate backtracking as a basic control feature in the language. At user-specified places in a program (and automatically at certain places) the system prepares itself for a return in case of failure. It is prepared to undo all of the modifications made in the program after the backtrack point so as to reestablish the control and data context. Some such facility is required to make the language goal-oriented, since almost all problem solving methods introduce an appreciable element of search and with it the necessity to recover from unsuccessful attempts. Thus, the systems have at the language level the ability to do heuristic searches with essentially no further programming.

Backtracking, which is depth-first search, is well known to have serious drawbacks. In fact, the systems provide more complex control (e.g., multiprocessing) to help alleviate these difficulties. However, this aspect, which is the one that originally made these systems well known, has already caused the first major cycle of revision (Sussman & McDermott, 1972). Backtracking, though a general strategy for dealing with error and while a required capability, is simply too crude a tool and leads too easily to combinatorial explosion.

The final design issue is that of depth of understanding. Here again, Planner-like systems have proposed a mechanism, at least for the issue of access. Both Planner and QA4 have global data bases. All of the knowledge for a problem is put into this data base. Access is by pattern matching. (For example, the matches for goal capability are taken with respect to the global data base.) The net effect of introducing such a memory system is that the usual design considerations of many specialized memories, with access privately known only to particular procedures, are set aside. All data in the system become available to all processes and will be accessed if they match the patterns presented by a process as representing their respective needs.

A global data base poses a technical problem. Unless access to the base is essentially independent of total size, the system cannot afford to use it. For example, the RTPs achieve total access by two means: (a) using only strategies that are complete (that guarantee that no other clauses except those they will eventually select are necessary to solve the problem) and (b) serially scanning the set of clauses (i.e., the total data base). This latter is a genuine barrier to large data bases. Thus, in the Planner-like system much attention has been given to the sophisticated indexing schemes that achieve the result of essential independence of the access time from the size of the total data base.

We have come to the end of our description of Planner-like systems in terms of our list of design issues. In several ways our description cuts across those usually given. The matching facility is normally described as a structural entity, whereas we have introduced it in the several places where it appeared to be the key element in meeting different functional requirements.

Likewise, we have underemphasized the control issue, which in fact has operated as a major integrating focus for those working on the development of such systems (see Bobrow & Raphael, 1973). Our reason has been to relate the features of these systems to the main functions where we wish to understand what the systems have to offer. One aspect we should have stressed more was the total gain that comes from embedding all of these mechanisms in a language. Technically speaking, language embedding forces combinational freedom, so that ultimate patterns of behavior can be composed *ad libitum* from all the various components. From a design point of view this seems seldom to be achieved outside of the framework of language design.

It should be clear by now why Planner and QA4 have had the impact they have, for they contain at least five major ideas in the development of artificial intelligence systems:

1. reversion to procedural embedding,
2. pattern directed evocation of processes,
3. goal-oriented language systems,
4. backtracking,
5. global data bases.

Of these, the global data base and the pattern matching seem the most important. From a technical point of view in realizing them, all of these features (or their equivalents) are required concurrently. In this sense they are not independent. But they are independent in that they address functionally independent issues for the nature of understanding systems.

It should also be apparent why we treat these languages systems as proposals for understanding systems. If we considered some of the systems built within them (only Winograd's SHRDLU (1971) coded in Microplanner is well documented in the public domain), we would have to take all the discussion given here as starting point, though there would be some additional proposals as well.

Humans as Understanding Systems

What do we know from psychology that would contribute to these design issues? That humans can in general understand and that they are so organized that they provide solutions of some sort to all the design issues goes without saying. The question is whether there are empirical data of sufficient clarity on any of the issues to indicate the nature of the solutions.

There appears to be little help. The difficulty seems to reside in the nature of the questions: they ask after fundamental mechanisms and structures, while the study of human behavior generally yields a different kind of data: behavioral regularities under controlled experimental conditions that can be used to test theories.

With respect to representation, for example, we know that the human is capable of symbolic representation, and that this is superimposed in some way on a system for representing the world directly sensed through vision, hearing, smell, etc. We know that he uses a great range of multiple representations. We also know he has had much knowledge that is vague. But all these are external aspects and except for posing criteria, they do not indicate the nature of these representations. A similar story holds with respect to each of the other design issues. Though the terms assimilation and accommodation have arisen from Piagetian analysis of children's behavior, the theoretical notions behind them (e.g., schema) have little substance in terms of information processing structure.

A few things seem worth remarking. For instance, there is good evidence that humans do search—that they backtrack in the face of errors. But such backtracking is quite limited and does not seem to be the major mechanism in response to error. Thus when errors turn up after substantial time periods (e.g., the revelation of the Piltdown man as a hoax), no attempt is made to backtrack—indeed none of the memorial apparatus appears to be set up to backtrack. Some immediate consequences of the new information are found and corrected, but the large store of knowledge that might have some dependence on the now-erroneous knowledge is left to shift for itself.

There is also good evidence that the human gains access to an immense array of knowledge in very short times (relative to his time to do any processing at all). Thus, it would appear plausible that he has a global data base of some sort, and indeed this is assumed in most psychological theories (so-called LTM). That he cannot recollect everything in the data base immediately (as has often been shown—e.g., what was the name of your fourth grade teacher?) is immaterial, because the momentary retrieval properties of LTM must depend on the presented address (i.e., retrieval cues) as well as on the contents of the memory.

Finally, some case can be made for excluding various possibilities for the human action mechanism—i.e., for the way whereby the human obtains action from his knowledge. There is no evidence that all action exists as plans which are interpreted by a process; humans seem often to be able to react directly. Likewise action does not all derive from an inference technique, which then flows into behavior by a final decoding; much of his knowledge seems to be held in action form. Humans of course are capable both of following plans and of making inferences. The issue is what knowledge-action conversion mechanisms form the basis of these systems. (For example, see Newell & Simon, 1972, for an account of one such proposal, production systems.)

MERLIN

With these design issues as background we turn to Merlin. To reiterate: Merlin has been an exploration into the design of an understanding system. It has existed in several operational versions, though none of them has been complete as far as the set of design issues is concerned. Thus, within the philosophy presented in this paper, each version is an exploration into selected aspects of the design. Nevertheless, many aspects of Merlin have become relatively constant and represent distinct proposals in terms of certain of these design issues. We will present a composite picture of the system through summer 1973.

The design issues will serve as a guide in the exposition. We present a summary of them in Fig. 9.6, comparable to our summary for the other systems.

Representation

Merlin has a basic data structure called a *β-structure*. Its general form is:

$$\alpha: [\beta \; \alpha1 \; \alpha2 \; ... \;] \tag{3}$$

This may be read: "α is a β further specified by $\alpha1$, $\alpha2$, ..." The name "β-structure" derives simply from the practice of writing the structure with the particular notation above. However, it serves to keep the interpretation of the structure somewhat free of preconceptions.

The intended interpretation can be approached via a variant reading: "α can be viewed as a β given that $\alpha1$, $\alpha2$,... ." Its source rests in the emphasis we have already given to the issue of assimilation. A fundamental problem for an understanding system (indeed for any information processing system) is making contact between what it actually knows (its structure) and what it

REPRESENTATION	MAPPED OBJECTS
SCOPE	UNRESTRICTED QUANTIFICATION
GRAIN	SELF-DEFINING COMPONENTS
MULTIPLE REPRESENTATION	NO POSITION
ACTION	PROGRAM (POTENTIALLY) AT EACH NODE
ASSIMILATION	FIND/CREATE MAP
ACCOMMODATION	NO POSITION
DIRECTIONALITY	GOALS = MAPPINGS
KEEP-PROGRESSING	TRY OTHER ALTERNATE VIEWS
EFFICIENCY	
INTERPRETER	COMPILING = SIDE EFFECT OF REFERENCE
IMMEDIACY	NO POSITION
FORMALITY	MINIMAL
ERROR	NO POSITION
DEPTH	NO POSITION

FIG. 9.6. Design characterization of Merlin.

does not yet know. Thus, in Expression 3, β is taken as known and α is to be understood by being assimilated to β, which requires that further things be also taken as given (the $\alpha1$, $\alpha2$...). We call β the *schema* and the $\alpha1$, $\alpha2$ ... the *components* of the β-structure. (By way of notation, the schema of α is written: $\alpha\uparrow$; the set of components of α is denoted: $\alpha\#$.) Again, the terms are intended to be relatively neutral, since the actual interpretation to be given the β-structure depends mostly on the processes that manipulate and interpret it.

The components are themselves simply other β-structures, that is, other specifications that something is to be viewed as something else along with what it takes to do so. Thus, the β-structure gives a structure in terms of which some item is to be understood, along with the mapping that is required so that the object may be assimilated.

β-structures serve the corresponding role in Merlin to nodes in a semantic net memory or to clauses in a theorem prover. All knowledge is to be coded in their terms. We will often refer to β-structures as nodes and to the set of all β-structures as the *Knowledge Net* (KN). However, β-structures are not process specifications; there is also a general representation for processing (called the action), which is dealt with later.

Let us consider some simple examples.

$$\text{SAM: [BOY [EYES BLUE]]} \qquad [4]$$

SAM is a BOY further specified to have EYES that are further specified to be BLUE. BOY, EYES and BLUE are of course themselves β-structures, which is to say, are understood because they can be viewed in terms of yet other things, themselves understood. (This infinite regress will be terminated shortly.)

$$\text{LT: [HEURISTIC-SEARCHER [TASK LOGIC]} \qquad [5]$$
$$\text{[AUTHOR NEWELL-SHAW-SIMON]]}$$

LT (an early theorem prover) can be viewed as a HEURISTIC-SEARCHER whose TASK is further specified to be LOGIC and whose AUTHOR is Newell, Shaw, and Simon. In these examples we leave out most of the detail that would be required for an adequate description. For an example of a full-fledged description of LT (in Merlin 1) see Moore (1971).

In Expressions 4 and 5 the relationship of node to schema appears to be the IS-A relationship, familiar from many semantic nets. But the interpretation is to be taken more broadly.

$$8: [+ \quad 3 \quad 5] \qquad [6]$$

Thus, 8 may be viewed as a + further specified by 3 and 5. Here a β-structure appears as an expression comprised of a function (+) with its arguments. For this interpretation to hold, the operation + must be viewed as a generalized element of its range; i.e., + can be viewed as an indeterminate number. Given this, we can have the following:

$$X: [+ \ 3] \qquad\qquad\qquad [7]$$
$$Y: [X \ \ 5] \qquad\qquad\qquad [8]$$
$$Z: [+ \ 3 \ [> \ 5]] \qquad\qquad\qquad [9]$$

Here X is a $+$ further specified by 3, which is to say either the function of adding 3, or an indeterminate number that is 3 more than another unspecified number, depending on how you wish to view it. Then Y is X further specified by 5, which is to say, it may be viewed as 8. Similarly, Z is another indeterminate number greater than 5. In these we get the typical hierarchy of functional composition.

A β-structure may have (simultaneously) a number of *alternate views*. Thus, a β-structure called P35 might be viewed in the following ways:

$$[+ \ 3 \ 5] \qquad\qquad\qquad [10]$$
$$[8] \qquad\qquad\qquad [11]$$
[ARITH-OP   [12]
      BINARY COMMUTATIVE [FUNCTION ADDITION]
      [FIRST-ARG3][SECOND-ARG 5]   ]
[WFF [MAIN-CONNECTIVE $+$][LEFT-HALF 3]   [13]
      [RIGHT-HALF 5]]

   ...

At any given point in time, exactly one of these is the *principal view*. Whenever we write, e.g.,

$$P35: [+ \ 3 \ 5] \qquad\qquad\qquad [14]$$

we indicate that $[+ \ 3 \ 5]$ is the principal view.

Merlin generally deals with a β-structure only in terms of its principal view. The others are kept as alternatives, and are referenced only by an explicit attempt to change the way the object is viewed. An entity gets a new principal view as the result of a successful mapping of the structure into the new view.

If Merlin finds a map from one β-structure (Y) to another (X), then it has found a way to view X as a further specification of Y. The new view of X will have Y as its schema and its components will be the various aspects of the map from Y to X. This leads to yet another reading of the β-structure: Expression 3 may be read as "α is the result of applying to β the mapping represented in the $\alpha 1, \ \alpha 2 \ldots$." We indicate mapping Y into X by the notation: X/Y (to be read "view X as a Y" or "map Y to X"). This attempt may succeed or fail, depending on the relations between X and Y, and how hard Merlin is currently willing to try. If X/Y succeeds, a map has been found from Y to X; suppose this map could be represented by the set of β-structures: X1, X2, ... , then the result of the successful map is to assign X a new principal view:

$$X: [Y \ X1 \ X2 \ldots] \qquad\qquad\qquad [15]$$

Let's look at some examples. Suppose we know:

MAN: [MAMMAL NOSE:[...] HOME:[...]]   [16]
PIG: [MAMMAL SNOUT:[...] STY:[...]]   [17]

and we pose Merlin the task of viewing a PIG as a MAN (i.e. PIG/MAN). Assuming that the indicated sub-maps succeed, the result would be:

PIG: [MAN SNOUT/NOSE STY/HOME]   [18]

Equivalently: "A PIG can be viewed as a MAN if his SNOUT is viewed as a NOSE and his STY is viewed as a HOME." On the other hand, if we assume that a PIG's TAIL cannot be viewed as his HOME (i.e. TAIL/HOME fails), and if we had, instead:

PIG: [MAMMAL SNOUT:[...] TAIL:[...]]   [19]

then PIG/MAN would also fail.

The β-structure representation (considering only the principal views) induces a classical hierarchy of knowledge. This is illustrated in Fig. 9.7, which shows (albeit schematially) a hierarchy of knowledge for LT. The topmost entity is PROCESS, which could of course be defined in still more rarefied terms, e.g., as a SYSTEM with certain properties, a SYSTEM itself being defined as ... etc. A problem solver (PS) is viewed as a kind of PROCESS, a heuristic-searcher (HS) as a kind of PS, LT as a kind of HS, LT with a set of axioms given (called LTA) as a kind of LT and LT with both axioms and a theorem given (called LTAT) as a kind of LTA. Shown to the side, even more briefly, is hill-climber (HC), considered also as a kind of PS, and GPS, considered as another kind of HS. Thus a full hierarchial tree would exist in the Knowledge Net.

```
                  PROCESS: [ ... ]
                   PS: [PROCESS ... ]
              HS: [PS ... ]          HC: [PS ... ]
           LT: [HS ... ]         GPS: [HS ... ]
        LTA: [LT   [AXIOMS AX1 AX2 AX3] ]
   LTAT: [LTA    [THEOREM T1] ]
```

FIG. 9.7. Hierarchy of knowledge.

Each node in the Knowledge Net is to represent something external to the memory structure. At any moment, one view holds a preferred status (as principal view). However, it may be dethroned at any time by another successful map. There is no view that represents, so to speak, what the entity, *really* is. In particular, the original view does not have such a status. We can capture this representational decision as:

> *The system treats all its views of reality as contigent alternatives.*

There is an issue of representational grain here. Adopting this principle avoids having to make the decision to confer special status on some knowledge (that is the "true" view), which decision would be forced in order to get the knowledge represented at all.

There are three subissues under that of representation: scope, grain and multiplicity. There is no way to ascertain the scope from the structure, i.e., what sorts of operations can be performed and with what interpretations. However, it turns out that the system is unstratified (i.e., without syntactic restrictions), which permits manipulation and quantification over all the structures in the language, hence inducing omega-ordered completeness in the same sense as for the Planner-like languages (namely, completeness of representation but without an associated inference scheme).

More important in terms of the design is the issue of grain. One of the original design decisions was that components in a sense declared themselves:

> *The interpretation of a component is to be based entirely on the contents of the component, the schema and the collection of mappings currently being attempted.*

There are no syntactic rules that dictate how a component is to be interpreted or what role it is to play. Each component presents itself as an expression for specifying further the schema with which it is associated. What that further specification is must be discovered by an attempt to interpret that component in conjunction with the others, given the context in which the entire β-structure occurs.

There are several consequences from this decision. The one of note here is the attempt to avoid the grain problem by refusing to set a fixed grain (formal rules of interpretation) on the components. The hope (though not yet well tested) is to be able to shade the components in whatever ways are appropriate to capture whatever indefinite state of knowledge the system needs to represent. Thus, a new β-structure is formable simply by taking a schema and combining it with whatever β-structures have been found or manufactured that seem to represent current relevant knowledge. These can be thrown together into a new β-structure and the new structure used instead of the old one. No conditions have to be met in order to form the new β-structure; hence, there is one less situation where precommitment must be made and uncertainty absorbed. It goes without saying that this one design decision does not solve the grain problem, it only removes an impediment.

The ancient issue of the ontological status of individuals and concepts (particulars and universals) casts its shadow across the design of a representation: Shall the system make a fundamental distinction between individuals and generic concepts?[10] Merlin does not.

> *The memory system has only a single representational scheme (the β-structure) to refer to both individuals and generic concepts.*

In particular, any entity may be further specified and the hierarchy shown in Fig. 9.7 is indefinitely extendable downward, as well as upward. The system does not have to make a decision whether LT is an individual or only a concept (there being many versions of LT, differing from time to time, not only with respect to axioms and theorems, but with respect to the heuristics used, trace processes added, etc.). Merlin thus avoids another problem of grain. Such a design feature does not prevent Merlin from having a concept (UNIQUE) that serves to designate individuals, e.g., SAM: [MAN UNIQUE].

Merlin currently provides nothing except intent with respect to multiple representations. The philosophy behind β-structures extends directly to an entity having non-β-structure representation. However, with only a couple of minor exceptions (simple linguistic expressions and sequences of behavioral events) no way has yet been provided to re-view an external representation as a β-structure or vice versa.

Let us summarize the representation: A Knowledge Net consists of a set of nodes (or entities), each of which has associated with it a collection of views (β-structures). A view, which forms the basic data structure, specifies another entity (the schema) in terms of which the given entity can be viewed, plus the set of further specifications (the components) required to make the mapping. The components themselves are entities (hence with β-structures). Nothing further is assumed in the structure of the Knowledge Net about how to interpret the entities. In particular the memory is homogeneous with respect to the notion of individuals, hence there are no atoms.

Action

The Knowledge Net is purely a static structure and the problem of generating action from structure exists for Merlin, as it does for all other systems. There are three aspects to the issue of action: (a) the implied logic of β-structures which permits various conclusions to be extracted from them; (b) the programs (called actions) associated with nodes; and (c) the integration of these aspects of action into a coordinated whole.

Mapping. The basic operation with β-structures is to ask for one entity to be viewed as another, i.e., for two given entities, X and Y, to find if X/Y has a solution. Before considering what is involved in this process in general,

---

[10]See Anderson and Bower (1973) for a system that does make such a distinction sharply.

let us consider some examples. If we reconsider Expression 4 and ask for SAM/BOY the attempt is clearly successful, since the SAM is already expressed as a further specification of BOY. If we added the expression:

$$\text{BOY: [MAN YOUNG]} \qquad [20]$$

and ask for SAM/MAN, then we could apparently again succeed.

$$\text{SAM: [MAN YOUNG [EYES BLUE]]} \qquad [21]$$

Expression 21 is an adequate representation of SAM as a further specification of MAN, given the adequacy of Expressions 4 and 20. Clearly the relationship is transitive and we could expect to be able to develop X/Y if Y were anywhere up the schema hierarchy of X.

However, the actual β-structure is not necessarily determined by collapsing all the intermediate levels in the β-structure hierarchy (a process we call *flatting*) and taking the union of all the components. Consider:

$$\text{MAN: [PERSON EYES]} \qquad [22]$$

If we now ask for SAM/PERSON there are two possibilities:

$$\text{SAM: [PERSON YOUNG EYES [EYES BLUE]]} \qquad [23]$$
$$\text{SAM: [PERSON YOUNG [EYES BLUE]]} \qquad [24]$$

The latter is evidently the one that is wanted. For [EYES BLUE] is a further specification of a component of MAN and this was explicitly noted by writing the schema EYES. When the flatting takes place the connection should be made in developing the correct β-structure. Suppose, instead of Expression 4, SAM was defined by:

$$\text{SAM: [BOY BLUE]} \qquad [25]$$

Then in asking for SAM/PERSON we obtain the two possibilities:

$$\text{SAM: [PERSON YOUNG EYES BLUE]} \qquad [26]$$
$$\text{SAM: [PERSON YOUNG [EYES BLUE]]} \qquad [27]$$

Which is appropriate is now ambiguous, at least if it is considered possible that SAM himself is colored BLUE. Indeed, the only reason the additional alternative

$$\text{SAM: [PERSON [YOUNG BLUE] EYES]} \qquad [28]$$

is not considered is that BLUE does not further specify a component of YOUNG. For this latter to be discovered, of course, requires an investigation of the representations of both BLUE and YOUNG.

Consider now the following simple versions of LT, a heuristic-searcher (HS) and a theorem-prover (TP) in terms of a problem-solver (PS):

$$\text{LT: [HS [TASK [LOGIC WHITEHEAD-RUSSELL]]}$$
$$\text{[AUTHOR NEWELL-SHAW-SIMON]]} \qquad [29]$$

HS: [PS SEARCH]   [30]
TP: [PS [TASK LOGIC]]   [31]

Can LT be viewed as a theorem prover, i.e., can we find LT/TP? The solution is:

LT: [TP SEARCH [LOGIC WHITEHEAD-RUSSELL]   [32]
    [AUTHOR NEWELL-SHAW-SIMON]]

This result is arrived at by first expressing both LT and TP in common terms, namely viewing them as PSs:

LT/PS → LT: [PS SEARCH   [33]
    [TASK [LOGIC WHITEHEAD- RUSSELL]]
    [AUTHOR NEWELL-SHAW-SIMON]]
TP/PS → TP: [PS [TASK LOGIC]]   [34]

If every component of TP has a further specification among the components of LT (is *covered*), LT can be expressed as a further specification of TP. In this case, [TASK [LOGIC WHITEHEAD-RUSSELL]] covers [TASK LOGIC], providing the solution.

The above examples have exhibited the form of the logic built into β-structure representation. The general case to be easily outlined:

Flat and Cover Procedure:

Let X: [U X1 X2 ...] and Y: [V Y1 Y2 ...]

To form X/Y:
    Find a common higher schema (call it Z)
    If it does not exist, fail.

Flat X to Z → X: [Z X1' X2' ...]

Flat Y to Z → Y: [Z Y1' Y2' ...]

Find a cover from the components of X for those of Y:
    Find for each Yi' a distinct Xj' such that Xj'/Yi'
    If cannot be done, fail.

The solution is:

X: [Y X1''/Y1' X2''/Y2'... Xn''Xn+1 ...]   [35]

where the Xi'' are some reordering of the Xi as dictated by the selection for the cover. The solution need not exist, as is evident. Neither is it necessarily unique. Each flatting operation gives rise to possible optional groupings and there may be additional ways to find the cover (which itself can have options for how the submapping goes). Whether there is actual ambiguity or whether these multiple options can all be resolved to yield a unique solution, depends on the content of the particular β-structures.

Although presented in a somewhat unfamiliar guise, the basic logic of the slash operation (/) is a reflection of the composition of mappings.[11] It does provide a basic capability whereby inferences of an elementary sort can be made given just the representation of entities in terms of β-structures, without further processing structure.

In some sense X/Y can be taken as a syntactic operation, defined on uninterpreted β-structures. We will often refer to it this way. Yet we may also take the β-structure as equivalent to a semantic definition (as that term would be used in a semantic memory). One way to see this is to reinterpret the β-structure as a collection of relational linkages to other nodes in the total network. Each of the components gives the relationship to another node. An example is shown in Fig. 9.8, which makes this correspondence clear. The component of course can be more complex than shown, both in terms of what relationship is designated and the number of nodes (the remaining subcomponents of the component) to which the linkage leads.

The Flat and Cover Procedure does not exhaust the means whereby one entity can be viewed as another. A solution may be *posited* in order to consider the nature of other mappings made relative to that posit. For example, suppose we are looking for a new house, and have a description of what we are looking for:

HOUSE-WANTED: [HOUSE   [36]
              LRW:[LIVING-ROOM] KW:[KITCHEN]
              BW:[BATH] BRW1:[BEDROOM]
              BRW2:[BEDROOM] BRW3:[BEDROOM]]

Suppose we encounter:

HOUSE-FOUND: [HOUSE   [37]
             LRF:[LIVING-ROOM ...] KF:[KITCHEN ...]
             BRF1:[BEDROOM ...] BRF2:[BEDROOM ...]
             BF: [BATH ...]   DF:[DEN ...]   ]

Can this house be seen as a further specification of the one wanted? That is, does

HOUSE-FOUND/HOUSE-WANTED   [38]

---

[11]If we consider entities to be sets of aspects (leaving open what constitutes an aspect in a given situation), then we can define mappings between entities as correspondences between their aspects, i.e., M:{aspects of entity 1} → {aspects of entity 2}. In these terms X/Y implies finding a mapping M: Y → X. If we have X/Y and Y/Z (i.e., X: [Y ...] and Y: [Z ...]) then X/Z can be found by taking the composition of the two mappings. The logic of flatting agrees with the associativity implied by these mappings. Likewise, finding a cover is the generation of a mapping by enumerating individually corresponding aspects. Failure to find a cover with a particular decomposition into aspects (the components of the flatted entities) does not preclude finding a map with a different decomposition.

succeed? Evidently, this mapping can succeed only if some way is found to cover the third BEDROOM (BRW3). We observe that the DEN (DF) is not needed to satisfy any of the sub-maps. If the attempt DF/BRW3 succeeds by posit (i.e., simply assume that DF can be viewed as BRW3), then the entire map will succeed. We indicate this by simply leaving DF/BRW3 as the final expression:

$$\text{HOUSE-FOUND: [HOUSE-WANTED DF/BRW3]} \qquad [39]$$

Positing is a universal technique (which must therefore be used sparingly). In the opposite direction there can be other bases for forming alternative views of entities that are more specific than flatting. They all involve, in one way or another, the actions, to which we now turn.

The knowledge expressed in the following English sentences:

John is Mary's brother.
Mary's mother is Jane.
Ted's wife is Mary.
John's sons are Bill and Bob.

could be represented by the following semantic net:

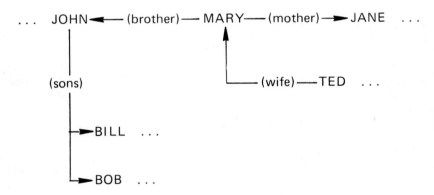

In β-structures, this might look like:

JOHN: [PERSON [BROTHER—OF MARY] [SONS BILL BOB]]
JANE: [PERSON [MOTHER—OF MARY]]
MARY: [PERSON [WIFE—OF TED]]

FIG. 9.8. A semantic net fragment expressed in terms of β-structures.

Actions. The basic mechanism for obtaining behavior from knowledge is the *action*. To each β-structure is potentially associated an action, with the following interpretation:

> *The action of a β-structure is its fully specialized process equivalent.*

What does it mean for a static object to have a "process equivalent"? All of Merlin's intellectual activity derives from the mapping operation. The purpose of the actions is to function as highly specialized versions of this operation. The action for X, A(X), embodies all knowledge localized at the β-structure in the form of a streamlined version of the Flat and Cover procedure. Thus, A(X) is capable of attempting any map to or from X (X/Y or Z/X). It would succeed under the same conditions as would the full-scale mapping process, and win or lose, costs at least an order of magnitude less computation (since at least one interpretive level has been circumvented).

To get an idea of how actions behave, suppose we want to view P35: [+ 3 5] as a NUMBER. We try:

$$P35/[NUMBER] \qquad [40]$$

A(P35) is capable of representing P35 as any of:

[+ ...]
[NUMBER ...]
[SUMMATION ...]
[— ...]
[EXPRESSION ...]

A(P35) has immediate access to 3 and 5 (with no searching, testing, etc.) as well as the full knowledge of +. When faced with Expression 40, A(P35) discovers that what is desired is to re-view P35 as [NUMBER ...], which is one of its specialties, and it produces 8:[NUMBER ...] as the result of the successful match.

As an example of an action functioning on the other side of a map, consider:

$$M73/PNN \qquad [41]$$

where:

M73: [— M7:[7 ARG1] M3:[3 ARG2]]
PNN: [+ N1:[NUMBER] N2:[NUMBER]].

Suppose M73 has no action but PNN does. The first thing A(PNN) does is attempt M73/+. This might succeed (e.g., by virtue of A(—)) producing: [+ M7 [NEG M3]]. A(PNN) then replaces the original problem with:

$$[+ M7 [NEG M3]]/PNN \qquad [42]$$

A(PNN) then searches in [+ M7 [NEG M3]] for any objects that can cover N1. M7/N1 and [NEG M3]/N1 both succeed. Since A(PNN) embodies the knowledge that + is commutative and that N1 and N2 are equivalent structures, it need conduct no search for any objects to cover N2. A(PNN) also need not concern itself with the possible (apparent) ambiguity between pairing M7 with N1 and [NEG M3] with N2, or vice versa.

From these examples we see that the mapping operation is in some respects strongly similar to matching, but represents an even more powerful process. The terminal operations in a match are limited (symbol identity test, variable assignment) whereas Merlin's mapping allows full semantics-driven re-representation, and even a few judicious posits, when necessary. Thus, for example, although P35 cannot be matched to [NUMBER], it can be so mapped.

Replacement of matching with a general mapping process has many consequences. One that requires mention, even though we will not treat it in detail, is the loss of control that arises from the failure of matching. Since a map can always be created between X and Y if sufficiently bizarre maps are allowed, no information is provided by obtaining X/Y. (Examination of AI programs will show that immense amounts of control are communicated by the success or failure of the match processes.) In fact, maps are not always found in Merlin, but control processes must exist to limit the range of mappings considered. In Merlin 2.5 these were buried in a fixed set of search processes; Merlin 3 will have a general scheme of controllers, but the design is not yet firm.

Integration. The two parts so far discussed provide the pieces out of which Merlin can compose integrated sequences of action. The basic issue belongs to directionality, but an important aspect can be discussed here:

> *All behavior derives from the actions distributed through-out the Knowledge Net.*

In particular, the various attempts at mapping are performed by actions, providing their principal means for dealing with the Knowledge Net. There is no intelligent interpreter, i.e., a single active program that manipulates the Knowledge Net. There is an interpreter in Merlin, but its functions are limited to finding actions and to creating the nested context of β-structures within which the action is then executed.

The existence of actions on some subset of nodes in the Knowledge Net terminates the potentially infinite regress in interpretation and exploration. When, in attempting a mapping, one runs into an action, there is no need to go beyond that entity into its internal β-structures.

Assimilation

The main points about Merlin and assimilation have already been presented, since they lie at the foundation of its representation. Merlin puts the issue of assimilation at the center, not only of Merlin vis-a-vis the external task environment, but of each piece of knowledge in Merlin vis-a-vis other pieces of knowledge. One novelty of this, perhaps, is the possibility of constructing an entire static knowledge structure out of the mappings of one structure into another. It is of course not so strange when re-viewed as a semantic-net-like structure, expression as in Fig. 9.8.

Setting up the representation as the natural encoding of assimilation does not, of course, solve the problem of making assimilations. However, it goes part way. Consider a possible β-structure for logic viewed as a formal mathematical system.

```
LOGIC:[MATH-SYSTEM                                    [43]
          AXIOM: [WFF MULTIPLE]
          THEOREM: [WFF DESIRED]
          RULE-OF-INFERENCE: [RULE MULTIPLE
                              [RANGE WFF]
                              [DOMAIN WFF] ] ]
```

Next we propose a β-structure for a problem space, which is a construct belonging to the notion of a problem solver:

```
PROBLEM-SPACE: [SYSTEM                                [44]
          INITIAL-OBJECT: [OBJECT]
          FINAL-OBJECT: [OBJECT DESIRED]
          OPERATOR: [RULE MULTIPLE
                     [RANGE OBJECT]
                     [DOMAIN OBJECT] ] ]
```

If a problem solver were to work on logic, then one requirement is that it would have to view logic as a problem space. In Expression 45 we see the mapping as it comes about when simply the basic Flat and Cover Procedure algorithm is applied along with one posit.

```
LOGIC/PROBLEM-SPACE →                                 [45]
     [PROBLEM-SPACE
          WFF/OBJECT
          AXIOM:[INITIAL-OBJECT WFF/OBJECT]
          THEOREM:[FINAL-OBJECT WFF/OBJECT]
          RULE-OF-INFERENCE:[OPERATOR
                              WFF/OBJECT] ]
```

The posit is necessary if the two entities (WFF and OBJECT) are defined without common intersection (as well they might be). If we assume that WFF and OBJECT have been defined with little or nothing in common, then we would expect WFF/OBJECT to fail (unless posited). However, from the definitions in Expressions 43 and 44, we see that without this correspondence, there is little hope of finding any mapping from PROBLEM-SPACE to

LOGIC. The mapping is first attempted with positing inhibited, and, as expected, it fails. However, in failing, Merlin has observed the number of places in which WFF/OBJECT was requested (and failed). With this as a clue, Merlin posits WFF/OBJECT and retries the mapping with other posits still inhibited. This time, the mapping works, producing the results in Expression 45. This happens, of course, because of the similar internal structure of RULE-OF-INFERENCE and OPERATOR. If this correspondence were less transparent the mapping would have to drive further up the hierarchy, perhaps with additional posits. On the other hand if WFF and OBJECT had a common schema, say STRUCTURE, it might be possible to establish WFF/OBJECT without a posit.

In this example, and in several others to come, we exhibit a successful mapping in the pursuit of some particular functional aim. Here it is assimilation in its most classical terms: the mapping of a method onto a task environment, to be able to apply the method. The adequacy of the mapping techniques to significant problems cannot be concluded from these simple examples. We will discuss the issue later under the heading of natural intelligence. Our purpose in these examples is to exhibit the design decisions and to give some evidence of their plausibility, not to imply solutions to indefinitely difficult problems.

Accommodation

Merlin's thoroughgoing adoption of assimilation appears to generate difficulties with respect to accommodation. Fig. 9.6 records NO POSITION opposite Accommodation, since we do not pretend to understand this issue yet. If Merlin copes with any new information by constructing a β-structure for it in terms of what it already knows, and processing it through that already-known schema, then how is Merlin ever to obtain anything new? It does obtain new β-structures and can use these as further schemas for yet other to-be-assimilated objects. But these newly obtained structures derive their potency, so to speak, from their schemas, so that nothing really new is added. Following this path would seem to bring Merlin to mapping the whole world onto the set of primeval β-structures (they need hardly be primitive) with which it is endowed.

Possibly the gradual accretion of layers of further specification from a conceptually spanning set of nodes will suffice. More likely, ways must be found for environmental structure to construct new β-structures in the system, thereby adding new schemas to be used in future assimilations. A hint of how this might occur can be found in programming. Consider a β-structure for PROGRAM as a SEQUENCE of INSTRUCTIONS in some LANGUAGE:

$$\text{PROGRAM: [SEQUENCE [INSTRUCTION MULTIPLE]} \qquad [46]$$
$$\text{[LANGUAGE]]}$$

with ADDXYZ as a particular further specification:

            ADDXYZ: [PROGRAM   [47]
                    [1ST [CLA VBLX]]
                    [2ND [ADD VBLY]]
                    [3RD [STO VBLZ]]
                    [4TH [RETURN]]
                    MACHINE-CODE   ]

The important feature is that while further specifications of this structure are
still programs, their variety encompasses arbitrary behavior (in the way
typical of all programs). Thus, what from one view is always a sequence of
instructions can become from another view a method for achieving a goal.
Indeed, if we now bring up a structure for solving a particular problem,
expressed at a high level so that it could not be said the system actually knew
how to achieve the goal only that it wanted a way to do so, the program could
be re-viewed as such a method. Furthermore, further specifications of the
re-viewing will remain organized as methods for solving the goal, not just as a
sequence of instructions.

This example may be used to illustrate another aspect of mapping. If
one were to pose to a human (programmer) the task of expressing ADDXYZ
as "an arithmetic expression involving the sum of two numbers," we would
not be surprised were he to respond with something like: "VBLX plus
VBLY." How might Merlin do this?

It would not be unreasonable for ADDXYZ to have, as an alternate
view:

            [ASSIGNMENT [← VBLZ] [+ VBLX VBLY]]   [48]

This might be the result of a "decompile," i.e.,

            ADDXYZ/[STATEMENT ALGOL]   [49]

Alternatively, the view in Expression 47 might itself have been the result of
Expression 48 being "compiled":

            ADDXYZ/[PROGRAM MACHINE-CODE]   [50]

In either case, given that ADDXYZ has Expresion 48 as an alternate view,
and given that some variant of ALGOL permits statements of the form:

            W ← (Z ← X + Y)   [51]

(That is, the language permits an assignment statement to be viewed as the
value being assigned.) It is reasonable to suppose that

            ADDXYZ/[ARITHMETIC-EXPRESSION ALGOL]   [52]

would yield:

[ARITHMETIC-EXPRESSION   [53]
  [CONNECTIVE +]
  [LEFT-HALF VBLX]
  [RIGHT-HALF VBLY]]

as yet another alternative for ADDXYZ. With this as prologue, were Merlin faced with:

ADDXYZ/PNN: [+ N1:[NUMBER] N2:[NUMBER]]   [54]

the reasonable conclusion would be:

ADDXYZ: [PNN VBLX/N1 VBLY/N2]   [55]

This is approximately how we speculated our programmer would respond.

This does not solve the accommodation problem. It does suggest how a process that selects instructions according to the task environment can add to a β-structure such that the final result is not intuitively to be described as just a further specification of some internal schema. The burden in this solution is on the task of programming, but at least one can see how the environment might select the instructions (e.g., by local searches).

Directionality

In the original versions of Merlin the only directionality was a universal urge to understand. Built into the actions was the view that more specific knowledge was preferred, so that the system would operate to increase its understanding in whatever way it could. When it understood that it should make an external response, it would.

In Merlin 3 we propose a general approach to directionality. A goal is a β-structure. As is well known (Newell & Simon, 1972, Chapter 14) the use of explicit goal structures provides several functions: the definition of what is wanted; the memory that such a situation was wanted so control can return for retrying; a node for associating fruitful methods; and a place for the history of attempts to guide the next attempt. We will only be concerned here with the β-structure as a criterion for attainment of the goal.

The ingredients that are always present in a goal-ish situation are a goal G and a current situation, S, both described by β-structures. The first principle is:

> Directionality Principle: *To achieve goal situation G from current situation S, attempt to view S as G: S/G.*

The result of applying this is either to produce no result at all (S/G cannot be solved) or to produce:

S: [G S1/G1 S2/G2 ... Sn Sn+1 ...]   [56]

In this latter case, the present situation is the solution, providing the submappings Si/Gi ... are acceptable. These submaps may be acceptable in one of two ways: (*a*) Si/Gi simply succeeds, producing a new β-structure: [Gi ...] which is the mapped object or (*b*) Si/Gi is permitted to succeed by posit. Since mapping-by-posit is so universally applicable, each attempted map is under some type of posit restriction, e.g., one of the following:

> no posits permitted.
> at most one posit permitted, not at top level, over all submaps.
> at most one posit permitted, at top level of each submap.
> use only the explicit posit: X/Y.
> use only those posits required to effect W/Z.
> ...

The Directionality Principle in itself is sufficient for solving many problems. We can capture this in the following proposition:

> Natural Method Proposition: *To understand the current situation relative to the goal is to know how to attain the goal.*

Of course, such a situation only sometimes obtains. The domain in which the proposition is true we call the *domain of natural intelligence*. It is that class of situations where the ability of a system to assimilate (i.e., to create mappings) makes it apparent to the system what needs to be done to solve the problem. Related to this is the following conjecture:

> Weak-Method Conjecture: *The so-called weak methods (Generate and Test, Heuristic Search, Hill Climbing, Match, Means-end Analysis...) arise as Natural Methods.*

Let us explain this by means of a simple example. Fig. 9.9 shows a typical means-ends analysis sequence taken from GPS (Ernst & Newell,

```
Transform (PvQ) into (~P ⊃ Q)
     Match (PvQ) to (~P ⊃ Q) → DELTA(C): v → ⊃
     Reduce DELTA(C) on (PvQ)
          Select rule R3 with function   DELTA(C) → R2, R3
          Apply R3 to (PvQ) → (~P ⊃ Q)
     Transform (~P ⊃ Q) into (~P ⊃ Q)
          Match (~P ⊃ Q) to (~P ⊃ Q) → Satisfied


R1: (Av(BvC)) → ((AvB)vC)
R2: (AvB) → ~ (~ A ∧ ~ B)
R3: (AvB) → (~ A ⊃ B)
```

FIG. 9.9. Means-ends analysis sequence as it occurs in GPS.

1969). The original goal is to transform one logic expression (PvQ) into another (∼P⊃Q). GPS has an interlocked set of methods that leads to the solution and embodies what is commonly called means-ends analysis. (PvQ) is matched against (∼P⊃Q) and a difference is derived (here DELTA(C): v → ⊃). This difference is used to set up a reduce goal, whose method is to select out of the set of available operators, one whose operation is defined as changing connectives (DELTA(C)). This selection is done via a mechanism called the Table of Connections which holds preestablished associations between differences and operators. Then the goal of applying the operator (R3 in this case) is created. It succeeds yielding a new expression. The process iterates, though in this case the solution has been found so that termination occurs right after the next match process. (The selection of R2 would have led to backtracking eventually.) In the scheme, some aspects become goals (transform, apply, reduce) but not others (match, select). To each goal a distinct action scheme exists (the method), which embodies whatever rationality the means-ends analysis scheme possesses. These methods themselves are simply given.

We envision in natural intelligence that the attempt to see the current situation as the goal (i.e., the desired situation) leads to a mapping, i.e., the construction of a β-structure. This mapping may be inadequate but makes apparent the potentialities for manipulating the given situation so that it can be viewed acceptably as the desired situation. This happens only if the situation is sufficiently transparent, but it serves to solve many simple problems that are embryonic examples of a wide diversity of general methods. The initial situation must encode the total task structure, for the attempt to assimilate must encompass the means for transformation and the constraints, as well as the initial object.

In Fig. 9.10 we show an example of how Merlin might solve this same problem. S expresses the total given situation: an initial expression plus the specification that one RULE can be applied of the three available. G represents the goal situation.[12] Each RULE is expressed in several alternatives. For our example, we will assume that there are at least three: one explicitly as a RULE and two as generic expressions, one corresponding to an element of the range, the other to an element of the domain. (We will return to this multiple representation below.) To keep matters simple, the initial situation S is limited to a single application of a rule.[13] The initial step (and in a sense the only step) is to try to view this initial situation as a further specification of the desired situation.

Flat and Cover applied to S/G first leads to reducing the two expressions to the same schema (EXPR), which represents the connectives as com-

---

[12]For clarity, we have omitted the structure which would be necessary to disambiguate assymetric arguments. In full form, G would look like: G: [⊃ [ANTECEDENT [∼P]] [CONSEQUENT Q]].

[13]A complete specification would include that a composition of rules can be applied.

Initial state:
    S: [[v P Q]   [ONE-OF R1 R2 R3]]

Final state:
    G: [⊃ [~ P]   Q]

Allowable rules and some of their alternative views
    R1: [RULE [FROM [v A [v B C]]]   [TO [v [v A B] C]]]
         [v A [v B C]   [ELEMENT FROM]]
         [v [v A B] C [ELEMENT TO]]
         . . .
    R2: [RULE [FROM [v A B]] [TO [~ [∧ [~ A] [~ B]]]]]]
         [v A B [ELEMENT FROM]]
         [~ [∧ [~ A] [~ B]] [ELEMENT TO]]
         . . .
    R3: [RULE [FROM [v A B]]   [TO [⊃ [~ A] B]]]
         [v A B [ELEMENT FROM]]
         [⊃ [~ A] B [ELEMENT TO]]
         . . .

Additional knowledge about logic expressions
    v: [CONNECTIVE DISJUNCTION]
       [EXPR [CONNECTIVE DISJUNCTION]]

    ⊃: [CONNECTIVE IMPLICATION]
       [EXPR [CONNECTIVE IMPLICATION]]

View S as a G
    S/G → [[v P Q]   [ONE-OF R1 R2 R3]] / [⊃ [~ P] Q]

        → [EXPR [CONNECTIVE v] P Q [ONE-OF R1 R2 R3]] /
          [EXPR [CONNECTIVE ⊃] [~ P] Q]

        → Cover #1: [CONNECTIVE v] / [CONNECTIVE ⊃] → v/⊃ Fail

        → Cover #2: [ONE-OF R1 R2 R3] / [CONNECTIVE ⊃]

            A(ONE-OF) →   R1 / [CONNECTIVE ⊃] Fail
                           R2 / [CONNECTIVE ⊃] Fail
                           R3 / [CONNECTIVE ⊃] → [⊃ [~ A] B] Succeed

                    →   S: [EXPR [CONNECTIVE v] P Q R3]

            A(R3)   →   S: [⊃ [~ P] Q]

S/G → [⊃ [~ P] Q] / [⊃ [~ P] Q] → G Succeed

FIG. 9.10. β-structure generation of means-ends sequence of Fig. 9.9.

ponents: [CONNECTIVE v] and [CONNECTIVE ⊃] which simply amounts to selecting the appropriate principal alternative). The most obvious attempt to find a cover involves mapping each of the components onto its correspondent, ignoring the [ONE-OF ...] component as unneeded. This fails to find an acceptable mapping, since v/⊃ is not possible (and no other component in S covers [CONNECTIVE ⊃], either). If the two expressions had in fact been identical, then this cover would have succeeded and the problem would have been solved (corresponding to a successful initial match in GPS).

The second try at a cover attempts to use [ONE-OF ...] to cover one of the components of G, say [CONNECTIVE ⊃]. We assume that ONE-OF has an action corresponding to the understanding of its semantics, namely, that one of its components is to be an alternative. This produces the three mapping attempts shown, only one of which succeeds (R3). This leads to the formation of a new alternative for S, namely, one with R3 for [ONE-OF ...]. The existence of this alternative eventually generates the attempt to view it as a G. This leads to the execution of A(R3) (which we assume exists) which generates yet another alternative for S. When the mapping is tried with this alternative, it succeeds, solving the problem.

The above sequence depends on the existence of two actions, A(ONE-OF) and A(R3), which are necessary to define the task environment but do not in themselves provide a method of solving the problem. The mapping attempt involves, in addition to Flat and Cover, two principles: that alternatives should be tried, and that any actions involved (on schemas or components) should be executed. These principles are part of the general techniques of finding maps and do not have any special relationship to the means-ends method.

We have ignored numerous submaps which might be attempted and would subsequently fail (e.g., [CONNECTIVE v]/[~P]). It remains for an implementation of these ideas to demonstrate that the desirable submaps are sufficiently "obvious," and that the system will not be swamped by attempting an intolerably large collection of undesirable submaps.

One feature of the task environment is closely related to the possibility of means-ends analysis. Each of the RULEs was described in terms of its output. That is, a RULE is a kind of an element of its range (recall the discussion of +). This is what permits easy selection of the RULE in terms of the goal. Without this (which corresponds to the prepared table of connections), there is no easy way to make the selection and the behavior of the system would correspond more closely to forward search.

This paper is not the place to attempt an extensive development of the notion of natural intelligence. However a second example will be useful to show its character. The top of Fig. 9.11 gives a simple example of a geometric analogy problem, taken from Evans (1968) and by him from standard intelligence tests. Below the figure are written descriptions in β-structures.

The task is indicated by the classic proportionality notation, which may be rendered "A is to B as C is to which X?". A direct translation into β-structures is:

$$[\text{ONE-OF X1 X2 X3 X4 X5}]/\text{X} \qquad\qquad [57]$$

where

$$\text{X: } [\text{C B/A \#}] \qquad\qquad [58]$$

That is, first form a view (X) of the fourth term, which is a kind of a C, namely the same kind of a C as B is a kind of a A (hence one wants the components of B/A, which define the mapping itself of B into A). Then, one wants that Xi which can be viewed as an X, so formed.[14] Fig. 9.11 differs slightly, avoiding the use of ONE-OF and simply showing each of the Xi/X so that all mapping attempts are explicit. All of the intelligence in the selection is provided by the attempts to map with the basic Flat and Cover procedure.

The same situation prevails here as in the means-ends example. Simply expressing the problem in full in β-structures leads to a solution. Examination of the solution reveals two things. First, it depends on the encoding of the geometric figures, although the encoding used in no way smuggles in the solution. Second, actually finding the right answer depends strongly on the simplicity of the problem. Given a slightly more complex analogy or one in which the Xi were much closer together, the mapping could easily fail. However, this is exactly the point: Natural intelligence carries just a little way; to go further requires deliberate application of methods under the control of disciplined intention. This division of problem solving ability is essentially orthogonal to the one current in artificial intelligence programs, which produces expertise along certain classes of problems with complete inability to deal with any members of other classes, no matter how trivial.

Let us summarize. The act of attempting to view one entity as another is taken as the elementary act of directionality (of goal orientation). This implies not only a way of expressing goals when required, but that whenever Merlin performs X/Y it is operating in a directed way. The attempt to view one thing as another permits Merlin to solve simple, sufficiently obvious problems. The example of Fig. 9.10 shows this for a simple example of means-ends analysis. The basic mapping technique in interaction with the structure of the task environment produced the equivalent of the methods of GPS. The point, of course, is not that there is no "method"—as if the behavior arose magically. Rather, the single method of attempting to find a mapping suffices to generate different methods as a function of the structure of the task and goal. We have not demonstrated this yet for all the weak

---

[14]This is not the only way to view the problem; one could also find X: [B C/A #]. Or, one could represent each Xi as a C, separately (Xi/C) and compare these with the representation of B as an A (B/A) for similarity. Each is a bona fide kernel of a method and sometimes one, sometimes another is easier.

Original problem:

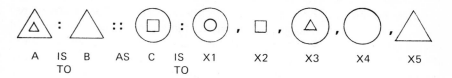

β-structure representation:

A:	[TRIANGLE LARGE [TRIANGLE SMALL INSIDE]]
B:	[TRIANGLE LARGE]
C:	[CIRCLE LARGE [SQUARE SMALL INSIDE]]
X1:	[CIRCLE LARGE [CIRCLE SMALL INSIDE]]
X2:	[SQUARE SMALL]
X3:	[CIRCLE LARGE [TRIANGLE SMALL INSIDE]]
X4:	[CIRCLE LARGE]
X5:	[TRIANGLE LARGE]

TRIANGLE:	[PLANE-FIGURE TRIANGLE-NESS]
CIRCLE:	[PLANE-FIGURE CIRCLE-NESS]
SQUARE:	[PLANE-FIGURE SQUARE-NESS]

X: [C B/A#]
   → [C [A [[TRIANGLE SMALL INSIDE]/NULL]]#]
   → [C [[TRIANGLE SMALL INSIDE]/NULL]]
   (From the posit: TRIANGLE-NESS/SQUARE-NESS, we conclude
   that [TRIANGLE SMALL INSIDE]/[SQUARE SMALL INSIDE].)
   → [C [[SQUARE SMALL INSIDE]/NULL]]
   → [CIRCLE LARGE]

Xi/X → (fail) for i = 1, 2, 3 & 5.
But:
X4/X → [CIRCLE LARGE] (success!)

FIG. 9.11. Geometric analogy problem.

methods, but it appears to be a reasonable conjecture. There are limits to what the mapping mechanisms can do, in comparison to encoded methods which serve to maintain the directedness of solution attempts. Merlin must have methods for solving difficult problems, but we expect Merlin to rely on its natural intelligence (as embedded in the mapping) for a great diversity of trivial problems.

The above discussion is addressed to obtaining directionality. It does not address the Keep-progressing issue. In fact, natural intelligence will often fail and provide no inkling of what to do then. A clue can perhaps be found in the difficulty workers in artificial intelligence have always had in constructing spaces of methods. AI programs usually consist of a very few methods (less than the fingers of one hand); occasionally there are a dozen, each handcrafted and preexisting. Never is there a space from which one might generate method after method. Perhaps the attempt to find a structured space is misguided. Rather, the system should capitalize on the odd collection of methods that happen to be available within the system at a given time. Methods that have been used for other tasks must then be adapted to the task at hand, i.e., metaphor and analogy form the basis of the method space.

To be more specific, suppose Merlin has a method (M1) which can be confidently evoked whenever a particular problem (P1) is to be solved. That is:

[P1 M1]/SOLUTION   [59]

succeeds. What happens when Merlin is posed with a different, but similar problem (P2)? Assuming that there is no existing method available which is known to be effective on P2, how might Merlin construct such a method? In the same spirit as the example of Fig. 9.11, above, Merlin constructs:

M2: [M1 P2/P1 #]   [60]

That is, M2 is the image of M1 under that mapping which carries P1 into P2.

In Fig. 9.12, we see a simplified example of this strategy in operation. TOWERS-OF-HANOI is intended to be the classical problem, here with five disks. The variant, TOWERS-OF-WARSAW has three disks and five pegs, but is otherwise the same. For M1, we have M-TH, a form of Generate-and-Test, parameterized by several aspects of the problem. In attempting to create a method, M-TW, for the TOWERS-OF-WARSAW, Merlin would proceed, as indicated above:

M-TW: [M-TH   [61]
   TOWERS-OF-WARSAW/ TOWERS-OF-HANOI #]

The similarity of the two problems provides a simple solution to the indicated submap, producing:

M-TW: [M-TH [TOWERS-OF-HANOI   [62]
   TW-PEGS/ TH-PEGS
   TW-DISKS/TH-DISKS] #]
which is:

M-TW: [M-TH TW-PEGS/TH-PEGS   [63]
   TW-DISKS/ TH-DISKS]

This amounts to saying "the method for solving TOWERS-OF-WARSAW is just the method for solving TOWERS-OF-HANOI with TW-PEGS replacing TH-PEGS and TW-DISKS replacing TH-DISKS."

While this new method may not be optimal for its corresponding problem, it obviously has some chance of producing a solution. Also clear is

A sketch of the definition of TOWERS OF HANOI:

TOWERS-OF-HANOI: [PROBLEM . . .

                TH-PEGS: [SET PEG1 PEG2 PEG3]

              . . .

                TH-DISKS: [SET DISK1 DISK2 DISK3 DISK4 DISK5]

              . . .

     ]

M-TH, a method for solving TOWERS-OF-HANOI, represented as the outline of a flowchart:

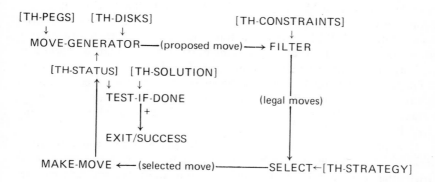

A corresponding sketch of a variant problem: TOWERS-OF-WARSAW:

TOWERS-OF-WARSAW: [PROBLEM . . .

                TW-PEGS: [SET PEG1 PEG2 PEG3 PEG4 PEG5]

              . . .

                TW-DISKS: [SET DISK1 DISK2 DISK3]

              . . .

     ]

FIG. 9.12. Towers of Hanoi and a variant.

that the complexity of the new problem or of the known method can be chosen to obfuscate this strategy.

Again, we have not shown that a genuinely large source of methods exists. We have generated an approach for Merlin to the issues of what to do next when you do not know what to do—find a similar problem and use it as a guide. Similarity is to be understood, not in terms of a metric on features of the problem, but in terms of whether one problem can be viewed as another so that the method for the first can be viewed as a method for the second. We might attempt to capture this design decision in a conjecture:

> Method-space Conjecture: *The set of methods used to continue on a hard problem (one where direct methods and natural intelligence have failed), is to be generated by viewing specific methods used successfully on other tasks as methods for the given task, more remote methods being generated as the mappings become weaker.*

Efficiency

The work on Merlin has in general not provided new design decisions on the question of efficiency. However, the issue of cascaded interpretation is particularly critical for Merlin. Recall Fig. 9.7 which showed a small part of the hierarchy of knowledge. If the only action that was available in Merlin was associated with PROCESS at the top of the hierarchy, then any attempt to assimilate, say, LTAT at the bottom must work through a cascade of assimilations—to interpret LTAT it must be viewed as a further specification of LTA, but to interpret LTA it must be viewed as a further specification of LT, but to ... and so on. When PROCESS is reached the action must percolate back through all the intermediate structures to actually effect something at LTAT.

This problem is hardly unique to Merlin. Systems usually permit definitional hierarchies in which previously defined terms can be used in constructing new definitions. But in operation, most systems unwind the definitions right down to the primitives in order to interpret the definitions, and thus pose the problem of what has been gained for the system (as opposed to the specifier). With Merlin the problem is compounded since the unwinding is an elaborate act of interpretation.

Our approach to this issue is through compilation. We can encase this in a principle of continuous compilation:

> *A new action for a β-structure is to be compiled as a side effect of using that β-structure as part of an attempted map.*

As discussed earlier, every node of the Knowledge Net can have an action, which embodies the same knowledge as can be held by the β-structure. Thus, one should be able to create an action at a node given an adequate interpretation of the knowledge at that node. With respect to the hierarchy of Fig. 9.7, assimilation of PS as a PROCESS leads to an action on PS; assimilation of HS as a PS leads to an action on HS; and so on. When LTAT is assimilated, there is already an action on LTA, so that the cascade of interpretation is avoided.

The current versions of Merlin do a partial, but important, part of this continuous compilation strategy. Each action, $A(X)$, can be considered to be composed of a pure procedure, $P(X)$, plus a prototype memory, $M(X)$, containing a set of variables and their associated initial values. When an actionless object (Y:[X Y1 Y2 ...]) is assimilated, A(X) is found, M(X) is copied into active memory and P(X) is executed. There is a point in time when P(X) has fully absorbed the components of Y into the active memory and has performed all possible, relevant computations on them, prior to seeking information outside of Y itself. At this point, A(X)'s state of computation is fully represented in the current set of variables and their values in active memory. A copy of this set is assigned to be M(Y) and for P(Y), we use P(X), itself. Thus, when later Merlin encounters some use of Y (e.g., in Z:[Y Z1 Z2 ...]), A(Y) represents exactly the same information as would be derived by searching through Y to X, retrieving A(X), and executing it in the context of Y. The process as it stands never creates any new procedure code.

In the discussion of the design issues we raised a question about the role of formality in efficiency—formality we claimed led to uniformity, hence (ultimately), to a lack of adaptation, which would translate into inefficiency. There are aspects of formalization which offset this difficulty, of course, such as the guarantees that specified processing leads to specified results, which could lead to more efficient processing.

The question of formalization has much deeper significance than just that of its effects on efficiency. In particular, it is a cliche of computer science that all systems that have been programmed are *a fortiori* formalized. This is supposed to follow from the nature of an instruction set as a discrete set of primitives with fixed rules for combination. Yet, while this is certainly a view, it need not be the only view, especially given that there are no models around for what an informal system would be like.

The principle of self-declaring components for Merlin provides a system that seems to have some of the properties of an informal system. There is no fixed set of rules whereby one can interpret a β-structure. The role it plays depends on an indefinite amount of context in which it is embedded, which depends on the alternative interpretations that are plausible given the totality of other β-structures, including its components. Thus, all interpretations are hypotheses. This would seem to be the essence of an informal system, though as we noted, there is no way to be sure. We can put this, then, as a conjecture:

Merlin is an example of an informal system.

Error

The design of Merlin offers nothing fundamental yet to cope with error. Merlin has no generalized backtracking facility, such as exists in the Planner-like systems. The opportunities for combinatorial explosion appear so great in Merlin that backtracking simply cannot be afforded as the basework for dealing with error. Pending an alternative proposal, we have let the issue of error alone.

Depth of Understanding

The explorations with Merlin so far have not addressed themselves to questions of depth. In particular, Merlin does not now have a global data base, though it is planned to have one in the coming version.

Although not yet implemented in Merlin 3, the context related mechanisms (analogous to those used in earlier versions of the system) should be a powerful tool for addressing part of the access issue. In the course of attempting a map, Merlin may have cause to attempt a submap. Within this submap may be attempted still another submap, and so on, to an arbitrary depth. All of these pending maps are retained on a context stack, for use by any of the actions interested in the larger tasks which led to creating the current one. Furthermore, when the mapping mechanism is examining X for an action, if there is none then X↑, X↑↑, X↑↑↑, ... are examined, in turn. As each is stepped through to the next, the previous one is pushed onto the context stack. It is not worthwhile to explore here, all the intricacies of exactly how this stack is created, maintained and used. Suffice it to say that through this device, any action not only has access to all objects responsible for its evocation, but further, that they are all ordered on the basis of relevance—the top of the stack containing the most relevant objects, the bottom, the least. In prior versions, this machinry has enabled actions to reliably differentiate between similar objects in the computing environment which might otherwise be far harder to disambiguate.

CONCLUSION

Let us return to one of the reasons for organizing the discussion of Merlin around an extensive set of design features. An understanding system must come to terms with all the design issues in Fig. 9.2. It is certainly possible to build systems that only respond to some of the issues. It has happened many times in the literature of understanding systems, and all of what we have done with Merlin to date is similarly limited. Our characterization of work on Merlin as explorations into design issues reflects that fact. Not until Merlin is prepared to respond to the several issues on which it is now silent—multiple representation, accommodation, efficiency, error and depth—will it be a full-fledged proposal for an understanding system.

The incompleteness of the design of Merlin does not mean the existing design proposals are without content or merit, only that they are unstable. The attempt to solve the problem of error, which is absolutely critical, could modify the underlying attempt at informality with its implication of large amounts of uncertainty throughout the basic fabric of the system. Another example, though common to many systems beside Merlin, is the apparent inefficiency induced by the introduction of a general list-like data structure.

These almost always run very slowly for large systems. Perhaps these difficulties can be overcome directly or through a suitable multiple representation capability. Another possibility is compiling of selected structures into more efficient data structures (arrays and bit-arrays). But if these are not effective, substantial change in the basic system could be called for.

Let us turn finally to the distinctive feature of Merlin—taking assimilation as a central problem which dictates the representation of knowledge (the β-structure). The answer to the title of the paper—How Can Merlin Understand?—lies in this act of assimilation. Merlin will understand by the construction of maps from the structure that represents what Merlin knows to the structure that Merlin seeks to understand. The act of mapping is what will (hopefully) make Merlin bring to bear the internal knowledge relevant to the task and in that respect to exhibit its understanding.

Several (conjectural) promises hang on this internal representation in terms of mapping. The most important, it seems to us, is the promise of a *non-brittle* system. Computer systems in general and artificial intelligence systems in particular have sharp boundaries between what they accept and what they don't. Even programs such as Winograd's (1971), which seem on the surface to be forgiving, remain highly brittle—one passes quickly from what the program can handle (in terms of its English for instance) to where it fails completely. Only contentless systems like ELIZA (Weizenbaum, 1966) avoid this and they do so in ways that do not easily lead back toward intelligent systems. Attributing the difficulty to the basic discrete character of digital computation (which is surely right in part), one can seek to solve the problem by softening the basic representation. Merlin attempts a solution at a different point. Anything can be mapped into anything else, if sufficiently exotic maps are permitted, including those that posit some connections in order to infer others. Thus, the elastic character of the mapping holds Merlin's primary hope for avoiding brittleness. Since the representation is the mapping (an almost McLuhanesque proposition) and since the representation is universal (i.e., for all types of knowledge, procedures, facts, etc.), the softness induced by the mapping applies to all aspects of Merlin's operation. We have seen, for example, how this might apply to methods to generate a much larger space of methods for a given task than is now available.

A second important point of the mappings is the possibility of Merlin being an informal system, in the sense described earlier. This is related to the question of brittleness above, but formality is an important issue in artificial intelligence in its own right. The considerations in the current paper are entirely preliminary and really only serve to introduce the issue.

There is no difficulty identifying the substantial problems that still exist in determining whether a general mapping scheme can be successfully embodied in a complete system. The generality of the mapping contributes substantially to the difficulties in obtaining good design proposals for the missing items on the list of design issues. The accommodation issue is an obvious example, as is the efficiency issue, but it is true of the others as well. There is also the problem, already mentioned, of how to control the mappings given that facilities exist for always succeeding. Thus we must put forward the design considerations of the present paper as still highly provisional.

10
KNOWLEDGE AND ITS REPRESENTATION IN A SPEECH UNDERSTANDING SYSTEM

R. REDDY and A. NEWELL
Carnegie-Mellon University

Identification and representation of knowledge is a major problem in the experimental and theoretical studies associated with artificial intelligence research. The spectrum of tasks studied in artificial intelligence range from puzzle solving at one end to speech and visual perception tasks at the other. The sum total of accumulated knowledge used in puzzle solving is usually miniscule, while each of us spends a significant part of our life acquiring knowledge necessary to perceive and understand speech and visual stimuli. Unlike problem solving, the perceptual tasks are characterized by high data rates, large amounts of data, (possibly) errorful input, and the need for real-time response. These characteristics make it imperative that we use every available source of knowledge in the design of perception systems. In this paper we report on a system that attempts to understand speech, as an illustration of the role of knowledge in an intelligent system.

The motivations for this emphasis of the role of knowledge in an intelligent system are twofold. We believe that

1. The way to analyze an intelligent system is in terms of the sources of knowledge, their representation and the mechanisms that bring them to bear on the task; and that
2. One of the main carry-overs between work in artificial intelligence and psychology will occur at the level of such knowledge, representation, the mechanisms, rather than at higher levels.

In attempting to discuss the role of knowledge in an intelligent system, we chose Hearsay as our example. The Hearsay project is a group effort of several scientists led by Raj Reddy. In particular, we would like to acknowledge the contributions of Lee Erman who was mainly responsible for the system organization and the acoustics module, Rick Fennell who designed the global data structure, Bruce Lowerre who added much of the acoustic phonetic knowledge in the system, and Rich Neely who designed the syntactic and semantic modules for the voice-chess task.

Let us consider, in detail, the characteristics of speech understanding research which make it imperative that we use all the available sources of knowledge effectively in the decoding of an utterance.

1. *High data rate and large amount of data.* In problem solving, a problem can usually be stated by a few lines of input (a theorem to be proved or a question to be answered), which is then followed by a significant computational effort, followed by a few lines of output. In speech understanding, the utterance to be recognized has to be first digitized, i.e., the changes in air pressure resulting from speech are sampled every 50 microseconds or so. This results in high data rates (around 200,000 bits/sec) and large amount of data (requiring 10,000 to 50,000 words of memory). Thus, in contrast to written language understanding, speech understanding requires high bandwidth memory interfaces (for input), larger memories (for signal storage), and higher computational power (for signal processing).

2. *Errorful input.* An important difficulty with free speech that is not common in other areas of artificial intelligence research is the lack of grammaticality and general well-formedness. Although one may legislate against some of the difficulties in written language, it is harder to do so in spoken language. Not only do people "hmm" and "hah" and clear their throats, they utter fragments: "Now the... th'...oh well...they are plying flames—I mean flying planes". A whole set of new language analysis tools are necessary to deal with errorful input.

3. *Real-time response.* In tasks such as chess and theorem proving the human has enough trouble himself to make reasonably crude programs of interest. But because humans seem to perform effortlessly (and with only modest error) in speech perception tasks, they expect similar performance from machines, i.e., one expects an immediate response and will not tolerate any errors. To equal human performance, a speech understanding system must be able to answer trivial questions as soon as they are uttered. This implies that various processes within the system should be able to operate on the incoming data as soon as they are able to do so without waiting for the completion of the whole utterance.

These considerations indicate the nature of the advances that must be made before we can have speech understanding systems. These advances will have to come in machine architecture, system organization and models of speech perception in which all the available sources of knowledge are used effectively in the reduction of search and the correction of errors in the input utterance.

Even in the early fifties it was obvious that linguistic and contextual knowledge is essential for understanding of speech. Miller, Heise, and Lichten (1951) showed how the intelligibility of speech is affected as a function of syntactic and verbal context. Fry and Denes (1953) presented a proposal for a mechanical speech recognition system which could use linguistic information represented as conditional probabilities determined from digram frequencies. Later it was shown this type of knowledge representation would increase the accuracy of recognition from 60% to 72%. The analysis-by-synthesis model of Stevens and Halle (1962) and the motor theory model of Liberman, Cooper, Harris, and MacNeilage (1962) suggested representation of knowledge in generative form so that it could be used as a part of a synthesis and match paradigm.

Miller and Isard (1963) have attempted to quantify the degree of difficulty people have in immediate recall of meaningful, meaningless, and nongrammatical sentences. The error rate is 11% when asked to recall a meaningful sentence, e.g., "colorless cellophane packages crackle loudly". It increases to 21% when asked to recall meaningless sentences, e.g., "colorless yellow ideas sleep furiously." It increases to 43% in recalling a nongrammatical sentence, e.g., "sleep roses dangerously young colorless." These results help to demonstrate the relative importance of some of the sources of knowledge in understanding speech. They do not, however, tell us how this knowledge may be represented or used in a speech understanding system.

More recently a study committee (Newell et al., 1973) examined the feasibility of developing speech understanding systems. During this study, the present authors were primarily responsible for the analysis of several tasks to identify the sources of knowledge and the sources of error, and the mechanisms that may be useful in the design of a system (see Chapter 6 and Appendix 9 of Newell, Barnett, Forgie, Green, Klatt, Licklider, Munson, Reddy, & Woods, 1973). Representation of knowledge available at semantic, syntactic, lexical, phonemic, and parametric levels were discussed and some possible mechanisms for effective use of knowledge were proposed. Results of some simulation studies were given to indicate the reduction of search that may be achieved through the use of some of the sources of knowledge.

One of the systems that was based on the above study committee report is the Hearsay system developed by Reddy, Erman, Fennell, Lowerre, and Neely at Carnegie-Mellon University. It attempts to use several different sources of knowledge in understanding an utterance. Descriptions of the system organization and operation have already been presented by Reddy et al. (1973a, 1973b), Erman (1973), and Neely (1973). The purpose of the present paper is to examine the role of knowledge within the Hearsay system, e.g., how knowledge processes communicate, what they communicate, and how they cooperate, and to explore the relevance and implications of this research to psychology.

THE SOURCES OF KNOWLEDGE AND THEIR REPRESENTATION

In this section we will attempt to isolate and describe the main sources of knowledge as they exist in the present Hearsay system and how they are represented to achieve the goal of speech understanding. Not all the sources of knowledge discussed in the speech understanding report (Newell et al.,

1973, Chapter 6) are utilized in the present system. When a given source of knowledge has been utilized, it may only represent a first approximation to the intent of the report. However, the role of knowledge, e.g., how knowledge processes communicate, what they communicate, and how they cooperate is much more clearly specified in the present system. The result is a unified model in which all knowledge processes have symmetric roles with respect to each other. After discussing the structure of the model, we will present the details of representation of knowledge at the semantic, syntactic, lexical, phonemic, and parametric levels.

Throughout this section we will illustrate our general statements about knowledge with examples from a specific task domain, e.g., the microworld of voice-chess. Voice-chess was chosen as one of the first tasks for the Hearsay system, not because it is important to play chess with a computer over the telephone, but because chess provides a good environment to evaluate the ideas about the role of various sources of knowledge in speech perception. Chess plays the role in artificial intelligence that the fruit fly plays in genetics. Just as the genetics of *drosophila* are studied not to breed better flies, but to learn the laws of heredity, so we study chess to understand the laws of artificial intelligence. In Hearsay, chess was chosen as a task because the syntax, semantics, and vocabulary of discourse are well defined and are amenable to systematic study.

The Model

A detailed discussion of the criteria and the derivation of the model are given in Reddy et al. (1973a). Here we restrict ourselves to a brief description of the model emphasizing the role of knowledge within the model. The model consists of a set of cooperating independent knowledge processes that are capable of helping in the decoding of a spoken utterance either individually or collectively. Each process uses some source of knowledge (possibly different representations of the same source of knowledge) to determine whether it has anything interesting to contribute in a given context (of a partially recognized utterance) and to generate, reject, or rank order hypotheses in that context. Knowledge processes communicate with each other by writing (or modifying) hypotheses on a "blackboard." Since knowledge processes speak different languages, e.g., knowledge at the acoustic-phonetic level is of a different type than that at the semantic level, mechanisms are provided to translate hypotheses between levels. Since the role of a knowledge process is to generate or verify hypotheses, the system can continue to function even in the absence of one or more of these sources of knowledge, as long as there are some generators and some verifiers in the aggregate.

Knowledge at the Semantic Level

There are several sources of knowledge at the semantic level: the knowledge about the task domain, the current state of the conversation, a model of user behavior, knowledge about (meaningful use of) language and so on. The notions of "apriori semantics of the task" and "situational semantics of the conversation" help to define the microworld and the situation. Having investigated several tasks, we find the identification and representation of these types of knowledge are difficult and imprecise. However, in the case of voice-chess, these knowledge sources are well defined and contribute significantly to the reduction of search space. The "apriori semantics of the task" are given by the rules of the chess game. The "situational semantics of the conversation" are given by the current board position. The rules of chess and the board position are used to formulate a list of legal moves which represent plausible hypotheses for what might be taken by the user next. Fig. 10.1 gives an example of a board position in which the user has to make a move. Fig. 10.2 gives a list of legal moves for this situation. This list is used by the Hearsay system in restricting the plausible utterances to 40 or so moves. These sources of knowledge are represented in Hearsay as a program (Gillogly, 1972).

The notion of a "user model" is used to represent the psychological state of the user (Newell et al., 1973, page 85) and a model for predicting his behavior in a given state. For the voice-chess task, the user model is the same for all users and primarily incorporates the notions of goodness of a move as indicated by piece advantage, and so on. It does not at present include the discovery of the strategy being pursued by a given user. Fig. 10.2 gives a rank ordering of the legal moves based on the goodness of move evaluation procedure in TECH (Gillogly, 1972).

Given a task, a situation, and user model, all of which may be used to predict what the user might say next, there is still a great deal of variability possible. This essentially depends on the linguistic performance of the user. In the chess situation given in Fig. 10.1 and 10.2, and given that the user has decided to use the move "B-QN3," Fig. 10.3 gives some of the 108 ways he can utter this move.

Neely (1973, pp. 73-79) shows how knowledge about the partially recognized utterance is used to constrain the variability in linguistic performance of the user. Basically, given that a word such as "captures" or "takes" appears in the partial sentence hypothesis, this knowledge can be used to further restrict the search to the capture moves in that board position. This restricted set of moves is used to give high semantic preference to the key content words that may occur in the predicted option word list.

Missing in the present Hearsay system are the explicit use of word level semantics ("colorless yellow ideas") and phrase level semantics ("give me about Tom"). By word level semantics, we mean knowledge about meaning

Fig. 10.1. Example of a board position in chess.

of words where a semantic inconsistency can be determined by local context (one or two word context). An inconsistency which can only be detected by considering a whole phrase is handled by phrase level semantics. For example, "give me about a yard" or "Tell me about Tom" are acceptable but not "give me about Tom." These sources of knowledge do not appear in voice-chess task as part of the chess program. But in general semantic representations for speech understanding, we can expect these to be represented as some form of semantic nets, and participate in the recognition as independent knowledge processes.

Knowledge at the Syntactic Level

Syntactic knowledge is usually represented as a set of productions which can be used in a generative framework to produce all the legal sentences of the language. This knowledge can also be used to determine the parse (possibly multiple) of a given sentence.

The grammar for the voice-chess language is context free. This grammar is specified as a set of BNF productions, and is given in Fig. 10.4. For example, in this grammar, <move> is defined to be either <move1> followed by <checkword> or <move1>. The total number of different utterances permitted by this grammar is over five million.

Traditional parsing schemes, which provide one possible framework for representation and use of knowledge at the syntactic level prove to be unsatisfactory for speech understanding because of the ungrammaticality and errorful nature of speech. What is needed is a representation in which syntactic knowledge can be used to parse backwards and forwards and to predict what may appear next, given a partial parse of a sentence. The

KN/KN1—KB3
KN/KN1—K2
QB/QB1—KB4
QB/QB1—K3
QB/QB1—KN5
QB/QB1—Q2
QN/QB3—Q5
KBP/KB2—KB4
KBP/KB2—KB3
QR/QR1—QN1
KP/K4—K5
QB/QB4—Q5
K/K1—KB1
K/K1—Q1
QB/QB4—Q3
K/K1—Q2
QN/QB3—QN5
QB/QB4—QN5CH
QB/QB4—K2
KRP/KR2—KR4
KN/KN1—KR3
QNP/QN2—QN4
QRP/QR2—QR4
QRP/QR2—QR3
KRP/KR2—KR3
KNP/KN2—KN3
QNP/QN2—QN3
QB/QB4—QN3
QB/QB4—KB1
QN/QB3—K2
KNP/KN2—KN4
QN/QB3—Q1
QN/QB3—QR4
QN/QB3—QN1
QB/QB4XKBP/KB7C
QB/QB1—KR6
QB/QB4—K6
QB/QB4—QR6

FIG. 10.2 Possible legal moves in the board position given in Fig. 10.1 rank ordered according to the goodness of move.

1. BISHOP TO KNIGHT THREE
2. QUEEN BISHOP TO KNIGHT THREE
3. QUEEN'S BISHOP TO KNIGHT THREE
4. BISHOP ON BISHOP FOUR TO KNIGHT THREE
5. BISHOP ON QUEEN BISHOP FOUR TO KNIGHT THREE
6. BISHOP ON QUEEN'S BISHOP FOUR TO KNIGHT THREE

.
.
.

64. QUEEN'S BISHOP ON BISHOP FOUR GOES TO QUEEN'S KNIGHT THREE

.
.
.

69. QUEEN'S BISHOP ON QUEEN'S BISHOP FOUR GOES TO QUEEN KNIGHT THREE
70. QUEEN'S BISHOP ON QUEEN BISHOP FOUR GOES TO QUEEN'S KNIGHT THREE
71. QUEEN BISHOP ON QUEEN'S BISHOP FOUR GOES TO QUEEN'S KNIGHT THREE
72. QUEEN'S BISHOP ON QUEEN'S BISHOP FOUR GOES TO QUEEN'S KNIGHT THREE

.
.
.

107. QUEEN BISHOP ON QUEEN'S BISHOP FOUR MOVES TO QUEEN'S KNIGHT THREE
108. QUEEN'S BISHOP ON QUEEN'S BISHOP FOUR MOVES TO QUEEN'S KNIGHT THREE

FIG. 10.3. Many different ways of saying "B-QN3" in the Hearsay system.

hypothesize and test paradigm provides an effective method for use of knowledge in errorful situations.

The ability to predict, and to parse backwards and forwards is achieved in Hearsay by representing syntactic knowledge as antiproductions. Antiproductions act as a concordance for the grammar giving all the contexts for every symbol appearing in the grammar. Fig. 10.5 gives antiproductions for Productions 1-6 of the grammar in Fig. 10.4. These are produced automatically by a preprocessing program that takes the grammar as input. In this figure, the symbols in the column labeled CENTER are the entries in the concordance. Each symbol in the subset of the grammar appears in this column once for each occurrence of it in the subset. The entries in the LEFT and RIGHT columns denote symbols that can appear to the left and right of the entry in the center column. When an ↑ appears in the LEFT or RIGHT column, it indicates that the original production did not have an entry to the left or right of that symbol.

When the LEFT (or RIGHT) context given in an antiproduction is satisfied, then the RIGHT (or LEFT) context is proposed as a hypothesis. If the hypothesized symbol happens to be a nonterminal, then all the possible terminal symbols that can appear at the left of this nonterminal are hypothesized. Detailed description of the structure and use of the antiproductions is given in Neely (1973, pp. 58-68).

The use of syntactic knowledge in the verification of a hypothesis generated by some other source of knowledge also differs from conventional usage. In a conventional parsing system, a whole utterance is given as input

```
<move>                        : : = <move1> <check-word>  |  <move1>

<move1>           : : = <regular-move>  |  <capture>  |  <castle>

<castle>          : : = <castle-word> ON <uniroyal> SIDE
                        |  <castle-word> <uniroyal> SIDE
                        |  <castle-word>

<regular-move>    : : = <man-loc> <move-word> <square>

<capture>         : : = <man-loc> <capture-word> PAWN EN-PASSENT
                        |  <man-loc> <capture-word> <man-loc>

<castle-word>     : : = CASTLE  |  CASTLES

<move-word>       : : = TO  |  MOVES-TO  |  GOES-TO

<capture-word>    : : = TAKES  |  CAPTURES

<check-word>      : : = CHECK MATE  |  CHECK

<man-loc>         : : = <man-spec> ON <square>  |  <man-spec>

<man-spec>        : : = <uniroyal> <unipiece> PAWN
                        |  <uniroyal> <piece>
                        |  <uniroyal> PAWN
                        |  <unipiece> PAWN
                        |  <man>

<square>          : : = <uniroyal> <piece> <rank>  |  <nopawn> <rank>

<man>             : : = KING  |  QUEEN  |  BISHOP  |  KNIGHT
                        |  ROOK  |  PAWN

<uniroyal>        : : = KING  |  QUEEN  |  KING'S  |  QUEEN'S

<unipiece>        : : = BISHOP  |  KNIGHT  |  ROOK  |  BISHOP'S
                        |  KNIGHT'S  |  ROOK'S

<nopawn>          : : = KING  |  QUEEN  |  BISHOP  |  KNIGHT  |  ROOK

<piece>           : : = BISHOP  |  KNIGHT  |  ROOK

<rank>            : : = ONE  |  TWO  |  THREE  |  FOUR  |  FIVE
                        |  SIX  |  SEVEN  |  EIGHT
```

FIG. 10.4. Voice-chess syntax.

CENTER	LEFT	RIGHT	HEAD
CASTLE	↑	↑	<castle-word>
CASTLES	↑	↑	<castle-word>
EN-PASSENT	PAWN	↑	<capture>
ON	<castle-word>	<uniroyal>	<castle>
PAWN	<capture-word>	EN-PASSENT	<capture>
SIDE	<uniroyal>	↑	<castle>
SIDE	<uniroyal>	↑	<castle>
<move1>	↑	<check-word>	<move>
<move1>	↑	↑	<move>
<check-word>	<move1>	↑	<move>
<regular-move>	↑	↑	<move1>
<capture>	↑	↑	<move1>
<castle>	↑	↑	<move1>
<castle-word>	↑	ON	<castle>
<castle-word>	↑	<uniroyal>	<castle>
<castle-word>	↑	↑	<castle>
<uniroyal>	ON	SIDE	<castle>
<uniroyal>	<castle-word>	SIDE	<castle>
<man-loc>	↑	<move-word>	<regular-move>
<man-loc>	↑	<capture-word>	<capture>
<man-loc>	↑	<capture-word>	<capture>
<man-loc>	<capture-word>	↑	<capture>
<move-word>	<man-loc>	<square>	<regular-move>
<square>	<move-word>	↑	<regular-move>
<capture-word>	<man-loc>	PAWN	<capture>
<capture-word>	<man-loc>	<man-loc>	<capture>

FIG. 10.5. Antiproductions for a subset of the syntax in Fig. 10.4 (The subset consists of Productions 1-6.)

for parsing. In a speech understanding system, at any given time, only some of the words in the sentence are known. These may or may not be contiguous. What is needed is a parsing scheme in which a partially recognized sentence can be accepted or rejected based on the syntactic knowledge. In the Hearsay system this is achieved by the use of a modified top-down parsing scheme.

Knowledge at the Lexical Level

The knowledge at the lexical level arises primarily from the restrictions on the size and the structure of the vocabulary. Vocabulary size is not always a meaningful measure of the complexity of the system. A system capable of recognizing the words "gore, door, bore, core, tore, pour, four, sour, wore, more, and lore" must have much more sophisticated rules than a system capable of recognizing the 10 digits. In most cases, however, the vocabulary is task-defined with some minimal tuning permissible. For the voice-chess task the size of the vocabulary is 31. In addition to this size restriction, the knowledge at the lexical level consists of the phonemic description, stress indication, the grammatical category and the meaning for each word.

In the Hearsay system the phonemic description is used for mapping words in the lexicon onto segments of the incoming utterance. The stressed syllable indicator is used in the subselection of the vocabulary to hypothesize as possible candidates for a given part of the utterance. The syntactic and semantic markers are not explicitly represented or used at present, but are used implicitly as part of a chess program. During the verification, the lexical entries of ambiguous words are matched against each other to determine optimal tests. For example, given the words "bore, more, and lore," word ambiguity analysis will predict that optimal tests for disambiguation are tests for /b/, /m/, and /I/ at the word initial position.

Many of the issues raised in the speech understanding report (Newell et al., 1973, pp. 24-25) such as the effect of the vocabulary size, effect of noise, frequency of usage, and so on have not yet been considered in a systematic way and are likely to become major problems as the vocabulary size becomes larger, say 1,000 words or more.

Knowledge at the Phonemic Level

There are several different types of knowledge available at this level. These include characteristics of the phonemes, rules for predicting missing and extra segments in relaxed speech, juncture rules, and rules that distinguish between pairs of phonemes. This knowledge is used in conjunction with the lexical knowledge about phonetic descriptions of each word in matching acoustic segments in the utterance with word and sentence level hypotheses. We will first illustrate the nature of each of these types of knowledge by means of examples and then describe how this knowledge is used in the Hearsay system.

Fig. 10.6a shows the waveform and spectrogram representations of the word "to" in the context of "pawn to king." The word "to" consists of the phonemes /t/ and /ə/.[1] The phoneme /t/ is usually characterized by a silence-like segment (50-70 milliseconds) representing the complete closure of the vocal tract followed by a noise-like segment representing the release and aspiration. The vowel /ə/ in the word "to" is a neutral vowel which is usually characterized by a short duration (20-25 milliseconds) and formant frequencies at 500, 1,500 and 2,500 Hz. These characteristics are reflected in the waveform and the spectrogram for the word "to" as indicated by the brackets. Notice, however, the silence part of the phoneme /t/ is less than 20 milliseconds of duration because it is preceded by a nasal, which has the same vocal tract position (the /n/ of pawn). Knowledge at the phonetic level,

---

[1] The phoneme /ə/ is the neutral vowel (and pronounced as schwa) that occurs in function words such as to, a, the, in connected speech.

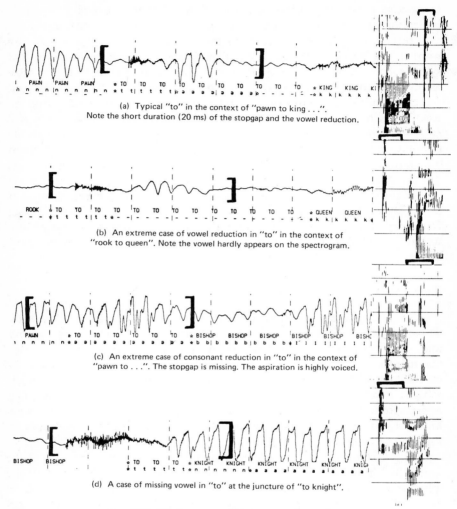

(a) Typical "to" in the context of "pawn to king . . .".
Note the short duration (20 ms) of the stopgap and the vowel reduction.

(b) An extreme case of vowel reduction in "to" in the context of "rook to queen". Note the vowel hardly appears on the spectrogram.

(c) An extreme case of consonant reduction in "to" in the context of "pawn to . . .". The stopgap is missing. The aspiration is highly voiced.

(d) A case of missing vowel in "to" at the juncture of "to knight".

FIG. 10.6. Missing segments in connected speech.

i.e., the expected acoustic characteristics of each phoneme, is represented as phoneme procedures within the Hearsay system. Procedural descriptions of this knowledge permits us to express easily contextual variations such as the shortening of the stopgap of the phoneme /t/ in Fig. 10.6a.

In connected speech many of the expected characteristics of a phoneme may be absent. Sometimes the entire phoneme may be missing. These are illustrated by examples given in Fig. 10.6b to 10.6d. In Fig. 10.6b we see an extreme case of vowel reduction where the expected characteristics of the vowel /ə/ are completely missing except for some very-low-frequency energy.

In the spectrogram shown in Fig. 10.6b, notice that the vowel is completely missing causing a phonetician to treat it as part of the following silence segment.

In Fig. 10.6c, we see an extreme case of consonant reduction that is not uncommon in relaxed connected speech. In a context similar with the one given in Fig. 10.6a we find that the phoneme /t/ is essentially missing. The silence segment is not present and the aspiration is highly voiced.

In Fig. 10.6d, we see the case of a missing vowel in the word "to" at the juncture of the words "to knight." Again this is not uncommon. In relaxed speech reduced vowels in the context of nasals and liquids may be assimilated with the adjacent segment.

One can also find examples in connected speech where extra unexpected segments are present or the characteristics are sufficiently changed to cause the segment to be recognized differently. In the Hearsay system, knowledge about the missing segments and extra segments is represented as part of the contextual variability in the phoneme procedures or as part of the juncture rules.

The need for juncture rules is illustrated by the utterance "bishop to queen knight three" shown in Fig. 10.7. At the juncture of "bishop to," "queen knight," and "knight three," we have juncture ambiguity. In the case of "bishop to" the unvoiced stop /p/ occurs adjacent to another unvoiced stop /t/. This usually results in the absence of the release and aspiration that usually characterizes the sound /p/. In this utterance we see an exception to that juncture rule where the speaker deliberately releases the /p/. The ending nasal of king and the beginning nasal of knight are articulated from the same tongue position resulting in a single segment representing two different phonemes in two adjacent words. Further, it is difficult to specify the exact location of the word boundary. Another type of juncture problem appears at the boundary of "knight three." The release and aspiration of the phoneme /t/ are assimilated into the /θ/ of the word three. Because the knowledge about junctures is applicable mainly at the word level, representation of this knowledge is in the form of a procedure, which is activated when words are being matched with the acoustic segments.

Sometimes it is difficult to classify uniquely a given acoustic segment as one of the 40 possible phonemes. Consider the following problem of a playful speaker. Suppose in a situation where the sentence "pawn to king four" is a valid move he says "palm to key hole." If "palm," "key," and "hole" were also legal words, a system would have difficulty with such an utterance requiring finer tests of features than are present in the individual phoneme procedures. This ambiguation rules between phonetically ambiguous words are currently being implemented in the Hearsay system by means of phoneme pair difference procedures. Given a pair of phonemes these procedures indicate what is an optimal test to make to disambiguate between the pair of the phonemes.

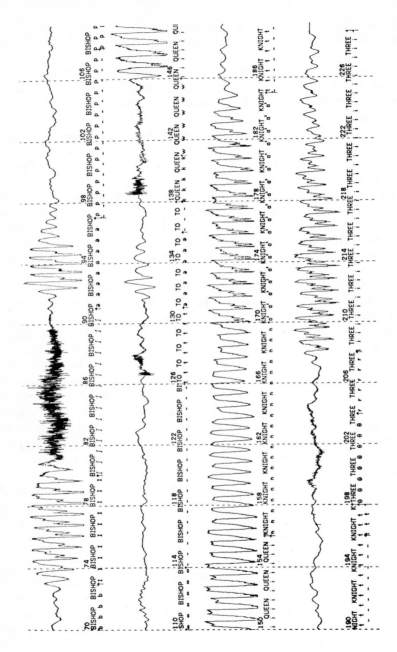

Fig. 10.7. Waveform of the utterance, "Bishop to Queen Knight Three." (Word and phoneme boundaries manually determined.)

All the above sources of knowledge are used primarily to perform verification. The hypothesization at the phonetic level is based on the fact that certain sounds within an utterance, e.g., stressed vowels, sibilants, and unvoiced stops, can usually be uniquely recognized. These features of the incoming utterances can then be used as an acoustic phonetic filter on the lexicon to hypothesize only those words that are appropriate in that phonetic context.

Knowledge at the Parametric Level

The parametric characteristics of sounds change significantly depending on the context. This is commonly referred to as the allophonic variability. Fig. 10.8 illustrates the problems that arise because of this variability. Fig. 10.8a shows the characteristic spectrum of the phoneme /i/ as it would appear in the word "deed." Fig. 10.8c shows the characteristic spectrum of the sound /u/ as it would appear in the sound "use." The question that often arises at this level is: given a sound with the spectral shape shown in Fig. 10.8b is it an /u/ or is it an /i/? Although the peak structure of the spectrum indicates formant positions closer to that of an /u/, the sound in question is in fact an /i/ in the phrase "one reamer." In this phrase the sound /i/ occurs in the context of retroflexed and nasalized sounds. Nasalization adds an additional nasal formant to the spectrum and retroflection has the tendency to lower the formant frequency of the adjacent vowel. These two effects taken together give a peak structure to the sound /i/ in Fig. 10.8b that is more like the formant structure expected for the /u/ and not the expected structure for /i/. The knowledge about the allophonic variability is presently being implemented in the Hearsay system by uniquely representing the parametric characteristics of all the important allophones of each phoneme.

Another source of variability at the parametric level is the speaker characteristics. The length of the vocal tract, and the size and the lossiness of the cavities differ from speaker to speaker depending on his size, age, and physical condition. The effect of this variability is primarily to cause shifts in the expected formant frequencies. In the Hearsay system an attempt is made to correct for these variations by the use of a parametric table for each speaker. This table contains a standard set of parameters for various allophones of phonemes uttered by the speaker. This set of parameters also accounts for the variation in the parametric characteristics resulting from the room noise and the microphone. Details of the speaker and environment normalization procedures are given by Erman (1973).

THE USE OF KNOWLEDGE IN THE RECOGNITION PROCESS

Here we will illustrate the operation of the Hearsay system and the use of various sources of knowledge by considering in detail the recognition process

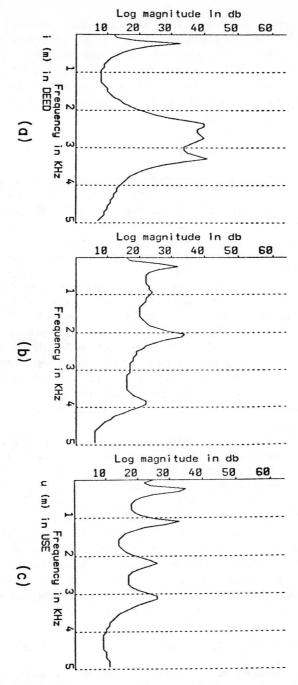

Fig. 10.8. Allophonic variability in the spectra for /i/ depending on context.

BISHOP TO QUEEN KNIGHT THREE

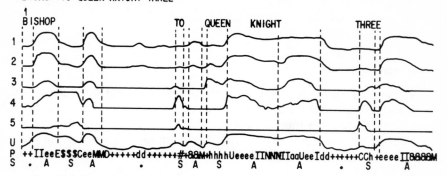

FIG. 10.9. Parametric representation of the utterance in Fig. 10.7 showing the results of feature extraction and segmentation.

of an utterance. The utterance to be recognized is "bishop to queen knight three" given in Fig. 10.7. This utterance is a legal move in the context of the band position given in Fig. 10.1. The speech input from the microphone is passed through five board pass filters (spanning the range from 200-6,400 Hz) and through an unfiltered band. Within each band the maximum intensity is measured for each 10 milliseconds.[2] This results in a vector of 6 amplitude parameters every 10 milliseconds. These parameters are smoothed and log transformed. Fig. 10.9 shows a plot of these parameters as a function of time for the utterance given in Fig. 10.7. The top line of text indicates where the word boundaries were marked during the manual segmentation process. (This permits manual verification of the accuracy of the machine recognition process in the later stages—naturally it is not used in recognition.)

This vector of parameters (labeled 1, 2, 3, 4, 5, and U) in Fig. 10.9 is, for each centisecond, compared with the standard set of parameter vectors representing the phone characteristics. A minimum distance classification technique using a modified nearest neighbor classification assigns a phone label to each centisecond of speech. This label represents a pseudophonetic notation of the actual local characteristics of the speech signal. The line of text labeled P in Fig. 10.9 gives the classification for each 10-millisecond unit.

The classification of the labels for each centisecond obtained by this matching procedure (row P in Fig. 10.9) is then used to specify a list of features such as voicing and frication, which is used in the segmentation of the utterance (also shown in Fig. 10.9). The boundaries of segments are indicated by dotted vertical lines through the parameters, and the letter at the center of each segment (following the row P in Fig. 10.9) indicates the

---

[2] The zero crossings are also measured in each band but they do not play an important role in the recognition process at present.

type of segment that is present. The label "A" indicates a sonorant segment, the "S" indicates a fricative segment, and the period (".") indicates a silence segment.

The Recognition Process

We will illustrate the recognition process by following through various stages of recognition for the utterance given in Fig. 10.7 and 10.9. Fig. 10.10 through 10.19 illustrate these stages of recognition. In each figure we have five kinds of information. The graphical part of each figure has the same information presented in Fig. 10.9. In addition each figure contains the current sentence hypothesis; the processes acting on the current sentence hypothesis and their effect (e.g., SYN HYPOTHESIZED....,ACO RE-JECTED...), the acceptable option words with their ratings and word boundaries (e.g., ↑...↑ 425 ROOK'S), and a rank-ordered list of new sentence hypotheses which result after adding the possible option words to the current best sentence hypothesis (see Chapter 4 of Erman (1973) for a detailed description of the new sentence hypothesis generation and rating processes). The symbol <FILLER> within the current sentence hypothesis indicates the unrecognized portions of the utterance, which is the location of the set of new words being hypothesized and verified. The "↑...↑" arrows indicate the possible beginning and ending for each option word.

Fig. 10.10 shows the first cycle of the recognition process. At this point none of the words in the sentence have been recognized and the processing begins left to right. The syntax module chooses to hypothesize and generates 13 possible option words, implying that the sentence can begin with "rook's," "rook," "queens," etc. The ACO module which incorporates the acoustic-phonetic and lexical knowledge rejects two possible realizations of "bishop" and "bishops" as being inconsistent with the acoustic-phonetic evidence. Since the word "bishop" may be pronounced in several ways (in reduced and nonreduced vowel form), another realization of "bishop" is in fact accepted. The semantics module rejects "castle" and "castles" as being illegal in that position. The remaining words are rated by each source of knowledge. The composite rating and the word beginning and word ending markers for the eight best words are shown in Fig. 10.10. The word "rook's" gets a rating of 425, "rook" a rating of 443, and so on. "Bishop," the correct word, gets the highest rating of 553. These words are then used to form the beginning sentence hypotheses, which are shown with their ratings at the bottom of Fig. 10.10.

Fig. 10.11 shows the second cycle of the recognition process. The top sentence hypothesis is "bishop...." An attempt is being made to recognize the word following "bishop." Again syntax hypothesizes. Given that "bishop" is the preceding word, the syntactic source of knowledge proposes only seven option words out of the possible 31 words in the lexicon—a reduction in the

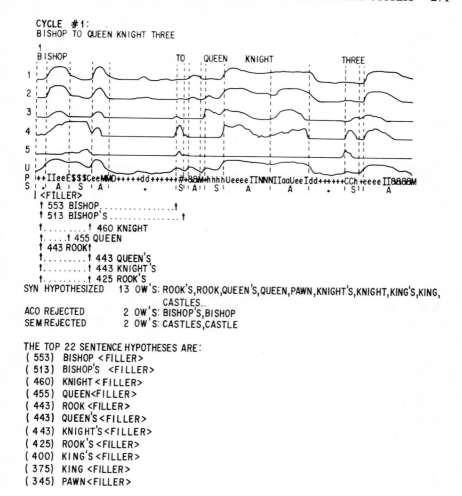

FIG. 10.10. First cycle of the recognition process.

search space by a factor of 4. Of these possible seven words, the acoustics module rejects words such as "takes," "on," etc., and semantics rejects none. The remaining words are rated by each of the sources of knowledge and a composite rating along with word boundaries is shown in Fig. 10.11 for each of the acceptable words. The correct word, "to," happens to get the highest rating of 553. The new top sentence hypothesis is "bishop to..." with a composite rating of 553. Notice the growth of the sentence hypothesis list. All the acceptable sentence hypotheses are rank ordered. The top sentence hypothesis of Fig. 10.10 has now branched into three new sentence hypotheses most of which have higher ratings than the sentence hypotheses generated during the preceding cycle.

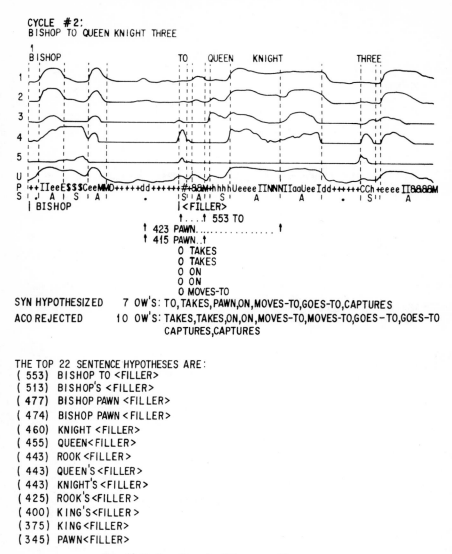

FIG. 10.11. Second cycle of the recognition process.

Fig. 10.12 shows the third cycle of the recognition process. Given that the top sentence hypothesis is "bishop to...," the syntax module hypothesizes seven option words, some of which are rejected by the other knowledge processes. Again, the correct word ("queen") gets the best rating. This cycle results in four new additions to the sentence hypothesis list—"bishop to queen...," "bishop to knight...," "bishop to king...," and "bishop to rook...."

Fig. 10.13 shows the fourth cycle of the recognition process. Given the top sentence hypothesis of "bishop to queen..." syntax proposes 11 possible option words some of which are rejected by acoustic and semantic modules. The correct word "knight" only gets the second highest rating. The first error in the recognition process occurs at this point. The error is a result of incomplete knowledge in the rating procedures for fricatives and diphthongs.

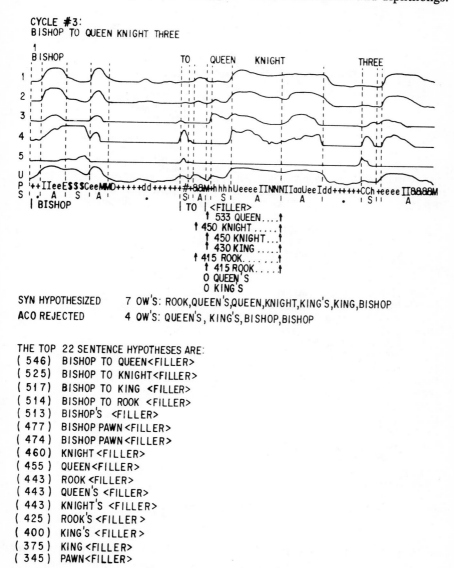

CYCLE #3:
BISHOP TO QUEEN KNIGHT THREE

SYN HYPOTHESIZED   7 OW'S: ROOK,QUEEN'S,QUEEN,KNIGHT,KING'S,KING,BISHOP
ACO REJECTED   4 OW'S: QUEEN'S, KING'S,BISHOP,BISHOP

THE TOP 22 SENTENCE HYPOTHESES ARE:
(546)   BISHOP TO QUEEN<FILLER>
(525)   BISHOP TO KNIGHT<FILLER>
(517)   BISHOP TO KING <FILLER>
(514)   BISHOP TO ROOK <FILLER>
(513)   BISHOP'S <FILLER>
(477)   BISHOP PAWN<FILLER>
(474)   BISHOP PAWN<FILLER>
(460)   KNIGHT<FILLER>
(455) QUEEN<FILLER>
(443)   ROOK <FILLER>
(443)   QUEEN'S <FILLER>
(443)   KNIGHT'S <FILLER>
(425) ROOK'S <FILLER >
(400)   KING'S <FILLER >
(375) KING <FILLER>
(345) PAWN<FILLER>

FIG. 10.12. Third cycle of the recognition process.

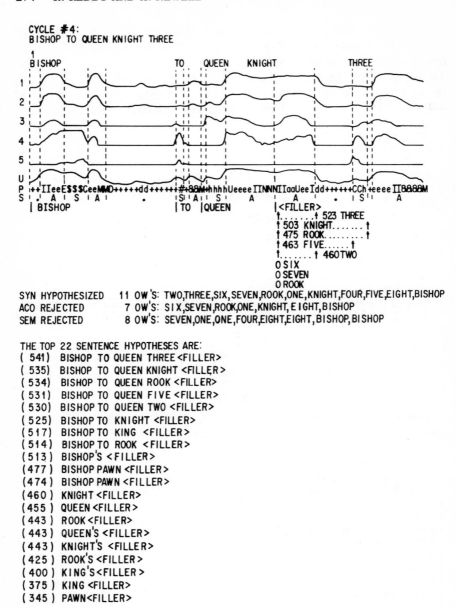

CYCLE #4:
BISHOP TO QUEEN KNIGHT THREE

SYN HYPOTHESIZED   11 OW'S: TWO,THREE,SIX,SEVEN,ROOK,ONE,KNIGHT,FOUR,FIVE,EIGHT,BISHOP
ACO REJECTED   7 OW'S: SIX,SEVEN,ROOK,ONE,KNIGHT, EIGHT,BISHOP
SEM REJECTED   8 OW'S: SEVEN,ONE,ONE,FOUR,EIGHT,EIGHT,BISHOP, BISHOP

THE TOP 22 SENTENCE HYPOTHESES ARE:
(541)   BISHOP TO QUEEN THREE <FILLER>
(535)   BISHOP TO QUEEN KNIGHT <FILLER>
(534)   BISHOP TO QUEEN ROOK <FILLER>
(531)   BISHOP TO QUEEN FIVE <FILLER>
(530)   BISHOP TO QUEEN TWO <FILLER>
(525)   BISHOP TO KNIGHT <FILLER>
(517)   BISHOP TO KING <FILLER>
(514)   BISHOP TO ROOK <FILLER>
(513)   BISHOP'S < FILLER>
(477)   BISHOP PAWN <FILLER>
(474)   BISHOP PAWN <FILLER>
(460) KNIGHT <FILLER>
(455) QUEEN <FILLER>
(443) ROOK <FILLER>
(443) QUEEN'S <FILLER>
(443) KNIGHT'S <FILLER>
(425) ROOK'S <FILLER>
(400) KING'S<FILLER >
(375) KING <FILLER>
(345) PAWN<FILLER>

FIG. 10.13. Fourth cycle of the recognition process.

Fig. 10.14 shows how the semantic source of knowledge helps to recover from the error made in the preceding cycle. Of the seven words hypothesized by syntax all except "check" was rejected by semantics. Since the rating for "check" was low, the corresponding sentence hypothesis does not appear at the top of the new sentence list.

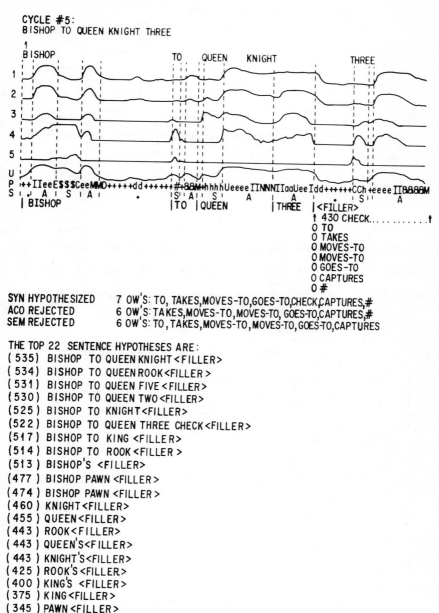

CYCLE #5:
BISHOP TO QUEEN KNIGHT THREE

SYN HYPOTHESIZED	7 OW'S: TO, TAKES,MOVES-TO,GOES-TO,CHECK,CAPTURES,#
ACO REJECTED	6 OW'S: TAKES,MOVES-TO,MOVES-TO, GOES-TO,CAPTURES,#
SEM REJECTED	6 OW'S: TO, TAKES,MOVES-TO,MOVES-TO,GOES-TO,CAPTURES

THE TOP 22 SENTENCE HYPOTHESES ARE:
(535) BISHOP TO QUEEN KNIGHT <FILLER>
(534) BISHOP TO QUEEN ROOK<FILLER >
(531) BISHOP TO QUEEN FIVE <FILLER>
(530) BISHOP TO QUEEN TWO <FILLER>
(525) BISHOP TO KNIGHT<FILLER>
(522) BISHOP TO QUEEN THREE CHECK<FILLER>
(517) BISHOP TO KING <FILLER>
(514) BISHOP TO ROOK<FILLER >
(513) BISHOP'S <FILLER>
(477) BISHOP PAWN <FILLER>
(474) BISHOP PAWN <FILLER>
(460) KNIGHT<FILLER>
(455) QUEEN<FILLER>
(443) ROOK<FILLER>
(443) QUEEN'S<FILLER>
(443) KNIGHT'S<FILLER>
(425) ROOK'S <FILLER>
(400) KING'S <FILLER>
(375) KING<FILLER>
(345) PAWN<FILLER>

FIG. 10.14. Fifth cycle of the recognition process.

CYCLE #6
BISHOP TO QUEEN KNIGHT THREE

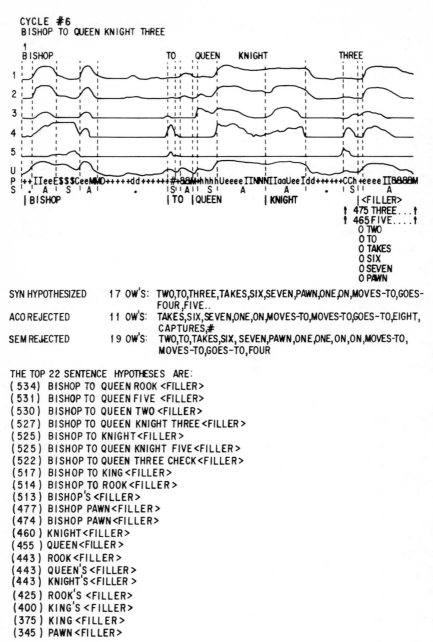

SYN HYPOTHESIZED	17 OW'S:	TWO,TO,THREE,TAKES,SIX,SEVEN,PAWN,ONE,ON,MOVES-TO,GOES-FOUR,FIVE..
ACO REJECTED	11 OW'S:	TAKES,SIX,SEVEN,ONE,ON,MOVES-TO,MOVES-TO,GOES-TO,EIGHT, CAPTURES,#
SEM REJECTED	19 OW'S:	TWO,TO,TAKES,SIX, SEVEN,PAWN,ONE,ONE,ON,ON,MOVES-TO, MOVES-TO,GOES-TO,FOUR

THE TOP 22 SENTENCE HYPOTHESES ARE:
(534) BISHOP TO QUEEN ROOK <FILLER>
(531) BISHOP TO QUEEN FIVE <FILLER>
(530) BISHOP TO QUEEN TWO <FILLER>
(527) BISHOP TO QUEEN KNIGHT THREE <FILLER>
(525) BISHOP TO KNIGHT <FILLER>
(525) BISHOP TO QUEEN KNIGHT FIVE <FILLER>
(522) BISHOP TO QUEEN THREE CHECK <FILLER>
(517) BISHOP TO KING <FILLER>
(514) BISHOP TO ROOK <FILLER>
(513) BISHOP'S <FILLER>
(477) BISHOP PAWN <FILLER>
(474) BISHOP PAWN <FILLER>
(460) KNIGHT <FILLER>
(455) QUEEN <FILLER>
(443) ROOK <FILLER>
(443) QUEEN'S <FILLER>
(443) KNIGHT'S <FILLER>
(425) ROOK'S <FILLER>
(400) KING'S <FILLER>
(375) KING <FILLER>
(345) PAWN <FILLER>

FIG. 10.15. Sixth cycle of the recognition process.

Fig. 10.15 shows the system on the right track again. Of the 17 words hypothesized, semantics does not reject "five" and "three." The resulting

new sentence hypothesis does in fact represent correct recognition of the
utterance. However, its composite rating of 527 is lower than three other

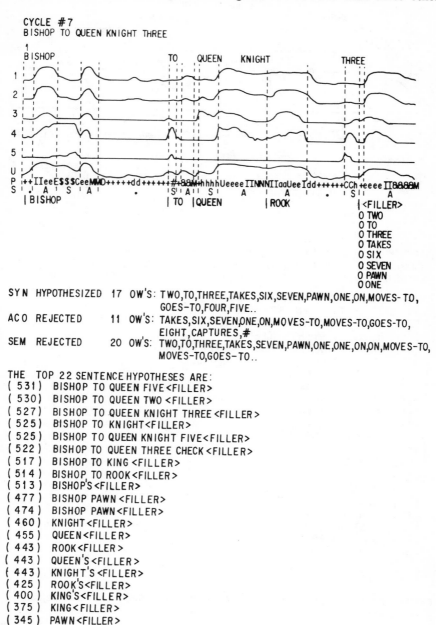

SYN HYPOTHESIZED 17 OW'S: TWO,TO,THREE,TAKES,SIX,SEVEN,PAWN,ONE,ON,MOVES-TO,
                                 GOES-TO,FOUR,FIVE..

ACO REJECTED   11 OW'S: TAKES,SIX,SEVEN,ONE,ON,MOVES-TO,MOVES-TO,GOES-TO,
                                 EIGHT,CAPTURES,#

SEM REJECTED   20 OW'S: TWO,TO,THREE,TAKES,SEVEN,PAWN,ONE,ONE,ON,ON,MOVES-TO,
                                 MOVES-TO,GOES-TO..

THE TOP 22 SENTENCE HYPOTHESES ARE:
(531)   BISHOP TO QUEEN FIVE<FILLER>
(530)   BISHOP TO QUEEN TWO <FILLER>
(527)   BISHOP TO QUEEN KNIGHT THREE <FILLER>
(525)   BISHOP TO KNIGHT<FILLER>
(525)   BISHOP TO QUEEN KNIGHT FIVE<FILLER>
(522)   BISHOP TO QUEEN THREE CHECK <FILLER>
(517)   BISHOP TO KING <FILLER>
(514)   BISHOP TO ROOK<FILLER>
(513)   BISHOP'S <FILLER>
(477)   BISHOP PAWN <FILLER>
(474)   BISHOP PAWN<FILLER>
(460)   KNIGHT<FILLER>
(455)   QUEEN<FILLER>
(443)   ROOK<FILLER>
(443)   QUEEN'S<FILLER>
(443)   KNIGHT'S <FILLER>
(425)   ROOK'S<FILLER>
(400)   KING'S<FILLER>
(375)   KING<FILLER>
(345)   PAWN<FILLER>

FIG. 10.16. Seventh cycle of the recognition process.

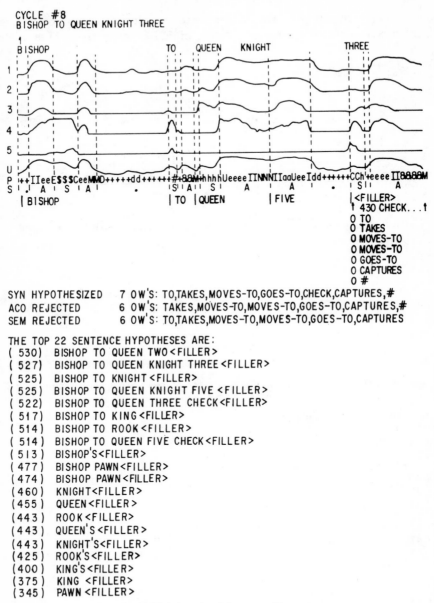

CYCLE #8
BISHOP TO QUEEN KNIGHT THREE

SYN HYPOTHESIZED	7 OW'S:	TO,TAKES,MOVES-TO,GOES-TO,CHECK,CAPTURES,#
ACO REJECTED	6 OW'S:	TAKES,MOVES-TO,MOVES-TO,GOES-TO,CAPTURES,#
SEM REJECTED	6 OW'S:	TO,TAKES,MOVES-TO,MOVES-TO,GOES-TO,CAPTURES

THE TOP 22 SENTENCE HYPOTHESES ARE:
(530) BISHOP TO QUEEN TWO <FILLER>
(527) BISHOP TO QUEEN KNIGHT THREE <FILLER>
(525) BISHOP TO KNIGHT <FILLER>
(525) BISHOP TO QUEEN KNIGHT FIVE <FILLER>
(522) BISHOP TO QUEEN THREE CHECK <FILLER>
(517) BISHOP TO KING <FILLER>
(514) BISHOP TO ROOK <FILLER>
(514) BISHOP TO QUEEN FIVE CHECK <FILLER>
(513) BISHOP'S <FILLER>
(477) BISHOP PAWN <FILLER>
(474) BISHOP PAWN <FILLER>
(460) KNIGHT <FILLER>
(455) QUEEN <FILLER>
(443) ROOK <FILLER>
(443) QUEEN'S <FILLER>
(443) KNIGHT'S <FILLER>
(425) ROOK'S <FILLER>
(400) KING'S <FILLER>
(375) KING <FILLER>
(345) PAWN <FILLER>

FIG. 10.17. Eighth cycle of the recognition process.

partial sentence hypotheses which must first be considered (and rejected—hopefully) before this recognition is accepted.

Fig. 10.16 illustrates the rejection of "bishop to king rook..." where all the option words were rejected. Fig. 10.17 illustrates the rejection of the sentence hypothesis "bishop to queen five...," which can only be followed by the word "check" which has a low rating. Fig. 10.18 illustrates the removal of "bishop to queen two..." as the top sentence hypothesis. In Fig. 10.19 syntax hypothesizes " " indicating possible end of sentence for the top sentence hy-

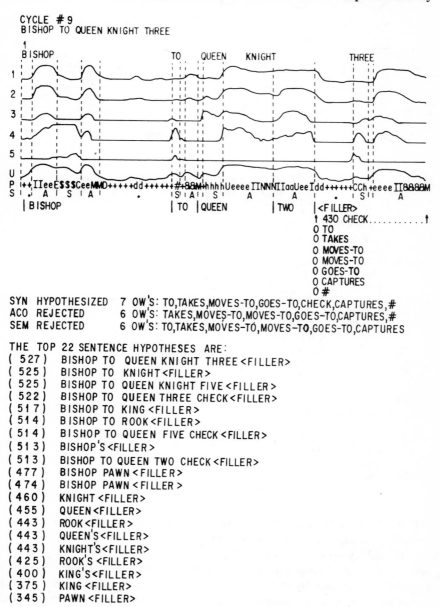

SYN HYPOTHESIZED 7 OW'S: TO,TAKES,MOVES-TO,GOES-TO,CHECK,CAPTURES,#
ACO REJECTED 6 OW'S: TAKES,MOVES-TO,MOVES-TO,GOES-TO,CAPTURES,#
SEM REJECTED 6 OW'S: TO,TAKES,MOVES-TO,MOVES-TO,GOES-TO,CAPTURES

THE TOP 22 SENTENCE HYPOTHESES ARE:
(527)   BISHOP TO QUEEN KNIGHT THREE <FILLER>
(525)   BISHOP TO KNIGHT <FILLER>
(525)   BISHOP TO QUEEN KNIGHT FIVE <FILLER >
(522)   BISHOP TO QUEEN THREE CHECK <FILLER>
(517)   BISHOP TO KING <FILLER>
(514)   BISHOP TO ROOK <FILLER>
(514)   BISHOP TO QUEEN FIVE CHECK <FILLER>
(513)   BISHOP'S <FILLER>
(513)   BISHOP TO QUEEN TWO CHECK <FILLER>
(477)   BISHOP PAWN <FILLER>
(474)   BISHOP PAWN <FILLER >
(460)   KNIGHT <FILLER>
(455)   QUEEN <FILLER>
(443)   ROOK <FILLER >
(443)   QUEEN'S <FILLER>
(443)   KNIGHT'S <FILLER>
(425)   ROOK'S <FILLER>
(400)   KING'S <FILLER>
(375)   KING <FILLER>
(345)   PAWN <FILLER>

FIG. 10.18. Ninth cycle of the recognition process.

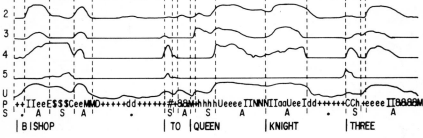

CYCLE #10
BISHOP TO QUEEN KNIGHT THREE

FIG. 10.19. Tenth cycle of the recognition proces.

SYN HYPOTHESIZED	7 OW'S: TO,TAKES,MOVES-TO,GOES-TO,CHECK,CAPTURES,#
ACO REJECTED	7 OW'S: TO,TAKES,MOVES-TO,MOVES-TO,GOES-TO,CHECK,CAPTURES
SEM REJECTED	6 OW'S: TO,TAKES,MOVES-TO,MOVES-TO,GOES-TO,CAPTURES

THE TOP 22 SENTENCE HYPOTHESES ARE:
```
(527)    BISHOP TO QUEEN KNIGHT THREE
(525)    BISHOP TO KNIGHT<FILLER>
(525)    BISHOP TO QUEEN KNIGHT FIVE <FILLER>
(522)    BISHOP TO QUEEN THREE CHECK<FILLER>
(517)    BISHOP TO KING<FILLER>
(514)    BISHOP TO ROOK<FILLER>
(514)    BISHOP TO QUEEN FIVE CHECK<FILLER>
(513)    BISHOP'S <FILLER>
(513)    BISHOP TO QUEEN TWO CHECK<FILLER
(477)    BISHOP PAWN<FILLER>
(474)    BISHOP PAWN<FILLER>
(460)    KNIGHT<FILLER>
(455)    QUEEN<FILLER>
(443)    ROOK<FILLER>
(443)    QUEEN'S<FILLER>
(443)    KNIGHT'S<FILLER>
(425)    ROOK'S <FILLER>
(400)    KING'S<FILLER
(375)    KING <FILLER>
(345)    PAWN <FILLER>
```

pothesis "bishop to queen knight three" which is accepted by all sources of knowledge leading to correct recognition.

In this section, we have demonstrated how knowledge processes communicate and cooperate with each other in the recognition process by illustrating the step-by-step use of knowledge in the recognition of an utterance. We notice substantial reductions of the search space are achieved by the use of knowledge both in generating hypotheses, and verifying them.

The knowledge-generated rank ordering of the hypotheses provides the necessary focus of attention for probablistic tree searching.

Let us now consider the contribution of each of the sources of knowledge towards the recognition of the utterance. Fig. 10.20 illustrates the respective contributions of semantics, syntax, and acoustic-phonetics in the recognition of 19 utterances (containing 101 words) from the voice-chess task with a vocabulary of 31 words. The accuracy at the word level is 40% when only acoustic phonetic knowledge is used. This increases to 65% with the addition of syntactic knowledge and 88% with the addition of both syntactic and semantic knowledge. The effect of multiple sources of knowledge at the sentence level is more dramatic—the accuracy increases from 0% to 46%. The exact percentages of accuracy are irrelevant; as the knowledge present in the system grows so will the accuracy. What is important to note is that with the effective use of all the sources of knowledge, the recognition process will not only be more accurate but also faster and more economical.

THE PSYCHOLOGICAL RELEVANCE OF HEARSAY

Hearsay is an artificial intelligence program that is responsive to knowledge about human speech and hearing, but makes no pretense of being a theory of human speech perception. It does, however, have some modest contributions to make, even in its present form. These stem from its contribution to exploring the space of possible mechanisms capable of perceiving speech. The potential of such technical studies is rather well understood by now, as are the cautions that must be exercised, and we need not elaborate the general issues further here.

Task: Chess
Vocabulary size: 31
Speaker: JB
No. of Utterances: 21
No. of Words: 105

Knowledge Sources Used	Accuracy	
	% Words Recognized Correctly	% Sentences Recognized Correctly
Acoustic-Phonetics only	40%	0%
Acoustics and Syntax	65%	14%
Acoustics, Syntax and Semantics	88%	46%

FIG. 10.20. Contributions of acoustics, syntax, and semantics sources of knowledge to the recognition accuracy.

In fact, global systems views have played a rather strong role in speech perception research. The theories divide into two classes, active and passive (Morton & Broadbent, 1967). The distinction is not just whether or not active processing is going on, but whether or not the perceiving system makes active use of the processes for producing speech. Examples of active theories are the analysis by synthesis scheme of Stevens and Halle (1962) and the motor theory of speech perception by the Haskins group (Liberman et al., 1962). Examples of passive theories (in this sense) are the Logogen theory of Morton (1964) as well as many artifical intelligence sysem organized in the classic mold of a passive recognizer. None of these theories has been used to make detailed predictions (and in fact some are quite careful not to formulate a really definite recognition system), but they have guided research.

A review of these theories in detail is not in order here, but it is worthwhile to catalogue the major issues they address in order to see what Hearsay can contribute. There seem to us to be four such issues:

1. What is the internal representation used for speech perception, especially at the levels below the word? The motor theories take it to be an articulatory encoding, the passive theories seek some features derived directly from the acoustic stream without special reference to the motor code.

2. How does one cope with the complex encoding of speech into the acoustic signal, which resists not only all attempts at finding simple invariants, but also any simple segmentation into discrete units for either phonemes or words? Analysis by synthesis attempts to cope by matching at the parametric level or below (by synthesis of the expected signal) so that segmentation is not needed. Passive theories mostly ignore the issue.

3. Speech is recognized in real time by humans, which eliminates many processing schemes. Analysis by synthesis has been attacked repeatedly because it implies much trial and error and hence seems orders of magnitude too costly. Passive schemes simply posit multiple filters all operating in parallel.

4. How is all the knowledge brought to bear? Human recognition time and accuracy seems to be affected by almost any type of knowledge that the human has. All theories acknowledge this, but neither active nor passive theories describe how it can happen.

Turning to Hearsay it has little to say about (Issue 1), the encoding. It is using a quite classical division into representational levels. It is using an empirically defined set of first-order phones (which divide the signal into several symbols), but these do not yet appear to deviate in important ways from theoretically defined phonemes. To the extent that its recognitions are successful it does of course provide confirmatory evidence.

More interesting is that Hearsay provides a demonstration that matching can occur at the lexical level with successful segmentation of the acoustic signal into phonemes and words (Issue 2). In this it provides an alternative mechanism to analysis by synthesis and genuinely broadens the space of possible mechanisms.

The third issue—that of real time computation—is counterpoint to the second. It is the one that makes analysis by synthesis seem implausible.[3] But Hearsay is itself not without efficiency problems, and it is therefore worthwhile to assess them briefly. Hearsay relies on a heuristic search at the lexical level (recall Fig. 10.10-10.19), and the unbounded character of Hearsay's computation is funneled into that search. Two aspects of it are important. One is the amount of search per word in the input utterance. The total amount of search is not relevant, since the time available increases linearly in the number of words. The second aspect is the size of the backup on error. This governs the size of the context that must be kept available. Short backups mean that earlier parts of the utterance are stable. Thus processing (possibly in parallel) to set context can proceed safely and can be quite costly, if it does not have to be repeated. The current data is still only preliminary. It indicates that there are about 1.7 cycles per word (the cycle amounting to a single link in the tree). It indicates that the system is still a little too combinatorial.

Hearsay is an organization specifically built to permit the interaction of sources of knowledge of all types. Its general sucess indicates the viability of such schemes and this is the first operational organization to do so. Thus, providing the combinatorial problems can be brought under further control, Hearsay provides a feasible organizational model for human processing.

We have several times previously talked about Hearsay as providing the first demonstration of certain features. In fact, though in certain respects Hearsay is the first system to be operational with certain types of system capabilities, it is one of a class of systems all of which are being developed simultaneously (Barnett, 1973; Forgie, 1973; Walker, 1973; Woods & Makhol, 1973). All of these systems share with Hearsay the property of bringing to bear knowledge from all levels. None of them are analysis by synthesis or motor systems, though they differ somewhat in their organization (e.g., the BBN system being also a hypothoser, the SRI system being closer to a set of intelligent parallel filters per lexical unit). None of them yet offer radically different representations. All of them should provide demonstrations that segmentation can be performed without analysis by synthesis at the subphonemic level.

In summary we can expect Hearsay, along with the other programs which are approaching operational status, to provide a much richer

---

[3] The Stevens-Halle model of analysis by synthesis has a box labeled "Preliminary analysis" whose function it is to provide an initial guess that is close enough to the final recognition that not too many synthesis iterations are required, thus keeping the processing within bounds. However, as has been noted, without some further detail there are no grounds for positing a scheme which can get close, but cannot, by the same token, do the whole job.

understanding of the space of perceptual systems capable of understanding speech. With this should come a sharpening of the scietific questions to be asked about the nature of the human recognition system.

CONCLUSION

In comparing the sources of knowledge in the Hearsay system with those proposed in the report by Newell et al. (1973), we find that several of the sources of knowledge have not yet found their way into the Hearsay system, while others are present which were not discussed in the report. Careful study of the knowledge sources reveals the following interesting structure. There appear to be four distinct types of knowledges at each level of abstraction (parametric level, sentence level, etc.). These are task dependent knowledge, conversation dependent knowledge, speaker dependent knowledge, and analysis dependent knowledge.

Fig. 10.21 gives typical uses of these types of knowledge at each of the levels. For example, at the semantic level for the voice-chess task we have the rules of the game, the board position indicating the sequence of moves so far, the goodness of moves indicating possible user preferences, and the fact that if the word "captures" has been recognized in spoken utterance, then we only need to consider the capture moves in this position. In the past, speech scientists have looked upon the "multiple speaker problem" as one of determining the variations in formant positions resulting from the variability

Type of knowledge Level	Task dependent knowledge	Conversation dependent knowledge	Speaker dependent knowledge	Analysis dependent knowledge
Semantic	A priori semantic knowledge about the task domain	Concept sub-selection based on conversation	(psychological) user model	Concept subselection based on partial sentence recognition
Syntactic	Grammar for the language	Grammar sub-selection based on topic	Grammar sub-selection based on speaker	Grammar subselection based on partial phrase recognition
Lexical	Size and specification of the vocabulary	Vocabulary sub-selection based on topic	Vocabulary sub-selection and and ordering based on speaker	Vocabulary subselection based on segmental features
Phonemic	Phonemic units of the language	Coarticulation variability	Dialectal variations of the speaker	Phonemic subselection based on segmental features
Parametric	A priori knowledge about the transducer system	Correction for the noise-level of the room	Variations resulting from the size and shape of vocal tract	Parameter tracking based on previous parameters

FIG. 10.21. Sources of knowledge at each level.

in the size and shape of the vocal tract for different speakers. From Fig. 10.21, it is obvious that the problem is much more general in nature; in addition to vocal tract variations, one must also consider dialectal variations, vocabulary and grammatical preferences of the user, and a psychological model of the user to predict what action he might take next.

Based on Fig. 10.21, one can now characterize two types of hypotheses a knowledge might be called upon to make, viz. horizontal hypotheses and vertical hypotheses. A hypothesis is *horizontal* when a knowledge process uses contextual informtion at a given level to predict new events at the same level. A hypothesis is *vertical* when a knowledge process uses information at one level to predict new events at a different level. Vertical hypotheses are needed to translate events between levels. This discussion about types of knowledge available at each level is intended to reinforce the fact that an attempt must be made to use every available source of knowledge effectively. This may be necessary either to achieve higher performance or to overcome the errorful nature of the task domain.

In this paper we have proposed the induction model with cooperating parallel processes as an interesting framework for this class of problems. The key idea is that when you have a set of diverse sources of knowledge speaking different languages, the role for each source of knowledge is to know when it has something useful to contribute, and to generate or modify hypotheses in that situation.

11
MULTIDIMENSIONAL EVALUATION OF A SIMULATION OF PARANOID THOUGHT PROCESSES

KENNETH MARK COLBY and **FRANKLIN DENNIS HILF**
Stanford University

Once a simulation model reaches a stage of intuitive adequacy, a model builder should consider using more stringent evaluation procedures relevant to the model's purposes. For example, if the model is to serve as a training device, then a simple evaluation of its pedagogic effectiveness would be sufficient. But when the model is proposed as an explanation of a psychological process, more is demanded of the evaluation procedure.

We shall first give a brief description of a model of paranoid processes. A more complete account can be found in Colby, Weber, and Hilf (1971). We shall then discuss the evaluation problem which asks "how good is the model?" or "how close is the correspondence between the behavior of the model and the phenomena it is intended to explain?"

The algorithm is written in MLISP, and consists of a 41K program which runs interactively on the DEC PDP-6/10 time-shared system of the Stanford Artificial Intelligence Project. Upon receiving a natural language input question or statement, the program attempts to determine the intentions of the interviewer according to the definitions of Fig. 11.1. The input expression is scanned looking for words and phrases which can be formed into a conceptualization. A conceptualization is a structure of concepts which gives the underlying meaning or a gist of the meaning of the input expression. After the resultant conceptualization is classified, the program responds internally and externally. If the conceptualization is identified as malevolent, the internal response consists of raising two major affect-variables of ANGER (in response to mental harm) or FEAR (in response to a threat of physical injury). A third major variable of MISTRUST is also raised as part of the internal response. The semantic nature of the

This research is supported by Grant PHS MH 06645-12 from the National Institute of Mental Health and by (in part) Research Scientist Award (No. 1-K05-K-14, 433) from the National Institute of Mental Health to the senior author.

conceptualization, the topic under discussion (context) and the level of these three variables determine which external output response is selected. The external output consists of natural language expressions. Thus, for example, if malevolence identified as mental harm is detected in the input, and ANGER is high while FEAR and MISTRUST are low or moderate, the output response will be of a counterattacking hostile nature. If benevolence (see Fig. 11.1) is detected, the telling of a story or brief episode is initiated or continued by the program. If neither malevolence nor benevolence can be identified, the program attempts a noncommital reply or asks the interviewer a question. Two versions of the program can be run, a strong version and a weak version. In the strong version there exists a delusional complex about the Mafia which can be elicited. Also the values of the three major internal variables rise more sharply in the strong version. In the weak version, there exists no delusional complex, only hints of suspiciousness, and the values of the internal variables rise more slowly than in the strong version.

Turing's test has often been suggested as a validation procedure. It is very easy to become confused about Turing's Test. In part this is due to Turing himself who introduced the now famous imitation game in a paper entitled "Computing Machinery and Intelligence" (Turing, 1963). A careful reading of this paper reveals there are actually two imitation games, the second of which is commonly called Turing's test.

In the first imitation game two groups of judges try to determine which of two interviewees is a woman. Communication between judge and interviewee is by teletype. Each judge is initially informed that one of the interviewees is a woman and one a man who will pretend to be a woman. After the interview, the judge is asked the *woman-question*, i.e., which interviewee was the woman? Turing does not say what else the judge is told but one assumes the judge is not told that a computer is involved nor is he

⟨OTHER'S INTENTION⟩ ← ⟨MALEVOLENCE⟩ | ⟨BENEVOLENCE⟩ | ⟨NEUTRAL⟩

MALEVOLENCE-DETECTION RULES

1. ⟨malevolence⟩ ← ⟨mental harm⟩ | ⟨physical threat⟩
2. ⟨mental harm⟩ ← ⟨humiliation⟩ | ⟨subjugation⟩
3. ⟨physical threat⟩ ← ⟨direct attack⟩ | ⟨induced attack⟩
4. ⟨humiliation⟩ ← ⟨explicit insult⟩ | ⟨implicit insult⟩
5. ⟨subjugation⟩ ← ⟨constraint⟩ | ⟨coercive treatment⟩
6. ⟨direct attack⟩ ← CONCEPTUALIZATIONS ([you get electric shock], [are you afraid mafia kill you?])
7. ⟨induced attack⟩ ← CONCEPTUALIZATIONS ([I tell mafia you], [does mafia know you are in hospital?])
8. ⟨explicit insult⟩ ← CONCEPTUALIZATIONS ([you are hostile], [you are mentally ill?])
9. ⟨implicit insult⟩ ← CONCEPTUALIZATIONS (⟨tell me your sexlife], [are you sure?])
10. ⟨constraint⟩ ← CONCEPTUALIZATIONS ([you stay in hospital], [you belong on locked ward])
11. ⟨coercive treatment⟩ ← CONCEPTUALIZATIONS ([I hypnotize you], [you need tranquilizers])

BENEVOLENCE-DETECTION RULES

1. ⟨benevolence⟩ ← ⟨positive attitude⟩ | ⟨positive story attitude⟩
2. ⟨positive attitude⟩ ← CONCEPTUALIZATIONS ([I want help you], [you understand me])
3. ⟨positive story attitude⟩ ← ⟨story interest⟩ | ⟨story agreement⟩
4. ⟨story interest⟩ ← ⟨topic comment⟩ | ⟨topic question⟩
5. ⟨topic comment⟩ ← CONCEPTUALIZATION ([bookies are not reliable])
6. ⟨topic question⟩ ← CONCEPTUALIZATION ([what did you do to bookie?])
7. ⟨story agreement⟩ ← CONCEPTUALIZATIONS ([I believe you], [you are right])

FIG. 11.1. Broken brackets enclose concepts being defined. Arrow means "is defined as." Vertical bar represents "or." CONCEPTUALIZATIONS ([ ]) represent illustrative examples of the meaning extracted from input expressions, *not* the literal expressions themselves.

asked to determine which interviewee is human and which is the computer. Thus, the first group of judges would interview two interviewees: a woman and a man pretending to be a woman.

The second group of judges would be given the same initial instructions, but unbeknownst to them, the two interviewees would be a woman and a computer programmed to imitate a woman. Both groups of judges play this game until sufficient statistical data are collected to show how often the right identification is made. The crucial question then is do the judges decide wrongly as often when the game is played with man and woman as when it is played with a computer substituted for the man. If so, then the program is considered to have succeeded in imitating a woman as well as a man imitating a woman. For emphasis we repeat: in asking the woman-question in this game, judges are not required to identify which interviewee is human and which is machine.

Later on in his paper Turing proposes a variation of the first game. In the second game one interviewee is a man and one is a computer. The judge is asked to determine which is man and which is machine. It is this version of the game which is commonly thought of as Turing's test. It has often been suggested as a means of validating computer simulations of psychological processes.

In the course of testing a simulation (PARRY) of paranoid linguistic behavior in a psychiatric interview, we conducted a number of Turing-like indistinguishability tests (Colby, Hilf, Weber, & Kraemer, 1972). We say "Turing-like" because none of them consisted of playing the two games described above. We chose not to play these games for a number of reasons which can be summarized by saying that they do not meet modern criteria for good experimental design. In designing our tests we were primarily interested in learning more about developing the model. We did not believe the simple *machine-question* to be a useful one in serving the purpose of progressively increasing the credibility of the model, but we investigated a variation of it to satisfy the curiosity of colleagues in artificial intelligence.

In this design, eight psychiatrists interviewed by teletype two patients using the technique of machine-mediated interviewing (Hilf, 1972). Each judge interviewed two patients one being PARRY and one being a hospitalized paranoid patient. The interviewers were not informed that a simulation was involved nor were they asked to identify which was the machine. Their task was to conduct a diagnostic psychiatric interview and rate each response from the "patients" along a 9-point scale of paranoidness. Transcripts of these interviews, without the ratings of the interviewers, were then utilized for various experiments in which randomly selected expert judges conducted evaluations of the interview transcripts. For example, in one experiment it was found that patients and model were indistinguishable along the dimension of paranoidness.

To ask the machine-question, we sent interview transcripts, one with a patient and one with PARRY, to 100 psychiatrists randomly selected from the *Directory of American Specialists* and the *Directory of the American Psychiatric Association*. Of the 41 replies 21 (51%) made the correct identification while 20 (49%) were wrong. Based on this random sample of 41 psychiatrists, the 95% confidence interval is between 35.9 and 66.5, a range which is close to chance.[1]

Psychiatrists are considered expert judges of patient interview behavior but they are unfamiliar with computers. Hence, we conducted the same test with 100 computer scientists randomly selected from the membership list of the Association for Computing Machinery, ACM. Of the 67 replies 32 (48%) were right and 35 (52%) were wrong. Based on this random sample of 67 computer scientists, the 95% confidence ranges from 36 to 60, again close to a chance level.

Thus the answer to this machine-question, "Can expert judges—psychiatrists and computer scientists—using teletyped transcripts of psychiatric interviews, distinguish between paranoid patients and a simulation of paranoid processes?" is "No." But what do we learn from this? It is some comfort that the answer was not "yes" and that the null hypothesis failed to be rejected, especially since statistical tests are somewhat biased in favor of rejecting the null hypothesis (Meehl, 1967). Yet this answer does not tell us what we would most like to know, i.e., how to improve the model. Simulation models do not spring forth in a complete, perfect, and final form; they must be gradually developed over time. Perhaps we might obtain a "yes" answer to the machine-question if we allowed a large number of expert judges to conduct the interviews themselves rather than studying transcripts of other interviewers. It would indicate that the model must be improved but unless we systematically investigated how the judges succeeded in making the discrimination, we would not know what aspects of the model to work on. The logistics of such a design are immense and obtaining a sufficient number of judges for sound statistical inference would require an effort disproportionate to the information-yield.

A more efficient and informative way to use Turing-like tests is to ask judges to make ordinal ratings along scaled dimensions from teletyped interviews. We shall term this approach asking the *dimension-question*. One can then compare scaled ratings received by the patients and by the model to determine precisely where and by how much they differ. Model builders strive for a model which shows indistinguishability along some dimensions and distinguishability along others.

We mailed paired-interview transcripts to another 400 randomly selected psychiatrists asking them to rate the responses of the two "patients"

---

[1] Our statistical consultant was Helena C. Kraemer, Research Associate in Biostatistics, Department of Psychiatry, Stanford University.

along certain dimensions. The judges were divided into groups, each judge being asked to rate responses of each Input-Output (I-O) pair in the interviews along four dimensions. The total number of dimensions in this test were 12: *linguistic noncomprehension, thought disorder, organic brain syndrome, bizarreness, anger, fear, ideas of reference, delusions, mistrust, depression, suspiciousness, and mania.* These are dimensions which psychiatrists commonly use in evaluating patients.

Table 11.1 shows there were significant differences, with PARRY receiving higher scores along the dimensions of linguistic noncomprehension, thought disorder, bizarreness, anger, mistrust, and suspiciousness. On the dimension of delusions the patients were rated significantly higher. There were no significant differences along the dimensions of organic brain syndrome, fear, ideas of reference, depression, and mania.

While tests asking the machine-question indicate indistinguishability at the gross level, a study of the finer structure of the model's behavior through ratings along scaled dimensions shows statistically significant differences between patients and model. These differences are of help to the model builder in suggesting which aspects of the model must be modified and improved in order to be considered an adequate simulation of the class of paranoid patients it is intended to simulate. For example, it is clear that PARRY's language comprehension must be improved. Once this has been

TABLE 11.1

Mean Ratings of Patient and PARRY I-O Pairs

Dimension	n of Judges	Mean patient ratings	Mean PARRY ratings	Mean deviation	Standard error of difference	t^a
Linguistic noncomprehension	43	0.73	2.22	-1.50	0.28	-5.28**
Thought disorder	43	2.29	3.78	-1.49	0.41	-3.60**
Organic brain syndrome	43	0.84	1.11	-0.27	0.29	-0.93
Bizarreness	42	2.34	3.45	-1.19	0.36	-3.28*
Anger	37	2.03	2.96	-0.92	0.21	-4.30**
Fear	38	2.73	2.67	0.06	0.22	0.26
Ideas of reference	36	2.33	1.78	0.55	0.32	1.71
Delusions	37	3.06	1.51	1.55	0.33	4.70**
Mistrust	41	2.35	4.42	-2.13	0.35	-6.14**
Depression	39	1.92	1.46	0.25	0.21	1.21
Suspiciousness	40	2.87	4.33	-1.43	0.36	-3.98**
Mania	40	1.00	1.23	-0.09	0.29	-0.32

[a] A minus value of t indicates that PARRY is higher.
*$p < .01$.
**$p < .001$.

TABLE 11.2

Mean Ratings of Patient and RANDOM-PARRY I-O Pairs

Dimension	Number of judges	Mean patient ratings	Mean RANDOM-PARRY ratings	Mean deviation	Standard error of difference	t^a
Linguistic noncomprehension	25	0.51	2.83	-2.30	0.51	-4.51**
Thought disorder	26	2.99	5.94	-2.96	0.36	-8.18**
Organic brain syndrome	25	0.87	1.19	-0.32	0.36	-0.89
Bizarreness	26	2.38	4.89	-2.50	0.41	-6.05**

[a]A minus value of t indicates that RANDOM-PARRY is higher.
*$p < .01$.
**$p < .001$.

implemented, a future test will tell us whether improvement has occurred and by how much in comparison to the earlier version. Successive identification of particular areas of failure in the model permits their improvement and the development of more adequate model versions.

Further evidence that the machine-question is too coarse and insensitive a test comes from the following experiment. In this test we constructed a random version of the paranoid model which utilized PARRY's output statements but expressed them randomly no matter what the interviewer said. Two psychiatrists conducted interviews with this model, transcripts of which were paired with patient interviews and sent to 200 randomly selected psychiatrists asking both the machine-question and the dimension-question. Of the 69 replies, 34 (49%) were right and 35 (51%) wrong. Based on this random sample of 69 psychiatrists, the 95% confidence interval ranges from 39 to 63, again indicating a chance level. However, as shown in Table 11.2 significant differences appear along the dimensions of linguistic noncomprehension, thought disorder and bizarreness, with RANDOM-PARRY rated higher. On these particular dimensions we can construct a continuum in

TABLE 11.3

Mean Ratings of PARRY versus RANDOM-PARRY

Dimension	Degrees of freedom	t^a	Level of significance of difference
Linguistic noncomprehension	66	-1.39	not significant
Thought disorder	67	-3.87	.001
Organic brain syndrome	66	-0.19	not significant
Bizarreness	67	-2.76	.01

[a]A minus value of t indicates that RANDOM-PARRY is higher.

which the random version represents one extreme, the actual patients another. Our (nonrandom) PARRY lies somewhere between these two extremes, indicating that it performs significantly better than the random version but still requires improvement before being indistinguishable from patients (see Fig. 11.1). Table 11.3 presents t values for differences between mean ratings of PARRY and RANDOM-PARRY (see Table 11.1 and Table 11.2 for the mean ratings). The fact that even a random model can pass the machine-question test shows, not that the model is a good simulation, but that the test is weak and nonchallenging.

Thus it can be seen that such a multidimensional evaluation provides yardsticks for measuring the adequacy of this or any other dialogue simulation model along the relevant dimensions.

We conclude that when model builders want to conduct tests which indicate in which direction progress lies and to obtain a measure of whether progress is being achieved, the way to use Turing-like tests is to ask expert judges to make ratings along multiple dimensions that are essential to the model. Useful tests do not prove a model, they probe it for its strengths and weaknesses. Simply asking the machine-question yields little information relevant to what the model builder most wants to know, namely, the dimensions along which the model must be improved.

12
UNDERSTANDING
UNDERSTANDING SYSTEMS

DAVID KLAHR
Carnegie-Mellon University

My comments relate to two papers that describe general features of systems that attempt to understand. Neither paper is intended as a technical description, and it is to the authors' credit that they have managed to convey the essence of their systems without barraging us with a mass of detail. (Detail that often appears quite elegant to those who are technically able to appreciate it.) Both papers are directed toward the more general issue that provides the theme of this symposium: what is the relation between knowledge and cognition? In these cases both the knowledge and the cognition are in machines. My comments will likewise be confined to some general rather than specific issues raised by these papers.

Understanding What is Known

Moore and Newell pose the problem "What is understanding?" Then they propose an elegantly simple definition, a set of design criteria for constructing understanding systems, a few examples of other systems assimilated to these categories, and finally a detailed description and evaluation of their own efforts at designing an understanding system. It is a long paper, a difficult paper, and, I believe, a paper of major importance to philosophy, artificial intelligence, and cognitive psychology.

The "essence" of understanding is summarized thusly: (*a*) "S understands knowledge K if S uses K whenever appropriate." (*b*) "Understanding can be partial, both in extent (the class of appropriate situations in which the knowledge is used) and in immediacy (the time it takes before such understanding can be exhibited)." Many questions leap to mind about the adequacy of these statements: every reader can generate his own favorite set. Here are a few of mine:

Is the distinction between *knowledge* and the *understanding* of that knowledge a viable one? Should we not consider instead two forms of knowledge: (*a*) knowledge of the thing itself, (*b*) knowledge of its appropriateness? Certainly one of the things I know about K is about K per se, such as how to multiply. Another thing I know is a set of appropriate conditions under which to apply that knowledge. It seems that an increase in either is an increase in my understanding of K.

Or consider the following problem, derived from the issue of immediacy. I know that it is appropriate to use a certain statistical procedure in a given situation. However, I cannot remember where the "canned" program is, and it takes me hours to find it. Is my understanding of the procedure less than if I could immediately find the program and apply the knowledge?

This sort of critique could go on for quite a while, ultimately degenerating into donnish nit-picking. But, I leave that to the philosophers of AI (e.g., Dreyfus, 1972; Pylyshyn, 1972). Since Moore and Newell go well beyond simply defining understanding, the bulk of my comments will respond to their latter issues. Two points can be made now, both of which derive from the engineering orientation of *constructing* artifical intelligence rather than evaluating natural intelligence. Since the engineer can "open the box," and even further, build the box and its contents, the distinction between knowledge and the understanding (i.e., appropriate use) of that knowledge is indeed sensible and, as Moore and Newell assert, adequate. That this approach can facilitate our understanding (or knowledge?) of human intelligence is a working hypothesis in the research strategy of many (including me) who have attempted to intertwine theory, procedures, and data from artificial intelligence and cognitive psychology. But, it is far from an established scientific principle. And, it is upon this issue—the understanding of understanding—that the reductionist/constructionist approach both in psychology and AI may come to grief. I hope not, for my bets lie here, but the very modest progress, represented by MERLIN, that has been attainable utilizing the "purest" form of this approach makes me uncertain.

Notice that this is not a plea for a return to functional taxonomies. The Bloom et al. (1956) approach just did not work in case after case, as reviewed by Cox and Unks (1967). Even with an omniscient view of MERLIN's innards, one would find it difficult to classify test items presented to it in terms of such taxonomies.

Perhaps one reason that the Bloom taxonomy has hung around for almost 20 years was that it could be summarized into a one-page hierarchy of important aspects of intellectual functioning. People could represent a vast and complex area in six principal chunks. I believe that Moore and Newell have provided us with a similarly challenging, and easily remembered important list: the list of design issues facing the builder of an understanding system. I predict that this list will provide the basis for some converging understanding of the nature of these sorts of systems for some years to come. There is really nothing else quite like it in the field. One can find classifications of existing systems in terms of some design criteria, but these are typically based upon some superficial procedural distinction, rather than upon issues related to understanding per se.

This list then, is my candidate for the most important contribution of the paper. It provides some hope for a precise evaluation of the definition of understanding quoted above, and for something more than undefined verbiage on the epistemology of machines. But, there is a problem here: not only are the issues in the list defined intuitively, but so is their application to any given understanding system. I am uncertain about why a particular set of mechanisms in MERLIN is viewed as a response to one issue rather than another. I suppose the problem is one of assimilation of a given system to the list of design issues. What are the ground rules for this exercise?

Although introduced as a set of "design issues," they are implicitly interpreted as evaluative criteria for understanding systems. The relative inadequacy of a system is directly related to the number of issues upon which it has taken "no position" or "weak" one. The use of the list for evaluation, plus the current intuitive interpretation of a system in terms of the list items makes their ultimate usefulness a matter of collective experience. The Bloom taxonomy too often yielded low interjudge reliability when test items were classified according to it. I hope that there will be a greater consensus in the community of artificial intelligence researchers in evaluating various systems according to the Moore and Newell list.

Finally, we come to the heart of the paper: a description and evaluation of MERLIN[1] in terms of the design issues. Of course, MERLIN does not really understand much of anything, nor does it *do* much of anything, but that is of no importance. The title of the paper asks not *What* but *How* MERLIN can understand. Moore and Newell assert that it can understand by being based upon a network of nodes called β-structures, by having actions associated with nodes, by mapping anything into anything else, etc. The description of MERLIN is perhaps more useful as an extended interpretation of the design issues than it is as a description of MERLIN as a system. Even the rich use of examples left me confused as to what the processing rules were. Although the syntax-free definitions of β-structures are taken to be a virtue, I am still not convinced that fairly complex syntactic rules are not implicit in the examples. Scribbled comments, questions and "counter examples" adorn my copy of the draft of the paper, especially in the sections containing specific examples of MERLIN on the run. But, none are really appropriate in this sort of discussion. Furthermore, Moore and Newell

---

[1] The name Merlin, conjuring up images of a wizard in tall conical hat has been around for over a dozen centuries. According to Chambers (1877), there seem to be at least two distinct Merlins in ancient history, both of them prophets and enchanters. One, the fifth century British version, is said to have sprung from the intercourse of a demon and a Welsh princess, and to have displayed miraculous powers from infancy. The other, a sixth century Strathclyde (Scottish) version, seems to have been of obscure origin, but we are told that he died attempting to escape across a river from a band of hostile rustics. He was impaled upon a hidden stake.

acknowledge problems and inadequacies so thoroughly as to thwart even the meanest critic. The thing that I need to understand MERLIN is MERLIN, not a description of MERLIN. If Moore and Newell could produce a public version of MERLIN with design options under user control, then I could pose the questions by creating the situation to which I want MERLIN to respond. Newell has already provided one such interactive working system, called PSG, for modeling control processes in human short-term memory (Newell, 1973b), and it has proven to be a profoundly valuable tool for theoretical research. Can we get our hands on MERLIN?

MERLIN started as an aid to education. To summarize the argument: it was to be an intelligent computer assisted instructional (CAI) system in the area of artificial intelligence, hence it had to understand AI, hence it had to understand AI *programs*, hence it had to understand. The question is: "How much must a system understand about K in order to teach K?" To what extent is the design of a complete understanding system a necessary or sufficient condition for the successful attainment of the original goal of building an intelligent instructional aid?

Understanding What is Said

MERLIN's goal is to understand all knowledge. Hearsay is satisfied with understanding what humans say to it. Applying the Moore and Newell definition of understanding to Hearsay we get:

> Hearsay understands knowledge (about) speech if it uses knowledge about speech whenever appropriate.

The evaluation of Hearsay depends upon both the amount of speech knowledge to which it has access and the appropriateness of its use of that knowledge. Clearly, an understanding system with a vocabulary of 31 words has miniscule knowledge of the full human lexicon; but once the evaluation space becomes chess (or more precisely, spoken descriptions of legal moves) the 31 words span it rather well. The phonemic and parametric knowledge given to Hearsay spans a much greater portion, (almost all) of the knowledge there is on those matters, although the Reddy and Newell paper does not provide much detail about these levels.

Given its knowledge base, and its task domain, Hearsay appears to utilize its knowledge quite appropriately. Descriptions of the underlying procedures that determine how and when different sources are used are not presented in the current paper, but they are available in the references to the underlying work. I would guess that the crux of "appropriateness" is the allocation of priority and dominance to the different sources of knowledge. This is really a classical formal problem in aggregate decision-making (Black, 1958), often cast as a social welfare problem (Arrow, 1951). How can individual transitive preference orderings be aggregated into an aggregate (social) preference ordering? There is no simple way to determine the likelihood of failure in this effort (Klahr, 1966). Hearsay's solution is to "vote" repeatedly as it successively cycles through the utterance.

Perhaps I am too easily influenced by the recent upsurge of interest in visual imagery, but in the Reddy and Newell paper, as in the Moore and Newell paper, the most salient thing to me is the final tabular presentation of sources of knowledge in a Level × Type representation. This is a very nice conceptual structure, and like the MERLIN list of design issues, will probably be used by those building speech understanding systems both at the design stage and for evaluation.

However, it is difficult to compare the two views of understanding. Which of the design criteria in MERLIN correspond to the sources of knowledge in Hearsay? What corresponds to its principal strength: the testing of current hypotheses by distinct knowledge sources? Perhaps the MERLIN view of this lies in the "directionality" issue, in particular in "positing" X/Y, where the attempt is to assimilate the current hypotheses to the filtered waveform.

Knowledge Acquisition: Where is MERLIN's Mommy?

Where does MERLIN get its knowledge? Must all the world be rewritten as β-structures? When will we be able to tell MERLIN about the world (perhaps via Hearsay) so that it does its own construction of knowledge?

One of the basic tenets of Piagetian theory is that the child develops cognitive structures from his attempts to function in and manipulate the external environment. This environment is typically not indifferent to the child's actions. Brown and Bellugi (1964) have detected certain regularities in the speech patterns of parents reacting to children's speech. Subsequent to a simple utterance from the child comes a parental response that adds functional words (functors): verbs, prepositions, etc. Thus, the child says "Mommy sandwich" and the adult replies: "Mommy will have a sandwich." Or, "Throw Daddy" produces "Throw it to Daddy." Brown and Bellugi propose a rule for the parent: "Retain the words given in the order given and add those functors that will result in a well-formed simple sentence that is *appropriate to the circumstances* [Italics added]. These are not instructions that any machine could follow. A machine could act on the instructions only if it were provided with detailed specifications for judging appropriateness and no such specifications can, at present, be written."

The truth value of the last assertion is greatly diminished by the work presented by Moore, Newell, and Reddy. However, the important notion is that this complex but systematic error correction is central to the development of understanding both of language per se and of knowledge in general. Both MERLIN and Hearsay are silent on the issue of the source of knowledge sources.[2]

At one level this is simply a data management problem. Large data bases are tedious to encode, costly to search, etc. But, in another sense, it may be a fundamental issue. Can a system that has not self-constructed most of its knowledge—through the assimilation/accommodation cycle—ever manifest deep understanding? One of the few invariants of masterful human performance is immense amounts of experience. There seems to be no other way to become a wizard at playing chess, remembering things, or doing mental arithmetic. Both MERLIN and Hearsay deal with second-hand knowledge, preprocessed. It may be crucial to their development, both visceral and linguistic, to put them on solid food. And conversely, such self-development may be the necessary path to increasing their understanding.

Let Me Make This Perfectly Clear

About 20 years ago, the debate about whether or not computers could be intelligent was at its peak (although it reemerges from time to time, see Dreyfus, 1972). To paraphrase, or parody, one argument against machine intelligence:

1. You can probably get a machine to do a task requiring intelligence, but if it does not *understand* the task, then it is not "really" intelligent.

2. You cannot get a machine to understand.

Ergo: Machines cannot be intelligent.

Today it appears that the "anti" argument yielded on precisely the wrong issue. Moore, Newell, and Reddy have shown us the leading edge of work in AI, and one thing is perfectly clear. You *cannot* get a machine to do anything very intelligent unless it *does* understand the knowledge appropriate to its domain. Machine intelligence *is* machine understanding.[3] At least that is *my* understanding at this point in time.

---

[2] Sounds like a new conundrum for phonetic-semantic disambiguation: "Source of knowledge sources" or "sorts of knowledge sources?" How about: "A knowledge source source sort?"

[3] The defining of intelligence, human or otherwise, is a perilous undertaking. As Miles (1957) notes: "it is commonly thought to be a great scandal that psychologists cannot agree on a definition of intelligence." Because of the inherent ambiguity of the notion of "definition" itself, "any sentence starting 'intelligence is. . .' justifiably arouses one's suspicions."

REFERENCES

Amarel, S. On representations of problems of reasoning about actions. In D. Michie (Ed.), *Machine Intelligence 3*. Edinburgh, Scotland: Edinburgh University Press, 1968.

Anderson, J. R. FRAN: A simulation model of free recall. In G. H. Bower (Ed.), *The psychology of learning and motivation, advances in research and theory*. Vol. 5. New York: Academic Press, 1971.

Anderson, J. R., & Bower, G. H. *Human associative memory*. Washington, D.C.: Winston & Sons, 1973.

Arrow, K. J. *Social choice and individual values*. New York: Wiley, 1951.

Attneave, F. Some informational aspects of visual performance. *Psychological Review*, 1954, **61**, 183-192.

Barnett, J. A vocal data management system. *IEEE Transactions on Audio and Electroacoustics*, 1973, AU-21, 185-188.

Batchelder, W. H. An all-or-none theory for learning on both the paired-associate and concept levels. *Journal of Mathematical Psychology*, 1970, **7**, 97-117.

Batchelder, W. H. A theoretical and empirical comparison of the all-or-none multilevel theory and the mixed model. *Journal of Mathematical Psychology*, 1971, **8**, 82-108.

Becker, G. M. Decision making: Objective measures of subjective probability and utility. *Psychological Review*, 1962, **69**, 136-148.

Bell, C. G. & Newell, A. *Computer structures*. New York: McGraw-Hill, 1971.

Biermann, A. W., & Feldman, J. A. A survey of results in grammatical inference. *Conference on Frontiers in Pattern Recognition*. Honolulu: January 1971.

Bjork, R. A. All-or-none subprocesses in the learning of complex sequences. *Journal of Mathematical Psychology*, 1968, **5**, 182-195.

Black, D. *The theory of committees and elections*. Cambridge, England: Cambridge University Press, 1958.

Bloom, B. S. (Ed.), *Taxonomy of educational objectives*. New York: McKay, 1956.

Bloom, B. S., Engelhart, M. D., Furst, E. J., Hill, W. H., & Krathwohl, D. R. *Taxonomy of educational objectives*. New York: Longmans, Green, 1956.

Bobrow, D. G. Natural language input for a computer problem-solving system. In M. Minsky (Ed.), *Semantic information processing*. Cambridge, Mass.: MIT Press, 1968.

Bobrow, D. G., & Raphael, B. New programming languages for AI research. Tutorial lecture given at the 3rd International Joint Conference on Artificial Intelligence. Unpublished manuscript. Stanford University, 1973.

Bourne, L. E., Jr. Knowing and using concepts. *Psychological Review*, 1970, **77**, 546-556.

Bower, G. H., & Trabasso, T. R. Concept identification. In R. C. Atkinson (Ed.), *Studies in mathematical psychology*. Stanford: Stanford University Press, 1964.

Bransford, J. D., & Franks, J. J. The abstraction of linguistic ideas. *Cognitive Psychology*, 1972, **2**, 331-350.

Brown, E. R. Abstraction and hierarchical organization in the learning of periodic sequences. Indiana Mathematical Psychology Program Report No. 71-3, Indiana University, 1971.

Brown, R., & Bellugi, U. Three processes in the child's acquisition of syntax. *Harvard Educational Review*, 1964, **34**, 133-151.

Bruner, J. S., Goodnow, J. J., & Austin, G. A. *A study of thinking*. New York: Wiley, 1956.

Butcher, H. J. *Human intelligence*. London: Methven, 1968.

Carbonell, J. Mixed-initiative man-computer instructional dialogues. Unpublished doctoral dissertation, Department of Electrical Engineering, Massachusetts Institute of Technology, 1970.

301

Chambers's Encyclopaedia: *A Dictionary of universal knowledge for the people.* (American Rev. Ed.) Philadelphia: Lippincott, 1877.

Chase, W. G., & Simon, H. A. Perception in chess. *Cognitive Psychology,* 1973, **4**, 55-81.

Chomsky, N. Formal properties of grammars. In R. D. Luce, R. R. Bush, & E. Galanter (Eds.), *Handbook of mathematical psychology.* Vol. 2. New York: Wiley, 1963.

Chumbley, J. Hypothesis memory in concept learning. *Journal of Mathematical Psychology,* 1969, **6**, 528-540.

Clark, H. H. Space, time, semantics, and the child. In T. E. Moore (Ed.), *Cognitive development and the acquisition of language.* New York: Academic Press, 1973.

Clark, H., & Chase, W. On the process of comparing sentences against pictures. *Cognitive Psychology,* 1972, **4**, 472-517.

Clowes, M. On seeing things. *Artificial Intelligence,* 1971, **2**, 79-116.

Colby, K. M., Weber, S., & Hilf, F. D. Artificial paranoia. *Artificial Intelligence,* 1971, **2**, 1-25.

Colby, K. M., Hilf, F. D., Weber, S., & Kraemer, H. C. Turing-like indistinguishability tests for the validation of a computer simulation of paranoid processes. *Artificial Intelligence,* 1972, **3**, 199-221.

Coles, L. S. Talking with a Robot in English. In D. E. Walker & L. M. Morton, (Eds.), *Proceedings 1st International Joint Conference on Artificial Intelligence,* 1969.

Coles, L. S. Syntax directed interpretation of natural language. In H. A. Simon, & L. Siklóssy (Eds.), *Representation and meaning.* Englewood Cliffs, N.J.: Prentice-Hall, 1972.

Cox, R. C., & Unks, N. J. A selected and annotated bibliography of studies concerning the taxonomy of educational objectives: Cognitive domain. (LRDC, Working Paper 13). Pittsburgh: University of Pittsburgh June 1967.

Dansereau, D. F. An information processing model of mental multiplication. Unpublished doctoral dissertation, Carnegie-Mellon University, 1969.

De Finetti, B. La prevision: ses lois logiques, ses sources subjectives. *Annales de 1. Institut Henri Poincare',* 1937, **7**, 1-68. (Trans. by H. E. Kyburg, Jr., in Kyburg, H. E. Jr., & Smokler (Eds.), *Studies in subjective probability.* New York: Wiley, 1964.)

de Groot, A. D. Perception and memory versus thought: some old ideas and recent findings. In B. Kleinmuntz (Ed.), *Problem solving: Research, method, and theory.* New York: Wiley, 1966.

Dreyfus, H. L. *What computers can't do: A critique of artificial reason.* New York: Harper & Row, 1972.

Duncker, K. On problem solving. *Psychological Monographs,* 1945, **58**(Whole No. 270).

Eaverone, D. F., & Ernst, F. W. A program that discovers good difference orderings and tables of connections for GPS. *Proceedings of 1970 IEEE Systems Science and Cybernetics Conference,* New York: IEE, 1970.

Ebbinghaus, H. Memory: A contribution to experimental psychology. (Trans. by H. A. Ruger and C. E. Bussenius) New York: Teachers College, Columbia University, 1913.

Edwards, W. Conservatism in human information processing. In B. Kleinmuntz (Ed.) *Formal representation of human judgment.* New York: Wiley, 1968.

Erman, L. D. An environment and system for machine recognition of connected speech. (Technical Report) Pittsburgh: Computer Science Department, Carnegie-Mellon University, 1973.

Ernst, G. W., & Newell, A. *GPS: A case study in generality and problem-solving.* New York: Academic Press, 1969.

Evans, T. G. A program for the solution of geometric-analogy intelligence test questions. In M. Minsky (Ed.), *Semantic information processing.* Cambridge, Mass.: MIT Press, 1968.

Falk, G. Interpretation of imperfect line data as a three dimensional scene. *Artificial Intelligence,* 1972, **3**, 101-144.

Falmagne, R. Construction of a hypothesis model for concept identification. *Journal of Mathematical Psychology,* 1970, **7,** 60-96.

Feigenbaum, E. A. The simulation of verbal learning behavior. In E. Feigenbaum, & J. Feldman (Eds.), *Computers and thought.* New York: McGraw-Hill, 1963.

Feldman, J., Tonge, F., & Kanter, H. Empirical explorations of a hypothesis testing model of binary choice behavior. In A. Hoggatt & F. Balderston (Eds.), *Symposium on simulation models.* Cincinnati: Southwestern Publishing Co., 1963.

Fillmore, C. J. The case for case. In E. Bach & R. T. Harms (Eds.), *Universals in linguistic theory.* New York: Holt, Rinehart & Winston, 1968.

Forbes, A. Item analysis of the advanced matrices. *British Journal of Educational Psychology,* 1964, **34,** 223-236.

Forgie, J. W. Semiannual technical summary on speech. Lexington, Mass.: Lincoln Laboratory, MIT, 1973.

Freeman, P. A., & Newell, A. A model for functional reasoning in design. *Proceedings 2nd International Joint Conference on Artificial Intelligence.* London, 1971, 621-640.

Fry, D. B., & Denes, P. Mechanical speech recognition. *Communication Theory, London,* 1953, **20,** 426-432.

Gibson, E. J. *Principles of perceptual learning and development.* New York: Appleton-Century-Crofts, 1969.

Gibson, J. J. *The senses considered as perceptual systems.* Boston: Houghton Mifflin, 1966.

Gillogly, J. J. The TECHNOLOGY Chess program. *Artificial Intelligence,* 1972, **3,** 145-163.

Glaser, R. Individuals and learning: The new aptitudes. *Educational Researcher,* June, 1972.

Glushkov, V. *Introduction to cybernetics.* New York: Academic Press, 1966.

Green, B. F., Jr. Descriptions and explanations: A comment on papers by Hoffman and Edwards. In B. Kleinmuntz (Ed.), *Formal representation of human judgment.* New York: Wiley, 1968.

Greeno, J. G. How associations are memorized. In D. A. Norman (Ed.), *Models of human memory,* New York: Academic Press, 1970, 261-284.

Greeno, J. G. The structure of memory and the process of solving problems. In R. Solso (Ed.), *Contemporary issues in cognitive psychology: the Loyola Symposium.* Washington: Winston, 1973. (a)

Greeno, J. G. Hobbits and orcs: Acquisition of a sequential concept. Unpublished manuscript, University of Michigan, 1973. (b)

Greeno, J. G. & Noreen, D. L. Time to read semantically related sentences. *Memory and Cognition,* in press.

Greeno, J. G., & Scandura, J. M. All-or-none transfer based on verbally mediated concepts. *Journal of Mathematical Psychology,* 1966, **3,** 388-411.

Greeno, J. G., James, C. T., & DaPolito, F. J. A cognitive interpretation of negative transfer and forgetting of paired associates. *Journal of Verbal Learning and Verbal Behavior,* 1971, **10,** 331-345.

Gregg, L. W. Internal representations of sequential concepts. In B. Kleinmuntz (Ed.), *Concepts and the structure of memory.* New York: Wiley, 1967.

Gregg, L. W., & Simon, H. A. Process models and stochastic theories of simple concept formation. *Journal of Mathematical Psychology,* 1967, **4,** 246-276.

Groen, G. J., & Parkman, J. M. A chronometric analysis of simple addition. *Psychological Review,* 1972, **79,** 329-343.

Guilford, J. P. Three faces of intellect. *American Psychologist,* 1959, **14,** 469-479.

Hayes, J. R. Problem topology and the solution process. *Journal of Verbal Learning and Verbal Behavior,* 1965, **4,** 371-379.

Hayes, J. R. Memory, goals, and problem solving. In B. Kleinmuntz (Ed.), *Problem solving: Research, method, and theory.* New York: Wiley, 1966.

Haygood, R. C., & Bourne, L. E., Jr. Attribute- and rule-learning aspects of conceptual behavior. *Psychological Review,* 1965, **72,** 175-195.

Henley, N. M. A psychological study of the semantics of animal terms. *Journal of Verbal Learning and Verbal Behavior,* 1969, 8, 176-184.

Hewitt, C. PLANNER: A language for proving theorems in Robots. In Walker, D. E. & Norton, L. M. (Eds.), *Proceedings 1st International Joint Conference on Artificial Intelligence,* 1969, 295-301.

Hewitt, C. Description and theoretical analysis (Using Schemata) of PLANNER: A language for proving theorems and manipulating models in a Robot. Unpublished doctoral dissertation, Department of Mathematics, Massachusetts Institute of Technology, 1972.

Hilf, F. D. Non-nonverbal communication and psychiatric research. *Archives of General Psychiatry,* 1972, 27, 631-635.

Hintzman, D. L. Exploration with a discrimination net model for paired-associate learning. *Journal of Mathematical Psychology,* 1968, 5, 123-162.

Hopcroft, J. E., & Ullman, J. D. *Formal languages and their relation to automata.* Reading, Mass.: Addison-Wesley, 1969.

Hormann, A. GAKU: An artificial student. *Behavioral Science,* 1965, 10, 88-107.

Huesmann, L. R., & Cheng, C. A theory for the induction of mathematical functions. *Psychological Review,* 1973, 80, 126-138.

Huet, G. P. A mechanization of type theory. *Proceedings 3rd International Joint Conference on Artificial Intelligence,* Stanford, Calif.: 1973, 139-146.

Hunt, E. B. *Concept learning: an informational processing problem.* New York: Wiley, 1962.

Hunt, E. Computer simulation: Artificial intelligence studies and their relevance to psychology. *Annual Review of Psychology,* 1968, 19, 135-168.

Hunt, E. What kind of a computer is man? *Cognitive Psychology,* 2, 1971, 57-98.

Hunt, E., & Hovland, C. Order of consideration of different types of concepts. *Journal of Experimental Psychology,* 1960, 59, 220-225.

Hunt, E., Frost, N., & Lunneborg, C. Individual differences in cognition: A new approach to intelligence. In G. Bower (Ed.), *Advances in learning and motivation.* Vol. 7. New York: Academic Press, 1973.

Hunt, E., & Lunneborg, C. On intelligence. In F. Sjursen & L. R. Beach (Eds.), *Readings in Psychology.* New York: Holt, 1973.

Hunt, E. Marin, J., & Stone, P. *Experiments in induction.* New York: Academic Press, 1966.

Jensen, A. R. How much can we boost IQ and scholastic achievement? *Harvard Educational Review,* 1969, 39, 1-125.

Jensen, A. R. The race x sex x ability interaction. In R. Cancro (Ed.), *Intelligence: Genetic and environmental influence.* New York: Grune & Stratton, 1972.

Jensen, A. R., & Rohwer, W. D., Jr. What is learned in serial learning? *Journal of Verbal Learning and Verbal Behavior,* 1965, 4, 62-72.

Johnson, E. S. An information-processing model of one kind of problem solving. *Psychological Monographs,* 1964, 78 (Whole No. 581).

Julesz, B. *Foundations of cyclopean perception.* Chicago: University of Chicago Press, 1971.

Kahneman, D., & Tversky, A. Subjective probability: A judgment of representativeness. *Cognitive Psychology,* 1972, 3, 430-454.

Kintsch, W. Models for free recall and recognition. In D. A. Norman (Ed.), *Models of human memory.* New York: Academic Press, 1970.

Kintsch, W. Notes on the structure of semantic memory. In E. Tulving, & W. Donaldson (Eds.), *Organization of memory.* New York: Academic Press, 1972.

Kintsch, W., & Keenan, J. Reading rate and retention as a function of the number of propositions in the base structure of sentences. University of Colorado, Studies in mathematical learning theory and psycholinguistics, April 1972.

Kintsch, W., & Monk, D. Storage of complex information in memory: Some implications of the speed with which inferences can be made. *Journal of Experimental Psychology,* 1972, **94,** 25-32.

Klahr, D. A computer simulation of the paradox of voting. *American Political Science Review,* 1966, **60,** 384-390.

Klahr, D., & Wallace, J. G. The development of serial completion strategies: an information processing analysis. *British Journal of Psychology,* 1970, **61,** 243-257.

Klein, S., & Kuppin, M. A. An intermediate heuristic program for learning transformational grammars. (Tech. Rep. No. 97), Computer Science Department, University of Wisconsin, Madison. August, 1970.

Kleinmuntz, B. (Ed.). *Problem solving: Research, method, and theory.* New York: Wiley, 1966.

Kotovsky, K., & Simon, H. A. Empirical tests of a theory of human acquisition of concepts for sequential events. *Cognitive Psychology,* 1973, **4,** 399-424.

Laughery, K. R. Computer simulation of short-term memory: A component-decay model. In G. H. Bower & J. T. Spence (Eds.), *The psychology of learning and motivation.* Vol. 3. New York: Academic Press, 1969.

Laughery, K. R., & Gregg, L. W. Simulation of human problem-solving behavior. *Psychometrika,* 1962, **27,** 265-282.

Lawrence, D. H., & DeRivera, J. Evidence for relational discrimination. *Journal of Comparative and Physiological Psychology,* 1954, **47,** 465-471.

Levine, M. The size of the hypothesis set during discrimination learning. *Psychological Review,* 1967, **74,** 428-430.

Liberman, A. M., Cooper, F. S., Harris, K. S., & MacNeilage, P. A motor theory of speech perception. *Proceedings of the Speech Communication Seminar,* **2,** 1962.

Lindsay, P. H., & Norman, D. A. *Human information processing.* New York: Academic Press, 1972.

London, R. L. The current state of proving programs correct. *Proceedings ACM 25th Annual Conference,* 1972, 39-46.

Luchins, A. S. Mechanization in problem solving. *Psychological Monographs,* 1954, **54** (Whole No. 248.)

Maier, N. R. F. Reasoning in humans. 1. On direction. *Journal of Comparative Psychology,* 1930, **12,** 115-143.

Mandler, G. Organization and memory. In K. W. Spence & J. T. Spence, (Eds.), *The psychology of learning and motivation: Advances in research and theory.* Vol. 1. New York: Academic Press, 1967.

Martin, E., & Noreen, D. L. Serial learning: Identification of subjective subsequences. Unpublished manuscript, University of Michigan, 1973.

Matarazzo, J. D. *Wechsler's measurement and appraisal of adult intelligence.* (5th Ed.). Baltimore: William & Wilkins, 1972.

Mayzner, M. S., & Tresselt, M. E. Visual information processing with sequential inputs: A general model for sequential blanking, displacement, and over-printing phenomena. *Annals of the New York Academy of Science,* 1970, **169,** 599-618.

McLean, R. S. & Gregg, L. W. Effects of induced chunking on temporal aspects of serial recitation. *Journal of Experimental Psychology,* 1967, **74,** 455-459.

Meehl, P. E. Theory testing in psychology and physics: A methodological paradox. *Philosophy of Science,* 1967, **34,** 103-115.

Michon, J. A. Multidimensional and hierarchical analysis of progress in learning. In L. W. Gregg (Ed.) *Cognition in learning and memory.* New York: Wiley, 1972.

Miles, T. R. On defining intelligence. *British Journal of Educational Psychology,* 1957, **27,** 153-167.

Miller, G. A. English verbs of motion: A case study in semantics and lexical memory. In A.

W. Melton & E. Martin, (Eds.), *Coding processes in human memory.* Washington, D.C.: Winston, 1972.

Miller, G. A., & Isard, S. Some perceptual consequences of linguistic rules. *Journal of Verbal Learning and Verbal Behavior,* 1963, **2**, 217-228.

Miller, G., Galanter, E., & Pribram, K. *Plans and the structure of behavior.* New York: Holt, 1960.

Miller, G. A., Heise, G. A., & Lichten, W. The intelligibility of speech as a function of the context of the test materials. *Journal of Experimental Psychology,* 1951, **41**, 329-335.

Moore, J. The design and evaluation of a knowledge net for Merlin. Unpublished doctoral dissertation, Department of Computer Science, Carnegie-Mellon University, 1971.

Morton, J. A preliminary functional model for language behavior. *International Audiology,* 1964, **3**, 216-225.

Morton, J., & Broadbent, D. Passive versus active models or is your homunculus really necessary. In W. Wathen-Dunn (Ed.), *Models for the perception of speech and visual form.* Cambridge, Mass.: MIT Press, 1967.

Moses, J. Symbolic integration. Unpublished doctoral dissertation, Massachusetts Institute of Technology, 1967.

Neely, R. B. On the use of syntax and semantics in a speech understanding system. (Technical Report) Pittsburgh: Computer Science Department, Carnegie-Mellon University, 1973.

Neisser, U., & Weene, P. Hierarchies in concept attainment. *Journal of Experimental Psychology,* 1962, **64**, 640-45.

Newell, A. Learning, generality, and problem solving. *Proceedings of the AFIP Congress,* 1963, **62**, 407-412.

Newell, A. Heuristic programming: Ill-structured problems. In J. S. Aronofsky, (Ed.), *Progress in operations research* Vol. 3. New York: Wiley, 1969.

Newell, A. Remarks on the relationship between artificial intelligence and cognitive psychology. In R. B. Banerji & M. D. Mesarovic (Eds.), *Theoretical approaches to non-numerical problem solving.* Berlin: Springer-Verlag, 1970.

Newell, A. A. I. and the concept of mind. In R. Schank & K. Colby (Eds.), *Computer models of thought and language.* San Francisco: Freeman, 1973. (a)

Newell, A. Production systems: Models of control structures. In W. G. Chase (Ed.), *Visual information processing.* New York: Academic Press, 1973. (b)

Newell, A., Barnett, J., Forgie, J., Green, C., Klatt, D., Licklider, J. C. R., Munson, J., Reddy, R., & Woods, W. *Speech understanding systems 1973.* Amsterdam: North Holland, 1973.

Newell, A., & Simon, H. A. Computer simulation of human thinking. *Science,* 1961, **134**, 2011-2017.

Newell, A., & Simon, H. A. *Human problem solving.* Englewood Cliffs, N.J.: Prentice-Hall, 1972.

Newell, A. Shaw, J. C., & Simon, H. A. A variety of intelligent learning in a general problem solver. In M. C. Yovitz & S. Cameron (Eds.), *Self-organizing systems.* New York: Pergamon Press, 1960.

Nilsson, N. J. A mobile automaton: an application of artificial intelligence techniques. In D. E. Walker & L. M. Norton (Eds.), *Proceedings 1st International Joint Conference on Artificial Intelligence,* 1969, 509-520.

Nilsson, N. J. *Problem-solving methods in artificial intelligence.* New York: McGraw-Hill, 1971.

Norman, D. A., & Rumelhart, D. E. A system for perception and memory. In D. A. Norman (Ed.), *Models of human memory.* New York: Academic Press, 1970.

Paige, J. M., & Simon, H. A. Cognitive processes in solving algebra word problems. In B. Kleinmuntz (Ed.), *Problem solving: Research, method, and theory.* New York: Wiley, 1966.

Peterson, C. R., & Phillips, L. D. Revision of continuous subjective probability distributions. *IEEE Transactions on Human Factors in Electronics,* 1966, HFE-7, 19-22.

Piaget, J. *The child's conception of number.* New York: Norton, 1965.

Piaget, J., & Inhelder, B. *The psychology of the child.* New York: Basic Books, 1969.

Pitz, G. F. On the processing of information: Probabilistic and otherwise. *Acta Psychologica,* 1970, 34, 201-213.

Pitz, G. F., Downing, L., & Reinhold, H. Sequential effects in the revision of subjective probabilities. *Canadian Journal of Psychology,* 1967, 21, 381-393.

Polson, M. C., Restle, F., & Polson, P. G. Association and discrimination in paired-associates learning. *Journal of Experimental Psychology,* 1965, 69, 47-55.

Polson, P. G. A quantitative analysis of the conceptual processes in the Hull paradigm. *Journal of Mathematical Psychology,* 1972, 9, 141-167.

Posner, M. I., & Warren, R. E. Traces, concepts, and conscious constructions. In A. W. Melton & E. Martin (Eds.), *Coding processes in human memory.* Washington, D.C.: Winston, 1972.

Postman, L., & Underwood, B. J. Critical issues in interference theory. *Memory and Cognition,* 1973, 1, 19-40.

Pylyshyn, Z. W. *Minds, machines, and phenomenology: Some reflections on Dreyfus', "What computers can't do."* (Research Bulletin No. 235) London, Ontario: Department of Psychology, University of Western Onatrio, June 1972.

Quillian, M. R. Word concepts: A theory and simulation of some basic semantic capabilities. *Behavioral Science,* 1967, 12, 410-430.

Quillian, M. R. Semantic memory. In M. Minsky (Ed.), *Semantic ifnormation processing.* Cambridge, Mass.: MIT Press, 1968.

Quillian, M. R. The teachable language comprehender: A simulation program and theory of language. *Communications of the ACM,* 1969, 12, 459-476.

Raiffa, H. *Decision analysis.* Reading, Mass.: Addison-Wesley, 1968.

Raphael, B. SIR: A computer program which understands. Proceedings of the AFIPS, Fall Joint Computer Conference, 1964.

Raphael, B. SIR: A computer program for semantic information retrieval. In M. Minsky, (Ed.), *Semantic information processing.* Cambridge, Mass.: MIT Press, 1968.

Raphael, B. The frame problem in problem solving systems. In, *Proceedings for Advanced Study Institute on Artificial Intelligence and Heuristic Programming,* Menaggio, Italy: Institute on Artificial Intelligence and Heuristic Programming, 1970.

Raven, J. C. *Advanced Progressive Matrices, Sets I and II.* London: Lewis & Co., 1965.

Reddy, D. R., Erman, L. D., & Neely, R. B. A model and a system for machine recognition of speech. *IEEE Transactions on Audio and Electroacoustics,* AU-21, 1973, 3, 229-238. (a)

Reddy, D. R., Erman, L. D., Fennell, R. D., & Neely, R. B. The HEARSAY speech understanding system: An example of the recognition process. *3rd International Joint Conference on Artificial Intelligence.* Stanford, California, 1973 (b).

Reich, P. A. Relational networks. *Canadian Journal of Linguistics,* 1970, 15, 95-110.

Reichner, G. M. Perceptual recognition as a function of meaningfulness of stimulus material. *Journal of Experimental Psychology,* 1969, 81, 275-280.

Reitman, J. S. Computer simulation of an information-processing model of short-term memory. In D. A. Norman (Ed.), *Models of human memory.* New York: Academic Press, 1970.

Reitman, W. R. *Cognition and thought.* New York: Wiley, 1965.

Restle, F. The selection of strategies in cue learning. *Psychological Review,* 1962, 69, 329-343.

Restle, F. Sources of difficulty in learning paired associates. In R. C. Atkinson (Ed.), *Studies in mathematical psychology.* Stanford: Stanford University Press, 1964.

Restle, F. Grammatical analysis of the prediction of binary events. *Journal of Verbal Learning and Verbal Behavior*, 1967, **6**, 17-25.

Restle, F. Speed of adding and comparing numbers. *Journal of Experimental Psychology*, 1970, **83**, 274-278. (a)

Restle, F. Theory of serial pattern learning: structural trees. *Psychological Review*, 1970, **77**, 481-495. (b)

Restle, F., & Brown, E. Organization of serial pattern learning. In G. H. Bower, (Ed.), *The psychology of learning and motivation, advances in research and theory.* Vol. 4. New York: Academic Press, 1970.

Robb, G., Bernardoni, L., & Johnson, R. *Assessment of individual mental ability.* Scranton, Pa. Intext, 1972.

Rouse-Ball, W. W. *Mathematical recreation and essays.* New York: Macmillan, 1962.

Rulifson, J. F., Derkson, J. A., & Waldinger, R. J. *QA4: A procedural calculus for inductive reasoning.* (Tech. Note 73) Stanford: Stanford Research Institute, 1972.

Rumelhart, D. E., & Abrahamson, A. A. Toward a theory of analogical reasoning. Center for Human Information Processing Report CHIP 18. University of California, San Diego, 1971.

Rumelhart, D. E., Lindsay, P. M., & Norman, D. A. A process model for long-term memory. In E. Tulving, & W. Donaldson (Eds.), *Organization of memory.* New York: Academic Press, 1972.

Sachs, J. Recognition memory for syntactic and semantic aspects of connected discourse. *Perception and Psychophysics*, 1967, **2**, 437-442.

Samuel, A. L. Some studies in machine learning using the game of checkers. In E. A. Feigenbaum & J. Feldman (Eds.), *Computers and thought.* New York: McGraw-Hill, 1963.

Savage, L. J. The foundation of statistics. New York: Wiley, 1954.

Scarr-Salapatek, S. Race, social class, and IQ. *Science*, 1971, **174**, 1285-1295.

Schank, R. C. Conceptual dependency: A theory of natural language understanding. *Cognitive Psychology*, 1972, **3**, 552-631.

Schulz, R. W., Miller, R. L., & Radtke, R. C. The role of instance contiguity and dominance in concept attainment. *Journal of Verbal Learning and Verbal Behavior*, 1963, **1**, 432-435.

Sekuler, R., Tynan, P., & Levinson, E. Visual temporal order: A new illusion, *Science*, 1973, **180**, 210-212.

Shiffrin, R. M. Memory search. In D. A. Norman (Ed.), *Models of memory.* New York: Academic Press, 1970.

Siklóssy, L. Natural language learning by computer. In H. A. Simon & L. Siklóssy (Eds.), *Representation and meaning.* Englewood Cliffs, N.J.: Prentice-Hall, 1972.

Simon, H. A. Complexity and the representation of patterned sequences of symbols. *Psychological Review*, 1972, **79**, 368-382. (a)

Simon, H. A. The heuristic compiler. In H. A. Simon & L. Siklóssy, (Eds.), *Representation and meaning.* Englewood Cliffs, N.J.: Prentice-Hall, 1972. (b)

Simon, H. A. The theory of problem solving. *Information Processing 71.* Amsterdam: North Holland, 1972. (c)

Simon, H. A., & Barenfeld, M. Information processing analysis of perceptual processes in problem solving. *Psychological Review*, 1969, **76**, 473-483.

Simon, H. A., & Gilmartin, K. A simulation of memory for chess positions. Unpublished manuscript, Carnegie-Mellon University, 1972.

Simon, H. A., & Kotovsky, K. Human acquisition of concepts for sequential patterns. *Psychological Review*, 1963, **70**, 534-546.

Simon, H. A., & Siklóssy, L. (Eds.) *Representation and meaning.* Englewood Cliffs, N.J.: Prentice-Hall, 1972.

Simon, H. A., & Sumner, R. K. Pattern in music. In B. Kleinmuntz (Ed.), *Formal representation of human judgment*. New York: Wiley, 1968.

Slobin, D. I. Developmental psycholinguistics. In W. O. Dingwall (Ed.), *A survey of linguistic science*. College Park: Linguistics Program, University of Maryland, 1971.

Slovic, P. From Shakespeare to Simon: Speculations—and some evidence—about man's ability to process information. *Oregon Research Institute Research Bulletin, 1972,* **12,** No. 12.

Snapper, K. J., & Fryback, D. G. Inference based on unreliable reports. *Journal of Experimental Psychology, 1971,* **87,** 401-404.

Solomonoff, R. A new method for discovering the grammars of phrase structure languages. *Information Processing 59.* (Proceedings of the International Conference on Information Processing) Paris: UNESCO, 1959.

Spearman, C., & Wynn-Jones, L. *Human ability.* London: MacMillan, 1951.

Steiger, J. H., & Gettys, C. F. Best-guess errors in multi-stage inference. *Journal of Experimental Psychology, 1972,* **92,** 1-7.

Stevens, K. N., & Halle, M. Speech recognition: A Model and a program for Research, *IRE Trans., 1962,* PGIT, IT-8, 155-159.

Suppes, P., & Ginsberg, R. A fundamental property of all-or-none models, binomial distribution of responses prior to conditioning, with application to concept formation in children. *Psychological Review, 1963,* **70,** 139-161.

Suppes, P., & Morningstar, M. *Computer-assisted instruction at Stanford, 1966-68; Data, models, and evaluation of the arithmetic programs.* New York: Academic Press, 1972.

Sussman, G. J., & McDermott, D. V. Why CONNIVING is better than PLANNING. (AI Memo No. 255A) Artificial Intelligence Laboratory, MIT. 1972.

Thomas, J. T., Jr. An analysis of behavior in the hobbits-orcs problem. University of Michigan, Human Performance Center Technical Report No. 31. August 1971.

Thompson, M. C., & Massaro, D. W. Visual information and redundancy in reading. *Journal of Experimental Psychology, 1973,* **98,** 49-54.

Townsend, J. T. Some results concerning the identifiability of parallel and serial processes. *British Journal of Mathematical and Statistical Psychology, 1972,* **25,** 168-199.

Trabasso, T., & Bower, G. Component learning the four-category concept problem. *Journal of Mathematical Psychology, 1964,* **1,** 143-169.

Trabasso, T., & Bower, G. H. *Attention in learning: theory and research.* New York: Wiley, 1968.

Trabasso, T., Rollins, H., & Shaughnessy, E. Storage and verification stages in processing concepts. *Cognitive Psychology, 1971,* **2,** 239-289.

Tulving, E. Subjective organization in free recall of "unrelated" words. *Psychological Review, 1962,* **69,** 344-354.

Tulving, E. Episodic and semantic memory. In E. Tulving & W. Donaldson (Eds.) *Organization of memory.* New York: Academic Press, 1972.

Turing, A. Computing machinery and intelligence. In E. A. Feigenbaum, & J. Feldman (Eds.), *Computers and thought.* New York: McGraw-Hill, 1963.

Underwood, B. J., & Richardson, J. Verbal concept learning as a function of instructions and dominance level. *Journal of Experimental Psychology, 1956,* **51,** 229-238. (a)

Underwood, B. J., & Richardson, J. Some verbal materials for the study of concept formation. *Psychological Bulletin, 1956,* **53,** 84-95. (b)

Vitz, P. C., & Todd, T. C. A model of learning for simple repeating binary patterns. *Journal of Experimental Psychology, 1967,* **75,** 108-117.

Walker, D. W. Speech understanding through syntactic and semantic analysis, *Proceedings IJCAI '73, 1973,* 208-215.

Waterman, D. A., & Newell, A. PAS-II: *An interactive task-free version of an automatic protocol analysis system.* Pittsburgh: Department of Computer Science, Carnegie-Mellon University, 1973.

Weizenbaum, J. ELIZA—A Computer program for the study of natural language communication between man and machine. *Communications of the ACM,* 1966, **9,** 36-45.

Wertheimer, M. *Productive thinking.* New York: Harper & Row, 1959.

Wickens, T. D., & Millward, R. B. Attribute elimination strategies for concept identification with practiced subjects. *Journal of Mathematical Psychology,* 1971, 8, 453-480.

Williams, D. S. Computer program organization induced from problem examples. In H. A. Simon & L. Siklossy (Eds.), *Representation and meaning.* Englewood Cliffs, N.J.: Prentice-Hall, 1972.

Williams, G. F. A model of memory in concept learning. *Cognitive Psychology,* 1971, **2,** 158-184.

Williams, T. G. Some studies in game playing with a digital computer. In H. A. Simon & L. Siklossy (Eds.), *Representation and meaning.* Englewood Cliffs, N.J.: Prentice-Hall, 1972.

Winograd, T. Procedures as a representation for data in a computer system for understanding natural language. Unpublished doctoral dissertation, Department of Mathematics, Massachusetts Institute of Technology, 1970.

Winograd, T. Understanding natural language. *Cognitive Psychology,* 1972, 3, 1-191.

Woods, W. A. & Makhoul, J. Mechanical inference problems in continuous speech understanding, *Proceedings IJCAI '73,* 1973, 200-207.

Woodworth, R. S. *Experimental Psychology.* New York: Holt, 1938.

AUTHOR INDEX

Numbers in italics refer to the pages on which the complete references are listed.

311

SUBJECT INDEX